The Radical Left Party Family in Western Europe, 1989–2015

This book provides an innovative analysis and interpretation of the overall trajectory of the Western European radical left from 1989 to 2015. After the collapse of really existing communism, this party family renewed itself and embarked on a recovery path, seeking to fill the vacuum of representation of disaffected working-class and welfarist constituencies created by the progressive neoliberalisation of European societies. The radical left thus emerged as a significant factor of contemporary political life but, despite some electoral gains and a few recent breakthroughs (SYRIZA in Greece, PODEMOS in Spain), it altogether failed to embody a credible alternative to neoliberalism and to pave the way for a turn to a different developmental model.

This book investigates why this was the case, combining aggregate (17 countries), case study (Germany, Italy, and France), and comparative methods. It accurately charts the evolution of the nature, strength, cohesion, and influence of the Western European radical left, offering new insights in explaining its behaviour, success, and limits. It is essential reading for scholars, students, and activists interested in the radical left and in contemporary European politics.

Paolo Chiocchetti holds a PhD in European Studies from King's College London. He is a Research Associate at the University of Luxembourg.

Routledge Studies in Radical History and Politics

Series editors: Thomas Linehan, *Brunel University*, and John Roberts, *Brunel University*

The series *Routledge Studies in Radical History and Politics* has two areas of interest. Firstly, this series aims to publish books which focus on the history of movements of the radical left. 'Movement of the radical left' is here interpreted in its broadest sense as encompassing those past movements for radical change which operated in the mainstream political arena as with political parties, and past movements for change which operated more outside the mainstream as with millenarian movements, anarchist groups, utopian socialist communities, and trade unions. Secondly, this series aims to publish books which focus on more contemporary expressions of radical left-wing politics. Recent years have been witness to the emergence of a multitude of new radical movements adept at getting their voices in the public sphere. From those participating in the Arab Spring, the Occupy movement, community unionism, social media forums, independent media outlets, local voluntary organisations campaigning for progressive change, and so on, it seems to be the case that innovative networks of radicalism are being constructed in civil society that operate in different public forms.

The series very much welcomes titles with a British focus, but is not limited to any particular national context or region. The series will encourage scholars who contribute to this series to draw on perspectives and insights from other disciplines.

Titles include:

Thomas More's *Utopia*
Arguing for social justice
Lawrence Wilde

Real Democracy in the Occupy Movement
No stable ground
Anna Szolucha

The Radical Left Party Family in Western Europe, 1989–2015
Paolo Chiocchetti

The Radical Left Party Family in Western Europe, 1989–2015

Paolo Chiocchetti

Taylor & Francis Group

LONDON AND NEW YORK

First published 2017
by Routledge
2 Park Square, Milton Park, Abingdon, Oxon OX14 4RN

and by Routledge
711 Third Avenue, New York, NY 10017

Routledge is an imprint of the Taylor & Francis Group, an informa business

© 2017 Paolo Chiocchetti

The right of Paolo Chiocchetti to be identified as author of this work has been asserted in accordance with sections 77 and 78 of the Copyright, Designs and Patents Act 1988.

All rights reserved. No part of this book may be reprinted or reproduced or utilised in any form or by any electronic, mechanical, or other means, now known or hereafter invented, including photocopying and recording, or in any information storage or retrieval system, without permission in writing from the publishers.

Trademark notice: Product or corporate names may be trademarks or registered trademarks, and are used only for identification and explanation without intent to infringe.

British Library Cataloguing in Publication Data
A catalogue record for this book is available from the British Library

Library of Congress Cataloging-in-Publication Data
A catalog record for this book has been requested

ISBN: 978-1-138-65618-5 (hbk)
ISBN: 978-1-315-62205-7 (ebk)

Typeset in Times New Roman
by Apex CoVantage, LLC

Printed and bound in Great Britain by
TJ International Ltd, Padstow, Cornwall

To Teresa

Contents

List of figures	viii
List of tables	x
Acknowledgements	xi
List of abbreviations	xiii
Introduction	1
1 Toward an analysis of the contemporary Western European radical left	6
2 The Western European landscape, 1914–1988	29
3 The Western European landscape, 1989–2015	60
4 The German radical left: a success story	81
5 The Italian radical left: the story of a failure	123
6 The French radical left: success or failure?	162
7 Filling the vacuum? The trajectory of the contemporary radical left in Western Europe	200
Conclusion	226
Index	232

Figures

2.1	Electoral strength, Western European radical left	38
2.2	Cross-national electoral trends	40
2.3	Electoral, parliamentary, and governmental strength, Western European radical left	42
2.4	Share of radical left members on the total electorate (m/e), eight countries	44
2.5	Sociology of radical left members, selected parties	47
3.1	Electoral strength, Western European radical left (1989–2015)	65
3.2	Cross-national electoral trends (1989–2015)	67
3.3	Electoral, parliamentary, and government strength, Western European radical left (1989–2015)	70
4.1	Strength evolution, German radical left	87
4.2	Support for German establishment parties	98
4.3	Net left-wing opinions, Germany (per cent of interviewed)	99
4.4	DIE LINKE vote (Bundestag, per cent of valid votes)	100
4.5	DIE LINKE vote in selected social groups (Bundestag, per cent of valid votes)	100
4.6	Cumulative net electoral flows of DIE LINKE (Bundestag, per cent of valid votes)	101
5.1	Family tree of the Italian post-communist left	126
5.2	Strength evolution, Italian radical left	128
5.3	Fragmentation (national level), Italian radical left	130
5.4	Support for Italian establishment parties (per cent of the electorate)	141
5.5	Net left-wing opinions, Italy (per cent of interviewed)	142
5.6	Italian radical left vote (Camera, per cent of valid votes)	144
5.7	Italian radical left vote in selected social groups (Camera, per cent of valid votes)	144
5.8	Cumulative net electoral flows of the Italian radical left (Camera, per cent of valid votes)	145
5.9	Membership ratios, Italian radical left	148
6.1	Strength evolution, French radical left	167
6.2	Fragmentation (national level), French radical left	169
6.3	Industrial conflicts in France (thousand days lost to strikes)	180

6.4	Support for French establishment parties (per cent of registered voters)	182
6.5	French radical left vote (per cent of valid votes)	184
6.6	Membership ratios, French radical left	187
7.1	Electoral strength, Western Europe	209
7.2	Electoral strength, Germany, France, and Italy	210
7.3	Parliamentary strength, Germany, France, and Italy	211
7.4	Governmental strength, Germany, France, and Italy	212
7.5	Membership strength, Germany, France, and Italy	214

Tables

1.1	Party strength: components and indicators	21
2.1	National vote shares in selected years (per cent)	39
3.1	National vote shares in selected years (per cent)	66
3.2	Fragmentation, Western European radical left (1994–2015)	76
4.1	Strength, German radical left	86
4.2	Sociology, German radical left	90
5.1	Strength, Italian radical left	127
5.2	Sociology, Italian radical left	133
6.1	Strength, French radical left	166
6.2	Sociology, French radical left	173
7.1	Core constituencies, Germany, France, and Italy	204
7.2	Significant determinants of the radical left vote, Germany, France, and Italy	205

Acknowledgements

I began researching the contemporary radical left in 2006, when the contradictions of neoliberal financialisation were still well hidden behind a global economic boom and the literature on the topic was rare and fragmented. The project has progressively grown from a comparison of five selected radical left parties (1999–2006) in my MA thesis at the University of Bologna, through the study of three national radical lefts (1989–2013) in my PhD thesis at King's College London, to the final form assumed in this book, which combines the investigation of the three case studies of Germany, France, and Italy (1989–2015) with that of the continental landscape across seventeen Western European countries (1914–2015). The prolonged observation of the real-time unfolding of events and scholarship and the broadening of the geographical and temporal scope of the analysis have helped me refine the theoretical and methodological tools, identify more precisely the key trends and dilemmas of the contemporary radical left, and strengthen my interpretation of its overall development. The narrative fittingly ends in 2015, when the electoral triumph and political debacle of SYRIZA in Greece gave a clear demonstration of both the potential and limits of the 'new' radical left, and the increasing instability of the political and economic situation seems to foreshadow major changes to come.

A number of people have supported, inspired, and put up with me during this long quest. I would like to express my sincere thanks to Jim Wolfreys, Stathis Kouvelakis, and Piero Ignazi for their guidance, productive comments, and assistance in the research phase. Many other scholars, examiners, reviewers, and conference participants have inspired me with their work and feedback. I have shared with my former colleagues of the Department of European and International Studies at KCL stimulating conversations and treasured experiences. King's College London has supported part of the research with a scholarship, its infrastructure, and a vibrant intellectual environment. The institutions ITANES and Istituto Cattaneo (Bologna), Centre de Données Socio-Politiques (Paris), and GESIS and Forschungsgruppe Wahlen (Mannheim) have kindly made available their survey data; countless other bodies and researchers have provided the primary data required for an accurate measurement of radical left strength. The cadres and activists of the parties included in the analysis have proved remarkably open to my questions, requests, and visits; special thanks goes to the branch of DIE

LINKE.SDS in Leipzig, the Rosa-Luxemburg-Stiftung in Berlin, and Pascale in Paris. My editor Emma Chappell, the two series editors Thomas Linehan and John Michael Roberts, my project manager Denise File and the staff of Routledge have provided an invaluable contribution in writing and producing this book. My parents Linda and Aldo, my grandparents Gisella and Tarcisio, and my friends have supported me materially and emotionally through this journey: thank you for everything. Last but not least, my girlfriend Teresa has stoically gone through the initial drafts of the book, patiently suffered my periodic bouts of misanthropy, filled my life with joy, and published her own first monograph: to her goes all my love and respect.

Abbreviations

Ab	Alþýðubandalagið
AET	L'Altra Europa con Tsipras
AfD	Alternative für Deutschland
AIT	International Workers' Association
AKEL	Anorthotikó Kómma Ergazómenou Laoú
ALLBUS	Allgemeine Bevölkerungsumfrage der Sozialwissenschaften
AN	Alleanza Nazionale
ANTARSYA	Antikapitalistikí Aristerí Synergasía gia tin Anatropí
APU	Aliança Povo Unido
ARAC	Association republicaine des anciens combattants et victimes de guerre
ARCI	Associazione Ricreativa e Culturale Italiana
ATTAC	Association pour une taxation des transations financières pour l'aide aux citoyens
AWO	Arbeiterwohlfahrt
BE	Bloco de Esquerda
BNG	Bloque Nacionalista Galego
CAGR	Compound Annual Growth Rate
CCA	Confederazione Comunisti/e Autorganizzati
CDSP	Centre de Données Socio-politiques
CDU (Germany)	Christlich Demokratische Union Deutschlands
CDU (Portugal)	Coligação Democrática Unitária [alliance of PCP and PEV (Partido Ecologista "Os Verdes")]
CGIL	Confederazione Generale Italiana del Lavoro
CGT	Confédération générale du travail
CIP	Contrat d'insertion professionnelle
CISL	Confederazione Italiana Sindacati Lavoratori
CNL	Confédération nationale du logement
CNT	Confederación Nacional del Trabajo
COBAS	Cobas per l'Autorganizzazione
Comintern	Communist International
CPE	Contrat première embauche
CPGB	Communist Party of Great Britain

CPN	Communistische Partij Nederland
CSU	Christlich-Soziale Union in Bayern
DC	Democrazia Cristiana
DÉI LÉNK	déi Lénk
DGB	Deutscher Gewerkschaftsbund
DIE LINKE	DIE LINKE
DGRV	Deutscher Genossenschafts- und Raiffeisenverband
DIKKI	Dimokratiko Koinoniko Kinima
DKP (Denmark)	Danmarks Kommunistiske Parti
DKP (Germany)	Deutsche Kommunistische Partei
DL (Ireland)	Democratic Left
DL (Italy)	Democrazia è Libertà – La Margherita
DMB	Deutscher Mieterbund
DNA	Det norske Arbeiderparti
DP	Democrazia Proletaria
DS	Democratici di Sinistra
EDA	Eniéa Dimokratikí Aristerá
E	Enhedslisten – De Rød-Grønne
EE	Euskadiko Ezkerra
EEC	European Economic Community
EH BILDU	Euskal Herria Bildu
EMS	European Monetary System
EMU	Economic and Monetary Union
ERP	European Recovery Plan
EU	European Union
FaS	Futuro a Sinistra
FASE	Fédération pour une Alternative Sociale et Écologique
FdG	Front de gauche
FDP (Germany)	Freie Demokratische Partei
FDP (Italy)	Fronte Democratico Popolare per la libertà, la pace, il lavoro
FdS	Federazione della Sinistra
FEPU	Frente Eleitoral Povo Unido
FI	Forza Italia
FIOM	Federazione Impiegati Operai Metallurgici
FN	Front national
FNACA	Fédération nationale des anciens combattants en Algérie, Maroc et Tunisie
FO	Confédération générale du travail - Force ouvrière
FRG	Federal Republic of Germany [West Germany]
FSGT	Fédération sportive et gymnique du travail
FSU	Fédération syndicale unitaire
FW	Die Freien Wähler
GATT	General Agreement on Tariffs and Trade
GDP	Gross Domestic Product
GDR	German Democratic Republic [East Germany]

GL	GroenLinks
GRÜNE	Bündnis 90/Die Grünen
GUE/NGL	European United Left/Nordic Green Left
HB	Herri Batasuna
ICV	Iniciativa per Catalunya Verds
IdV	Italia dei Valori
IASP	International Working Union of Socialist Parties
ILP	Independent Labour Party
IRMC	International Revolutionary Marxist Centre
ITANES	Italian National Election Studies
IU	Izquierda Unida
IWMA	International Workingmen's Association
KKE	Kommounistikó Kómma Elládas
KOS	Koordinierungsstelle gewerkschaftlicher Arbeitslosengruppen
KP	Kommunistische Partij
KPD	Kommunistische Partei Deutschlands
KPL	Kommunistesch Partei Lëtzebuerg
KPÖ	Kommunistische Partei Österreichs
LCR	Ligue communiste révolutionnaire
LE	Laïkí Enótita
LN	Lega Nord
LO	Lutte Ouvrière
L.PDS	Die Linkspartei.PDS
LR	Les Républicains
M5S	MoVimento 5 Stelle
MAS	Movimiento al Socialismo – Instumento Político por la Soberanía de los Pueblos
MCU	Movimento dei Comunisti Unitari
MDP	Movimento Democrático Português / Comissões Democráticas Eleitorais
MDC	Mouvement des citoyens
MJCF	Mouvement Jeunes Communistes de France
MLPD	Marxistisch-Leninistische Partei Deutschlands
MP	Member of Parliament
NATO	North Atlantic Treaty Organisation
ND	Nouvelle Donné
NGLA	Nordic Green Left Alliance
NGS	Nouvelle Gauche Socialiste
NKP	Norges Kommunistiske Parti
NPA	Nouveau parti anticapitaliste
OKV	Ostdeutsches Kuratorium von Verbänden
PASOK	Panellinio Sosialistiko Kinima
PBC	Per il Bene Comune
PBPA	People Before Profit Alliance
PC – SFIC	Parti communiste – Section française de l'Internationale communiste

xvi *Abbreviations*

PCd'I	Partito Comunista d'Italia
PCE	Partido Comunista de España
PCF	Parti communiste français
PCI (Italy)	Partito Comunista Italiano
PCL	Partito Comunista dei Lavoratori
PCP	Partido Comunista Português
PCS	Partito Comunista Sammarinese
PCTP-MRPP	Partido Comunista dos Trabalhadores Portugueses
PD	Partito Democratico
PdA	Partei der Arbeit der Schweiz
PdAC	Partito di Alternativa Comunista
PdCI	Partito dei Comunisti Italiani
PDS (Germany)	Partei des Demokratischen Sozialismus
PDS (Italy)	Partito Democratico della Sinistra
PEL	Party of the European Left
PG	Parti de Gauche
PIRATEN	Piratenpartei Deutschland
PODEMOS	Podemos
POI	Parti ouvrier indépendant
Possibile	Possibile
POUM	Partido Obrero de Unificación Marxista
PRC	Partito della Rifondazione Comunista
PS	Parti socialiste
PSA	Partito Socialista Autonomo
PSI	Partito Socialista Italiano
PSIUP	Partito Socialista Italiano di Unità Proletaria
PSOE	Partido Socialista Obrero Español
PSP	Pacifistisch Socialistische Partij
PSS	Partito Socialista Sammarinese
PSU (France)	Parti socialiste unifié
PSUC	Partit Socialista Unificat de Catalunya
PSUV	Partido Socialista Unido de Venezuela
PT	Parti des Travailleurs
PTE-UC	Partido de los Trabajadores de España-Unidad Comunista
PUP	Parti d'unité prolétarienne
PVDA-PTB	Partij van de Arbeid van België - Parti du Travail de Belgique
RC	Rivoluzione Civile
RL	Radical left
RØDT	Rødt
RPR	Rassemblement pour la République
RSDLP(b)	Russian Social Democratic Labour Party (Bolsheviks)
RSP	Revolutionair Socialistische Partij
RV	Rød Valgallianse

Abbreviations xvii

S	solidarités
SA	La Sinistra – L'Arcobaleno
SA-S	Sameiningarflokkur alþýðu – Sósíalistaflokkurinn
SC	Sinistra Critica
SD	Sinistra Democratica
SDAPDÖ	Sozialdemokratische Arbeiterpartei Deutschösterreichs
SEA	Single European Act
SED	Sozialistische Einheitspartei Deutschland
SEL	Sinistra Ecologia Libertà
SF (Denmark)	Socialistisk Folkeparti
SF (Ireland)	Sinn Féin
SF (Norway)	Sosialistisk Folkeparti
SFIO	Section française de l'Internationale ouvrière
SI	Sinistra Italiana
SKDL	Suomen Kansan Demokraattinen Liitto
SKP (Finland)	Suomen Kommunistinen Puolue
SKP (Sweden)	Sveriges Kommunistiska Parti
SoVD	Sozialverband Deutschland
SP (the Netherlands)	Socialistische Partij
SP (Sweden)	Socialistiska partiet
SPD	Sozialdemokratische Partei Deutschlands
SPF	Secours populaire français
STASI	Ministerium für Staatssicherheit der DDR
SV	Sosialistisk Venstreparti
SYN	Synaspismós tīs Aristerás tōn Kinīmátōn kai tīs Oikologías
SYRIZA	Synaspismós Rizospastikís Aristerás
TAV	Treno Alta Velocità
TINA	There is no alternative
Treuhand	Treuhandanstalt
UCPN-M	Unified Communist Party of Nepal (Maoist)
UDF	Union pour la démocratie française
UFF	Union des femmes françaises [after 1998 FS, Femmes solidaires]
UIL	Unione Italiana del Lavoro
UMP	Union pour un mouvement populaire
UNEF	Union nationale des étudiants de France
UNRPA	Union nationale des retraités et des personnes âgées
USPD	Unabhängige Sozialdemokratische Partei Deutschlands
USI	Unione Sindacale Italiana
USSR	Union of Soviet Socialist Republics
V	Vänsterpartiet
VAS	Vasemmistoliitto
VdK	Sozialverband Vdk (Verband der Kriegsbeschädigten, Kriegshinterbliebenen und Sozialrentner Deutschlands)

Verdi	Federazione dei Verdi
Verts	Les Verts, Confédération écologiste – Parti écologiste
VPK	Vänsterpartiet Kommunisterna
WASG	Arbeit & soziale Gerechtigkeit – Die Wahlalternative
WP	The Workers' Party
WTO	World Trade Organisation

Introduction

The nineties opened with a near-universal declaration of death of the Western European radical left. Scholars took note of the fall of the Soviet bloc and of the collapse of Western communist parties, declaring the experience of twentieth-century communism concluded (Bell 1993; Bull and Heywood 1994; Wilson 1993). Formerly a living political tradition, the radical left suddenly became a merely historical object (Agosti 1999; Dreyfus et al. 2004; Kowalski 2006) or a somewhat anachronistic vestige of the past, squeezed between decline and adaptation (Botella and Ramiro 2003; Moreau et al. 1998).

More broadly, the continued relevance of traditional forms of ideological debate and political conflict seemed to be radically questioned by the historical developments of the eighties and early nineties. The neo-conservative intellectual Fukuyama (1989) hailed them as representing 'the end of history', paving the way for a shift toward a de-ideologised, pacified, and consensual policy-making built on the cornerstones of free-market capitalism, liberal democratic institutions, and technocratic policies. The social democratic scholar Kitschelt (1994) agreed, claiming that the left-right conflict remained important on cultural and post-materialist issues but was made substantially redundant on socio-economic issues by the success of the welfare state, the constraints of globalisation, and the shift to a post-industrial society. Radical left thinkers, in turn, decried a drastic narrowing of the boundaries of legitimate debate to the horizon of capitalism and neoliberalism (TINA, the 'single thought', the Washington consensus).

The subsequent decades, however, were more contradictory than expected.

First, mainstream political parties indeed converged in terms of intellectual references and socio-economic policies, but their electoral support and rates of approval became more volatile and declined, while political disengagement, dissatisfaction, and anti-establishment parties rose (Crouch 2004; Mair 2006).

Secondly, the neoliberal trends and reforms progressively eroding the pillars of the post-war European social model were largely successful, but met with sustained popular resistance. Labour militancy remained low at the workplace and sectoral level, but general strikes and union-led mass demonstrations increased and became the main driver of anti-government protest (Kelly et al. 2013; Kouvelakis 2007; Vandaele 2011). And social movement activism was vibrant, with movements of squatters (López 2013), the unemployed (Lahusen and Baumgarten 2006), students (Fernàndez 2014), migrants (Nyers and Rygiel 2012), digital activists (Karatzogianni 2015), pacifists (Walgrave and Rucht 2010), marginalised strata (Mouchard 2009), alter-globalists (Della Porta 2007), and the precarised youth (*Current Sociology* 2013) periodically sparking large-scale extra-parliamentary mobilisations.

Thirdly, the promises of prosperity extolled by the ideologues of capitalism, globalisation, neoliberal reforms, and Europeanisation became less and less credible, as growth rates and wages continued their long-term downward decline, unemployment remained high, social inequalities grew, and periodic financial and economic crisis shook the global economy (Duménil and Lévy 2004, 2011).

Fourthly, the academia and the public discourse remained dominated by mainstream discourses, but critical voices did not disappear (Bidet and Kouvelakis 2005; Keucheyan 2013).

In this context, the Western European radical left did not boom, but nevertheless experienced a certain revival of its sympathy, electoral support, governmental influence, and scholarly attention. As I will show in more detail in chapter three, the aggregate electoral strength of radical left parties went through ups and downs, but almost doubled from its trough in 1993 (5.1 per cent) to its peak in 2015 (9.6 per cent). A few countries experienced major electoral breakthroughs, in particular Sweden in 1998 (12.1 per cent), the Netherlands in 2006 (16.6 per cent), Denmark in 2007 (15.4 per cent), Germany in 2009 (12 per cent), Greece in 2012 and 2015 (31.8 and 45 per cent), Spain in 2015 (25.8 per cent), and Portugal in 2015 (21.5 per cent). Radical left parties also became increasingly involved in national and subnational governments. Their aggregate governmental strength remained low, in average 1.8 per cent between 1994 and 2015, but they directly participated or externally supported centre-left cabinets in several countries, and took the leading position in two cases (AKEL in Cyprus in 2008–13, and SYRIZA in Greece since 2015). Finally, the contemporary radical left became again an important object of scholarly interest, with a large number of scholarly articles, monographs, book chapters, and edited volumes (Escalona et al. 2017; March 2012; March and Mudde 2005).

The overarching goal of the book is to provide a *convincing interpretation of the overall trajectory of the Western European radical left since 1989*, explaining its internal tensions, behaviour, and success (or lack thereof). More specifically, the analysis focuses on the description and explanation of the evolution of three key aspects: the *cohesion* of the radical left, its *strength*, and its *influence* on the political and social system.

In order to answer these questions, I integrate the tools of various sub-fields of political science and some cues of related disciplines (political sociology, contemporary history, political economy, and political theory) into an *original holistic approach*.

While building on the existing literature on party politics and the radical left, I put to the forefront of the analysis a number of themes which are often underemphasised, undertheorised, or treated in isolation from each other. First, the existence in each country of a radical left field affecting with its tensions the behaviour of the individual radical left parties belonging to it. Secondly, an understanding of radical left parties as complex tools enabling collective action, whose nature depends on the specifics of their constituency, short-term and long-term political project, organisational mediations, and strategic mediations. Thirdly, an accurate quantification of the strength of the Western European radical left at different levels (continental, national, and sub-national), units of analysis (party family and individual parties), and dimensions (electoral, parliamentary, governmental, membership, and more). Fourthly, the question of radical left success, both in terms of the mere accumulation of resources of power and in terms of actual policy influence. Fifthly, the paramount importance of party system rules and dynamics and party competition. Finally, the interplay between party agency, national contexts, and cross-national trends.

Armed with this approach, I show that the contemporary Western European radical left party family must be understood as a reaction to the triple crisis of communism, of the Fordist social model, and of neoliberalism. The first was at once the greatest asset and the greatest liability of the radical left: a systemic alternative to capitalism, which, however, proved politically indefensible and economically problematic. The second was relentlessly dismantled since the eighties by neoliberal trends and reforms, but the defence of its achievements became the focal point of left-wing dissatisfaction and resistance. The third was successful in restoring the income and power of the top capitalist strata, but meant socio-economic stagnation or regression for the vast majority of the population. In short, a vacuum of representation of working-class and welfarist constituencies opened up in the political systems, which the radical left sought to turn to its benefit. Through an analysis of both the continental trends and three case studies (Germany, Italy, and France), I show that this endeavour led to a certain renewal and recovery of the Western European radical left, which emerged from its initial crisis in the early nineties as a vital and relevant political tradition. At the same time, this party family failed to measure up to its own high expectations, remaining a partial thermometer of the crisis of neoliberalism but no bearer of a viable alternative.

The envisaged contribution to the scholarship is twofold. On the one hand, the analysis will improve our understanding of the Western European radical left party family, in particular the definition of its nature, the identification of its main trends and tensions, and the explanation of some of its paradoxical properties (strategic and programmatic uncertainty, a failure to regroup in a coherent party or coalition, abrupt electoral oscillations, and a weak overall impact on the political system). On the other hand, it will provide a coherent conceptual and empirical framework to study party families and political parties, enriching the tools available to students of party politics.

The structure of the book is the following.

The first part (chapter one) deals with theoretical and methodological issues. I present here the theoretical framework guiding the analysis. The treatment of the radical left as a party family is theorised and justified. The boundaries of the anti-neoliberal field are defined and its main features and tensions identified. The methodology for the analysis and comparison of the radical left at the continental, national, and party levels is explained. Finally, the main research questions are expanded upon.

The second part explores the roots and evolution of the radical left at a continental level, that is, across seventeen Western European countries. In chapter two, I review the evolution of the communist, left-socialist, and far left predecessors of the contemporary radical left from 1918 to 1988, showing how their nature and strength evolved under the pressure of internal, national, and international events and trends. In chapter three, I track instead the evolution of the 'new' radical left since 1989.

The third part carries out an in-depth analysis of the three case studies of Germany, Italy, and France, selected for their central importance within the European Union and for the diversity of their starting points and trajectories. In chapter four, I investigate the relative success story of the German radical left, characterised by the uneven but generally successful consolidation of a medium-sized radical left party (PDS and DIE LINKE) in a country of weak or discredited radical traditions. In chapter five, I examine the disastrous case of the Italian radical left, which moved from the initial defection of the PCI, to a recovery of the PRC up to 1996, through splits and oscillations up to 2007, to a final state of unprecedented weakness and fragmentation afterwards. In chapter six, I assess the contradictory case of the French radical left, which remained relatively strong but failed to profit from the recurrent social and political crises, oscillating between fragmentation and regroupment, prominence and marginality.

The final part brings together the different analytical threads and offers a final assessment of the contemporary radical left party family. In chapter seven, I explicitly compare the three national trajectories with the Western European benchmark, reaching robust conclusions on the nature, success, and limitations of this party family. In the conclusion, I summarise the main findings of the analysis and discuss their implications.

References

Agosti, Aldo (1999). *Bandiere rosse. Un profilo storico dei comunismi europei*. Roma: Editori Riuniti.

Bell, David Scott (ed.) (1993). *Western European communists and the collapse of communism*. Oxford: Berg.

Bidet, Jacques, and Stathis Kouvelakis (2005). *Critical companion to contemporary Marxism*. Leiden: Brill.

Botella, Juan, and Luis Ramiro (eds.) (2003). *The crisis of communism and party change: The evolution of Western European communist and post-communist parties*. Barcelona: ICPS.

Bull, Martin J., and Paul Heywood (eds.) (1994). *West European Communist parties after the revolutions of 1989*. London: Macmillan.

Crouch, Colin (2004). *Post-democracy*. Cambridge: The Polity Press.

Current Sociology, 61(4)/2013. Special issue: 'From indignation to occupation: A new wage of global mobilization'.

Della Porta, Donatella (ed.) (2007). *The global justice movement. Cross-national and transnational perspectives*. Boulder: Paradigm Publishers.
Dreyfus, Michel, Bruno Groppo, Claudio Sergio Ingerflom, Roland Lew, Claude Pennetier, Bernard Pudal, and Serge Wolikow (eds.) (2004). *Le siècle des communismes*. Paris: Éditions de l'Atelier.
Duménil, Gérard, and Dominique Lévy (2011). *The crisis of neoliberalism*. Cambridge: Harvard University Press.
Duménil, Gérard, and Dominique Lévy (2004). *Capital resurgent. Roots of the neoliberal revolution*. Cambridge: Harvard University Press.
Escalona, Fabien, Luke March, and Mathieu Vieira (2017). *The Palgrave handbook of radical left parties in Europe*. London: Palgrave.
Férnandez, Joseba (2014). 'Facing the corporate-university: The new wave of student movements in Europe', *Journal for Critical Education Policy Studies* 12(1): 191–213.
Fukuyama, Francis (1989). 'The end of history?', *The National Interest*, Summer: 3–18.
Karatzogianni, Athina (2015). *Firebrand waves of digital activism, 1994–2014. The rise and spread of hacktivism and cyberconflict*. Basingstoke: Palgrave Macmillan
Kelly, John, Kerstin Hamann, and Alison Johnston (2013). 'Striking concessions from governments: the success of general strikes in Western Europe, 1980–2009', *Comparative Politics* 46(1): 23–41.
Keucheyan, Razmig (2013). *The left hemisphere: Mapping critical theory today*. London: Verso.
Kitschelt, Herbert (1994). *The transformation of European social democracy*. Cambridge: Cambridge University Press.
Kouvelakis, Stathis (2007). *La France en révolte. Luttes sociales et cycles politiques*. Paris: Textuel.
Kowalski, Ronald (2006). *European communism: 1848–1991*. Basingstoke: Palgrave Macmillan.
Lahusen, Christian, and Britta Baumgarten (2006). 'Die Fragilität kollektiven Handelns: Arbeitslosenproteste in Deutschland und Frankreich', *Zeitschrift für Soziologie* 35(2): 102–119.
López, Miguel A. Martínez (2013). 'The squatters' movement in Europe: A durable struggle for social autonomy in urban politics', *Antipode* 45(4): 866–887.
Mair, Peter (2006). 'Ruling the void? The hollowing of Western Democracy', *New Left Review* 42: 121–129.
March, Luke (2012). *Radical left parties in contemporary Europe*. Abingdon: Routledge.
March, Luke, and Cas Mudde (2005). 'What's left of the radical left? The European radical left after 1989: Decline *and* mutation', *Comparative European Politics* 3: 23–49.
Moreau, Patrick, Marc Lazar, and Gerhard Hirscher (eds.) (1998). *Der Kommunismus in Westeuropa. Niedergang oder Mutation?* Landsberg: Olzog.
Nyers, Peter, and Kim Rygiel (eds.) (2012). *Citizenship, migrant activism and the politics of movement*. Abingdon: Routledge.
Vandaele, Kurt (2011). Sustaining or abandoning 'social peace'? Strike development and trends in Europe since the 1990s [working paper]. Brussels: ETUI.
Walgrave, Stefaan, and Dieter Rucht (2010). *The world says no to war. Demonstrations against the war on Iraq*. Minneapolis: University of Minnesota Press.
Wilson, Frank (1993). *The failure of West European communism: Implications for the future*. New York: Paragon.

1 Toward an analysis of the contemporary Western European radical left

This chapter presents the theoretical and methodological framework that will guide the analysis of this book.

The first section delimits the research object to the development of the partisan radical left in Western Europe from 1989 to 2015.

The second section spells out in detail my holistic approach to the conceptualisation and analysis of the contemporary radical left. First, I propose a slightly modified definition of the boundaries of the radical left, highlighting its internal pluralism and historicity. Secondly, I build on the existing literature on party politics to conceptualise the nature of radical left parties in terms of constituency, political project, organisational mediations, and strategic mediations. Thirdly, I point to the existence of an underlying anti-neoliberal political field produced by the transformations of the social and political system, whose contradictory properties largely overdetermine the dilemmas and behaviour of radical left parties. Finally, I argue for a multi-level, aggregate approach taking into account all three levels (party families, individual parties, and political fields) and putting the discussion of the party family level to the centre stage.

The third section expands on the main research questions and the methodology used to answer them. The former focus on assessing and explaining radical left cohesion, strength, and influence. The latter combine quantitative methods and qualitative observations. The consistent and accurate measurement of radical left strength in its various electoral, parliamentary, governmental, and extra-parliamentary components, in particular, will represent one of the main contributions of the analysis.

The concluding section, finally, summarises and discusses the main features of the framework.

Delimiting the research object

The object of this book is the development of the partisan radical left in Western Europe over the period 1989 to 2015. All three qualifiers – organisational type, geographical scope, and temporal span – must be briefly justified.

The radical left, just like all other political traditions, cannot be reduced to its partisan dimension. In his masterly survey of the long-term evolution of the 'class left', Bartolini (2000) identifies two main components: a 'political channel' (parties) and a 'professional channel' (trade unions). March and Mudde (2005), for their part, distinguish within the radical left a political component (parties), a civil society component (non-party organisations such as trade unions, associations, or social movement networks), and a subcultural component.[1] Raynaud (2006), similarly, explores the French far left from the point of view of both political parties and their intellectual inspiration.

My analysis will focus on the partisan radical left, looking at other components from the point of view of political parties: their capacity to represent the concerns of their wider subculture at the electoral and institutional levels; their ability to bind sympathisers to their organisations as members or activists; the organisational linkages they establish with civil society and social movement organisations; and their collaboration with non-party actors in extra-parliamentary mobilisations.

The choice is motivated by an interest in the crisis and renewal of partisan forms of participation and representation, and should not be taken as a sanction of a general primacy of party or institutional politics. On the one hand, non-party organisations and movements routinely intervene in the political decision making through privileged links with specific parties, transversal lobbying, referendums, extra-parliamentary mobilisations, public opinion campaigns, and the creation of new parties. On the other hand, political parties themselves straddle the boundary between state and civil society, working within representative institutions but at the same mobilising citizens in electoral campaigns, anti-government demonstrations, and even armed insurrections. Although their primary preoccupation is indeed concerned with influencing state policies, they also often try to directly shape the functioning of civil society institutions (companies, universities, cooperatives, families) and people's ideas and behaviours (identity building, value change, interpersonal relations). Political parties are just one part of a broader subculture made of civil society and social movement organisations, informal groups, physical spaces, media, companies, intellectuals, minority tendencies of non-radical parties or associations, and individual citizens, all of them interacting to various degrees of closeness and coherence.

Contrary to an influential strand of the recent literature (Backes and Moreau 2008; Hudson 2012; March 2012), I will limit the analysis to the radical left of Western Europe – that is, all European countries that belonged to the Western sphere of influence during the Cold War.

There are good arguments in favour of the former option. Until 1989, the relationship between Western communist parties and their Eastern counterparts was tight, despite the progressive drift away from Moscow of Eurocommunist and other tendencies. Relations temporarily collapsed in the nineties but partially resumed with the EU enlargements of the noughties and twenty-tens, with many Eastern parties joining the GUE/NGL and the PEL as full members or observers. Nevertheless, the political cultures and systems of the two sides still remain fundamentally different (Hloušek and Kopeček 2010). An all-European approach would obscure rather than illuminate the analysis of the nature and behaviour of the radical left, which is shaped by very different forces in Western and Eastern Europe.

The Western European radical left will be approached from two vantage points: a general analysis of the continental landscape, and three detailed national case studies. The continental landscape is defined as the sum of seventeen Western European countries: Austria, Belgium, Denmark, Finland, France, Germany, Greece, Ireland, Italy, Luxembourg, the Netherlands, Norway, Portugal, Spain, Sweden, Switzerland, and the United Kingdom. This covers the whole area with the exclusion of the microstates (Andorra, Monaco, Liechtenstein, San Marino, and the Vatican City) and some small states of late independence (Iceland in 1944, Cyprus in 1960, Malta in 1964).[2] The only exception to the Western focus is the case of former East Germany (GDR), which reunified in 1990 with West Germany (FRG) and will therefore be included from that point onwards. The three case studies are Germany, Italy, and France. The rationale for their selection is not the strength and relevance of the radical left, which was high in previous decades but was surpassed by several countries in the post-1989 period (Cyprus, Greece, Portugal, Denmark, and, more recently, Spain). It is instead the central demographic, economic, political, and cultural weight of the countries themselves, which lends to their radical lefts an objectively superior importance for the course of Western European politics. The three countries accounted in 1989–2015 for 50.5 per cent of total registered voters, 56.9 per cent of total radical left voters, 50.8 per cent of the total GDP, and a dominant influence within EU and Eurozone institutions. Not accidentally, their main parties (PRC, PDS/DIE LINKE, PCF, LCR/NPA, and PG) have until recently dominated the transnational discussion, coordination (GUE/NGL, PEL, Transform!), and mobilisation of the Western European radical left. This prominence has receded since the extraordinary electoral successes of SYRIZA in Greece (2012–15) and PODEMOS in Spain (2015), but developments in Germany and France (less in Italy) still remain the key to a shift of the continental social and political balance of forces.

The temporal span of the analysis covers the period from 1989 to 2015. The main characteristics of the contemporary Western European radical left are, to a large extent, the product of processes initiated in the seventies and eighties: the explosion of left-libertarian and green themes; the post-Fordist and post-industrial shift of advanced capitalist economies; the neoliberalisation of economic mechanisms, public policy, culture, and politics; the erosion of working-class identification, militancy, and power; and the multi-faceted crisis of world communism. The fall of the Soviet bloc in 1989–91, however, acted as an accelerator of these processes, precipitated a violent crisis of the radical left, and paved the way for a new beginning of this party family after 1993. The choice of a starting point between 1989 and 1993 is therefore the most natural one. Previous developments (1917–88) will nevertheless be briefly reviewed in chapter two.

Theorising the Western European radical left

The radical left as a party family: boundaries, definition, and implications

Does it make sense to treat radical left parties in Western Europe as a *party family*? Mair and Mudde (1998) have highlighted both the essential role of this concept for comparative political analysis and the pitfalls of its empirical use. No broad agreement on the most appropriate discriminating criteria currently exists. A number of alternatives, such as party name, transnational links, policy, ideology, origin, sociology, organisation, and position within the matrix of political cleavages, are possible, each leading to different classification results. More specifically, the concept of a Western European radical left party family is well established in the literature (De Waele and Seiler 2012; Hudson 2000, 2012; March 2012; March and Mudde 2005; Tannahill 1978; Waller and Fennema 1988), but opinions somewhat diverge on two critical points: the extent to which the concept applies beyond traditional communist parties to include alternative organisations (of a far-left or left-socialist bent), and the (dis)continuity of the radical left before and after the shock of 1989–91.

Until 1989, scholars of the radical left focused almost exclusively on a specifically *communist party family*. This was an obvious choice, as official communist parties generally dominated the space to the left of social democracy and, at least initially, represented an ideal-typical case of cohesive party family: a common origin as a split of the socialist workers' movement in the 'critical juncture' of 1917 (Lipset and Rokkan 1967: 47–48); a uniform ideology in the Soviet Marxist-Leninist worldview; tight transnational links first in the Comintern, the 'world party of revolution', and later in Moscow-inspired networks; very similar policies, organisational models, constituencies, strategies, and tactics. The categorisation, however, had its problems. Firstly, it ignored the fact that communist parties often closely cooperated with left socialists and other fellow travellers in permanent fronts such as the Finnish SKDL (1945–90) or in temporary electoral alliances such as the Italian FDP (1948) or the French *union de la gauche* (1972–77). Secondly, it underestimated the progressive loss of ideological and relational cohesion of Western communism, which moved from the monolithism of Stalin's reign to a tentative 'polycentrism' after 1956, a marked differentiation between Eurocommunist and orthodox sensibilities after 1968, and an effective disintegration in 1989–91. Thirdly, it ignored alternative leftist traditions such as anarchism, Trotskyism, Maoism, the post-1968 new left, and radicalised minority nationalisms, despite their partial similarity of origin and/or ideology with orthodox communist parties. The reactions of Western European communist parties to the collapse of the Eastern bloc forced a rethinking of the dominant classification, but left observers puzzled with regards to possible alternatives. Bull (1994: 211) claimed that 'the erstwhile fragmentation has become separation and [. . .] it will no longer be possible to generalise about these parties as a "family", nor fruitful to study them within the same analytical framework'. Other authors concurred, approaching their subsequent diverging choices as a post-communist coda of a history which was in fact over (Botella and Ramiro 2003; Marantzidis 2004). In the noughties, however, several authors began to argue that while the 'old' communist movement was indeed dead and buried, some form of reconfigured 'new' *radical left party family* had been emerging from its ruins (Hudson 2000, 2012; March and Mudde 2005). This insight has since become an accepted premise of the literature on the contemporary radical left, and rightly so, as a composite yet relatively distinct and coherent political space to the left of the socialist and green party families does clearly exist, both in terms of objective commonalities and in terms of subjective relations between parties in fora such as the European United Left/Nordic Green Left (GUE/NGL) European Parliament group, the Party of the European Left (PEL) and Nordic Green Left Alliance (NGLA) international party federations, the Transform! think tank, transnational social movements such as the global justice movement, and bilateral contacts.

More problematic are instead the attempts to find an appropriate definition of the distinguishing features of this party family and its relation with its communist predecessor. All authors categorise these parties primarily on the basis of their assumed anti-capitalism, loosely understood as a generic critique of contemporary relations of social and political power (Ducange et al. 2013; March and Mudde 2005; Seiler 2012). The term, however, is too vague to be useful. On the one hand, anti-capitalism is precisely one of those elements which the post-1989 radical left has generally tended to downplay, focusing instead on a medium-term anti-neoliberal programme centred on defending and reviving the welfare state and labour rights against the present onslaught. On the other hand, the application of this criterion to earlier periods would completely blur the distinction with mainstream social democrats, since they as well often upheld a formal commitment to an ultimate overcoming of capitalism and always expounded some form of opposition to the inequalities, insecurity, and power structures produced by capitalism.

In my opinion, the solution to these dilemmas lies in the definition of the radical left as a party family (a) situating itself in the tradition of the 'class left', a historical tradition determined to reform or overcome capitalism from the standpoint of universalistically conceived working-class interests, and (b) identifying and organising itself as a separate tendency from and to the left of mainstream social democracy. The formula is similar to that of Seiler (2012: 13–14), but loosens the anti-capitalist qualification and clarifies that the adjective 'radical' must be understood not as a substantive but as a predominantly relational qualifier.

What may at first sight appear as a very formalistic definition actually presents a number of key advantages on the existing alternatives. It clearly delimits the boundaries of the radical left, distinguishing it unambiguously both from party families primarily concerned with the representation of other classes and transversal cleavages, and from mainstream social democracy, with which it nevertheless shares a common origin in the nineteenth-century labour movement. It also highlights the constitutive pluralism of the radical left, where different ideological traditions and political currents such as Marxists and non-Marxists, reformists and revolutionaries, moderates and radicals, statists and anti-statists, and workerists and left-libertarians have coexisted side by side in varying degrees of cooperation or competition. Finally, it allows the precise ideological, sociological, and relational content of the radical left to vary over time, thus enabling a historically-grounded understanding of its evolution and adaptation to changing national and international environments. Schematically, the 'revolutionary' radical left born of the trauma of World War I and the October Revolution was predominantly characterised by a Leninist worldview, a manual working-class constituency, and an overt enmity toward the moderate left based on domestic radicalism and proletarian internationalism. From the thirties to the eighties, however, these elements evolved: the ideology was first thoroughly Stalinised, then went through a slow but extensive rethinking of liberal democracy, the road to power, and the socialist goal; non-manual social constituencies, such as the traditional petty bourgeoisie, public-sector employees, white-collar workers, students, and the economically inactive, acquired a subordinate but growing weight; and elements of competitive cooperation with social democratic and other political forces were found in the common battle for the expansion of democratic and socio-economic rights. Since the nineties, finally, the characteristic features of the communist tradition were greatly diluted and hybridised in a 'broad left' matrix: long-term anti-capitalist concerns receded further into the background, while a pragmatic focus on a mid-term anti-neoliberal programme took the centre stage; the centrality of productive workers was replaced by a looser welfarist constituency, appealed to more as citizens and human beings than as producers; and the separation from social democracy was justified not on the grounds of its moderate reformism but on its alleged conversion to neoliberalism. Seen in these terms, the contemporary radical left thus appears as the fruit of the convergence of three distinct elements: the de-emphasised traditions of its communist, left-socialist, and far-left predecessors; the ideal legacy of much of the social democratic and green-alternative thought of the seventies and early eighties; and newer anti-neoliberal concerns.

Radical left parties: the analysis of party nature

Regardless of their degree of uniformity and cohesion, party families are still necessarily composed by a plurality of organisations with specific orientations and features. Political parties are understood here as *complex tools* enabling collective action and mediating between civil society and public authoritative decision making. Which constellation of social interests does a given party represent, to which end, and how? Reorganising a number of established lines of inquiry on party politics, I analyse the *nature* of political parties as the interaction of four main components: their social constituency; their political project; their organisational mediations; and their strategic mediations.

The first component, the *social constituency*, refers to the constellation of groups directly operating within a party or linked to it by relations of support and representation.

This theme is often approached by the sub-disciplines of political sociology and electoral studies, with the aim of identifying the socio-demographic characteristics, identities, values, opinions, practices, and other characteristics of party members and voters. However, cleavage-based and Marxist approaches correctly argue (Lipset and Rokkan 1967; Marx 1969) that the relation between a party and its constituency has two faces: an empirical-sociological one (actual constituency supporting the party) and a normative-ideological one (ideal constituency that the party strives to represent). For instance, a party can have a broad popular support but primarily pursue the interests of a small power elite or, on the contrary, advocate the interests of the mass of wage earners but have little support among them.

An analysis of the party constituency must therefore identify its components and dominant elements straddling between empirical and normative elements, and moving along a multi-layered structure. Any political party encompasses several partially overlapping layers of people characterised by varying degrees of attachment and influence (Van Haute 2009). Within the boundaries of the party-organisation proper, it is possible to distinguish the top-level elite (the leader, members of executive bodies, national elected representatives), the middle-level elite (full-time cadres, holders of local party or elected offices, congress delegates), the activists, and the ordinary members. Outside of it, there are external layers of financial backers, members of collateral and sympathising organisations, active fellow-travellers, party identifiers, and ordinary voters. Thus, tensions inevitably emerge between the social composition, interests and values, and relative weight of each layer. Territorial differences further complicate the picture (Carty 2004; Hopkin 2003).

Evidence on the characteristics of the party constituency can be found in sociological data (surveys and administrative figures, ethnographic studies), organisational data (internal distribution of power), ideological data (party documents and rhetoric), and policy data.

The second component, the *political project*, refers to the articulation of the interests of the social constituency of a party in a coherent set of medium-term and long-term objectives.

The analysis of ideology is one of the established fields of party politics research and is approached in terms of broad political traditions (Seiler 1980; Von Beyme 1985) or finer ideological (Mudde 2002) and policy (Bakker et al. 2015; Klingemann 2006) differences. In my perspective, it is important to underline the connection between a political project and its (explicit or implicit) social constituency. The former is, however, relatively autonomous from the latter. First, the interests of a given constituency are not ideologically univocal, but are instead open to a plurality of conceptualisations. Working-class interests, for instance, can be legitimately construed as implying a fair distribution of the social product or the overcoming of capitalism, class struggle or cross-class collaboration, nationalism or internationalism, universalism or particularism (for instance, by bolstering the position of wageworkers of the dominant gender, ethnicity, nationality, religion, status, and so on against underprivileged strata or newcomers). Secondly, parties with the same constituency and the same broad ideological orientation can still develop very different political projects in terms of the institutional mechanisms, the temporal horizons, and the necessary intermediate steps envisaged. Thirdly, the contours of the political project of a party are the object of continuous political and power struggles between groups, layers, factions, and tendencies, and are affected by the impact of the external environment, party competition, and broad cultural trends. Fourthly, positions on new issues are a further element of variation between otherwise similar parties: an example is the slow and uncertain adaptation of traditional parties to post-materialist and left-libertarian themes. Typically, political parties encompass a multiplicity of distinct orientations and accents: clear formulations or compromise solutions are sometimes reached at the level of formal programmatic documents, but the overall political project is necessarily shifting (following the outcome of internal and external debates) and contains large margins of ambiguity (in order to conciliate political differences).

The political project of a party is expressed, with various degrees of coherence, in internal documents, the public discourse of the party, theoretical works by party intellectuals or external sources of inspiration, and the inner beliefs (sometimes expressed, sometimes implicit) of party leaders, members, and supporters.

The third component, the *organisational mediations*, refers to the ways a party structures itself from an organisational point of view in the pursuit of its own goals, and of the goals of its constituency.

A first strand of the literature focuses on organisational issues in the narrow sense, embodying diachronic change and innovation in a succession of party models: from cadre parties in the nineteenth century to mass parties in the twentieth century (Duverger 1951; Weber 1968); from the latter to catch-all (people's) parties (Kirchheimer 1966) or electoral professional parties (Panebianco 1988) in the post-war decades; and a proliferation of new models since the eighties, such as new politics parties (Poguntke 1987), modern cadres parties (Koole 1994), cartel parties (Katz and Mair 1995), business firm parties (Hopkin and Paolucci 1999), network parties (Heidar and Saglie 2003), franchise parties (Carty 2004), and personal parties (Calise 2010). The systematisation of these models in a coherent classificatory framework has been attempted (Gunter and Diamond 2003; Wolinetz 2002) but still lacks in comprehensiveness and discriminatory power (Krouwel 2006).

A second strand of the literature also deals with organisational issues, but from the point of view of internal power relations (Rye 2014).

A third strand focuses instead on a broader analysis of the mediating function that political parties play between citizens and the state. Neumann (1956) distinguishes between parties aggregating disparate opinions or interests (individual representation), integrating subcultural blocs in the democratic political system (democratic integration), and organising the latter against liberal democracy (total integration). Kirchheimer (1966) differentiates between three main functions of political parties: the selection and circulation of the political class; the aggregation and articulation of popular consent; and the democratic participation of citizens. Lawson (1980) mentions five types of linkages: participatory, electoral, policy-responsive, clientelistic, and directive; Poguntke (2002) adds a sixth type, the organisational linkage. Mair (1994) and Katz and Mair (1995), finally, describe the historical trajectory of Western political parties as moving from agents of civil society (up to the fifties), through brokers between civil society and the state (the Fordist period), to agents of the state (since the eighties).

All these perspectives are important for the analysis of organisational mediations. On the one hand, organisational solutions have feedback effects on the constituency and political project of parties, favouring the dominance or marginality of specific groups and layers. On the other hand, the specific forms in which parties ensure internal coordination and cohesion, develop ties of identification and attachment, communicate with their potential constituency, articulate social demands, organise their membership, structure social linkages, collect financial and material resources, and mobilise their supporters at the extra-parliamentary level affect their success and failure.

The main sources for the analysis of organisational mediations are data on statutes, internal rules and practices, membership figures, collateral organisations, the party apparatus and its resources, communication channels, and party activities.

The fourth component, the *strategic mediations*, refers to the means, strategies, and tactics employed by parties in the pursuit of their political project.

The literature on these issues is also extensive, dealing with legitimate and illegal means, electoral-institutional and extra-parliamentary activities, political and social alliances, conciliatory or intransigent attitudes, temporalities, and complex sequential plans.

The analysis of strategic mediations can be gleaned partly from explicit party 'doctrines', and partly from actual party behaviour.

An adequate analysis of the nature of radical left parties – above a certain threshold of relevance – is usually possible, due the existence of abundant primary data and secondary literature on the key features of their social constituency, political project, and organisational and strategic mediations. However, this task exceeds the scope of this book, requiring a monograph or chapter for each party. I will instead limit myself to sketching the key features of the most relevant parties, emphasising their similarities and differences with the general radical left norm.

The anti-neoliberal field of forces

Parties and party families sometimes evolve according to internal impulses (party agency), but are profoundly shaped by the effects of other parties (party competition) and broader social and political forces (external environment). The structured nature of these effects can be conceptualised in terms of *fields of forces*.

In the case of the contemporary radical left, the triple crisis of international communism, of the Fordist social model, and of neoliberalism gave rise to a peculiar *anti-neoliberal field of forces*, whose contradictory tendencies both stimulated the recovery and renewal of the radical left (existing radical left parties, social-democratic splinter groups, and new organisations), and overdetermined its dilemmas and behaviour.

The first two crises, broadly covering the period from the late seventies to the early nineties, had important consequences: a swift decline of the radical left and of other working-class and welfarist currents; a steady rightward shift of the political systems; and a progressive neoliberal turn of economic mechanisms, public policy, and culture. At the same time, the promises of prosperity of neoliberalism were time and time again refuted by facts. Neoliberal reforms and trends elicited the opposition and active resistance of important sections of the population, provoked a slow and hesitant decline of mainstream parties, and opened up new growth prospects for the radical left, particularly since their acceleration in the early nineties and during the great recession.

The notion of neoliberalism has gained a widespread currency in the recent critical literature, although its use is often ambiguous (Mudge 2008; Thorsen 2011). Accounts of its origin, nature, and political implications also differ (Cahill et al. 2012; Foucault 2008; Harman 2007; Harvey 2005; Saad-Filho and Johnston 2005). Following the neo-Marxist interpretation of Duménil and Lévy (2004, 2011), I view neoliberalism as a pragmatic political project of the upper strata of the capitalist class, in alliance with top managerial strata, to restore their power, wealth, and incomes. In advanced economies these groups, far from striving for a return to the utopian 'minimal state' advocated by some market fundamentalists, generally preserved a strong role of the state while changing the goals and priorities of its intervention: profits over accumulation; high over middle and low incomes; the financial sector over the real economy; low inflation over growth; a regulatory over a dirigiste state; and so on. In fact, states continued to forcefully intervene in the economy to support aggregate demand[3] and investments, improve national competitiveness, ensure social peace, and rescue ailing banks, with levels of revenues, expenditures, and debt remaining at historically peak levels. A broad agreement reigned on a specific set of policies, such the imposition of shareholder value criteria within companies, trade and capital liberalisation, tax competition between states, privatisations, welfare retrenchment, and labour market flexibility, but preferences on specific enforcement mechanisms varied according to the concrete circumstances, ranging from outright de-regulation to an active neoliberal re-regulation via national legislation, independent central banks and authorities, international treaties, and international institutions such as the WTO or the EU. Moreover, important national and political differences remained on issues such as interest and exchange rates, fiscal and monetary austerity, import- or export-led orientation, and social partnership with the trade unions.

In Western Europe, the neoliberal project was gradually embraced and implemented at all levels, although strong popular opposition and resistance influenced and slowed down its course. The final result was an accumulation of barriers to progressive national economic policies, an erosion of the post-war model of the welfarist mixed economy, a strong upward redistribution of income and wealth, a weak macro-economic performance (low accumulation, investment, and growth; high unemployment), and an absolute stagnation or regression of the living conditions and prospects of large social strata.

The political parties and traditions that had been at the forefront of the construction of the European social model gradually converted to these new policy orientations, while retaining some commitment to varied levels of welfare provisions. Social democratic and labour parties trashed their traditional policies centred on Keynesianism, dirigisme, social protection, decommodification, downward redistribution of income, wealth, and power, and (in some cases) a long-term overcoming of the capitalist mode of production (Bailey 2009; Moschonas 2002; Nachtwey 2013). Other party families – Christian democrats, left-liberals, conservatives – did the same. This determined the emergence of a *potential vacuum of political representation of working-class and welfarist constituencies*, straining the relations between the modernising elites and their traditionalist supporters. At the same time, social democratic and other mainstream parties generally managed to retain the allegiance of most of these constituencies thanks to a variety of mechanisms: the memory and present effects of past policies; the differentiated impact of neoliberalism on different social groups; the continued support of key civil society groups (such as the trade unions); a gradual and delayed implementation of negative reforms; their successful framing as limited or inevitable; the lowering of expectations; the impact of bipolarism; and so on.

The consequence of these complex developments was the emergence of an anti-neoliberal field of forces including the plurality or majority of Western European voters, which exposed the radical left to three key contradictory tendencies.

The first and most important one was the contradiction between *anti-neoliberal coherence and centre-left unity*. The moderate left (and other mainstream parties) had largely adopted a neoliberal policy orientation, but retained an important level of anti-neoliberal image and support. Choosing the right attitude was therefore extremely difficult. A conciliatory course, motivated by a pessimistic option against the greater evil (the right) or by an optimistic belief in one's ability the (pull the moderate left to the left), usually ended up involving radical left parties in the implementation of policies directly opposed to their own principles (privatisations, deregulation, fiscal austerity, the precarisation of labour, foreign military interventions) and harmed its anti-neoliberal credibility. An intransigent course, motivated by the regressive policy orientation of the 'new' social democracy, exposed instead radical left parties to accusations of sectarianism and the danger of tactical voting.

The second one was the contradiction between *anti-neoliberalism and anti-capitalism*. Traditionally strongly linked to anti-capitalist perspectives, the radical left was now encouraged to pick up the banners of reformism and welfarism that mainstream parties had let fall to the ground. This was not a big problem in itself, as the two could be easily reconciled in principle. The overwhelming majority of radical left parties argued that anti-neoliberal reforms were a necessary first step toward a future socialist transformation, focusing on the former but maintaining a vague commitment to the latter. Many far-left parties, in turn, claimed that reform objectives, by stimulating popular mobilisation and clashing against the limits of the capitalist system, could be used to directly transcend them. Finally, concrete policy differences were not so relevant until an offensive stage was reached, and most tendencies (anti-neoliberals and anti-capitalists, moderates and radicals, gradualists and immediatists) were therefore open to collaborate in the defensive stage of resistance to the neoliberal onslaught. In practice, however, an outspoken communist identity generally limited the short-term chances of winning over new disaffected voters and organised groups, leading most parties to gradually de-emphasise it and provoking contrary reactions within their ranks.

The third one was the contradiction between *old traditions and new realities*. The ideological, sociological, organisational, and strategic foundations of the twentieth-century radical left were radically questioned by historical developments since the seventies: the political and economic bankruptcy of the 'really existing socialisms' of the Soviet bloc; the crisis of working-class identification, organisation, and militancy; post-Fordism, deindustrialisation, and globalisation; the global shift from developmentalist and redistributive (Keynesianism, welfarism, dirigisme, socialist planning) to neoliberal forms of socio-economic regulation; the rightward shift of mainstream political parties, including social democratic ones; the rise of left-libertarian values and issues; and so on. Radical left parties remained divided both on their willingness and ability to respond to these developments, and on the direction of the necessary change: a stubborn defence of traditional legacies; their revitalisations under new forms; an embrace of new possibilities; or a mere adaptation to the new trends.

Crucially, the contemporary radical left never managed to escape from the contradictory effects of the anti-neoliberal field described above, at least up to the great recession.

On the one hand, it did not split in clearly identifiable sub-groups. Divergences were important but fluid. All parties were traversed by the same tensions and constantly oscillated between the two poles of each contradiction, experimenting with various elements of a common matrix, rising and falling, breaking up and regrouping. For this reason, the ideological sub-categories developed by some authors (Gomez et al. 2016; March 2012) – radical vs. far left; traditional vs. new left; conservative vs. reform communist; democratic vs. populist socialist – have proved to be unstable and largely artificial, and are only occasionally retained in this analysis.

On the other hand, it never succeeded in monopolising the representation of working-class and welfarist constituency (a recent exception is SYRIZA in Greece). It thus remained trapped in an uneasy relationship with the moderate left, oscillating between conciliatory and intransigent attitudes, disastrous collaborations, and sterile denunciations.

A multi-level, aggregate analysis

The conceptual work carried out in this section suggests that the analysis of the radical left must take into account *three distinct but interrelated levels*: party families, individual parties, and underlying political fields.

Political parties form larger party families, competing for control and – in the extreme cases – switching allegiance. They also compete with members of other party families. The terrain of the competition is structured by political fields with distinctive boundaries and properties, which overdetermine the behaviour of parties.

In the case of the contemporary radical left parties, these forms of interaction can be summarised as follows. First, radical left parties competed with each other for the (small) existing radical left constituency. Secondly, they competed with other party families and the abstention on their core issue (anti-neoliberalism) and other transversal issues (for instance, ecology, pacifism, civil rights, the 'protest vote', anti-establishment populism, and national or regional interests). Thirdly, the nature of the anti-neoliberal field of forces, which went well beyond the traditional anti-capitalist and communist milieus, offered them promising growth prospects but simultaneously created unresolvable tensions.

The *aggregate level* will be privileged in the analysis.

The radical left will be approached as a relatively coherent but plural party family, within which various partisan organisations (big and small, parliamentary and extra-parliamentary, old and new) and ideological tendencies operate, interact, and compete. This choice has three inevitable corollaries.

First, both the Western European radical left and each national radical left must be analysed (and compared) as wholes. This will allow a better discussion of their overall strength, cohesion, fragmentation and regroupment, nature (common trends and party specificities), and ideological and strategic debates.

Secondly, the exclusion of specific parties on the ground of ideology or relevance must be minimized, as it distorts the overall picture. While the analysis will necessarily focus on the largest players, all organisations that can be identified as part of the radical left will in principle be included, avoiding any *a priori* threshold of relevance.[4] This will improve the accuracy and consistency of the evidence, enabling a better comparison between cohesive (Germany, the Netherlands), fragmented (France, Portugal), and scattered (Belgium, the UK) radical lefts and between cohesive and fragmented periods (such as Italy before and after 1998).

Thirdly, individual parties must be treated not in isolation but as members of the radical left party family. This affiliation has specific effects on the nature and behaviour of parties, both in terms of mutual influences (imitation, transfer, joint elaboration) and in terms of the influence of underlying forces emanating from the social and political system: in the case of the radical left, the contradictory tensions of the anti-neoliberal field of forces.

Summary

In this section, I have built on the existing literature on party politics and on the observation of empirical trends to propose a new holistic approach to the conceptualisation and analysis of the radical left party family. This relies on the interaction of three main levels (party family, individual party, underlying political fields).

On the first account, the radical left has been defined as a party family situating itself in the tradition of the 'class left' and organising as a separate tendency from mainstream social democracy. This flexible definition allows one to distinguish it from other party families, acknowledge its internal pluralism, and recognise the variation of its exact content in space and time. Previously rooted in the communist movement and other far-left and left-socialist traditions, the contemporary Western European radical left has gradually moved since the nineties toward a 'broad left' synthesis centred on opposition to neoliberalism, thus putting a claim on the legacy of both of its direct organisational predecessors and of much of the social democratic and left-libertarian traditions.

On the second account, a new framework has been proposed for the analysis of the nature of individual radical left parties. This is based on the interaction of four key aspects, identified through a reformulation of existing politological lines of inquiry: their constituency, their political project, their organisational mediations, and their strategic mediations. In the empirical analysis of the rest of the book it will emerge that the vagueness of the long-term anti-capitalist goals of contemporary radical left parties does not currently represent a big problem, but the weaknesses of their constituency, organisation, and strategies do contribute to their instability and ineffectiveness.

On the third account, the properties of an anti-neoliberal field of forces have been identified as essential to understand the development and dilemmas of the contemporary radical left. Produced by the triple crisis of international communism, the Fordist social model, and neoliberalism itself, this field shapes the behaviour of radical left parties and exposes it to three key contradictions: between anti-neoliberal coherence and centre-left unity; between anti-neoliberalism and anti-capitalism; and between old traditions and new realities. These tensions help to explain many important features of the contemporary radical left: its uneasy relation with other 'left' (social democratic and green) party families; the potential and limits of its growth; the vagueness and instability of its content; and its continued movement between fragmentation and regroupment.

All three levels will be considered in the empirical analysis, privileging the party family one. This will mean to treat the Western European radical left and each national radical left as wholes (aggregate approach), to include all radical left organisations without thresholds of relevance, and to analyse the latter as members of a party family shaped by common social and ideological similarities, webs of relations, and underlying socio-political forces.

Research questions and methodology

Cohesion

The first question deals with the *cohesion* of the Western European radical left. On the one hand, I will look at the way in which resources, in particular voters and members, are concentrated in the hands of one dominant party or are on the contrary distributed among competing parties. On the other hand, I will examine the processes of fragmentation (as in the case of the Italian PRC) and regroupment (as in the case of the German DIE LINKE). Finally, I will try to identify the drivers and conditions of a cohesive radical left.

The analysis will be based on an observation of quantitative trends, historical processes, and public debates. No particular methodological remarks are needed.

Strength

The second question deals with an accurate measurement of the *strength* of the Western European radical left, followed by an exploration of the causes of the success and failure of the radical left mobilisation. The measurement of the strength and relevance of the radical left is an important concern of the literature, but results so far have been uneven: the contribution of minor parties is generally ignored; data and time series are rarely consistent and comprehensive; indicators are sometimes incoherent; and the exploration is often characterised by a unidimensional focus on electoral results.

My contribution here is three-fold. First, I have collected and harmonised a large amount of existing quantitative data on the contemporary radical left in Germany, France, Italy, and other fourteen Western European countries. The figures, together with their sources, methodological notes, and further elaborations, are made accessible through the Western European Radical Left Database (Chiocchetti 2016a). Secondly, I provide a systematic, coherent, comprehensive, and fine-grained framework for the analysis of party strength. The model and indicators follow the innovative methodology developed in Chiocchetti (2016b), with minor amendments to improve the comparability and clarity of the findings. Thirdly, I use these data and tools to measure levels and trends of radical left strength, to compare it across time and space, to assess its overall relevance and specific features, and to point to possible explanatory factors.

The *toolkit of indicators* used to measure radical left strength is summarised in Table 1.1 below.

The strength of a party (or party family) is defined as its capacity to accumulate *resources of political power*, the assets needed to ensure its existence and its potential influence on the political and social system. Many of these resources exist; only a few of them are both universally recognised as having a paramount importance in the political competition and are adequately operationalisable and measurable with quantitative indicators.

Four main components are retained: the electoral, parliamentary, governmental, and membership component. Electoral strength is operationalised in terms of votes won in free elections for legislative (and in some cases presidential) offices. The indicator of governance strength proposed in Chiocchetti (2016b) is split into its two original sub-components, in order to better show the differences between electoral, parliamentary, and governmental results. Parliamentary strength is operationalised in terms of seats won in legislative bodies. Governmental strength is operationalised in terms of relevant parliamentary seats: that is, the seats of parties belonging to the ruling coalition (regardless of their direct participation or external support to the seating cabinet). The party affiliation of the president is

Table 1.1 Party strength: components and indicators

COMPONENT	ABSOLUTE STRENGTH (n)	SYSTEMIC STRENGTH (%)	SOCIETAL STRENGTH (%)
ELECTORAL STRENGTH	votes	votes / total valid votes	votes / registered voters
PARLIAMENTARY STRENGTH	parliamentary seats	seats / total seats	parliamentary systemic strength* state expenditures / GDP
GOVERNMENTAL STRENGTH	relevant parliamentary seats	relevant seats / total relevant seats	parliamentary systemic strength* state expenditures / GDP
MEMBERSHIP STRENGTH	members	members / total members	members / registered voters
OVERALL STRENGTH	-	average of all dimensions	average of all dimensions (index with base-year)

also counted in the case of France, but ignored in the remaining 'weak' or disputed semi-presidential systems. Membership strength is operationalised in terms of declared or estimated party members. Overall strength is operationalised in terms of an unweighted average of the above-mentioned indicators. Further important components that cannot be operationalised or where data are not reliable or comparable (financial resources, communicative resources, and social linkages) are not included in the model but discussed separately.

Each indicator is offered in *three forms*: in absolute terms (resources), in relative terms compared to the party system (systemic strength), and in relative terms compared to society at large (societal strength).

All figures are harmonised and expressed in *end-of-year yearly rolling figures*. This means that the values of parliamentary, governmental, and membership indicators are measured each year on the date of 31 December (some missing membership data are interpolated and estimated), while the values of the electoral indicator are set for each year at the level of the last available election: of the same year (real) or of previous years (rolling).

Indicators are generally calculated in a *composite form* including all relevant institutions at the national and regional level (regional parliaments and governments, second chambers, elected presidents), weighted for their relative importance.

Cross-national and cross-regional results are produced through the *weighted aggregation* of national and sub-national results: that is, not through a simple average, but through a weighted average based on the share of total valid votes of each unit (for electoral strength) or on the share of total registered voters of each unit (for parliamentary and governmental strength).

Finally, party strength is generally calculated with reference to the *whole radical left*, adding the values of all existing parties belonging to this party family in a given country (national values) or in Western Europe (continental values).

A full model is employed for the analysis of the German, Italian, and French case studies (chapters four to six), while a simplified model including only three dimensions – no membership strength – and excluding sub-national levels and second chambers is used for the analysis of the Western European landscape (chapter two and three).

The methodology described above provides a number of important advantages over existing methods. First, it provides the first systematic framework to measure the levels and variations of party strength over time, in space, and across components. Most indicators are in fact directly drawn or inspired by existing options, but their adaptation and harmonisation into a single coherent model greatly enhances their use and significance. Secondly, it enables both an accurate tracking of short-term (year-on-year) variations of strength over time, and a better calculation of medium-term (say, ten-year) or long-term diachronic averages, accounting for the varying duration of legislatures and cabinets. Thirdly, it improves the coverage of the measures through the use of yearly (as opposed to occasional) data, the addition of all parties without thresholds of relevance, and (when needed) the inclusion of the regional level of governance. Fourthly, it resolves aggregation problems, allowing the creation of weighted aggregate series from individual sub-series: for instance, continental strength from national results, or national strength from central and regional results.

The improvement is particularly evident with regard to the estimation of the continental electoral strength of a given party family. So far, the common practice has been to calculate first ten-year averages of the (non-rolling) national results of the 'relevant' members of the party family, and then the simple average of the resulting national values (De Waele and Vieira 2012; March 2012; Moschonas 2011). That procedure underestimates the strength of fragmented party families, cannot identify short-term cross-national trends, does not account for the varying frequency of elections, and attributes the same weight to countries of a very different size (in 2013, for instance, the size of national electorates in Western Europe varied from 239,668 in the Luxembourg to 61,946,900 in Germany). The proposed methodology, on the contrary, remedies these problems and offers an accurate and flexible instrument to analyse both short-term and long-term trends, with the only proviso that the movement of the aggregate continental curve is necessarily slower than possible underlying trends, as it reflects electoral results harking back up to five years in the past (in average about two years).

Influence

The third question refers to the actual *influence* of the radical left on the social and political system. First, I will look at the means, strategies, and tactics deployed by radical left parties to influence the dynamics of political competition and the social and political balance of forces. Secondly, I will assess their success or failure. Thirdly, I will point to possible explanations of these outcomes.

The analysis will be based on a qualitative observation of policy orientations and outcomes. Again, no particular methodological remarks are needed.

Explanatory variables

Explaining political processes is an uncertain endeavour: because of the role played by human (individual and collective) agency; because of the non-repeatability of historical events; because of the complexity of causal interactions (a multiplicity of agents, structures, and processes); and because of gaps in the empirical evidence. Nevertheless, this book will try to contribute to the explanation of radical left behaviour and success by highlighting the importance of *four key variables*.

The first one is the process of neoliberalisation of Western European societies. By creating a potential vacuum of representation of working-class and welfarist interests, this process opened up interesting growth prospects for the radical left and encouraged its renewal. Radical left parties were pulled out of their narrow milieus and preoccupations and started to compete to 'fill the vacuum' of anti-neoliberalism.

The second one is the role of party competition. The behaviour and success of the radical left was particularly affected by the competition with the moderate left. The Janus-like character of the 'new' social democracy, which decisively turned toward neoliberal policy orientations but maintained a strong hold on welfarist strata, the organised labour movement, and the 'left' public opinion, largely shaped the potential and the limits of radical left success and its strategic predicaments.

The third one is the role of party system rules and dynamics. The fine-prints of national electoral systems, party financing regimes, media access, and modes of competition (for instance, bipolarism) had a major effect on the success and behaviour of the radical left, affecting tightly its strength, cohesion, electoral tactics, public perception, and growth.

The fourth one is the role of mass mobilisations. The occurrence of a large-scale popular movement structured around left-wing demands is one of the strongest predictors of subsequent radical left growth: from the revolutionary wave of 1917–23 to the great strikes of the thirties; from the armed anti-fascist resistance during World War Two to the 'long 1968'; from the anti-governmental protests of the nineties and noughties to the square occupations of the great recession. The problems with the movements from 1980 to 2010 were that they erupted almost exclusively against right-wing governments, and that they never managed to institutionalise the initial bouts of popular participation in permanent organisational mediations: as a consequence, they reflated moderate left parties more than radical left ones, and their effects were usually short-lived.

Viewed in this context, the role of party agency and subjective brilliant moves or mistakes appears relativised: they remained important, but were largely overdetermined by factors beyond the control of radical left parties.

Summary

The analysis of the Western European radical left party family will focus on tracking, assessing, and explaining the evolution of three key dependent variables: its cohesion, its strength, and its systemic influence. The approach will blend quantitative and qualitative observation, highlighting the impact on the success and behaviour of the radical left of five explanatory variables: the process of neoliberalisation of Western European societies; the impact of party competition, particularly that of social democratic parties; the effects of party system rules and dynamics; the role of left-wing mass mobilisations; and subjective choices. An important independent contribution will be the accurate estimation of radical left strength through the collection and homogenisation of a large amount of quantitative data and a new systematic framework of analysis.

Concluding remarks

The book aims to provide a convincing interpretation of the overall trajectory of the Western European radical left from 1989 to 2015.

The analysis will be guided by an original holistic approach, characterised by the following elements: an improved definition of the radical left, allowing for its constitutive pluralism and historicity; a revised conceptualisation of political parties as complex tools enabling collective action, each having a specific constituency, political project, organisational mediations, and strategic mediations; a multi-level approach focusing on the interaction between the party families, individual parties, and an underlying field of forces; and an aggregate approach, giving primacy to the party family level.

First, I will identify the key elements of the nature of the radical left party family, pointing to the structuring effects of what I define as the anti-neoliberal field of forces. Next, I will track, assess, and try to explain the evolution of its cohesion, strength, and influence. The analysis will combine quantitative and qualitative observation, existing and improved tools, and the contribution of a number of disciplinary fields and subfields (political science, political sociology, contemporary history, political economy, and political theory). Hypothesised key explanatory variables are neoliberalism, party competition, party systems, extra-parliamentary mobilisations, and party agency.

The next two chapters will discuss the pre-1989 roots and post-1989 development of the radical left at a continental level (seventeen countries). The following three chapters will discuss the three case studies of Germany, Italy, and France.

Notes

1 The use of the term by the authors is slightly confusing, as they seem to refer to organised activist networks (already included in the previous component), instead of the broader mass of people sharing with parties beliefs, values, practices, and forms of sociability.
2 The countries excluded are quantitatively irrelevant, but some of them have strong radical lefts with extremely interesting histories: the communist AKEL in Cyprus has never fallen below 27 per cent of votes (Charalambous 2007); in Iceland, the communist-socialist organisations SA-S and Ab have generally been stronger than their mainstream social democratic counterparts; in San Marino, finally, a popular front of communists (PCS) and left-socialists (PSS) actually ruled the country from 1945 to 1957 – the only case in Western Europe.

3 Less through direct state spending and investment and more through subsidies to the private economy, indirect fiscal and monetary policies, and the encouragement of a 'privatised Keynesianism' based on the indebtedness of families (Bellofiore 2013).
4 March and Mudde (2005) and March (2008) set it at 3 per cent of the vote and one seat in at least one parliamentary election; De Waele and Vieira (2012) set it at one parliamentary seat.

References

Backes, Uwe, and Patrick Moreau (eds.) (2008). *Communist and post-communist parties in Europe.* Göttingen: Vandenhoeck and Ruprecht.
Bailey, David J. (2009). *The political economy of European social democracy: A critical realist approach.* London: Routledge.
Bakker, Ryan, Catherine de Vries, Erica Edwards, Liesbet Hooge, Seth Jolly, Gary Marks, Jonathan Polk, Jan Rovny, Marco Steenbergen, and Milada Anna Vachudova (2015). 'Measuring party positions in Europe: The Chapel Hill expert survey trend file, 1999–2010', *Party Politics* 21(1): 143–152.
Bartolini, Stefano (2000). *The political mobilization of the European left, 1860–1980: The class cleavage.* Cambridge: Cambridge University Press.
Bellofiore, Riccardo (2013). '"Two or three things I know about her": Europe in the global crisis and heterodox economics', *Cambridge Journal of Economics* 37(3): 463–477.
Botella, Juan, and Luis Ramiro (eds.) (2003). *The crisis of communism and party change: The evolution of Western European communist and post-communist parties.* Barcelona: ICPS.
Bull, Martin J. (1994). 'The West European communist movement: Past, present, future', in Martin J. Bull and Paul Heywood (eds.). *West European communist parties after the revolutions of 1989.* London: Macmillan, 203–222.
Cahill, Damien, Lindy Edwards, and Frank Stilwell (eds.) (2012). *Neoliberalism. Beyond the free market.* Cheltenham: Edward Elgar.
Calise, Mauro (2010). *Il partito personale. I due corpi del leader.* Bari: Laterza.
Carty, R. Kenneth (2004). 'Parties as franchise systems. The stratarchical organizational imperative', *Party Politics* 10(1): 5–24.
Charalambous, Giorgos (2007). 'The strongest communists in Europe: Accounting for AKEL's electoral success', *Journal of Communist Studies and Transition Politics* 23(3): 425–56.
Chiocchetti, Paolo (2016a). Western European radical left database. Version 2.0 (30.04.2016). Available at: www.paolochiocchetti.it/data.
Chiocchetti, Paolo (2016b). 'Measuring party strength: A new systematic framework applied to the case of German parties, 1991–2013', *German Politics* 25(1): 84–105.
De Waele, Jean-Michel, and Daniel-Louis Seiler (eds.) (2012). *Le partis de la gauche anticapitaliste en Europe.* Paris: Economica.
De Waele, Jean-Michel, and Mathieu Vieira (2012). 'La famille de la gauche anticapitaliste en Europe occidentale', in Jean-Michel De Waele and Daniel-Louis Seiler (eds.). *Le partis de la gauche anticapitaliste en Europe.* Paris: Economica, 50–70.
Ducange, Jean-Numa, Philippe Marlière, and Louis Weber (2013). *La gauche radicale en Europe.* Paris: Éditions du Croquant.
Duménil, Gérard, and Dominique Lévy (2011). *The crisis of neoliberalism.* Cambridge: Harvard University Press.
Duménil, Gérard, and Dominique Lévy (2004). *Capital resurgent. Roots of the neoliberal revolution.* Cambridge: Harvard University Press.

Duverger, Maurice (1951). *Les partis politiques*. Paris: Armand Colin.
Foucault, Michel (2008). *The birth of biopolitics*. New York: St. Martin's Press.
Gomez, Raul, Laura Morales, and Luis Ramiro (2016). 'Varieties of radicalism: Examining the diversity of radical left parties and voters in Western Europe', *Western European Politics* 39(2): 351–379.
Gunther, Richard, and Larry Diamond (2003). 'Species of political parties: A new typology', *Party Politics* 9(2): 167–199.
Harman, Chris (2007). 'Theorising neoliberalism', *International Socialism Journal* 117: 87–121.
Harvey, David (2005). *A brief history of neoliberalism*. Oxford: Oxford University Press.
Heidar, Knut, and Jo Saglie (2003). 'Predestined parties? Organizational change in Norwegian political parties', *Party Politics* 9(2): 219–239.
Hloušek, Vít, and Lubomír Kopeček (2010). *Origin, ideology and transformation of political parties: East-Central and Western Europe compared*. Farnham: Ashgate.
Hopkin, Jonathan (2003). 'Political decentralization, electoral change and party organizational adaptation: A framework for analysis', *European Urban and Regional Studies* 10(3): 227–237.
Hopkin, Jonathan, and Caterina Paolucci (1999). 'The business firm model of party organisation: Cases from Spain and Italy', *European Journal of Political Research* 35(1): 307–339.
Hudson, Kate (2012). *The new European left. A socialism for the twenty-first century?* Basingstoke: Palgrave Macmillan.
Hudson, Kate (2000). *European communism since 1989: towards a new European left?* Basingstoke: Palgrave Macmillan.
Katz, Richard S., and Peter Mair (1995). 'Changing models of party organization and party democracy: The emergence of the cartel party', *Party Politics* 1(1): 5–28.
Kirchheimer, Otto (1966). 'The transformation of the Western European party systems', in Joseph LaPalombara and Myron Weiner (eds.). *Political parties and political development*. Princeton: Princeton University Press, 177–200.
Klingemann, Hans-Dieter (ed.) (2006). *Mapping policy preferences II. Estimates for parties, electors, and governments in Eastern Europe, the European Union and the OECD, 1990–2003*. Oxford: Oxford University Press.
Koole, Ruud (1994). 'The vulnerability of the modern cadre party in the Netherlands', in Richard S. Katz and Peter Mair (eds.). *How parties organize. Change and adaptation in party organizations in Western democracies*. London: Sage, 278–303.
Krouwel, André (2006). 'Party models', in Richard S. Katz and William Crotty (eds.). *Handbook of party politics*. London: Sage, 249–269.
Lawson, Kay (1980). *Political parties and linkage: A comparative analysis*. New Haven: Yale University Press.
Lipset, Seymour Martin, and Stein Rokkan (1967). 'Cleavage structures, party systems and voter alignments: An introduction', in Seymour Martin Lipset and Stein Rokkan (eds.). *Party systems and voter alignments: Cross-national perspectives*. New York: The Free Press, 1–64.
Mair, Peter (1994). 'Party organizations: From civil society to the state', in Richard S. Katz and Peter Mair (eds.). *How parties organize: Change and adaptation in party organizations in Western democracies*. London: Sage, 1–22.
Mair, Peter, and Cas Mudde (1998). 'The party family and its study', *Annual Review of Political Science* 1: 211–229.

Marantzidis, Nikos (2004). 'Exit, voice or loyalty? Les stratégies des partis communistes d'Europe de l'Ouest après 1989', *Communisme* 76/77: 169–184.
March, Luke (2012). *Radical left parties in contemporary Europe.* Abingdon: Routledge.
March, Luke (2008). *Contemporary Far Left Parties in Europe: From Marxism to the Mainstream?* [report]. Berlin: Friedrich-Ebert-Stiftung.
March, Luke, and Cas Mudde (2005). 'What's left of the radical left? The European radical left after 1989: Decline *and* mutation', *Comparative European Politics* 3: 23–49.
Marx, Karl (1969). *Class struggles in France, 1848 to 1850.* Moscow: Progress Publishers. Available at: www.marxists.org/archive/marx/works/1850/class-struggles-france/ [accessed on 01.04.2016].
Moschonas, Gerassimos (2011). 'Historical decline or change of scale? The electoral dynamics of European social democratic parties, 1950–2009', in James Cronin, George Ross, and James Shock (eds.). *What's left of the left: Democrats and social democrats in challenging times.* Durham: Duke University Press, 50–85.
Moschonas, Gerassimos (2002). *In the name of social democracy: the great transformation from 1945 to the present.* London: Verso.
Mouchard, Daniel (2009). *Être représenté. Mobilisations d' 'exclus' dans la France des années 1990.* Paris: Economica.
Mudde, Cas (2002). *The ideology of the extreme right.* Manchester: Manchester University Press.
Mudge, Stephanie Lee (2008). 'What is neo-liberalism?', *Socio-Economic Review* 6(4): 703–731.
Nachtwey, Oliver (2013). 'Market social democracy: The transformation of the SPD up to 2007', *German Politics* 22(3): 235–252.
Neumann, Sigmund (1956). *Modern political parties.* Chicago: University of Chicago Press.
Panebianco, Angelo (1988). *Political parties: Organisation and power.* Cambridge: Cambridge University Press.
Poguntke, Thomas (2002). 'Party organisational linkage: Parties without firm social roots?', in Kurt Richard Luther and Ferdinand Müller-Rommel (eds.). *Political parties in the new Europe. Political and analytical challenges.* Oxford: Oxford University Press, 43–62.
Poguntke, Thomas (1987). 'New politics and party systems: the emergence of a new type of party?', *West European Politics* 10(1): 76–88.
Raynaud, Philippe (2006). *L'extrême gauche plurielle. Entre démocratie radicale et révolution.* Paris: CEVIPOF.
Rye, Danny (2014). *Political parties and the concept of power.* Basingstoke: Palgrave.
Saad-Filho, Alfredo, and Deborah Johnston (eds.) (2005). *Neoliberalism. A critical reader.* London: Pluto Press.
Seiler, Daniel-Louis (2012). 'Panorama de la gauche anticapitaliste en Europe: essai de typologie', in Jean-Michel De Waele and Daniel-Louis Seiler (eds.). *Le partis de la gauche anticapitaliste en Europe.* Paris: Economica, 7–31.
Seiler, Daniel-Louis (1980). *Partis et familles politiques.* Paris: PUF.
Tannahill, R. Neal (1978). *The communist parties of Western Europe: A comparative study.* Westport: Greenwood Press.
Thorsen, Dag Einar (2011). 'The neoliberal challenge. What is Neoliberalism', *Contemporary Readings in Law and Social Justice* 2(2): 188–214.
Van Haute, Emilie (2009). *Adhérer à un parti. Aux sources de la participation politique.* Bruxelles: Editions de l'Université de Bruxelles.

Von Beyme, Klaus (1985). *Political parties in Western democracies*. Aldershot: Gower.
Waller, Michael, and Meindert Fennema (eds.) (1988). *Communist parties in Western Europe: Decline or adaptation?* Oxford: Basil Blackwell.
Weber, Max (1968). *Economy and society* (vol. 1). New York: Bedminster Press.
Wolinetz, Steven B. (2002). 'Beyond the catch-all party: Approaches to the study of parties and party organization in contemporary democracies', in Richard Gunther (ed.). *Political parties: Old concepts and new challenges*. Oxford: Oxford University Press, 136–165.

2 The Western European landscape, 1914–1988

This chapter discusses the roots of the contemporary Western European radical left, looking at the evolution of its predecessors at the continental level (seventeen countries) in the period 1914–88.

Decade after decade, a variety of orthodox communist parties, communist variants and dissidences, left-socialist organisations, and far-left or 'new left' grouplets entered and exited the stage, clashed and cooperated with each other, and evolved in response to internal decisions, international impulses, the national political competition, and general economic, social, and political trends. An adequate treatment of this history would exceed the scope of this book, and a number of good general overviews are already available on specific periods and topics: Hobsbawm (1995) on global events; Mazower (1998) and Judt (2005) on European events; Dreyfus et al. (2004) and Priestland (2009) on world communism; Bartolini (2000), Eley (2002), and Sassoon (2010) on the European left as a whole; and Agosti (1999) and Kowalski (2006) on European communism. What I will do instead is offer a brief overview of the long-term evolution of the Western European radical left, highlighting in a schematic way its key continuities, discontinuities, and junctures.

The discussion is structured as follows. First, I offer a brief narrative account and periodisation of the overall trajectory of the Western European radical left since 1914, focusing on the interaction between parties and their external environment. Secondly, I examine the evolution of radical left aggregate strength, using the methodology described in chapter one to provide the first ever estimate of levels and variations of its electoral, parliamentary, and governmental strength at a continental level. Thirdly, I summarise the key shifts of radical left nature. Fourthly, I briefly discuss radical left cohesion. Finally, I summarise and discuss the key elements of this history.

Historical narrative: parties and contexts

The origins of the Western European radical left as a distinct political tradition are to be found in the split of the pre-World War I socialist labour movement under the impact of war, revolution, and mass democratisation. Its composition, field of action, and fortunes repeatedly changed over the years. This section provides a brief narrative overview of the key developments until 1988.

Prelude: the socialist labour movement, 1845–1913

The prehistory of the modern radical left can be said to start in the middle of the nineteenth century, when a burgeoning proletariat produced by the spread of capitalist relations in industry and agriculture met with socialist ideas elaborated by intellectuals (Charles Fourier, Henri de Saint-Simon, Robert Owen, Pierre-Joseph Proudhon, Louis Auguste Blanqui, Louis Blanc, Mikhail Bakunin, Ferdinand Lassalle, Karl Marx, and Friedrich Engels, and so on) or spontaneously developed by working-class activists (Cole 1953, 1954). Previous European history had known major emancipatory movements of the subaltern classes: slave revolts in the Antiquity, peasant and urban revolts in the Middle Ages and Early Modern Era, and plebeian activities in the Age of Revolution. However, their rootedness in largely pre-capitalist social relations made them qualitatively different from the subsequent socialist labour movement, whose emancipatory project was based on a novel horizon of generalised material and cultural abundance potentially opened up by capitalist development.

The emergence, structuration, and politicisation of a class cleavage separating workers from capitalists was a complex and uneven affair (Bartolini 2000; Hellemans 1990; Lipset and Rokkan 1967; Thompson 1980; van der Linden 2008). Over time, the working class developed a distinct social identity and a tight subcultural network of trade unions, cooperatives, mutual and recreational associations, spaces, and political parties. Different political tendencies competed for the hegemony over this world. Marxism, anarchism, and reformist socialism gradually gained the upper hand, but other forms of interclassist ideologies – national, confessional, republican, conservative – remained an important factor in working-class politics. High points in the development of a specifically socialist labour movement were the early labour mobilisations in the Revolutions of 1848–49, the activities of the International Workingmen's Association (IWMA) in 1864–72, the Paris Commune in 1871, and the progressive emergence of mass national trade unions and parties after the eighteen-eighties, many of which converged in 1889 in the social democratic (and largely Marxist) Second International.

In the nineteen-tens, the international socialist movement seemed to be on the verge of breakthrough, with social democratic parties rising above 25 per cent of valid votes in Germany, Finland (still part of the Russian Empire), Denmark, Sweden, and Norway. The outbreak of World War I, however, proved its fragility, as the vast majority of its leaders ditched their promises to oppose an armed conflict and rallied to their national elites. This shocking turn of events was the root of a split between moderate, 'social-patriotic' wings and radical, 'internationalist' wings that would divide the socialist movement for the rest of its history.

War and revolution, 1914–23

The carnage of the Great War acted as the incubator of a revolutionary wave that swept all over Europe from 1916 to 1923 (Carr 1979; Cronin 1980; Haimson and Sapelli 1992; Wrigley 1993). During the war, the mounting popular yearning for peace, social justice, and democratisation exploded in a number of army mutinies and strike movements. Pre-revolutionary mobilisations took place in Ireland, Spain, Switzerland, and the Netherlands. Full-blown socialist revolutions and civil wars developed in the Russian Empire, Finland, Hungary, and Germany, ultimately paving the way to the armistice of 1918. After the war, the same aspirations fed an impetuous growth of industrial unrest, trade union membership, workers' councils, and leftist parties. Germany repeatedly came close to a new revolution (Broué 2004), and vast confrontations took place in other countries around social and democratic demands.

This context brought a new revolutionary left to the centre stage. The loose tendency embodied since 1915 by the anti-war Zimmerwald movement was emboldened by the October Revolution and steadily moved toward a separation from mainstream social democracy (Nation 1989). The process was chaotic, as the intense confrontations between radical and moderate wings of the labour movement only gradually settled into clear political and organisational differentiations. What emerged was not a cohesive revolutionary tendency, but a broad palette of radical sensibilities (Braunthal 1986; Broué 1997; Darlington 2013; Steiner 1991; van der Linden and Thorpe 1990). The main pole of attraction was the Communist International (Comintern), created in 1919 by the Russian Bolsheviks, and its affiliated communist parties. The political intransigence of the communists, however, ultimately won over only a minority of the radicals. Many social democratic parties initially envisioned a participation in the Comintern, but only three officially joined (the French SFIO, the Italian PSI, and the Norwegian DNA), paying the price of heavy splits and defections. Diverse left-socialist currents took control of existing or new socialist parties (notably, the German USPD) and briefly converged in 1921–23 in the International Working Union of Socialist Parties (IASP). Anarcho-syndicalist currents, which were strong in several countries (notably, the Spanish CNT and the Italian USI), were also attracted to the Comintern, but later splintered between a conversion to Leninism and an allegiance to the revived International Workers' Association (AIT). Finally, many members and leaders of mainstream social democratic parties remained radicals at heart, but considered a shift to communist parties impracticable or misguided.

This composite radical left played an important role in the revolutionary wave of the period but, with the exception of Soviet Russia, failed to steer the events in the direction of successful socialist revolutions. The ruling classes responded with a mix of concessions, co-optation, isolation, and violent repression, and the movement rapidly abated after 1923.

Between bourgeois stabilisation and fascism, 1924–39

The end of the revolutionary wave left Soviet Russia isolated, while a new liberal-democratic order emerged in Western Europe (Maier 1975). The settlement, however, was fragile and progressively collapsed under the impact of international Fascism and the Great Depression (Overy 2007; Payne 1995; Winkler 1993). The contradictions of the Paris treaties fostered geopolitical and internal instability in

Germany, Italy, and Central Europe. The moderation of mainstream social democratic parties paved the way for their progressive acceptance as legitimate governmental partners, but isolation and repression still prevailed in many countries. The tensions between a strengthened and radicalised labour movement and the conservative sections of the ruling classes remained high, flaring up into impressive strikes waves (UK in 1926, Norway and Sweden in 1931, France in 1936), insurrections (Austria and Spain, 1934), and a sequence of civil war, social revolution, and international conflict in Spain between 1936 and 1939 (Broué and Témime 2007). An increasingly popular answer to the problems of labour militancy, economic crisis, political instability, and geopolitical claims was offered by authoritarian and fascist regimes, which were established in Spain in 1924–30 and again in 1939, in Italy and Portugal in 1926, in Germany and Austria in 1933, and in Greece in 1936. In 1938–39, finally, Nazi Germany launched its bid for European hegemony and soon left most of the continent annexed, occupied, or ruled by German allies or puppets.

In the interwar period, the radical left was reduced to relatively marginal communist parties keeping alive the flame of proletarian revolution against liberal stabilisation and fascist reaction. Many of the early supporters of the Comintern left, and communist parties were reduced to medium-small organisations (the German KPD, the French PC-SFIC, the Italian PCd'I, and Finnish SKP, and the Swedish SKP) or insignificant sects. Left-socialist or dissident communist organisations maintained an autonomous existence for a while, but were progressively absorbed in the social democratic mainstream or crushed by World War Two (Alexander 1981, 1991; Braunthal 1986; Buschak 1985; Prat 1984). The former IASP parties gradually rejoined the revived Second International.[1] The Norwegian DNA was expelled from the Comintern in 1924, and did the same in 1938. In the late twenties and thirties, a number of new communist dissidences (the Italian Bordigists, the Bukharinian 'right opposition', and the Trotskyist 'left opposition') and left-socialist splits (the British ILP) emerged, but usually remained weak and short-lived.[2]

The radical left strongly declined in the twenties. In the thirties, it grew in free elections, with major surges in Germany (1932), France (1936), and Spain (1936–37), but was progressively smashed by fascist coups, forced underground in most of the surviving liberal democracies[3], and ultimately overwhelmed by the expansion of the Axis powers (1939–40).

The brief anti-fascist golden age, 1944–46

In 1945, the Axis powers were defeated by a coalition of liberal-democratic and communist states – USA, UK, and USSR – with the help of important armed resistance movements (Hawes and White 1975). The initial phase of reconstruction was dominated by a progressive mood. Provisional governments of anti-fascist unity, under the supervision of the victors, were installed across the continent and busied themselves with the cleansing of former fascists and collaborators, the re-establishment and extension of democratic institutions, and important socio-economic reforms (Henke and Woller 1991; Judt 2005).

The years between 1944 and 1946 represented a brief golden age for the Western European radical left, which suddenly acquired unprecedented mass roots, legitimacy, and political influence (Almond 1947; Sassoon 1992). Communist parties surged across the continent, acquiring an equal or superior standing to that of mainstream social democracy in France (PCF) and Italy (PCI) (Lazar 1992). Sizeable left-socialist currents agreed to a close cooperation in semi-permanent fronts (the Italian FDP in 1947–48; the Finnish SKDL since 1944; the Greek EDA in 1951–67) or looser alliances (the Italian PSI, which retained a radical and pro-Soviet line until the late fifties). Alternative radical traditions such as anarcho-syndicalism or anti-Stalinist Marxism were instead completely marginalised.

The Cold War backlash, 1947–59

Already in 1947, however, the differences between Washington and Moscow led to the outbreak of the Cold War (Gaddis 2005; Gilbert 2014). The politics of anti-fascist unity was superseded by the imperatives of containing the Soviet threat in the East and rolling back domestic communism in the West. Western Europe was integrated into a loose US-led sphere of influence through bilateral ties and multilateral agreements and institutions such as the European Recovery Plan (ERP, 1948–52), the General Agreement on Tariffs and Trade (GATT, 1947), and the North Atlantic Treaty Organisation (NATO, 1949). In addition, processes of closer European integration (Gilbert 2012) were pursued by most countries within the framework of organisations such as the Council of Europe (CoE 1949) and the European Economic Community (EEC 1957). Communist parties were outlawed only in Greece (1948) and West Germany (1956), but all states agreed to isolate them politically and to curb their influence with varying combinations of social reforms, institutional changes, and repression. Economically, the continent experienced the beginning of a long post-war boom that lasted until the early seventies (Brenner 2006). These processes were not steered by uniform political coalitions: conservatives dominated in the UK, Christian democrats in Italy and Germany, and social democrats in Scandinavia; consociational grand coalitions ruled in Benelux, Austria, Finland, Switzerland, and France; and authoritarian regimes survived in Spain and Portugal. Socio-economic policies also varied, following distinct welfare regimes (Esping-Andersen 1990), more dirigiste or more regulatory forms of state intervention, and different combinations of capitalist, managerial, petty-bourgeois, and working-class interests. In all cases, however, the trend broadly followed a model of welfarist mixed economy with rising living standards and levels of social protection.

In this period, the radical left was again reduced to a network of communist parties of strict Stalinist obedience (Claudin 1975). Economic growth and the welfare state dampened the appetite for radical alternatives to capitalism, and the effort of communist parties to present themselves as national and democratic forces was belied by their close association with the Soviet Union. Radical left influence declined strongly, with heavy losses in its strongholds (Italy, France, and Finland) and a violent downsizing elsewhere, where it came close to fading into irrelevance. Titoist or anti-Stalinist dissidences failed to take root, but the 1956 Hungarian crisis contributed to the realignment of its strongest non-communist party, the Italian PSI.

For and beyond the welfare state, 1960–79

After 1960, however, the tide turned and the radical left moved again to the centre stage of Western European politics. The sixties and seventies were marked both by the apogee of the Fordist model, and by attempts to overcome its limits. Growth, accumulation, and technological progress remained effervescent, but by 1973 the long post-war boom had morphed into a more uncertain phase of transition. Increasing sections of the population started to push the boundaries of the post-war compromise, envisaging its radicalisation, the transition to some form of socialist society, or the restoration of capitalist hegemony (Duménil and Lévy 2004; Esping-Andersen 1985; Gordon et al. 1987; Horn 2007; Klimke and Scharloth 2008).

On the one hand, the shifting social, political, and international balance of forces rapidly undermined the model 'to the left'. American hegemony was crumbling under the weight of economic imbalances and the Vietnam War. The surge of leftist national liberation movements led to a rapid political decolonisation and threatened the international position of Western states and multinationals with various brands of 'third-worldist' developmental models (Rothermund 2006). The European working class, now shielded by labour protections, welfare provisions, and full employment, embarked on an escalation of industrial and political struggles that won massive conquests and started to challenge the very core of capitalist/managerial control over individual enterprises and society as a whole. Already visible in the early sixties, labour militancy reached its peaks in the French May 1968, the Italian 'hot autumn' of 1968–69 (Balestrini and Moroni 1997), and the Portuguese revolution of 1974–75, and remained high in all countries until the end of the decade. The youth revolts of 1968, finally, questioned traditional values and structures, mixing anti-capitalist and libertarian impulses and reinvigorating a whole range of old and new emancipatory movements. On the other hand, the upper classes reacted by radicalising to the right, toying with authoritarian solutions (France 1958 and 1961, Greece 1967, various planned coups in Italy) and working vigorously toward the preparation of a major reversal.

A resolution of this conflict remained uncertain for the whole decade of the seventies: macro-economic policies oscillated between Keynesian intervention and austerity; wage growth was undermined by ballooning inflation and unemployment; and left-wing parties were torn between a traditional course of moderate reforms, pressures for a pro-business turn, and dreams of nationalisations and workers' self-management (as in the French *Programme commun* or the Swedish *Löntagarfonder*). The tide rapidly turned after 1978, with workers' power in the workplaces eroded by mass unemployment and productive restructuring and left-wing radicalism in retreat at the cultural and political level. A new neoliberal consensus centred on shareholder value, wage restraint, welfare retrenchment, privatisations, and globalisation emerged, but imposed itself only gradually, and did not fundamentally alter the nature of the European welfarist mixed economies until the nineties.

The period was marked by a strong renewal of the radical left. The sixties saw the emergence of a number of new medium-small left-socialist organisations: the Dutch PSP in 1959, the Danish SF in 1960, the Norwegian SF in 1961, the French PSU in 1962, and the Italian PSIUP in 1964. The post-1968 decade, in turn, saw a flourishing of smaller but combative far left organisations of a Maoist, Trotskyist, workerist, and left-nationalist bent, particularly in Portugal, Spain, Italy, France, Ireland, and Switzerland (Alexander 1991, 2001; Harman 1988). More importantly, the still dominant communist parties started to drift away from Moscow (Boggs and Plotke 1980; Starobin 1965; Tannahill 1978). This evolution resulted in the seventies in an open rift, with most parties converging around the moderate, democratic, and pro-EEC 'Eurocommunist' positions of the Italian PCI, others (such as the Greek KKE and the Portuguese PCP) maintaining an orthodox and pro-Soviet line, and a third group (such as the French PCF) sitting on the fence.

Radical left influence grew strongly. Electoral results rose in the sixties and again in the mid-seventies; extra-parliamentary strength was bolstered by a large influx of new party members, the activities of the hyperactive far left grouplets, and a general radicalisation of workers, intellectuals, and the new social movements; and important episodes of governmental participation took place in Portugal, Italy, and the Nordic countries.

Through its parliamentary and extra-parliamentary activities, the radical left contributed to a large improvement of living, social protection, and democratic standards. However, it failed to point a way forward to a socialist transition, and was ultimately outmanoeuvred in a moderate normalisation and a neoliberal reaction.

The neoliberal turn, 1980–88

In the eighties, the social and political balance of forces shifted slowly but surely to the right (Abdelal 2007; Brenner 2006; Duménil and Lévy 2004; Harman 2009; Reinhart and Sbrancia 2011). At the international level, a wide-ranging reversal imposed itself. The game changer was probably the hike of US interest rates in 1979–82 (the so-called 'Volcker shock'), that spread unemployment in the industrialised world, undermined the economies of communist and third-worldist states, and reflated American hegemony. Productive restructuring gained momentum. The economic profession and the political class rapidly turned from a support for dirigiste and Keynesian policies to neoliberal solutions. The first major steps toward the liberalisation of international trade and finance were taken. Within Western Europe, the scope for expansionary national policies was increasingly curtailed by trade, financial, and monetary integration, with innovations such as the European Monetary System (EMS) in 1979, the Single European Act (SEA) in 1986, and the capital liberalisation directive in 1988. Both centre-right and centre-left parties started to turn against the institutions and policies of the post-war settlement and to prioritise market solutions and the needs of international and domestic private capital, although this reconversion was uneven and often hesitant, not excluding initial counterexamples.[4] Finally, processes such as industrial restructuring, mass unemployment, the post-industrial transition, and value change sapped the identity and confidence of wageworkers, weakening the traditional forms of organisation and representation that had structured the labour movement since the mid-nineteenth century (trade unions, associations, and political parties).

The radical left proved incapable to resist these trends and struggled with a long, profound, and multi-faceted crisis, which undermined its influence and very identity (Waller and Fennema 1988). Far left groups declined and often disappeared. The former 'Eurocommunist' grouping lost much of its coherence, with key groups (notably, the Italian PCI) seeking a rapprochement with the Socialist International and other groups stressing their continued radical goals or reverting to orthodoxy. Several communist parties – both reforming and orthodox – started running for office as part of semi-permanent alliances with other radical left and green organisations: in Portugal since 1979 (FEPU, APU, CDU), in Spain since 1986 (IU), and in the Netherlands (GL) and Greece (SYN) since 1989. Radical left influence strongly declined, with most radicals drifting toward social democratic and green parties or political disengagement.

Summary

From 1914 to 1988, both the Western European radical left and its external environment went through important transformations. The capitalist system moved from moments of profound crisis to prolonged phases of vibrant growth. Regimes of accumulation and regulation morphed from the semi-competitive model of the interwar period, to the Fordist model of 1945–73, to the neoliberalisation, financialisation, and globalisation trends of the post-Fordist decades. Political forms varied from liberal, authoritarian, totalitarian, democratic, and perhaps post-democratic regimes. Moscow-aligned communism usually dominated the radical left, but coexisted with alternative left-socialist and far-left traditions and gradually lost its internal coherence since the seventies. The relations between the radical and the moderate left oscillated between competition, fundamental opposition, cooperation, and a few reunification attempts. Finally, radical left strength experienced strong variations, from the peaks of 1920, 1946, and 1978 to the troughs of 1924, 1943, 1959, and 1988.

The following sections will examine in more detail the long-term evolution of three key aspects: radical left strength, radical left nature, and radical left fragmentation.

Strength

This section investigates the evolution of the electoral, parliamentary, governmental, and membership strength of the Western European radical left from 1919 to 1988, both in their aggregate dynamics and in their national variations.

The analysis follows the methodology described in chapter one. Aggregate electoral strength is weighted by valid votes; aggregate parliamentary and governmental strength are weighted by population (instead of by registered voters). The latter choice flows from the scant significance of electoral rolls in periods of restricted suffrage and authoritarian regimes. A credible estimation of aggregate membership strength is prevented by gaps in the primary data; an alternative series based on seven countries, however, is provided. The primary data for all seventeen countries, together with sources, notes, and elaborations, are available in the Western European Radical Left Database (Chiocchetti 2016).

Electoral strength

The measurement of the aggregate electoral strength of the Western European radical left is unproblematic for the period 1977–2015, when general restrictions to free and universal suffrage were few and specific restrictions against the radical left rare. The period 1919–76, instead, poses a number of problems. First, in several countries free elections and democratic institutions were suppressed by authoritarian regimes: the share of the Western European population affected rose from 8.3 per cent in 1923 to a peak of 77.5 per cent in 1943, declined to 12.8 per cent in 1945, and remained roughly around that level until 1974. Secondly, some years often elapsed between the end of authoritarian rule and the first democratic election, particularly in 1943–49 and in 1974–77. Thirdly, radical left parties were repeatedly outlawed, although reconstituted legal fronts were usually subsequently allowed to run for office. Fourthly, vote shares of individual parties are uncertain for the early elections in Greece and Portugal (1918–25) and Spain (1918–23). Fifthly, the extension of the franchise remained highly uneven until the late forties, ranging from universal to universal male or restricted suffrage; in Switzerland, women obtained the right to vote only in 1971.[5] A number of different estimates of party strength in this period are therefore possible. I have chosen to report two curves, which deal differently with these 'missing values'. Both always include all seventeen countries. The first (compound line) sets radical left votes to zero as soon as democracy is suppressed or the radical left outlawed. The second (dash line) keeps radical left votes fixed to the level of the last available free election. The two curves greatly diverge from 1924 to 1946, when poor aggregate results were caused more by an impossibility of the radical left to run for office than by a decline in its popular support. The discussion will be mainly based on the first curve.

The evolution of *aggregate electoral strength* is depicted in Figure 2.1. The average for the whole period is 9 per cent, with big variations over time.

Data for the early twenties are not very significant, as moderates and radicals still coexisted in the same organisations in most of the countries. A possible estimate including communist parties, left-socialist splinter groups, and social democratic parties where the radicals were predominant indicates a healthy 14.9 per cent in 1920.[6] Strength then retreated to 5.4 per cent in 1924, when only communist and other minor radical parties are included. The value stagnated until 1929 but then rose under the impact of the Great Depression, reaching 8.1 per cent in 1932. The

38 Western European landscape, 1914–1988

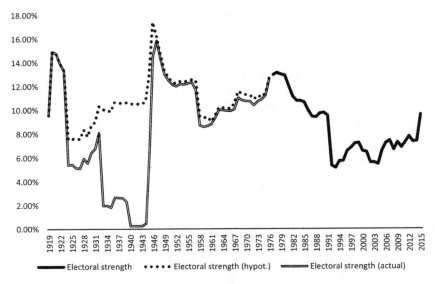

Figure 2.1 Electoral strength, Western European radical left

mounting of international fascism, however, rapidly pushed the curve to a trough of 0.3 per cent in 1943, despite continued electoral growth in the thirties in the remaining liberal democracies. The impetuous surge of the immediate post-war years is evident in the all-time peak of 15.8 per cent reached in 1947. The point of maximum influence was actually reached in 1946, but it does not show due to the delayed electoral cycle in Germany; in the remaining sixteen countries, aggregate strength soared a stunning 19.2 per cent. From 1948 to 1959, the radical left steeply declined to 8.6 per cent. In the sixties and seventies, however, it made up half of the lost terrain, recovering until 1968 (11 per cent), stalling until 1975 (11.2 per cent), and growing again until 1978 (13.1 per cent). From 1979 to 1988, finally, a new decline set in, bringing aggregate electoral strength down to 9.4 per cent.

This evolution was not homogeneous across the continent. The importance of *national variations* is evident in Table 2.1, which reports the rolling vote share of the radical left in each country for selected key years.

Results in the immediate aftermath of World War I were determined by the outcome of the struggle between moderate and radical wings for the control of the flourishing 'old' social democratic parties. Parties where radical factions had the upper hand obtained 44.8 per cent in Finland (1917), 31.6 per cent in Norway (1918), 32.3 per cent in Italy (1919), 23.5 per cent in Switzerland (1919), 21.2 per cent in France (1919), and 6.2 per cent in Spain (1918). Independent left-socialist parties won 20.5 per cent in Germany (1920) and 8.0 per cent in Sweden (1917). In all other countries, moderate factions maintained the control and communist splits remained small or tiny. By 1924, when the dust settled, the

Table 2.1 National vote shares in selected years (%)

	1920	1924	1932	1947	1959	1967	1978	1988	AVERAGE 1919–88
AGGREGATE	14.9	5.4	8.1	15.8	8.6	10.0	13.1	9.4	9.0
AUSTRIA	0.9	0.7	0.6	5.4	3.3	0.4	1.2	0.7	1.8
BELGIUM	0.0	0.0	2.9	12.7	1.9	6.3	4.1	2.1	3.2
DENMARK	0.4	0.5	1.1	6.8	3.1	11.6	10.2	14.5	6.2
FINLAND	0.0	10.5	1.0	23.5	23.2	21.2	19.2	13.6	14.3
FRANCE	21.2	9.8	9.1	28.6	18.9	24.7	23.9	11.7	18.6
GERMANY	20.5	9.3	17.0	9.3	0.0	1.3	0.4	0.0	3.7
GREECE	-	-	5.0	-	24.4	-	12.3	12.0	6.4
IRELAND	-	0.4	0.4	0.0	0.2	0.0	1.8	4.2	0.7
ITALY	32.3	3.7	-	39.8	22.7	25.3	36.0	28.3	21.2
LUXEMBOURG	0.0	0.0	0.4	11.1	7.2	10.4	8.8	4.4	5.6
NETHERLANDS	3.6	2.3	2.6	10.8	4.3	6.5	3.0	2.3	4.4
NORWAY	31.6	6.1	1.7	11.9	3.4	7.4	5.2	6.2	7.0
PORTUGAL	-	-	-	-	-	-	19.4	15.4	4.0
SPAIN	6.2	-	0.9	-	-	-	11.5	9.1	2.4
SWEDEN	6.4	5.1	8.3	10.4	3.4	5.2	5.1	6.3	5.9
SWITZERLAND	23.5	0.0	1.9	5.1	2.7	2.9	3.7	2.6	3.7
UK	0.2	0.2	1.8	0.7	0.1	0.2	0.2	0.1	0.4

relative weakness of the Comintern sections compared to the social democratic mainstream became clear: radical left results were around 10 per cent in France, Germany, and Finland; more modest in Norway, Sweden, and Italy; and below 3 per cent in all remaining countries. In the thirties, notable surges took place in Finland (13.5 per cent in 1929), Germany (17.0 per cent in 1932), Greece (9.6 per cent in 1935), and France (17.1 per cent in 1936), but were invariably followed by a legal suppression of the parties. By 1940, the radical left had been forced underground everywhere except for Sweden (3.6 per cent in 1940) and the UK (0.8 per cent in 1935). Results soared everywhere in the brief post-war golden age, reaching exceptional levels in Italy (39.8 per cent in 1946), France (28.6 per cent in 1946), and Finland (23.5 per cent in 1945), and scores above 9 per cent in Belgium, Denmark, the (unsovereign) West German regions, the Netherlands, Norway, and Sweden. The Cold War retrenchment slashed vote shares below 3.5 per cent in most countries, but the radical left retained a weakened central position in Finland (23.2 per cent in 1958), Italy (22.7 per cent in 1958), and France (18.9 per cent in 1958) and rose in Greece (24.4 per cent in 1958). The subsequent recovery was generalised until 1967, but very uneven afterwards. At its peak, the strongholds had expanded to Italy (36.0 per cent in 1976), France (24.7 per cent in 1973), Portugal (23.4 per cent in 1979), Finland (19.2 per cent in 1975), Spain (16.3 per cent in 1979), Denmark (15.2 per cent in 1981), and Greece (13.2 per cent in 1981); elsewhere, values remained much lower. Finally, the decline of the eighties did not affect all countries in the same way, leaving Italy in a leading position (28.3 per cent in 1987), hitting especially hard the remaining former strongholds, and sparing Scandinavia and Ireland.

40 Western European landscape, 1914–1988

These national variations were further accompanied by important local variations, as communist parties often managed to entrench themselves in localised strongholds: for instance, the 'red regions' of Central Italy for the Italian PCI, the '*banlieue rouge*' near Paris for the French PCF, and the rural Alentejo for the Portuguese PCP (Bellanger and Mischi 2013; Ramella 2005).

Despite these variations, the analysis shows the presence of strong *cross-national trends* entailing a synchronous rise and decline – albeit of a variable universality and intensity – of both aggregate results and the vast majority of national ones. Figure 2.2 reports two types of net trends. These are defined as the number of countries improving their performance minus those worsening it. The first refers only to the countries holding a legislative election in the year; the second to the rolling trend of all seventeen countries (in relation to the last or the second to last election); changes below 0.1 per cent are ignored. The overlap with the movement of the aggregate curve is clear, showing the cross-national character of most phases of growth, decline, and stagnation. The big exception is the period 1968–81, which was instead marked by countries rising and falling in an uncoordinated and often violent fashion.

To sum up, the electoral history of the Western European radical left can be shown to consist in an alternation of relatively coherent *cross-national phases of development*: tumultuous growth in 1917–20; steep decline in 1921–24; stagnation in 1925–29; growth after 1930, which was, however, progressively frustrated by right-wing coups, party bans, and Axis occupations; a new brief surge in 1943–46; severe decline in 1947–59; partial recovery in 1960–67; trendless volatility in 1968–81; and a final decline in 1982–88. Most of these periods were

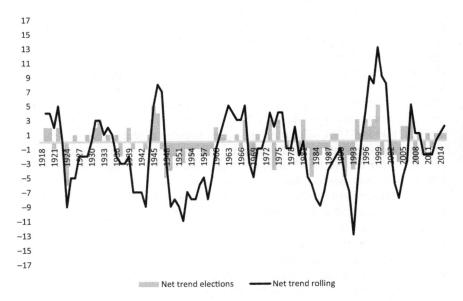

Figure 2.2 Cross-national electoral trends

characterised by strong cross-national trends leading to a relatively consistent and synchronised rise and decline of the radical left across the continent; exceptions are the 1930s (when the radical left was outcompeted by fascism) and the 'long 1968' (when patterns and temporalities diverged across countries). These trends perfectly coincide with well-documented historical shifts of cultural elites and public opinions 'to the left', 'to the right', and toward polarisation.

Nevertheless, electoral *success was primarily determined at the national level*. The gaps between countries were yawning: some radical lefts evolved into important political players (most of the period in France, Italy, and Finland; Norway until the mid-twenties; Germany until 1933, Portugal in the seventies); others remained confined to a medium-small size; and a third group was generally condemned to electoral insignificance. These outcomes were determined by the interaction of the national contexts, the actions of specific parties, and the reactions of their competitors. Particularly important was the ability of the radical left to profile itself at crucial junctures of a nation's history. In these conjunctures political time accelerated, sudden leaps became possible, and party choices could lead to either long-lasting influence or permanent marginality.

Parliamentary strength

Radical left parliamentary strength followed quite closely the evolution of its electoral strength, but at a substantially lower level (Figure 2.3). The average over the whole period was 6.9 per cent, almost a quarter less than the latter. It peaked at 11.2 per cent in 1920, when the radical left was represented in only half of the countries. It then fell to 3.2 per cent in 1926, despite a growth of countries with representation to eleven out of seventeen. Subsequent oscillations led to a low point of 0.2 per cent in 1941, when the radical left remained represented only in Sweden and the UK. An all-time high was reached in 1946, with 13.9 per cent and representation in twelve countries, then a long decline until 1961 (5.1 per cent), a recovery until 1978 (10.8 per cent), and a new decline until 1988 (7.0 per cent).

The discrepancy between parliamentary and electoral strength varied across space and time and had three main causes: the workings of electoral laws, which penalised medium-small non-aligned parties through majoritarian formats (the UK, France since 1958), explicit electoral thresholds (Germany, Austria), small constituency sizes and/or restrictive allocation formulas (Belgium, Greece, Ireland, Norway, Spain), and majority premiums (France in 1951); the fragmentation into rival organisations, which forfeited several potential seats (particularly since the sixties); in some cases, a level of electoral support insufficient to win any seat (particularly in the UK, Ireland, West Germany, and Austria).

Governmental strength

Radical left governmental strength was usually low or insignificant (Figure 2.3), with an average value of just 1.0 per cent over the whole period and long stretches at zero or close to zero.

42 Western European landscape, 1914–1988

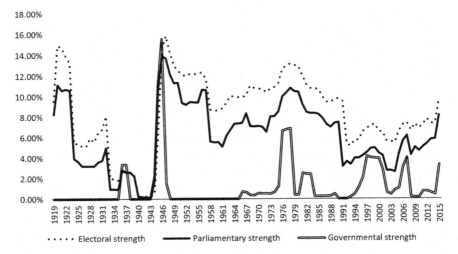

Figure 2.3 Electoral, parliamentary, and governmental strength, Western European radical left

Important experiences of governmental participation nevertheless took place. In 1918–19, the radical left headed provisional revolutionary socialist cabinets in Finland, Bavaria, and Hungary, which were, however, soon crushed militarily. In Germany, the left-socialist USPD shared the control of the provisional revolutionary government until November 1918. The radical left taboo on governmental participation with bourgeois forces was broken in 1936 by the formation of Popular Front governments in France (1936–37), where the communist PC-SFIC offered only an external support, and Spain (1936–39), where the communist PCE and the anarchist CNT were represented with ministers. In the second half of World War I, the radical left was a leading force in the armed anti-fascist resistance and took part in provisional governments in several countries, notably in France, Italy, and Greece. This shift was generalised after the war, as communist parties were included in governments of anti-fascist unity in Austria, Belgium, Denmark (briefly), Finland, France, most German regions, Italy, Norway (briefly), and Luxembourg. Aggregate governmental strength rose to an all-time peak of 15.5 per cent in 1946, but plunged back to zero in 1948, when all leftist parties were kicked out of office and labelled 'uncoalitionable' on geopolitical grounds. Governmental involvement resumed in 1966 but remained usually confined to the Nordic countries, with several experiences of direct participation in Finland and of external support in Denmark, Norway, and Sweden.[7] Three important exceptions stand out: the direct participation of PCP and MDP in revolutionary Portugal (1974–76), where sections of the population and of the military even leant toward the establishment of a socialist state; the external support of the PCI in Italy (1976–79), which was instead characterised by regressive measures in socio-economic policies and civil liberties; and the involvement of the PCF in the Mitterrand cabinets (1981–84), which started out with an ambitious programme of structural reforms but flip-flopped in 1983 with the famous *'tournant de la rigueur'*.

Governmental participation always remained a controversial theme for the radical left, which tended to view the state apparatus as a tool of the bourgeoisie (which, according to Lenin, needed to be smashed and replaced by new forms of council democracy), social democratic parties as betrayers of the working class, and most other parties as class enemies. In turn, national and international elites were suspicious of the radical left, even when it followed a prudent course of moderation (as in the Popular Fronts of the mid-thirties and in the National Fronts of the forties). The balance sheet of these experiences was equally controversial. There is no doubt that the perspective of a left government captured the popular imagination, led to electoral and membership surges of the radical left, and was often accompanied (preceded or followed) by large-scale grassroots mobilisations: general strikes in Germany (1920), Spain (1934), and France (1936); factory occupations in Italy (1919–20); land occupations in Italy (1945–47) and Portugal (1974–75); and full-blown revolutions in Finland (1918), Germany (1918–19), and Spain (1936–37). The record of these governments in office, however, was mixed, as they did often implement important democratic, social, and economic reforms, but simultaneously worked to defuse the popular unrest and prevent a radicalisation of the process. Finally, governmental experiences since the late-seventies were entirely deceiving, involving the radical left in the implementation of austerity policies and undermining the cohesion of its electorate (particularly in France, where the PCF fell from 16.1 per cent in 1981 to 9.8 per cent in 1986).

Membership strength

Radical left membership strength cannot be measured with precision, due to gaps in the primary data and the general unreliability of membership figures. Moreover, being a party member had a different meaning and entailed a different level of loyalty and commitment in each historical period, country, and individual party.

Nevertheless, an idea of the shifts occurred in aggregate levels can be given by available data on a representative sample of seven countries (Figure 2.4), which encompasses about three quarters of the total Western European electorate (Austria, Finland, France, Germany, Italy, the Netherlands, Sweden, and the UK).[8] If the figures are to be trusted, the aggregate share of radical left members on the total electorate (M/E) was very high in 1920 (1.7 per cent), collapsed to about 0.2 per cent in 1924, remained below 0.3 per cent until 1939, soared to an extraordinary 3.3 per cent in 1947, declined to 1.6 per cent in 1957 and to 1.3 per cent in 1973, somewhat increased to 1.4 in 1977, and then fell again to 1.0 in 1988. The figures are certainly inflated, especially in the forties and fifties, and underestimate the

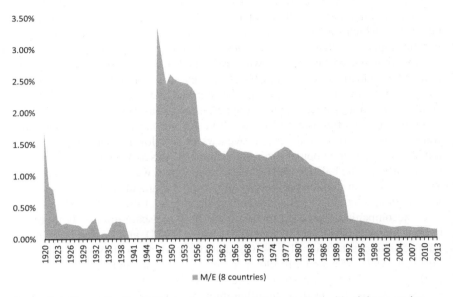

Figure 2.4 Share of radical left members on the total electorate (m/e), eight countries

recovery of the seventies (the myriad of far-left organisations and collectives that emerged alongside official parties is not counted), but the broad shape of the curve seems congruent with other historical sources and accounts. A reliable aggregate share of radical left members on total party members (M/Mtot) is not available, but was certainly much higher than electoral strength, reaching in some cases and periods (Italy and France from the late forties to the early eighties) half or more of all party members.

Three features must be emphasised. First, variations in time were huge, from the relative weakness of 'vanguard communism' in the interwar period to the extraordinary strength of 'mass communism' after 1945. Secondly, membership figures were crucially affected by the specific political culture and historical development of each country. Thirdly, individual radical left parties greatly varied in their ability to develop a veritable mass character: a few communist parties gained an equal or stronger membership than that of their social democratic competitors (in the mid-thirties in France and Spain; in the forties in Italy and Finland; in the seventies in Portugal, Spain, and Greece); other communist and left-socialist parties remained medium-sized; a third category of radical left actors never went beyond the stage of small group or tiny sect. In fact, five parties encompassed between 85 and 95 per cent of total radical left members in most years: the German USPD (0.9 million members in 1920) and KPD (0.3 million in 1947); the Italian PCI (2.2 million in 1947) and PSI (0.9 million in 1946); and the French PCF (0.6 million in 1978).

Summary

In average, aggregate radical left strength between 1919 and 1988 can be estimated at 9.0 per cent in electoral terms, 6.9 per cent in parliamentary terms, and 1.0 per cent in governmental terms. Membership strength cannot be measured with precision, but was substantially higher than all of the above both in quantitative and in qualitative terms.

These levels greatly varied over time. Radical currents failed to consolidate their initial surge (1917–20), leading to a swift recovery of the mainstream social democracy and a relative marginality of communist parties (1920–29). A smaller surge after 1929 shattered against the rise of domestic and international fascism. A third, stronger surge in the years of the anti-fascist resistance and reconstruction (1943–46) was contained and rolled back by Cold War politics – although the radical left remained strong in a few countries (Italy, France, and Finland) and medium-small but viable in others. Finally, a long recovery in the sixties (near-universal) and seventies (more variegated) was outmanoeuvred by the neoliberal turn of the early eighties, leading to a steep decline until 1988.

Strength was also very uneven in geographical terms. A handful of parties – the French PCF, the Italian PCI and PSI, and the German KPD and USPD – constantly concentrated three-quarters of all radical left votes and seats, and nine-tenths of all radical left members. Electoral strength varied from strongholds above 15 per cent of valid votes (France, Italy, and Finland for most of the period; Norway until the mid-twenties, Germany until 1933, Greece in 1958–60, Portugal since 1974, Spain in 1979–81, Denmark in the eighties) to virtual wastelands (the UK, Ireland until the seventies, Germany since 1957, Austria before 1945 and after 1965), with all other countries in medium-weak intermediate positions. Parliamentary strength varied from large to weak, and was absent in several countries. Governmental participation was generally rare, but more frequent in the Nordic countries.

Altogether, the radical left became truly central for the fate of Western European politics only in three moments (1917–23, 1943–47, and 1968–81), but remained throughout the century a relevant, medium-sized party family.

Nature

The nature of the Western European radical left also changed over time.

Its social constituency was based on the active working class and more broadly the 'popular classes', but the relative weight of specific groups varied, and actual support was limited to radicalised minorities. Its political project was informed by a commitment to a fundamental transformation of the productive and social systems (capitalism and bourgeois domination), but the goal of a communist society steadily receded into the background outside of periods of revolutionary enthusiasm (such as 1918–23 or the seventies), the transitional steps to get there remained controversial, and the principles of proletarian internationalism were only partially followed through. Its organisational mediations oscillated from vanguard to mass solutions. Finally, its strategy progressively shifted from the solitary pursuit of a working-class majority and the advocacy of a violent revolutionary break to the acceptance of coalition politics and a parliamentary road to socialism.

Social constituency: the proletariat and the people

The core of the ideological interpellation of radical left parties did not change much over time and centred on the idea of *broad popular alliances led by the working class*.

Marx (1967) clearly identified the emancipatory subject in the proletariat, defined as the totality of wageworkers engaged in capitalist production, manual and intellectual, skilled and unskilled, 'from manager down to the last day-labourer'. This was the only class with both an interest and the capacity to overthrow capitalism and replace it with an alternative social system. The theory, however, was confronted with two problems. On the one hand, the working class was never reduced to a homogeneous mass, as tendencies toward industrial concentration and social levelling were constantly accompanied by countervailing tendencies. Thus, growing upper layers of salaried managers, supervisors and 'experts' replaced the traditional petty-bourgeoisie, and were often pitted against the mass of ordinary wageworkers by their social background, privileged position, and actual social tasks. Moreover, the interests of workers in modern industrial sectors and large companies were generally prioritised by the radical left, but small-scale productions always retained an important weight and a new atomisation of the workforce into smaller workplace units, complex subcontracting chains, and a myriad of contractual relations set in after the seventies. On the other hand, employed wageworkers represented in the nineteenth century a small minority of the adult population, which was dominated by people engaged in subsistence and reproductive labour and small semi-independent producers. Their subsequent growth, with the generalisation of capitalist relations to all productive sectors and the erosion of the sole breadwinner model, was massive within the economically active population, but counterbalanced within the adult population by the emergence of large layers of pensioners, students, and unemployed.

Thus, radical left politics was characterised from the outset by the effort to forge broad popular alliances against common feudal and bourgeois enemies. Independent workers, such as peasants, artisans, shopkeepers, and professionals, could be won over by protecting them against the encroachment of big business. Students and intellectuals were often spontaneously attracted to socialist and communist ideas, which carried on and radicalised many key rationalist and humanist values. Currently inactive individuals (old people, sick and disabled, students, homemakers, unemployed, and so on) were linked to the active working class by biographical or family ties, being past or future wageworkers and members of proletarian households. All these groups suffered under capitalism, performed essential (paid or unpaid) labour, and had to be won over to the perspective of a future socialist commonwealth of 'associated producers', where their distinction from wageworkers would cease to exist.

In general terms, the primacy of the active working class was most evident in the internal and extra-parliamentary discourse, while more attention to other components of the broader popular alliance was given in the electoral discourse.

The actual *sociology of members*, instead, changed much (Figure 2.5). Data exists only for a few parties and years. Existing evidence suggests that industrial workers made up the overwhelming majority of the radical left membership until World War Two, but subsequently fell below 50 per cent in the fifties and below 40 per cent in the seventies. The remaining share was filled by a variety of social groups: agricultural workers and peasants (particularly between the thirties and the sixties); pensioners and other inactive persons (in constant growth since the fifties); white-collar employees, intellectuals, and students (since the seventies); and the unemployed (in the thirties and since the seventies). Members were also overwhelmingly male, although women gradually increased toward 20 per cent in the forties and toward 30 per cent in the eighties.

Importantly, radical left parties constantly sought to involve individuals with a manual working-class background in the middle-level and top leadership positions, fighting the natural predominance of intellectuals with preferential selection policies and specific educational institutions. This specificity, however, started to fade after 1968 to the benefit of students and university-educated persons.

The actual *sociology of voters*, finally, was much more similar to that of the general electorate. Employed industrial workers were always strongly overrepresented, but after World War Two rarely rose beyond 40 per cent of the radical left electorate. The broader working class, in turn, was generally a clear majority,

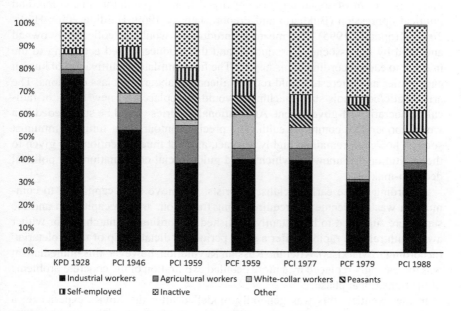

Figure 2.5 Sociology of radical left members, selected parties

but increasingly heterogeneous (blue-collar and white-collar, uneducated and educated, private and public sector, employed and unemployed) and flanked by a large number of self-employed and the inactive persons.

To sum up, the Western European radical left remained from the twenties to the eighties a party family firmly anchored in the class cleavage, mobilising a popular coalition composed of the active working class, its dependents (students, homemakers, and pensioners), and some allies (intellectuals, professionals, the peasantry, and the petty-bourgeoisie) against the feudal and bourgeois elites. The homogeneity of this coalition, however, declined over time, from an overwhelming predominance of employed male manual workers to a more heterogeneous mixture of class fractions, professions, qualifications, educational backgrounds, and genders. In addition, the radical left only managed to win over radicalised minorities of the labour movement, which predominantly continued to identify with social democratic and other political ideologies (Catholic or Protestant confessionalism, liberal republicanism, nationalism, and so on).

Political project: abstract communism, concrete transitions, and socialist internationalism

Right from its emergence as the radical wing of the socialist labour movement, the radical left has conceived the core of its political project in the *overcoming of capitalism and its replacement with a new communist society*. The daily struggle for partial social and democratic demands was considered important, but could not be separated from the final goal of working-class emancipation. The ultimate goal was a form of social organisation freed from exploitation, alienation, and political oppression (Bukharin and Preobrazhensky 1969; Harding 2009; Hudis 2013; Kropotkin 1995). The means of production would be collectively owned and used by the associated producers, and the produce shared according to the maxim 'to each according to his needs'. The free omnilateral cultivation of human capabilities and interests would replace alienated labour and class divisions. The aristocratic/bourgeois state machinery would be replaced by new forms of radical democratic self-government. And national rivalries would be superseded in a world cooperative commonwealth. The precise contours of a future communist society, however, remained highly abstract, and not much attention was given to the institutional framework which could guide social coordination and political decision-making.

According to the early socialist theorists, the move from capitalism to communism was not deemed to require a long transition, as both capitalism and the state were supposed to be instantly abolished (according to anarchists) or wither away with relative rapidity after a short period of 'dictatorship of the proletariat' (according to Marxists). After the Russian Revolution, however, this immediatism was increasingly replaced by a more detailed exploration of the concrete problems of the transitional phase.

In the twenties, this was generally modelled after the Soviet experience: a violent revolutionary break, a council-based democracy (the 'dictatorship of the proletariat'), a leading political role of communist parties (with or without allies), and a centrally-planned economy. Minority voices, however, criticised these principles or their authoritarian and hyper-centralistic application, advocating a stronger role for the councils, trade unions, and cooperatives (Broué 1997).

In the thirties, a yawning gap developed between the theory of a classless, stateless, and democratic society and the realities of the bureaucratic, state-led, and totalitarian Russian society. The original vision remained as a vague long-term goal, but the necessity of a transitional period shaped after the ideas of Joseph Stalin was successfully imposed by the orthodox communist parties (van Ree 2002). The negation of the socialist character of Stalinist societies remained minoritarian and uncertain, with views ranging from partial criticisms (the orthodox Trotskyist analysis of 'degenerated workers' states' as bureaucratic deformations over a fundamentally sound economic structure) to deeper attacks ('bureaucratic collectivisms' or 'state capitalisms') (van der Linden 2007). More generally, the steady rise of industrial concentration and state intervention across the industrial world progressively marginalised the widespread pre-war beliefs in the possibility of a direct transfer of economic management from capitalists to the associated producers, enhancing the faith in the central role of the state as coordinator, redistributor, welfare provider, and direct producer (for democratic socialists, through nationalisations and the welfare state; for communists, through a thoroughly planned economy).

The Popular Front turn (1935), the German invasion of the Soviet Union (1941), and the end of World War Two (1945) gradually juxtaposed to this model of socialist transition a different model, variously defined as 'progressive democracy' or 'popular democracy'. This foresaw a medium-term persistence of political freedoms, liberal-democratic institutions, and the mixed economy in the framework of a gradual implementation of ameliorative and structural reforms by broad anti-monopoly governmental coalitions. The concept remained, however, highly ambiguous, as its implementation in Eastern Europe soon proved to be a mere fig leaf for Stalinist planned economies and the variants promoted in Western Europe were accused of being smokescreens of communist parties biding their time before a solitary power grab.

In the sixties and seventies, these ambiguities were removed by Eurocommunist thinkers, which started advocating a peaceful, gradual, and democratic road to socialism not so different from that of left-leaning social democrats (Boggs and Plotke 1980; Esping-Andersen 1985; Weber 1978). Far-left organisations went instead the opposite way, reviving classic debates on revolutionary violence, workers' self-management, and socialist democracy.

In the eighties, finally, the crisis of both revolutionary hopes in the West and really-existing socialisms in the East conjured to put to the centre stage the mere defence of the existing model of welfarist mixed economy, pushing reflections on communism and transitional phases into the background.

A final key element of the radical left political project was *proletarian or socialist internationalism* (Waterman 1991). The radical left aspired to represent the general interests of the world working class; this did not mean disregarding national specificities, particularly those of 'oppressed nations', but involved a clear refusal to pit one section of the working class against the other for the sake of the interests of national ruling classes. In contrast, mainstream social democracy was accused precisely of this kind of 'social patriotic' bandwagoning, from its original support to the imperialist massacre of World War One to its subsequent compromises on national defence, the colonial question, migrants, military alliances, and foreign military interventions. Within the communist movement, however, this original meaning of internationalism soon morphed into an unquestioned loyalty toward the Soviet Union and the 'socialist camp'. Orthodox communist parties, thus, turned a blind eye to the oppression and repression of the working class in really-existing socialist countries: most glaringly, in occasion of the popular revolts in East Germany (1953), Hungary (1956), Czechoslovakia (1968), Poland (1981), and across Eastern Europe (1989). They also toned down their militancy, anti-militarism, and anti-imperialism whenever Soviet foreign policy required it (as during World War Two). Eurocommunist parties, in turn, became more critical of the Soviet Union after 1968 (Bracke 2007), but less of their own country, the European Union, and NATO. The position of far-left groups, finally, varied from 'third campism', to a critical support for the USSR, to an alignment with the foreign policy of minor powers (China, Cuba, Vietnam, Libya, or Albania).

To sum up, anti-capitalism always remained the polar star of the radical left, but intermediate phases of transition from a capitalist to a communist system progressively assumed an increasing importance and duration. Three main models existed: a Commune-like state based on council democracy *and* the leading role of a communist party with eventual allies (in the twenties); a Stalinist state based on one-party rule and a planned economy (since the thirties); and a progressive democracy based on the gradual deepening of the European model of welfarist mixed economy (most clearly since the seventies). In all cases, final and intermediate goals increasingly diverged, as democratic mechanisms remained poorly developed (Glaser 1999), aspirations toward a wide-ranging popular control clashed with the needs of technocratic rule, and material improvements for the working class passed through the extension of those very mechanisms (wage labour and state power) that communism was supposed to abolish. Finally, the principles of proletarian internationalism remained fragile and often perverted into a blind allegiance to the foreign policy interests of 'socialist' states or camps.

Organisational mediations: the vanguard and the masses

The radical left of 1917–23 inherited the organisational models of the pre-war socialist labour movement: an organisation based on territorial branches, a developed internal democracy, and strong links with the labour movement. The Comintern imposed a turn toward discipline, clandestine activities, and military preparations, but did not suppress internal pluralism and participation.

The streamlining of the communist parties in the 'Bolshevization' (1924–27) and 'third period' (1928–34) campaigns gradually led to a very different organisational model (LaPorte et al. 2008). Membership shrunk to a 'vanguard' of the faithful. A smaller basic unit, the cell, was introduced, but workplace cells never encompassed more than a third of the membership. Internal democracy was rapidly compressed in the name of 'democratic centralism' (Waller 1981), expelling groups resisting the directives of the Comintern and ultimately banning every open organisation of oppositional tendencies. Subcultural links, whose forms had greatly varied in the pre-war period (from formal affiliation to sympathetic autonomy, and from trade union to party predominance), were all brought back to a top-down subordination of collateral organisations or their communist factions to the central party leadership. The clandestine and paramilitary work was strengthened. All these measures were supposed to increase the efficacy of party activities, but alienated many members and potential supporters and proved incapable both of bringing insurrections to a successfully end (as in the 1923 fiasco in Germany) and of resisting fascist takeovers (as in 1924-26 in Italy and 1933-34 in Germany). They, however, played an important role in allowing the dogged survival of communist groups within authoritarian and totalitarian regimes and favouring their ascendancy over armed anti-fascist resistances.

In the Popular Fronts and after 1945 these elements were reproduced, but in the context of veritable mass parties, which opened the doors to a large influx of members and took into account their diverse needs, ideas, and modes of activism, as long as these did not result into open dissidence.

The elements of a strong and committed membership, a weak internal democracy ruled by the principles of democratic centralism, and a tight central control of the party over its subcultural networks weakened in the eighties, but were still largely in place in 1988.

Strategic mediations: from revolution to coalition

The means envisaged by the radical left for the attainment of its goals were initially far-removed from those of mainstream party families, but progressively lost specificity and conformed to the realities of normal liberal democratic politics. Three themes may be singled out: the advocacy of insurrectional means; an intransigent coalition policy; and the primacy of extra-parliamentary work over institutional activities.

On the first account, the radical left was initially divided from reformist social democracy by the belief in the inevitability of a final violent revolutionary confrontation between the proletariat and its party (or parties) on the one side, and the bourgeoisie and its state on the other side. Early radical left theorists considered the gradual legal and semi-legal accumulation of forces possible and necessary, but an entirely peaceful transition unlikely (Egan 2014; Nimtz 2010). In some cases, confrontation was actively pursued through strategies based on the creation of 'dual powers', popular insurrections, targeted military coups, or prolonged armed struggles (Bensaid 2007). In other cases, confrontation was not sought but it was expected to result from a violent right-wing reaction to a democratically-elected socialist government, as a long series of subsequent experiences seemed to confirm: the coups of Kapp in Germany (1920), Franco in Spain (1936), and Pinochet in Chile (1973). These theories, however, gradually lost their salience after World War Two. During the war, the Western European communist parties took the lead in the armed resistance against fascism, but – under the impulse of Stalin – refrained from steering it toward the establishment of socialist regimes, accepting instead a smooth liberal-democratic transition (Pons 2011). Insurrectional violence was not rejected in itself, but was considered premature or futile, as it could be easily crushed with the help of Western powers (the Greek Civil War of 1944–49) and threatened the geopolitical equilibrium between the two superpowers. Communist parties thus shifted to the advocacy of a 'peaceful road to socialism' through elections and alliances, retaining clandestine structures only as a safeguard against authoritarian threats. Since the seventies, the possibility of gradual and peaceful transition to socialism was envisaged with more boldness by Eurocommunist and other radical left currents (Weber 1978). Insurrectional strategies were revived by some far-left groups, but repression and political failure confined them to isolated fringe groups in a largely non-violent and electoralist environment.

On the second account, the radical left was initially very intransigent in its alliance policies. Electoral or governmental alliances with bourgeois parties were categorically rejected in the name of the political independence of the working class. Moreover, the only veritable alliances envisaged by the Comintern were with parties sharing the goals of a socialist revolution and of the 'dictatorship of the proletariat', therefore excluding most social democratic parties and including only small left-socialist, far-left, and left-nationalist forces. A 'united front' policy toward mainstream social democracy was envisaged in the twenties, but it was plagued with theoretical and practical difficulties and failed to be implemented in the crucial battles against fascism in Italy and Germany (Broué 1997). After the mid-thirties, these principles were thoroughly revised under the rising threat of international fascism. The communist parties first pushed for the formation of 'popular fronts' with reformist socialists and republicans (1935), and then accepted the need of 'national fronts' including all anti-fascist forces, including socialists, liberals, Christian democrats, and even conservatives (1943). This course was pursued until 1947 with the participation in all-party cabinets of anti-fascist unity. In the heat of the Cold War, positions radicalised toward an opposition against all Western-oriented forces. Since the sixties, finally, radical left positions varied freely between intransigence (mostly due to the refusal of potential partners), the pursuit of broad left-wing coalitions (as in the French *union de la gauche* of the seventies), and national unity alliances (as in the Italian *compromesso storico*). The relationship with mainstream social democracy became more cooperative, but heavy tensions remained (Smith 2012).

On the third account, radical left parties generally prioritised mobilisation in the workplaces, neighbourhoods, streets, trade unions, mass organisations, and social movements over activities in parliaments and cabinets. While some minority currents (anarchism, left-communism, parts of the post-1968 far left) went as far as rejecting electoral participation altogether, the vast majority valued both kinds of work. Extra-parliamentary activities, however, were considered essential for two reasons: on the one hand, immediate conquests for the working class were deemed to largely hinge upon the class struggle outside the state institutions, with legislative and policy measures following suit and rationalising its outcomes; on the other hand, popular participation was required both for the creation and survival of a communist government (through insurrectional or parliamentary means) and to move forward the process of socialist transformation. This specificity partially discoloured over time. Contrary to the theory, communist parties did encourage grassroots mobilisations when in opposition but actually used their cohesive organisation to suppress them whenever they found themselves in government, both in the East and in the West. The pursuit of a parliamentary road to socialism and of political allies increased the importance of institutional politics and advised against excessively radical struggles. The post-1968 wave of militancy briefly revived the belief in the potentialities of extra-parliamentary action, but ultimately abated. By the mid-eighties, the articulation between parliamentary and extra-parliamentary work resembled that of 'normal' political parties, although workerist and movementist features remained conspicuous.

Summary

The Western European radical left was born as an *anti-capitalist working-class party family* striving to represent the immediate interests of the proletariat, its dependents, and its allies and to lead the way from capitalism to an alternative communist society. This aspiration, however, proved elusive and gave way to a complex historical development punctuated with tensions and deviations.

Its actual social constituency was generally limited to radical minorities, giving rise to a violent competition with the reformist social democracy and other traditions for the allegiance of the same social groups. Moreover, these minorities were in themselves often heterogeneous, leading to frictions between active wageworkers and the broader popular classes, an industrial blue-collar core and other professional figures, sociological divisions (such as those based on gender, age, education, and employment status), and value orientations (materialist and post-materialist, traditional and left-libertarian).

Against the predictions of early socialists, the systemic transformation from capitalism to communism proved to be an unlikely and complex endeavour, which could be partially prefigured in the high points of revolutionary mobilisation but never institutionalised into viable socialist democracies. Thus, the radical left increasingly refocused its attention on long-lasting transitional periods modelled after really-existing forms of societies that seemed to do away with the worst elements of capitalism: the Russian model of authoritarian planned economies and the European model of welfarist mixed economies. Both guaranteed good levels of employment, living standards, and social protection, but neither ultimately proved amenable to anti-capitalist goals. As a consequence, the anti-capitalism of the radical left largely remained a vague aspiration, while the actual content of its political mobilisation was a *radical welfarist developmentalism* led by the state. Similarly, the unity of the world working class around the principles of proletarian internationalism was pursued only intermittently, while a pro-Soviet alignment and national imperatives often got the upper hand.

In organisational terms, radical left parties were distinctive in their cohesion, levels of activism, effective intervention at the extra-parliamentary level, and resilience under authoritarian regimes. This very discipline, however, had important drawbacks, as it limited internal democracy, repelled dissidents and potential allies, and suffocated grassroots mobilisation whenever the parties reached the threshold of governmental power.

In terms of strategy, the radical left moved from an intransigent, revolutionary, and predominantly extra-parliamentary course in the twenties to practices not so different from those of mainstream liberal democratic parties in the eighties, despite some residual reservations.

Cohesion

Radical left cohesion also varied over time.

In organisational terms, orthodox communist parties generally held a large majority of total radical left votes, seats, and members, but their supremacy was not complete and universal. In the first years (1918–23), the scene was actually dominated by 'centrist' factions. After 1924, communist parties established a solid control on a much weakened radical left, but alternative traditions did not entirely disappear and remained strong in a few countries (the Netherlands, Spain, Sweden, and the UK).[9] After 1945, the dominance of communist parties and communist-led fronts became almost complete, with the exception of the special case of Italy in 1946–56 (where the socialist PSI was allied to the communists but retained an independent organisation). After 1960, fragmentation rose steadily. A variety of left-socialist, far-left, and left-nationalist organisations emerged alongside official communist parties, sometimes replacing them as the main radical left player (Denmark, Ireland, Norway, Netherlands, Switzerland, and the UK), in other cases converging with them in temporary coalitions.

In ideological terms, the cohesion of the Western European communist parties gradually loosened. It was exceptionally strong under the Comintern (1919–43) and Cominform (1947–56), when dissidents were marginalised and uniformity easily imposed. It, however, quickly decreased in the seventies and eighties, when Eurocommunist parties distanced themselves from Moscow while a minority of orthodox organisations continued on a pro-Soviet line.

Concluding remarks

This chapter has sketched the key elements of the development of the Western European radical left from 1914 to 1988. It was a history of (failed) revolutions and struggles for social and democratic reforms; tranquillity and persecutions; foreign dependence and national adaptation; ideological, sociological, organisational, and strategic change; hostility and cooperation with the moderate left; cohesion and fragmentation; rise and decline. Born as a revolutionary anti-capitalist tendency of the socialist labour movement, the Western European radical left was subsequently torn between the advocacy of Stalinist models of 'really existing socialism' and an essentially social democratic path of gradual redistributive and welfarist reforms. While some features remained roughly constant for long periods, others changed in gradual or spectacular fashions in response to internal decisions, international impulses, the national political competition, and broader economic, social, and political trends.

The deep crisis of the eighties deepened in the years 1989–93, leading to the defection of most radical left members and voters and to the almost extinction of the party family. The 'new' radical left that emerged from its ashes was fundamentally different from its predecessors, although it overwhelmingly consisted of long-standing members of communist, left-socialist, Trotskyist, Maoist, and other far left organisations. The complex historical legacy it inherited was both an asset and a liability, as I will show in the following chapters.

Notes

1 Most members in 1923, the Portuguese PSP in 1925, the Swiss SPS in 1927, and the Italian PSI in 1930.
2 Beyond the large and already-mentioned Norwegian DNA, partial exceptions were the smallish Swedish SP, Spanish POUM, Dutch RSP, French PUP, and British ILP. Most of these radical groups affiliated after 1932 to the International Revolutionary Marxist Centre (IRMC), which however ceased to exist in 1940.
3 Radical left parties were outlawed in Finland (1918, 1923, and 1930), France (1939), Switzerland (1940, 1941), and Ireland (1940); Luxembourg unsuccessfully tried to do the same in 1937; Sweden (1940–44) and the UK (1941–42) limited themselves to outlawing the communist press.
4 Notably, the initial phases of the governments of Mitterrand in France (1981–82), Papandreou in Greece (1981–85), and Palme in Sweden (1982–84).
5 Actually, national legislations still vary in their treatment of certain categories of potential voters (citizens living abroad, the youth, prisoners, and former felons), automatic registration, the naturalisation of foreign residents, and other details.
6 Not-yet-divided social democratic parties with a radical majority and IASP left-socialist parties are retained until 1923 for Italy, France, Norway, Switzerland, and Spain, and are excluded afterwards. The Austrian SDAPDÖ is always excluded, despite its formal membership in the IASP. Radical currents, however, remained quite influent in many social democratic parties both before and after 1923.
7 Only cases of explicit governmental agreements are here retained; in other cases, the radical left also provided weaker forms of support to minority social democratic governments by allowing them to survive investiture votes, no-confidence motions, and budgetary votes.
8 Biver (2015) provides a good estimate for twenty countries since 1974; the profile of the curve is very similar.
9 The methodology used actually underestimates fragmentation by excluding former IASP parties and the Norwegian DNA after 1924.

References

Abdelal, Rawi (2007). *Capital rules: The construction of global finance.* Cambridge: Cambridge University Press.
Agosti, Aldo (1999). *Bandiere rosse: un profilo storico dei comunismi europei.* Roma: Editori Riuniti.

Alexander, Robert J. (2001). *Maoism in the developed world*. Westport: Praeger.
Alexander, Robert J. (1991). *International Trotskyism, 1929–1985: A documented analysis of the movement*. Durham: Duke University Press.
Alexander, Robert J. (1981). *The right opposition: The Lovestoneites and the international Communist opposition of the 1930s*. Durham: Duke University Press.
Almond, Gabriel A. (1947). 'The resistance and the political parties of Western Europe', *Political Science Quarterly* 62(1): 27–61.
Balestrini, Nanni, and Primo Moroni (1997). *L'orda d'oro 1968–1977. La grande ondata rivoluzionaria e creativa, politica ed esistenziale*. Milano: Feltrinelli.
Bartolini, Stefano (2000). *The political mobilization of the European left, 1860–1980: The class cleavage*. Cambridge: Cambridge University Press.
Bellanger, Emmanuel, and Julian Mischi (eds.) (2013). *Les territoires du communisme. Élus locaux, politiques publiques et sociabilités militantes*. Paris: Armand Colin.
Bensaïd, Daniel (2007). 'The return of strategy', *International Socialism* 113: 139–155.
Biver, Nico (2015). 'Verschwindet die Linke? Mitgliederentwicklung und Wahlergebnisse linker Parteien in Westeuropa seit den 1970er Jahren', *Z – Zeitschrift Marxistische Erneuerung* 101: 141–153 and 102: 141–151.
Boggs, Carl, and David Plotke (eds.) (1980). *The politics of Eurocommunism: Socialism in transition*. Boston: South End Press.
Bracke, Maud (2007). *Which socialism, whose détente? West European communism and the Czechoslovak crisis of 1968*. Budapest: Central European University Press.
Braunthal, Julius (1986). *Geschichte der Internationale: Band 3*. Hanover: Dietz.
Brenner, Robert (2006). *The economics of global turbulence: The advanced capitalist economies from long boom to long downturn, 1945–2005*. London: Verso.
Broué, Pierre (2004). *The German revolution, 1917–1923*. Chicago: Haymarket.
Broué, Pierre (1997). *Histoire de l'Internationale communiste (1919–43)*. Paris: Fayard.
Broué, Pierre, and Emile Témime (2007). *The revolution and the civil war in Spain*. Chicago: Haymarket.
Bukharin, Nikolai and Evgenii Preobrazhensky (1969). *The ABC of communism*. Baltimore: Penguin.
Buschak, Willy (1985). *Das Londoner Büro. Europäische Linkssozialisten in der Zwischenkriegszeit*. Amsterdam: IISG.
Carr, E.H. (1979). *The Russian revolution from Lenin to Stalin, 1917–1929*. Basingstoke: Macmillan.
Chiocchetti, Paolo (2016). Western European radical left database. Version 2.0 (30.04.2016). Available at: www.paolochiocchetti.it/data.
Claudin, Fernando (1975). *The communist movements: From Comintern to Cominform*. Harmondsworth: Penguin.
Cole, G.D.H. (1953, 1954). *A history of socialist thought. Vol. 1 and 2*. Basingstoke: Macmillan.
Cronin, James E. (1980). 'Labor insurgency and class formation: Comparative perspectives on the crisis of 1917–1920 in Europe', *Social Science History* 4(1): 125–152.
Darlington, Ralph (2013). *Radical unionism: The rise and fall of revolutionary syndicalism*. Chicago: Haymarket.
Dreyfus, Michel, Bruno Groppo, Claudio Sergio Ingerflom, Roland Lew, Claude Pennetier, Bernard Pudal, and Serge Wolikow (eds.) (2004). *Le siècle des communismes*. Paris: Éditions de l'Atelier.
Duménil, Gérard, and Dominique Lévy (2004). *Capital resurgent. The roots of the neoliberal revolution*. Boston: Harvard University Press.

Egan, Daniel (2014). 'Rethinking war of maneuver/war of position: Gramsci and the military metaphor', *Critical Sociology* 40(4): 521–538.
Eley, Geoff (2002). *Forging democracy: The history of the left in Europe, 1850–2000.* Oxford: Oxford University Press.
Esping-Andersen, Gøsta (1990). *The three worlds of welfare capitalism.* Princeton: Princeton University Press.
Esping-Andersen, Gøsta (1985). *Politics against markets: The social democratic road to power.* Princeton: Princeton University Press.
Gaddis, John Lewis (2005). *The Cold War: A new history.* New York: Penguin Press.
Gilbert, Mark (2014). *Cold War Europe: The politics of a contested continent.* Plymouth: Rowman & Littlefield.
Gilbert, Mark (2012). *European integration: A concise history.* Plymouth: Rowman & Littlefield.
Glaser, Daryl (1999). 'Marxism and democracy', in Andrew Gamble, David Marsh, and Tony Tant (eds.). *Marxism and social science.* Basingstoke: Palgrave Macmillan, 239–258.
Gordon, David M., Thomas E. Weisskopf, and Samuel Bowles (1987). 'Power, accumulation and crisis: The rise and demise of the post-war social structure of accumulation', in Robert Cherry (ed.). *The imperiled economy.* New York: URPE, 43–57.
Haimson, Leopold, and Giulio Sapelli (eds.) (1992). *Strikes, social conflict and the first world war. An international perspective.* Milano: Feltrinelli.
Harding, Neil (2009). *Lenin's political thought.* Chicago: Haymarket.
Harman, Chris (2009). *Zombie capitalism: Global crisis and the relevance of Marx.* London: Bookmarks.
Harman, Chris (1988). *The fire last time: 1968 and after.* London: Bookmarks.
Hawes, Stephan, and Ralph White (eds.) (1975). *Resistance in Europe: 1935–45.* London: Viking.
Hellemans, Staf (1990). *Strijd om de moderniteit. Sociale bewegingen en verzuiling in Europa sinds 1800.* Leuven: Leuven University Press.
Henke, Klaus-Dietmar, and Hans Woller (eds.) (1991). *Politische Säuberung in Europa: Die Abrechnung mit Faschismus und Kollaboration nach dem zweiten Weltkrieg.* München: DTV.
Hobsbawm, Eric (1995). *The age of extremes: The short Twentieth Century, 1914–1991.* London: Abacus.
Horn, Gerd-Rainer (2007). *The spirit of '68. Rebellion in Western Europe and North America, 1956–1976.* Oxford: Oxford University Press.
Hudis, Peter (2013). *Marx's concept of the alternative to capitalism.* Chicago: Haymarket.
Judt, Tony (2005). *Postwar: A history of Europe since 1945.* London: Vintage.
Klimke, Martin, and Joachim Scharloth (eds.) (2008). *1968 in Europe: A history of protest and activism, 1956–77.* London: Palgrave.
Kowalski, Ronald (2006). *European communism: 1848–1991.* Basingstoke: Palgrave Macmillan.
Kropotkin, Peter (1995). *The conquest of bread and other writings.* Cambridge: Cambridge University Press.
LaPorte, Norman, Kevin Morgan, and Matthew Worley (eds.) (2008). *Bolshevism, Stalinism and the comintern. Perspectives on Stalinization, 1917–1953.* Basingstoke: Palgrave Macmillan.
Lazar, Marc (1992). *Maisons rouges. Les Partis communistes français et italien de la Libération à nos jours.* Paris: Aubier.

Lipset, Seymour M., and Stein Rokkan (1967). 'Cleavage structures, party systems and voter alignments: An introduction', in Seymour M. Lipset and Stein Rokkan (eds.). *Party systems and voter alignments: Cross-national perspectives.* New York: The Free Press, 1–64.

Maier, Charles S. (1975). *Recasting bourgeois Europe: Stabilization in France, Germany, and Italy in the decade after World War I.* Princeton: Princeton University Press.

Marx, Karl (1967). *Capital. Vol. III.* New York: International Publishers.

Mazower, Mark (1998). *Dark continent: Europe's twentieth century.* London: Penguin.

Nation, R. Craig (1989). *War on war: Lenin, the Zimmerwald Left, and the origins of communist internationalism.* Durham: Duke University Press.

Nimtz, August H. (2010). 'Marx and Engels's electoral strategy: The alleged versus the real', *New Political Science* 32(3): 367–387.

Overy, Richard J. (2007). *The inter-war crisis.* 2nd ed. Harlow: Pearson Longman.

Payne, Stanley G. (1995). *A history of Fascism: 1914–1945.* Madison: University of Wisconsin Press.

Pons, Silvio (2011). 'Stalin and the European communists after World War Two (1943–1949)', *Past and Present* 6: 121–138.

Prat, Michel (1984). 'L'echec d'une opposition internationale de gauche dans le Komintern, 1926', *Communisme* 5: 61–75.

Priestland, David (2009). *The red flag: Communism and the making of the modern world.* New York: Groove Press.

Ramella, Francesco (2005). *Cuore rosso? Viaggio politico nell'Italia di mezzo.* Roma: Donzelli.

Reinhart, Carmen M., and M. Belen Sbrancia (2011). The liquidation of government debt [working paper]. NBER Working Papers, 16893. Available at: www.imf.org/external/np/seminars/eng/2011/res2/pdf/crbs.pdf [accessed on 01.04.2016].

Rothermund, Dietmar (ed.) (2006). *The Routledge companion to decolonization.* London: Routledge.

Sassoon, Donald (2010). *One hundred years of socialism: The West European left in the Twentieth Century.* 2nd ed. London: I.B. Tauris.

Sassoon, Donald (1992). 'The rise and fall of West European communism, 1939–48', *Contemporary European History* 1(2): 139–169.

Smith, W. Rand (2012). *Enemy brothers: Socialists and communists in France, Italy, and Spain.* Plymouth: Rowman & Littlefield.

Starobin, Joseph R. (1965). 'Communism in Western Europe', *Foreign Affairs* 44(1): 62–77.

Steiner, Herbert (1991). 'Die Internationale Arbeitsgemeinschaft Sozialistischer Parteien (II 1/2. Internationale) 1921–1923', *Beiträge zur Geschichte der Arbeiterbewegung*, 1: 13–24.

Tannahill, R. Neal (1978). *The communist parties of Western Europe: A comparative study.* Westport: Greenwood Press.

Thompson, E.P. (1980). *The making of the English working class.* 2nd ed. Harmondsworth: Penguin.

van der Linden, Marcel (2008). *Workers of the world: Essays toward a global labor history.* Leiden: Brill.

van der Linden, Marcel (2007). *Western Marxism and the Soviet Union. A survey of critical debates and theories since 1917.* Leiden: Brill.

van der Linden, Marcel, and Wayne Thorpe (eds.) (1990). *Revolutionary syndicalism: An international perspective.* Aldershot: Scolar Press.

van Ree, Erik (2002). *The political thought of Joseph Stalin: A study in twentieth-century revolutionary patriotism.* London: Routledge
Waller, Michael (1981). *Democratic centralism: An historical commentary.* Manchester: Manchester University Press.
Waller, Michael, and Meindert Fennema (eds.) (1988). *Communist parties in Western Europe: Decline or adaptation?* Oxford: Basil Blackwell.
Waterman, Peter (1991). 'Understanding socialist and proletarian internationalism', *ISS Working Paper Series* 97.
Weber, Henri (1978). 'Eurocommunism, socialism and democracy', *New Left Review* 110: 3–14.
Winkler, Heinrich August (1993). *Weimar 1918–1933. Die Geschichte der ersten deutschen Demokratie.* München: C.H. Beck.
Wrigley, Chris (ed.) (1993). *Challenges of labour: Central and Western Europe 1917–1920.* London: Routledge.

3 The Western European landscape, 1989–2015

This chapter sketches the key transformations of the Western European radical left since 1989, from a short initial phase of identity crisis and material collapse to a long subsequent period of uneven renewal and recovery. What progressively emerged after 1994 was a 'new' radical left, where each party tried to chart its way between the contradictions of the anti-neoliberal field of forces described in chapter one: anti-neoliberal coherence and centre-left unity, anti-neoliberalism and anti-capitalism, and old traditions and new realities.

The discussion is structured as follows. First, I provide a brief narrative introduction to the historical context and the main radical left trends and players. Secondly, I analyse the evolution of aggregate radical left strength and its main quantifiable components (electoral, parliamentary, governmental, and membership strength), partially revising the assessments found in the existing literature. Thirdly, I explore the key shifts that occurred in the nature of the radical left. Fourthly, I highlight the growing fragmentation of this party family. Finally, I summarise and discuss the main findings of the analysis.

Historical narrative: parties and contexts

The post-1989 trajectory of the Western European radical left can be usefully divided in three main periods. From 1988 to 1993, this party family was hit hard by the collapse of the Soviet bloc and saw its coherence and societal strength decline markedly. From 1994 to 2007, it tried to reinvent itself as a representative of the working-class and welfarist constituencies affected by neoliberalism, and experienced a fragile but real recovery. After 2008, the effects of the economic crisis increased the dissatisfaction and volatility of national electorates, but clear breakthroughs were achieved only in a handful of peripheral countries (Greece, Spain, and Portugal), while the main beneficiaries in the rest of the continent were right-wing populist and other kinds of opposition parties.

The collapse of world communism, 1988–93

The late eighties and early nineties were marked by wide-ranging changes of the international and European context. The Soviet bloc and other communist regimes (such as Yugoslavia and Albania), already weakened by a decade of economic decline, collapsed in 1989–92 under the impact of popular revolutions, nationalist tensions, and the attraction exerted by global capitalism on sections of the ruling communist elites. Germany was reunified in 1990. The process of European integration moved toward both a deepening of its content (establishment of the European Union in 1993, completion of the single market, blueprint for a single currency) and an enlargement of its geographical scope (accession of the neutral Austria, Finland, and Sweden in 1995, negotiations on association agreements and future membership with the Eastern European countries). Economic globalisation gained momentum, with a growth of international trade and finance, the lowering of legislative and practical barriers, and an expansion of global supply chains. Europe was at the forefront of these trends, with a complete liberalisation of capital movements (1990) and internal trade (1992–94), a global web of free-trade agreements, and a growing productive integration and centralisation of European firms and banks. Finally, the world entered into a unipolar moment, with the start of a massive expansion of US foreign bases, alliances, and interventions across the world.

The collapse of the Soviet bloc accelerated the crisis tendencies already operating within the Western European radical left since the eighties, and almost led to the death of this party family. All actors were stunned by the events in Eastern Europe, regardless of their orthodox, reform (Eurocommunist and pro-Gorbachev), or anti-Stalinist sympathies. The reactions of communist parties have been widely investigated in the literature (Botella and Ramiro 2003; Bull and Heywood 1994; Marantzidis 2004). Five broad groups can be distinguished. Some of the weakest parties dissolved (the British CPGB in 1991) or virtually ceased to exist as autonomous electoral organisations (the Flemish KP, the Norwegian NKP, and the German DKP). Some parties abandoned their communist identity and switched to other party families: the majority faction of the Italian PCI, which rebranded as PDS in 1991 and joined the Socialist International in 1992; the Dutch CPN, which merged with other forces in the ecologist GL in 1989; the minority of the Irish WP, which rebranded as DL in 1992 and joined the Irish Labour Party in 1999; and the Spanish PTE-UC and EE, which joined the socialist party in 1991. A third group moved toward non-communist forms of leftism. These parties changed name, moderated their ideology, took over social democratic and green themes, and reconverted into 'broad left' parties or coalitions, while remaining part of the radical left: the Finnish SKDL (rebranded as VAS in 1990), the Swedish VPK (rebranded as V in 1990), the East German SED (rebranded as PDS in 1990), the Danish DKP (merged in E in 1989), the Spanish PCE (active since 1986 in the IU coalition), the Catalan PSUC (gradually dissolved after 1987 in the IC/ICV coalition, which later oscillated between the radical left and green party families), and a minority of the Greek communists (converged in SYN in 1991). A fourth group continued to refer to communism, but pursued a path of ideological and organisational reforms similar to those of the previous group, albeit more cautiously: notably, the French PCF, the minority faction of the Italian PCI (which established the PRC in 1991), and the Austrian KPÖ. Finally, some parties stuck to a more or less orthodox course: notably, the majority faction of the Greek KKE and the Portuguese PCP. The reactions of far-left organisations (Pina 2005) were actually very similar and ranged between dissolution, adaptation to social democracy and ecologism, convergence into broader radical left parties or coalitions, a difficult renewal, and loyalty to traditional positions. Left-socialist organisations were also affected: the French PSU dissolved in 1990; other parties merged into larger green (the Dutch PSP in 1989) or social democratic (the Swiss PSA in 1991) competitors; the Danish SF and Norwegian SV stayed their course, while deepening the ecologist and libertarian elements of their ideologies.

This identity crisis was coupled with a profound weakening of the radical left. Its aggregate electoral strength fell from 19.1 million votes (9.4 per cent) in 1988 to 11.2 million votes (5.1 per cent) in 1993. Most of this decline was due to the events in the Italian PCI, which in 1988 had 10.3 million votes – more than half of the total. If we account for the effects of defections and new entries in the party family,[1] aggregate data are instead stable around 4.8 per cent, but the almost totality of radical left parties still lost moderately or heavily. Membership levels, financial resources, and organisational linkages also strongly declined.

A new radical left against neoliberalism, 1994–2007

The general trends in the social and political balance of forces described above continued in the following two decades, which were characterised by a progressive unfolding of neoliberal mechanisms and reforms over the Western European societies (Cafruny and Ryner 2003; Featherstone 2001; Mayer 2006; Saad-Filho and Johnston 2005; Vail 2010). The traditional tools of national macro-economic policy (control over monetary creation, financial repression, restrictions to the free movement of goods and capitals, exchange rate adjustment, deficit spending, and state-owned enterprises and banks) were dismantled or redirected from the goals of growth and full employment to the pursuit of the financial profitability of the private sector. Legislative reforms pushed toward a flexibilisation of the labour market, the containment of future pension expenditures, and a selective retrenchment of the welfare state. The living standards of the majority of the population stagnated due to low wage growth, high unemployment rates, and a higher tax burden, while a minority benefitted from the rise of redistributed profits and top salaries, the wealth effects of growing real estate and financial prices, and tax avoidance. European states continued to offer comprehensive public services and safety nets, but considerations of well-being and social justice receded into the background. Mainstream political parties fully embraced neoliberal positions, although they implemented them gradually and selectively to decrease their public opinion impact.

These trends created the conditions for a recovery of radical left parties, which reinvented themselves as the most decided opponents of neoliberalism and the new representatives of working-class and welfarist constituencies neglected by the political establishment (Backes and Moreau 2008; Bensaid et al. 2011; Daiber et al. 2012; De Waele and Seiler 2012; Hudson 2000, 2012; March 2012). This process was helped by the revival of social movements, in particular union-led anti-governmental campaigns, pacifist demonstrations, and the new alter-globalist galaxy. At the same time, objective constraints and subjective failings kept its success limited and fragile. Aggregate electoral strength rose from 5.1 per cent in 1993 to 7.2 in 1999, sank back to 5.5 in 2004, and recovered to 7.4 in 2007. The growth in the nineties was near-universal, but trends after 2000 varied widely according to national specificities. Communist parties sometimes consolidated their position but more frequently continued to decline, and most of the gains were made by a variety of alternative organisations. The crisis of non-electoral dimensions was rarely reversed. Finally, the fragmentation of the radical left in rival parties and tendencies rose steadily, depressing its coherence, parliamentary representation, and overall influence.

The Great Recession, 2008–15

The start of the Great Recession in 2007–08 further exacerbated the problems of the neoliberal model (Bellofiore 2013; Duménil and Lévy 2011). Trends in the European Union and in the Eurozone were harsher than in the rest of the world, as the absence of internal exchange rate adjustments, the full mobility of capital, and fiscal austerity added to the effects of the global conjuncture. Parts of the financial sector collapsed and had to be saved through joint efforts of national governments, central banks, and the multilateral institutions. Private and sovereign debt levels soared and became increasingly hard to refinance. Capitals flowed back from the troubled periphery to the more stable core. Fiscal austerity was tightened by instruments like the 2012 Fiscal Compact that imposed a pro-cyclical balanced budget framework. The stagnation of labour costs and prices in Germany and the presence of a single currency (in the Eurozone) forced other countries to a strategy of internal devaluation, compressing domestic demand to recover competitiveness. The combined effects of these factors were dire. European GDP and wage growth came to a standstill, unemployment and poverty rates rose, and industrial production strongly declined. In 2015, eight years into the crisis, the domestic product of Greece, Italy, Spain, and Portugal was still lower than before its start.

Crisis and austerity elicited important protests, progressively eroded the support of government parties, and opened up a window of opportunity for anti-establishment challengers. The radical left found itself in a very favourable position, but managed to exploit it only in a limited number of countries (Ducange et al. 2013; Escalona et al. 2017; Gerbaudo 2016; March and Keith 2016). Aggregate electoral weight oscillated trendlessly between 6.7 and 7.8 per cent until 2014, and soared to 9.6 per cent in 2015. Results in Greece rose from 13.9 (2007) per cent to 45.0 per cent (2015) of valid votes, bringing SYRIZA to power. Results in Spain increased from 4.9 per cent (2008) to 25.8 per cent (2015), pushed by the rise of the new party PODEMOS and its allied regionalist coalitions. Results in Portugal oscillated from election to election between 15 and 22 per cent. In all other countries, electoral outcomes varied and were not uniformly positive; in the three largest countries (German, France, and Italy), they remained stagnant or declining.

64 *Western European landscape, 1989–2015*

Summary

After the collapse of 1989–93, the Western European radical left renewed itself and recovered on the back of its opposition to neoliberalism. Until 2014, however, it failed to fully benefit from the growing popular dissatisfaction with establishment parties, oscillating in aggregate terms between 5 and 8 per cent of valid votes. In 2015, it finally experienced major breakthroughs in some of the countries most affected by the Great Recession (Greece, Spain, and Portugal), but the rest of the continent did not follow suit.

Radical left strength

The methodology described in chapter one enables one to measure the strength of the contemporary Western European radical left in a more comprehensive, accurate, and fine-grained way than existing methods. First, the inclusion of minor parties and lists improves the measurement of electoral strength, particularly in countries characterised by weak or fragmented radical lefts. Secondly, the aggregation of national results through weighted averages – instead of simple averages – provides an adequate reflection of the continental strength of this party family. Thirdly, the use of yearly rolling figures permits the detection of short-term movements and improves the accuracy of medium-term averages. Fourthly, the simultaneous observation of the yearly development of aggregate and national figures allows an accurate periodisation of the overall trajectory of radical left strength and a differentiation between phases characterised by strong cross-national trends and phases of trendless fluctuations. Finally, the consistency of indicators of electoral, parliamentary, and governmental strength enables a systematic cross-dimensional comparison of strength variations.

The analysis confirms several assertions of the literature: the relative weakness of the contemporary radical left compared to the pre-1989 period; mixed electoral trends; a continued decline of communist parties; a growing level of governmental involvement; and large national variations. At the same time, it reveals some new elements: a real but unstable post-1994 recovery, characterised by an alternation of short-term phases of cross-national growth, cross-national decline, and trendless fluctuation; a major but uneven spike in 2015, with a divergence between a Northern core and a Mediterranean periphery; and a growing organisational fragmentation of the radical left.

The primary data for all seventeen countries, together with sources, notes, and elaborations, are available in the Western European Radical Left Database (Chiocchetti 2016).

Electoral strength

The evolution of *aggregate electoral strength* from 1989 to 2015 is depicted in Figure 3.1. Two additional curves are reported: the first represents aggregate values excluding results in the Eastern German regions (former GDR and West

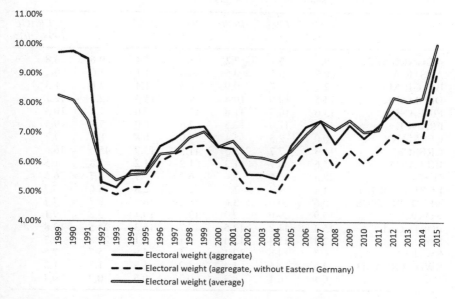

Figure 3.1 Electoral strength, Western European radical left (1989–2015)

Berlin), thus preserving a full comparability of the territorial scope of the analysis; the second represents unweighted average values. The dynamics of all three curves are quite similar, although their discrepancies clearly show the key role played by the Italian PCI until 1991 and by the German PDS since 1990 in shaping aggregate results.

Aggregate electoral strength initially halved, from 9.6 per cent in 1989 to 5.1 per cent in 1993. It then recovered to 7.2 per cent in 1999, but retreated to 5.5 per cent in 2004. A new recovery to 7.4 per cent in 2007 was followed by stagnation until 2014, and a final big push to 9.6 per cent in 2015. The uncertainty of the literature in declaring a decline, stagnation, or recovery of the radical left since the early nineties is explained by its focus on ten-year averages which do not coincide with actual trends (De Waele and Seiler 2012; March 2012; March and Mudde 2005). The use of yearly figures clarifies the picture. On the one hand, aggregate strength in 1994–2015 (6.8 per cent) was substantially lower than before 1989 (10.7 per cent in the eighties, 9.4 per cent in 1988). Electoral peaks in 1999 (7.2 per cent), 2007 (7.4 per cent), and 2012 (7.8 per cent) also remained below the bar of 1988. A full recovery from the crisis of the early nineties was reached only in 2015, largely thanks to the surge of PODEMOS in Spain. On the other hand, however, aggregate strength since 1994 was generally substantially higher than the 1993 trough (5.1 per cent), with the partial exception of the weak results of 2002–04 (around 5.5 per cent).

National results in selected years are reported in Table 3.1. While somewhat inferior than in the pre-1989 period, national differences remained large even after

Table 3.1 National vote shares in selected years (%)

	1989	1993	1999	2004	2007	2015	AVERAGE 1994–2015
AGGREGATE	9.7	5.1	7.2	5.5	7.4	9.6	6.8
AUSTRIA	0.7	0.5	0.5	0.6	1.1	1.0	0.7
BELGIUM	2.1	0.7	0.9	0.5	1.4	3.8	1.3
DENMARK	14.5	10.0	10.4	9.0	15.4	12.2	12.1
FINLAND	13.6	10.3	11.8	11.2	9.6	7.5	10.3
FRANCE	11.7	11.0	12.5	7.6	8.0	7.9	9.3
GERMANY	0.0	2.5	5.1	4.0	8.8	8.7	7.2
GREECE	11.3	7.7	15.5	11.5	13.9	45.0	16.6
IRELAND	5.6	0.7	1.2	1.2	1.2	2.8	1.5
ITALY	28.3	5.6	8.6	6.7	7.9	5.7	6.5
LUXEMBOURG	4.4	4.4	3.3	2.8	2.8	6.6	3.7
NETHERLANDS	0.6	0.6	3.6	6.4	16.6	9.7	7.7
NORWAY	10.9	9.0	7.7	13.8	10.1	5.2	9.1
PORTUGAL	15.4	11.2	12.5	10.7	15.3	21.5	13.8
SPAIN	12.4	11.3	12.4	6.1	6.1	25.8	9.3
SWEDEN	6.3	4.6	12.1	8.5	5.9	5.7	7.5
SWITZERLAND	2.6	1.6	1.4	1.2	1.3	1.2	1.3
UK	0.1	0.1	0.3	0.7	0.6	0.2	0.4

1994. The 1994–2015 average was above 10 per cent in four countries (Greece, Portugal, Denmark, and Finland), above 6 per cent in seven (France, Germany, Italy, the Netherlands, Norway, Spain, and Sweden), and below 4 per cent in the other six (Austria, Belgium, Ireland, Luxembourg, Switzerland, and the UK).[2] The volatility of national results was naturally higher than that of aggregate results, with a number of remarkable (often short-lived) breakthroughs: 15.5 per cent in Greece (1996), 12.1 per cent in Sweden (1998), 13.8 per cent in Norway (2001), 16.6 per cent in the Netherlands (2006), 15.4 per cent in Denmark (2007), 12.0 per cent in Germany (2009), 45.0 per cent in Greece (2015), 25.8 per cent in Spain (2015), and 21.5 per cent in Portugal (2015). Interestingly, the historical strongholds of Italy, France, and Finland stagnated or declined, dragged down by the negative baggage and governmental involvement of the local communist and post-communist parties, while a few countries with medium or weak recent radical traditions largely exceeded the results of the seventies and eighties (Germany, the Netherlands, and Greece).

Nevertheless, the movements of the aggregate curve were often associated with strong *cross-national trends* (Figure 3.2). Both the decline of 1989–93 and the recovery of 1994–99 were nearly universal. The 2000–04 dip and the 2005–07 recovery were marked by still recognisable but weaker trends, with a growing role played by national specificities. After 2008, finally, all regularities broke down, with individual countries and parties rising and falling in an uncoordinated fashion, sometimes with dramatic variations. Like the structural crisis of the seventies, the Great Recession enhanced the role of party agency, rewarding effective mobilisation strategies and heavily punishing mistakes (in particular, governmental

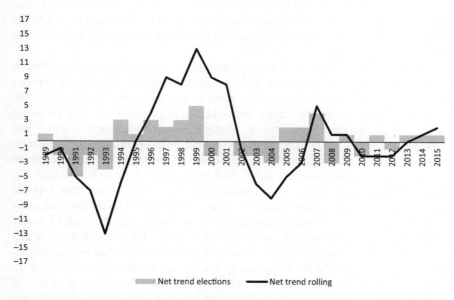

Figure 3.2 Cross-national electoral trends (1989–2015)

participation), eroding the hold of establishment parties but increasing the appeal of a variety of anti-establishment competitors.

What are the causes of these variations in time and space? Some attempts to explain the electoral success and failure of the contemporary radical left already exist in the literature. Several relevant causal variables with statistically significant and strong effects have been identified (March and Rommerskirchen 2015; Ramiro 2016): specifically, contextual (unemployment rates), ideological (self-positioning on the left-right axis, absent or weak religiosity, anti-globalisation sentiment, Euroscepticism, dissatisfaction with democracy), milieu (working-class identity, trade union membership), and politological (past results, high electoral thresholds, parliamentary representation, governmental participation, competition from Green and radical right parties) factors. Ramiro (2003) rejects a strong role of sociological variables in the eighties, pointing to the importance of party agency in shaping outcomes among different class sections and value groups. Visser et al. (2014) point to a number of sociological, ideological, and contextual variables affecting the strength of radical left self-positioning: the most relevant are non-religiosity, support for income distribution, unemployment, low and medium income levels, and tertiary education. Taken together, these variables constitute a constellation of favourable conditions for the electoral success of the radical left, but do not rigidly determine its actual development nor can explain its large national variations and sudden movements. Firstly, the above-mentioned variables explain only a small portion of the country-level variance. Secondly, the quantitative gaps between actual radical left voters and people placing themselves on the far left of the political spectrum or broadly supporting anti-neoliberal positions are huge. Thirdly, each party attracts a different kind of support: workerist and post-materialist; lower-class and middle-class; older and younger; radical and moderate; and so on.

My analysis contributes to this literature by highlighting the interaction between party agency, national factors, and cross-national trends in shaping radical left results. First, what radical left parties make of the above-mentioned favourable or unfavourable conditions clearly depends to a large extent on their projected image, spokespersons, programmes, strategies, communication resources, and interactions with allies and competitors. Two examples will suffice here: the relative resilience of the Italian PCI to the decline of the eighties (compared to its French and Portuguese counterparts), and the failure of the Italian radical left to profit from the Great Recession (contrary to the Spanish one). This variable is, however, difficult to operationalise, as comprehensive data on the total communication outreach of parties through the mass media, members, and friendly organisations are not available, and the effectiveness of a given strategy or discourse is only recognisable *ex post*. Secondly, national histories are fundamental both in determining the stickiness of radical left results, and in opening up important windows of opportunities. What we see at play throughout the electoral history of the radical left since 1917 is the coexistence of two kinds of temporalities: during periods of deep economic and political crisis, sudden leaps or falls in electoral results become possible (1918, 1945, 1968, 1989, 2015); in 'normal' periods, results tend to follow past levels and gains and losses are usually limited and gradual. Thirdly, the analysis helps understand the nature of an unexpected finding of Ramiro (2016): the effects of the 'year' variable. Far from being exclusively determined by national factors, radical left results are often affected by cross-national trends shaping their simultaneous rise and decline across the continent. These seem to coincide with well-documented European and global shifts in the strength of left-wing ideas and militancy. Interestingly, periods of structural crisis (the thirties, the seventies, and the twenty-tens) are instead characterised by trendless and volatile fluctuations, which continue until one of the possible solutions to the crisis decisively imposes itself. Further historical research, however, is needed to clarify the precise combination of cultural, structural, geopolitical, generational, and imitation factors behind these public opinion trends.

In addition, three new factors are identified as playing an important role. The first is the strength of subcultural linkages (Bellucci and Heath 2012). The failure to dent the supremacy of mainstream social democratic parties over the 'red' subculture proved to be a major obstacle to the radical left in the interwar period. Success, in turn, ensured the stability of the communist vote in Italy, France, and Finland until the eighties. The subsequent crisis of traditional mediations, finally, largely contributed to an increase in the volatility of overall and radical left results. The second is the level, thematic focus, and political leaning of extra-parliamentary mobilisations. In general, mass mobilisations usually exert a strong short-term impact on election results, although long-term effects are rarer. In the case of the contemporary radical left, anti-neoliberal mass movements have regularly been followed by small or large electoral spikes, most prominently in Greece and Spain after 2011. The third is the political composition of seating governmental coalitions. Involvement of the radical left in experiences of direct or external governmental participation (Bale and Dunphy 2011; Olsen et al. 2010) is, since the late seventies, invariably associated with heavy losses, sometimes leading to truly catastrophic outcomes (the French PCF in 1997–2002, the Italian radical left in 2006–08, and the Danish SF in 2011–14). Opposition to centre-right governments is often associated with short-term gains (March and Rommerskirchen 2015), partly because of the unpopularity of the former and partly because of a higher frequency of anti-governmental mass mobilisations. These conjunctures, however, increase the pressures toward centre-left unity, cancelling out the benefits in the medium term. Opposition to centre-left governments does not have clear effects. Gains among disaffected centre-left voters are usually limited, as some potential supporters choose to stick with governmental parties as the 'lesser-evil', others are demoralised and move toward abstention, and a third group ends up associating (neoliberal) governmental policies with the left *tout court*, shifting toward populist parties or the traditional right. Finally, opposition to grand coalition governments seems to be the most promising option, but cases are still few and empirical results mixed.

To sum up, radical left success largely appears as the delicate outcome of a complex interaction between party agency, party competition, national contexts, and cross-national trends. This issue will be explored more in detail in the analysis of the German, French, and Italian case studies.

Parliamentary strength

As in the previous period, the evolution of *aggregate parliamentary strength* broadly mirrored electoral developments, but at a markedly lower level (Figure 3.3). The 1994–2015 average was 4.7 per cent, with troughs in 1993 (3.4 per cent) and 2004 (2.6 per cent) and peaks in 1999 (4.9 per cent), 2007 (5.7 per cent), and 2015 (8.1 per cent).

The radical left was represented at any one time in twelve to fourteen of the seventeen states, with a permanent absence in Austria and an intermittent one in another eight countries: Belgium (1985–2013), the United Kingdom (1974–2004, 2010–11, 2015), Luxembourg (1994–97 and 2004–08), Ireland (1992–96, 2007–10), the Netherlands (1989–93), Italy (2008–11), Switzerland (2011–14), and Germany (1977–89). The number rose to fifteen in 2014. The gap between parliamentary and electoral strength was almost one third (−30.8 per cent), substantially higher than in the post-war decades; it ranged from an almost perfectly proportional representation in Denmark, Germany, the Netherlands, and Sweden to massive disproportionalities in Luxembourg, France, and Spain. These outcomes resulted from the combined effects of electoral legislations, radical left weakness, and radical left fragmentation.

70 *Western European landscape, 1989–2015*

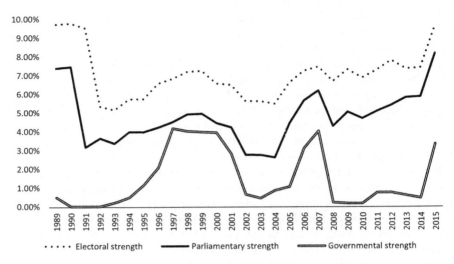

Figure 3.3 Electoral, parliamentary, and governmental strength, Western European radical left (1989–2015)

Governmental strength

The evolution of *aggregate governmental strength* is depicted in Figure 3.3. The 1994–2015 average remained low (1.8 per cent), although it doubled compared to the 1947–88 period (0.9 per cent). It ranged from values close to zero to non-negligible peaks in 1997 (4.4 per cent), 2006 (3.1 per cent), and 2015 (3.3 per cent). Contrary to the post-war period, when the governmental involvement of communist parties was severely limited by geopolitical considerations, after 1989 these experiences increased both quantitatively (nine countries, sixty-four years) and qualitatively (more direct cabinet participations). In 2015, SYRIZA won the election in Greece and became the leading party of a coalition government (Ovenden 2015).[3]

All these experiences ranged from negative to catastrophic. Firstly, radical left parties rarely managed to shape governmental socio-economic policies in a recognisably progressive direction, at best mitigating their regressive content. Until 2015, it was widely thought that this essentially depended on an insufficient balance of parliamentary and social forces, but the case of Greece proved otherwise: despite a strong anti-austerity mandate, with a solid parliamentary majority and the overwhelming popular support gained in the July referendum, after months of inconclusive negotiations with its European partners SYRIZA ultimately backed down and accepted the implementation of harsh neoliberal policies. This experience demonstrated the extent to which the framework of EU institutions and policies tightly constrains the feasibility of anti-neoliberal programmes, and the fundamental incompatibility of the two. Only a small minority of the Western

European radical left, however, has so far opted for a Eurorejectionist course, the majority continuing to advocate 'critical Europeanist' (also known as 'soft Eurosceptic') positions.

Secondly, radical left parties regularly experienced moderate to heavy electoral losses in the next election, with part of their electorate leaving toward abstention or further protest options and another part directly shifting to the moderate left.

Thirdly, governmental experiences often tested the very cohesion of radical left parties, provoking internal crises and organisational splits. Given this balance sheet, it is not easy to understand the continued popularity of governmental participation among radical left leaderships. In the analysis of the three cases I will show that this orientation depends not only on an overestimation of their own possibilities but, more importantly, on the bipolar mentality of most of the radical left electorate (which would struggle to understand an explicit refusal to elect and support a centre-left government against the right) and on material incentives and disincentives provided by the political system.

Membership strength

As already remarked in chapter two, membership data are incomplete and not entirely reliable. Nevertheless, all sources and estimates agree on a sudden collapse of the aggregate radical membership between 1989 and 1992 (mainly but not exclusively due to the defection of the PCI majority in Italy), a slower decline until 2008, and stagnation afterwards. My estimate for thirteen countries – excluding Ireland, Luxembourg, Norway, and Switzerland – shows a decline from 2.2 million members in 1989 (0.85 per cent of the total electorate) to 0.8 million in 1992 (0.29 per cent) and less than 0.5 million in 2012 (0.16 per cent). Biver's (2015) estimate for twenty countries shows a similar pattern.

The trajectories of individual parties were not uniform, ranging from unambiguously negative (the French PCF), positive (the Dutch SP), and mixed (the Danish SF); however, the gains (usually, of new and small parties) rarely compensated the losses (usually, of larger communist parties).[4]

Summary

The analysis of the continental evolution of four dimensions of strength (electoral, parliamentary, governmental, and membership) shows that the collapse of the 'old' radical left in 1989–93 was followed after 1994 by a strong cross-national recovery of a 'new' radical left, revived by internal reforms and a growing popular opposition to neoliberalism. This growth path, however, stopped in 1999 and turned into a succession of short-term oscillations and increasingly divergent national trends. The growing involvement of the radical left in centre-left alliances and governments – at both national and regional levels – played an important role in breaking its initial momentum, associating it to the unpopularity of the 'third way' governments of the nineties, and denting its anti-neoliberal and anti-establishment credentials. It also represented one of the main causes of national divergences since 2000. Still, these 'mistakes' were partly unavoidable, as a number external factors pushed toward a policy of left unity and made the option of a long-term isolation look fraught with graver dangers: the bipolar mind-set of many radical left voters, that could have led to a massive pro-socialist tactical voting (as indeed later happened in France after 2002); the effects of disproportional electoral systems, which threatened non-aligned forces with the loss of parliamentary representation and financial resources; and a honest revulsion toward seating right-wing governments (further strengthened by the consequences of anti-neoliberal mass mobilisations). This and other factors constrained a further development, which never crossed the threshold of 8 per cent until 2014. The Western European radical left arrived at the appointment with the Great Recession politically compromised, organisationally weakened, programmatically and strategically uncertain, and often fragmented in rival organisations. The opportunities offered by the crumbling support for establishment parties were thus largely wasted, with veritable breakthroughs in three Mediterranean countries (Greece, Spain, and Portugal) but stagnation or decline across most of the remaining states. In addition, the limits of the critical Europeanism of most parties were laid bare by the experience of the SYRIZA government, revealing a major credibility gap between their political project and its actual feasibility.

Radical left nature

The radical left re-emerged from the ruins of the 1989 crisis as a profoundly refashioned party family. Some legacies of twentieth-century communism continued to operate in a de-emphasised way within contemporary radical left parties, but only a small minority actively cultivated them. The vast majority, on the contrary, experimented with a broad matrix of communist, Marxist, Keynesian, anarchist, social democratic, left-libertarian, radical democratic, ecologist, and populist references, seeking to reinvent themselves as modern, inclusive, and pluralist anti-neoliberal forces (Fagerholm 2016; Hudson 2012; March 2012). Specific solutions, however, varied, and no dominant model has so far imposed itself.

The *political project* of the radical left retained a vague idea of a long-term socialist transition, but its contours became evanescent. Almost all parties continued to refer to a final anti-capitalist goal, variously defined as communism, democratic socialism, full democratisation, or the primacy of human beings over profits. At the same time, they studiously refrained from developing concrete proposals on its possible economic and political organisation, which had so spectacularly failed under the Stalinist regimes. These references played the role of identitarian distinctions and general aspirations, but were of little import as guides for day-to-day practice.

The centre stage was instead taken by a *medium-term anti-neoliberal programme* centred on the defence of the welfare state, the representation of working-class and popular interests, and the promotion of left-libertarian values. The list of proposals was often coherent and detailed, typically focusing on employment, social protection, redistribution, re-regulation, pacifism, and (more timidly) structural measures. Two problems, however, somewhat undermined its credibility. On the one hand, the efforts to build bridges with potential centre-left allies regularly led to a watering down of structural reforms (say, treasury control over the central bank, nationalisations, or the exit from NATO) and a focus on minor redistributive issues and transversal non-economic themes. On the other hand, the constraints imposed by EU law and institutions on the implementation of an anti-neoliberal programme were recognised and harshly criticised, but the solution was generally identified in vague negotiations not backed by serious threats of an exit (Charalambous 2011; Dunphy 2005). Two experiences are particularly significant: in the nineties, radical left parties of three countries (Italy, France, and Finland) actively contributed to the introduction of the European single currency in their role of junior partners in centre-left governments; after 2015, the SYRIZA government in Greece chose compliance with the Treaties and a virtual loss of socio-economic sovereignty to the Troika over the wager of a Grexit.

The *social constituency* of the radical left remained broadly anchored among working-class and welfarist strata, but further lost part of its homogeneity. Parties continued to focus their primary attention on ordinary wageworkers, but increasingly appealed to them as citizens and human beings rather than as producers. Blue-collar workers, the unemployed, and to a lesser extent white-collar workers continued to be over-represented among the radical left electorate, but the weight of the economically inactive and the cultural elites (intellectual workers, professionals, students) tended to increase. The traditional privileged links with the core working class largely vanished at the level of the party-organisation, with a growing weight of university-educated individuals among cadres and leaders and of pensioners among ordinary members (plus, in some cases, sectors of the youth). Finally, social linkages gradually shifted from the trade unions to the galaxy of social movement activism. In short, the social constituency of the contemporary radical left tentatively moved toward a broad welfarist identity, which tried to keep together (with varying degrees of success) all social groups affected by neoliberalism: private-sector and public-sector workers; the unemployed; pensioners and the inactive; students and the young precariat; migrants; and intellectual strata.

The level of *organisational mediations* was affected by wide-ranging transformations. Communist monolithism was largely ditched in favour of internal democracy and pluralism. Memberships shrank, with a rapid transition from mass to intermediate or cadre organisations. Sub-cultural links with collateral organisations loosened, replaced by more unstable punctual collaborations on specific campaigns and movements. The dependency from state funding strongly increased. These tendencies interested the vast majority of radical left parties, but organisational models remained highly diversified. Beside a majority of modern membership-based parties (such as the Italian PRC or the German DIE LINKE), other models existed: traditional communist parties (such as the Greek KKE) and Trotskyist small groups (such as the French LO); different kinds of coalitions (such as the Spanish IU, the Greek SYRIZA, and the French FdG); more recently, loose 'network' parties (the Spanish PODEMOS). None of these models was entirely up to the tasks implied by a consequent anti-neoliberal (let alone anti-capitalist) project and strategy. On the one hand, radical left parties generally failed to structure short-term bouts of sympathy and electoral support into stable links of attachment and participation. On the other hand, the lack of solid connections within mass civil society organisations (notably, the trade unions) prevented radical left parties to influence the course of social conflicts and anti-governmental mobilisations.

The level of *strategical mediations* remained the most controversial one. On the one hand, some minority groups advocated strategies of anti-capitalist alternative geared at a short-term clash with capitalist structures, but most parties argued for more gradual strategies of left-ward pull aimed at a medium-term anti-neoliberal turn. Broadly speaking, this was thought to involve three phases: first, the electoral growth of the radical left and the revival of workers' and social mobilisations; second, a 're-social democratisation' of moderate left parties; third, the electoral victory of a left-wing coalition and the implementation of the anti-neoliberal programme. Not much thought was given to the next task, the long-term transition to socialism. The general idea was that of a progressive decommodification of entitlements, socialisation of production, and democratisation of decision-making processes, but no details on the mechanisms, time-frame, and depth of these processes were provided.

On the other hand, opinions sharply diverged on the appropriate strategy to achieve the wished-for reversal of neoliberal orientations. Virtually all parties agreed on a peaceful road combining parliamentary and extra-parliamentary pressures (strikes, demonstrations, ideological battle). Disagreements on the question of the opportunity of alliances with the moderate left, however, dominated the debate. Some parties were conciliatory, seeking to influence developments from within centre-left coalitions and governments. Other were intransigent, refusing any organic alliance in absence of substantial policy concessions, and thinking that only a long period of hostile pressures could lead to a defeat of 'third way' positions within social democratic parties. Most organisations were divided on the issue, including a broad range of opinions and charting an elusive middle course between the two extremes – for instance, favouring case-by-case electoral alliances and external support rather than direct governmental participation.

To sum up, the nature of the contemporary Western European radical left progressively moved away from the typical features of twentieth-century communism (in its various third period, popular front, and Eurocommunist variants) and toward a modern broad left orientation. Radical left actors partly adapted to the general societal trends and partly experimented with different solutions, while retaining some birthmarks of their pre-1989 history. However, no single successful and replicable blueprint emerged, unlike in previous historical periods (the German SPD before World War I, the Russian RSDLP(b) after 1917, the Italian PCI after World War Two). The political projects of the radical left remained vague, its strategies controversial, its organisational models ineffectual, and its constituencies numerically small and internally heterogeneous. Its parties enriched the public debate, offered important contributions to extra-parliamentary struggles, and frequently made some short-term or long-term electoral gains, but did not make much progress in their attempts to bring about an anti-neoliberal turn in state policies and social relations. In 2015, two radical left organisations were catapulted into power (SYRIZA in Greece) or near it (PODEMOS in Spain) by the combined effects of national conjunctures and interesting innovations, advancing the discussion on effective forms of anti-neoliberal policies. They too, however, have not transcended the key weaknesses of the contemporary radical left.

Radical left cohesion

The evolution of *radical left cohesion* went through three main phases. The crisis and renewal of communist parties created favourable conditions for a confluence of different radical left traditions and sensibilities into 'broad left' parties or coalitions (1989–97). Past divides between communists, Trotskyists, Maoists, left-socialists, and left-wing ecologists were overshadowed by the reality of a common struggle against neoliberal trends and the need to pool together resources to preserve parliamentary representation and political viability. This process of regroupment had already started in the late eighties (the Spanish IU in 1986) but accelerated after the fall of the Soviet bloc, with successful unifications in Germany (PDS in 1990), Finland (VAS in 1990), and Italy (PRC in 1991), a short-lived coalition in Greece (the 'first' SYN in 1989–91), partial mergers in Denmark (E in 1990) and Portugal (BE in 1999), and a general bandwagoning of smaller groups to larger allies. The number of radical left lists running for election decreased; the average vote share of the main list in each country rose from 78.7 per cent in 1988 to 83.2 in 1995; and the average seat share increased in the same period from 89.1 to 95.9 per cent.

This model, however, showed its limits in the following phase (1998–2004). Most problems derived from the question of the attitude to be taken toward centre-left alliances and governmental participations. The electoral growth of the nineties made the votes and seats of the radical left increasingly vital for the formation of centre-left governmental majorities, forcing clear choices between intransigent and conciliatory strategies. As a result, several parties suffered heavy splits (most clearly in Italy) or opened up their flank to the rise of alternative challengers (most clearly in France). The breadth of the spectrum of anti-neoliberal interests and lingering political and organisational rivalries further complicated the picture, contributing to a steep rise in radical left fragmentation. The number of radical left lists increased; the average vote share of the main radical left list in each country declined from 81.4 per cent to 72.7 per cent; and the average seat share followed suit, from 91.8 per cent to 82.0 per cent.

In the third phase (2006–15), more decisive steps toward regroupment were taken, but were only partially successful. In Germany, the PDS and its new competitor WASG allied in 2005 and merged in 2007 in DIE LINKE. In France, unity processes failed in 2007 and succeeded in 2009–12, but the FdG remained nothing but a fragile cartel. In Italy, unity was reached in 2008 with the SA coalition, but its electoral collapse led to a renewed explosion of rival organisations and coalitions. In Greece, the post–2012 electoral rise of SYRIZA marginalised its competitors, but the orthodox KKE and important far-left groupings stayed out. In Spain, IU was outclassed by PODEMOS in 2015, but the situation remained one of multiple parties and regionally-based coalitions. These developments led to a recovery of the average vote share (79.0 per cent) and seat share (86.8) in 2014, but this was largely an optical illusion, with ideological and organisational divisions living on behind the external screen of formal coalitions.

An overview of national differences in the period 1994–2015 is provided in Table 3.2. In average, both the vote share (77.2 per cent) and the seat share (86.9) of the main radical left list in each country was quite low, considering that in several cases the ranking of lists changed and different parties converged into

Table 3.2 Fragmentation, Western European radical left (1994–2015)

COUNTRY	LISTS (aver., n)	VOTE SHARE OF FIRST LIST (aver., %)	SEAT SHARE OF FIRST LIST (aver., %)	OVERTAKINGS & COALITIONS	MAIN PARTIES
AGGREGATE		82.0	84.8		
AVERAGE	4.1	77.2	86.9		
AUSTRIA	1.6	95.8	-		KPÖ
BELGIUM	2.9	71.6	100.0		PVDA-PTB
DENMARK	4.0	69.0	68.8	Y	SF, E
FINLAND	3.3	93.6	100.0		VAS
FRANCE	4.8	73.2	100.0	Y	PCF, LO, LCR/ NPA, PG
GERMANY	3.0	99.3	100.0	Y	PDS/DIE LINKE, *WASG*
GREECE	7.1	55.9	66.4	Y	KKE, SYN/ SYRIZA, LE, ANTARSYA, *DIKKI*
IRELAND	3.2	60.7	80.0	Y	SP, PBPA
ITALY	2.8	78.7	81.6	Y	PRC, SEL, *PdCI*
LUXEMBOURG	1.8	76.9	100.0	Y	DÉI LÉNK, KPL
NETHERLANDS	1.7	96.6	100.0		SP
NORWAY	3.0	84.1	99.0		SV, RV/RØDT
PORTUGAL	4.4	63.8	76.6	Y	PCP, BE, PCTP-MRPP
SPAIN	7.7	78.1	68.0	Y	IU, PODEMOS, BNG, HB/ EH BILDU
SWEDEN	4.5	98.9	100.0		V
SWITZERLAND	2.1	71.6	83.3	Y	PdA, S
UK	10.5	44.8	68.8	Y	-

Notes: In *italics:* currently dissolved or irrelevant.

broader coalitions. Five countries were represented by one virtually unchallenged radical left party: Austria, Finland, Germany, the Netherlands, and Sweden. The other fifteen countries, however, were characterised by the competition of two or more radical left players. The highest level of fragmentation was reached in three countries: the UK, where a multitude of largely irrelevant organisations competed in a selected number of parliamentary constituencies only; Greece, where competition happened between two main actors (KKE and SYN/SYRIZA) plus a variety of smaller organisations; and Portugal, which lived a similar situation (CDU, BE, and a number of smaller groups).

This high level of fragmentation did not damage the radical left from an electoral point of view, as the increased offer could cater for larger and more composite constituencies, but had highly negative effects on its parliamentary representation and overall relevance.

Concluding remarks

The collapse of the Soviet bloc in 1989–92 shook the Western European radical left to the core, despite the critical attitude of many far-left and Eurocommunist parties toward the Soviet Union and its satellites. The Italian PCI reconverted to mainstream social democracy; other organisations did the same or dissolved; most parties embarked on a path of hurried internal reforms while losing voters, members, linkages, and overall social influence. The simultaneous acceleration in the neoliberalisation of European societies, however, paved the way for a renaissance of the radical left as an anti-neoliberal party family competing for the representation of the large working-class and welfarist constituencies neglected by the establishment parties.

Radical left strength recovered from 1994 to 1999, but later oscillated in unstable and increasingly asynchronous trends. The 1994–2015 average levels of electoral (6.8 per cent), parliamentary (4.7 per cent), and governmental (1.8 per cent) strength define a medium-small party family, weaker than in the eighties, relevant in most of the countries but regularly dwarfed by its social democratic competitors. National breakthroughs took place, but were often short-lived. An exception is the year 2015, when extraordinary results in Greece, Spain, and Portugal suddenly enhanced its importance.

Radical left nature swiftly moved toward a new anti-neoliberal orientation, but neither old nor new parties managed to embody it into effective ideological, sociological, organisational, and strategical mediations. Radical left parties were more likeable than in the past, but struggled with a poorly defined vision, small and ineffectual organisations, weak roots in the traditional working-class and the new precariat, and heartrending strategic choices.

Radical left fragmentation rose from relatively low levels in the nineties to concerning ones in the noughties, which subsequent regroupment attempts did not entirely rein in. Party splits and the rise of small and new competitors partly depended on ideological differences and organisational jealousies, but were fundamentally determined by conflicts on the strategy of centre-left alliances.

In conclusion, the analysis highlights both the recovery and renewal of the radical left since the early nineties, and the limits of its development. Despite some advances, it won over only a small part of the discontent toward neoliberal policies and trends, and (so far) failed to chart a credible way toward an anti-neoliberal (or anti-capitalist) turn.

Notes

1 Beyond the Italian PCI, other defecting parties in Ireland, the Netherlands, Spain, and Switzerland had 0.6 million voters in 1988. The sole new entry, the German PDS, had instead 1.0 million votes in the eastern regions in 1990.
2 Data for Denmark include the left-socialist SF. The party has an unambiguously radical history and official programme, but since the mid-noughties has progressively moved away from the radical left and toward the greens. It is currently a member of the (radical left) Nordic Green Left Alliance, a member of the Green/EFA group in the European Parliament, and an observer in the European Green Party. Data for the UK and Ireland exclude the republican SF (Sinn Féin). A left-nationalist party, it makes references to democratic socialism in its official documents and maintains loose ties with radical left parties, sitting since 2004 in the GUE/NGL group of the European Parliament.
3 The Greek case was actually preceded by the Christofias presidency in Cyprus (AKEL, 2008–13), which lies beyond the geographical scope of this analysis. An English-language critical assessment can be found in Charalambous and Ioannou (2015).
4 Since 2014 the Spanish PODEMOS has experienced an incredible boom of 'members', more than 400,000 in April 2016. Their classification is uncertain, as no barrier or duty (crucially, the traditional payment of membership fees) is connected to the online act of joining, but all members can nevertheless fully participate to the decision-making processes of the party.

References

Backes, Uwe, and Patrick Moreau (eds.) (2008). *Communist and post-communist parties in Europe*. Göttingen: Vandenhoeck and Ruprecht.

Bale, Tim, and Richard Dunphy (2011). 'In from the cold? Left parties and government involvement since 1989', *Comparative European Politics* 9(3): 269–291.

Bellofiore, Riccardo (2013). '"Two or three things I know about her": Europe in the global crisis and heterodox economics', *Cambridge Journal of Economics* 37(3): 497–512.

Bellucci, Paolo, and Oliver Heath (2012). 'The structure of party-organisational linkages and the electoral strength of cleavages in Italy, 1963–2008', *British Journal of Political Science* 42(1): 107–135.

Bensaïd, Daniel, Alda Sousa, Alan Thornett, and others (2011). *New parties of the Left: Experiences from Europe*. London: Resistance Books.

Biver, Nico (2015). 'Verschwindet die Linke? Mitgliederentwicklung und Wahlergebnisse linker Parteien in Westeuropa seit den 1970er Jahren', *Z – Zeitschrift Marxistische Erneuerung* 101: 141–153 and 102: 141–151.

Botella, Juan, and Luis Ramiro (eds.) (2003). *The crisis of communism and party change: The evolution of Western European communist and post-communist parties*. Barcelona: ICPS.

Bull, Martin J., and Paul Heywood (eds.) (1994). *West European communist parties after the revolutions of 1989*. London: Macmillan.

Cafruny, Alan W., and Magnus Ryner (eds.) (2003). *A ruined fortress? Neoliberal hegemony and transformation in Europe*. London: Rowman and Littlefield.
Charalambous, Giorgos (2011). 'All the shades of red: Examining the radical left's Euroscepticism', *Contemporary Politics* 17(3): 299–320.
Charalambous, Giorgos, and Gregoris Ioannou (2015). 'No bridge over troubled waters: The Cypriot left in government, 2008–2013', *Capital & Class* 39(2): 265–286.
Chiocchetti, Paolo (2016). Western European radical left database. Version 2.0 (30.04.2016). Available at: www.paolochiocchetti.it/data.
Daiber, Birgit, Cornelia Hildebrandt, and Anna Striethorst (eds.) (2012). *Von Revolution bis Koalition. Linke Parteien in Europa*. Berlin: Dietz Verlag.
De Waele, Jean-Michel, and Daniel-Louis Seiler (eds.) (2012). *Le partis de la gauche anticapitaliste en Europe*. Paris: Economica.
Ducange, Jean-Numa, Philippe Marlière, and Louis Weber (2013). *La gauche radicale en Europe*. Paris: Éditions du Croquant.
Duménil, Gérard, and Dominique Lévy (2011). *The crisis of neoliberalism*. Cambridge: Harvard University Press.
Dunphy, Richard (2005). *Contesting capitalism: Left parties and European integration*. Manchester: Manchester University Press.
Escalona, Fabien, Luke March, and Mathieu Vieira (2017). *The Palgrave Handbook of radical left parties in Europe*. London: Palgrave.
Fagerholm, Andreas (2016). 'What is left for the radical left? A comparative examination of the policies of radical left parties in Western Europe before and after 1989', *Journal of Contemporary European Studies*. Advance online publication, doi:10.1080/1478280 4.2016.1148592.
Featherstone, Kevin (2001). The political dynamics of the *vincolo esterno*: The emergence of the EMU and the challenge to the European Social Model [working paper]. Queen's Papers on Europeanisation 6.
Gerbaudo, Paolo (2016). *The mask and the flag. The rise of anarcho-populism in global protest*. London: Hurst.
Hudson, Kate (2012). *The new European left. A socialism for the Twenty-First century?* Basingstoke: Palgrave Macmillan.
Hudson, Kate (2000). *European communism since 1989: Towards a new European left?* Basingstoke: Palgrave MacMillan.
Marantzidis, Nikos (2004). 'Exit, voice or loyalty? Les stratégies des partis communistes d'Europe de l'Ouest après 1989', *Communisme* 76/77: 169–184.
March, Luke (2012). *Radical left parties in contemporary Europe*. Abingdon: Routledge.
March, Luke, and Daniel Keith (eds.) (2016). *Europe's radical left. From marginality to the mainstream?* London: Rowman and Littlefield.
March, Luke, and Cas Mudde (2005). 'What's left of the radical left? The European radical left after 1989: Decline *and* mutation', *Comparative European Politics* 3: 23–49.
March, Luke, and Charlotte Rommerskirchen (2015). 'Out of left field? Explaining the variable electoral success of European radical left parties', *Party Politics* 21(1): 40–53.
Mayer, Florian (2006). *Vom Niedergang des unternehmerisch tätigen Staates. Privatisierungspolitik in Großbritannien, Frankreich, Italien und Deutschland*. Wiesbaden: VS Verlag.
Olsen, Jonathan, Michael Koß, and Dan Hough (2010). *Left parties in national governments*. Basingstoke: Palgrave Macmillan.
Ovenden, Kevin (2015). *SYRIZA: Inside the labyrinth*. London: Pluto.
Pina, Christine (2005). *L'extrême gauche en Europe*. Paris: La Documentation Française.

Ramiro, Luis (2016). 'Support for radical left parties in Western Europe: Social background, ideology and political orientations', *European Political Science Review* 8(1): 1–23.

Ramiro, Luis (2003). The crisis of Western Communist parties: Reconsidering socio-structural explanations [working paper]. Madrid: UAM. Available at: www.uam.es/ss/Satellite/Derecho/es/1242658791834/listadoCombo/Working_Papers.htm [accessed on 01.04.2016].

Saad-Filho, Alfredo, and Deborah Johnston (eds.) (2005). *Neoliberalism. A critical reader.* London: Pluto Press.

Vail, Mark I. (2010). *Recasting welfare capitalism. Economic adjustment in contemporary France and Germany.* Philadelphia: Temple University Press.

Visser, Mark, Marcel Lubbers, Gerbert Kraaykamp, and Eva Jaspers (2014). 'Support for radical left ideologies in Europe', *European Journal of Political Research* 53(3): 541–558.

4 The German radical left

A success story

In this chapter I analyse the trajectory of the German radical left from 1989 to 2015. This can be characterised as an electoral success story, as the radical left managed to grow to medium-sized levels in a country where communism had been wiped out by Nazism and the Cold War (in the West) and largely discredited by the authoritarian rule and poor economic performance of the SED regime (in the East). On the other hand, it failed to become a fully credible alternative to the established parties, and its efforts to stop and reverse neoliberal policies led at best to indirect and palliative improvements.

The developmental path of the contemporary German radical left has aroused considerable interest from commentators and political scientists alike, and its history presents many enticing features for students of contemporary European politics.

First, the Party of Democratic Socialism (PDS) was one of the few former Soviet-bloc ruling parties that successfully survived the post-1989 democratic transition as a *radical leftist* parliamentary force. This simple anomaly was transformed into a political enormity by the 1990 incorporation of the German Democratic Republic (GDR) in the Federal Republic of Germany (FRG), which thereby transferred a piece of communist history in a country with deep anti-communist traditions.

Secondly, the developments of the period 2003–09 remain to this day the clearest example of success of the radical left in a *large* European nation. Mass discontent toward the socio-economic policies of the Schröder government led to the creation from scratch of a new radical left organisation, the WASG, and the success of the joint L.PDS/WASG lists in the 2005 federal election. The result of their merger in 2007, DIE LINKE, went on to win 11.9 per cent of the national vote in 2009. Moreover, the WASG and the Western branches of DIE LINKE represent so far the most significant European case of left-ward split of the 'new' social democracy: while in other European countries the radical left won over only marginal figures and tendencies, in Germany it acquired Oskar Lafontaine, the popular and skilful former member of the top SPD leadership (candidate for chancellor, party chairman, and finance minister).

Thirdly, this electoral success had the effect of destabilising the overall dynamics of the German party system. Whereas in the eighties the rise of the GRÜNE had gradually transformed the traditional 'two-and-a-half-party system' (Blondel 1968) into a bipolar competition between centre-right (CDU/CSU and FDP) and centre-left (SPD and GRÜNE) coalitions, the emergence of a fifth relevant party worked to prevent both camps from reaching a parliamentary majority and to force CDU/CSU and SPD into awkward 'grand coalitions'. This became a common occurrence for Eastern governments since 1994 and for the federal government since 2005 (2005–09 and 2013–present). The theoretically feasible option of 'red-red-green' alliances was experimented with in the East but categorically rejected by the SPD at the federal level.

Fourthly, the German radical left has arguably become a sort of role model for its brother parties across the EU. The PDS played a central role both in the radical left political group within the European Parliament (GUE/NGL) and in establishing the transnational Party of the European Left (PEL) in 2004; its political foundation Rosa-Luxemburg-Stiftung has become an important site of theoretical debate; the experience of DIE LINKE, finally, has been a source of inspiration for the radical left of other countries, such as Italy and France.

The discussion is structured as follows. First, I briefly introduce the historical context and radical left responses. Secondly, I track more in detail the evolution of the systemic strength, fragmentation, and political nature of the contemporary German radical left. Thirdly, I explain its remarkably low level of fragmentation through a combination of six external and internal factors. Fourthly, I analyse the validity of the 'vacuum thesis' with reference to the German case. I show that radical left growth unquestionably relied on the neoliberal turn of established parties and the resulting vacuum of political representation of working-class and welfarist interests. However, a number of factors constrained this expansion to a minority of its potential constituency. Fifthly, I assess its 'strategy of leftward pull', showing that it failed to noticeably influence either the social balance of force, state policies, or the overall dynamics of political competition. Finally, I summarise and discuss the main findings.

The analysis is based on a large amount of primary evidence. Due to space constraints, references in the text are generally limited to the secondary literature. Primary data, together with sources, notes, and elaborations, are instead made accessible through the Western European Radical Left Database (Chiocchetti 2016b).

The national context

The seemingly unlikely success story of PDS and DIE LINKE cannot be understood but in the context of *three major historical shocks* that destabilised the traditional alignments between individual citizens, social organisations, and political parties.

The first shock was the crisis of the GDR in 1989–90, its rapid incorporation in the FRG, and the lasting consequences of reunification. The East German communist regime showed increasing signs of economic and political distress in the eighties, which morphed into a full-fledged political revolution in the autumn of 1989 (Dale 2004, 2006; Föster and Roski 1990; Gehrke and Hürtgen 2001; Lohmann 1994; Segert 2009; Steiner 2010). The movement briefly propelled at its helm a variety of left-wing oppositional organisations (*Bürgerbewegungen*), but the mood soon shifted in favour of pro-unification centre-right forces. These triumphed at the 18 March 1990 Volkskammer election and rapidly led the country toward a currency union with West Germany (1 July) and full unification (3 October). Successive developments, however, did not entirely live up to the hopes of 'blossoming landscapes' promised by the Western establishment (Kohl 1990). The East German economy was thoroughly de-industrialised and large sections of its populations were forced into unemployment, early retirement, and internal migration, although a huge influx of public transfers ensured a simultaneous improvement of monetary living standards (Burda 2013; Roesler 1994; Wiesenthal 2003). Moreover, the modalities of the unification process left marginalised Eastern specificities and interests. While discontent was initially limited to the downwardly-mobile former bureaucracy, more and more *Ossis* (Easterners) came to resent the 'colonisation' of their regions by Western institutions and personnel, their discrimination as 'second class citizens', the devaluation of their academic titles and biographies, and the disregard for their history and current needs (Abromeit 1993; Brie 2000; Bürklin and Rebenstorf 1997; Fuchs 1999; Goedicke 2003; Hodgin and Pearce 2011; Kunze 2008; Neller and Thaidigsmann 2002; Wiesenthal 1998; Wollmann 1996). The former GDR thus came to occupy a peculiar place within the landscape of the new Berlin republic and acquired economic, social, political, and cultural features which persist to this day. The extent of post-unification dissatisfaction reached its apex in 1992–93, when a large wave of industrial and street mobilisation erupted in response to the final stages of the privatisation of the Eastern state-owned sector by the Treuhandanstalt, which resulted not in the revitalisation but in the winding-up of much the companies (Garms 1994; Gehrke 1997; Roesler 1991). It was in this context that the initially discredited PDS managed to revive its fortunes as a left-wing regional party, claiming to be the sole true representative of East German interests against the Western 'Bonn parties'.

The second shock was the return to power of the Social Democratic Party (SPD) in 1998, after sixteen years of opposition, and the staunchly neoliberal course pursued by it in its seven years of office (Beck and Scherrer 2005; Nachtwey 2013). The turn away from traditional social democratic values and solutions began early, as exemplified by the replacement of the Keynesian Oskar Lafontaine as Minister of Finance (1999), the Kosovo military mission (1999), and tax and pension reforms (2000–01), but during its first term in office dissatisfaction remained limited to left-wing activist circles and did not result in heavy electoral losses. It was only after March 2003, when the re-elected Schröder cabinet unveiled its ambitious plans for a reform of the labour market (*Agenda 2010*) that a veritable rift opened up between the SPD and its traditional welfarist constituency. The biggest wave of street protests since unification occupied the forefront of the political scene in 2003–04, with union demonstration and weekly marches of the unemployed and their supporters (Lahusen and Baumgarten 2006). Although the movement failed to prevent the implementation of the reform, it provided the backdrop for the formation of the WASG and for the electoral successes of the radical left along the whole 2005–09 electoral cycle.

The third shock was the great financial crisis of 2008–09. While milder than in other European countries, the crisis further undermined the stability of the German party system. Its immediate impact was to erode the support for the grand coalition parties, which collapsed in 2009 to their lowest vote share since 1949 (CDU/CSU at 33.8 per cent, SPD at 23.0 per cent). It also prompted some important and often successful social movements and campaigns against tuition fees, austerity, and for the introduction of a legal minimum wage (Hildebrandt and Tügel 2010; Kolisang 2013; Nowak 2015). Its long-term political effects, however, are still unclear. Electoral volatility has remained high but has not followed a consistent anti-establishment pattern, provoking surges of oppositional (DIE LINKE, GRÜNE, FDP) and new (PIRATEN, AfD, FW) parties but also their rapid fall and a spectacular comeback of the CDU/CSU in the 2013 general election. The public debate and social mobilisations, similarly, soon shifted from the issue of responsibilities of and solutions to the crisis to themes less congenial for the radical left, such as environmental protection (Brettschneider and Schuster 2013; Roose 2010), the sovereign debt crisis in the European periphery, Islamic terrorism, and mass immigration.

The German radical left was relatively successful in reacting and adapting to these generally favourable trends. The starting situation of 1989 seemed to forebode a rapid disappearance of radical left ideas and organisations. In the West, communist and far-left groups had been marginal since the fifties, and their influence further collapsed in the eighties and early nineties (Fülberth 1990; Jünke 2001; Schultze and Gross 1997; Steffen 2002). In the East, the scene was monopolised by the ruling Sozialistische Einheitspartei Deutschlands (Socialist Unity Party of Germany, SED), whose totalitarian and inefficient regime was successfully challenged by a popular revolution (Herbst et al. 1997; Weitz 1997). Some of the oppositional movements that mushroomed in the Autumn of 1989 had a left-wing or radical left profile, but their hostility toward the SED gradually pushed them away from democratic socialist aspirations and toward the Western Greens or SPD (Kamenitsa 1998; Timmer 2000).

Unexpectedly, however, a new radical left formed around the reformed rump of the SED, the Partei des Demokratischen Sozialismus (Party of Democratic Socialism, PDS) (Bortfeldt 1992; Gerner 1994; Gysi and Falkner 1990; Segert 2008). External and internal pressures forced the Eastern Stalinist party through a rapid process of adaptation and a complete reinvention as a peculiar 'democratic socialist' party. While its historical pedigree made it unpalatable in the West and little appealing in the East, its success in gaining parliamentary representation and the ability and openness of its new modernising leadership made it into an inescapable future pole of attraction for disaffected left-wingers. In the following years, the PDS survived the initial attempts of political and economic strangulation and, by 1992, experienced a turnaround in its electoral fortunes. The party started to intercept the grievances of large sectors of the Eastern population and by 1998 it had become a successful regional socialist party (Barker 1998; Brie et al. 1995;

Brie and Woderich 2000; Gerth 2002; Neugebauer and Stöss 1996; Oswald 2002). The PDS, however, was not able to profit from the tensions produced by the neoliberal orientation of the Schröder government (Bortfeldt 2003; Brie 2003; Hough 2002; Meuche-Mäker 2005; Olsen 2002; Thompson 2005). Despite promising gains in the preceding European and regional elections, it suffered a severe setback in the 2002 federal election. The outcome was unexpected and was largely the product of a last-minute swing toward the SPD in response to extraordinary circumstances: chancellor Schröder's skilful management of the Iraq War controversy and of the Elbe floods, and Gysi's sudden retreat from the political scene (Stöss and Neugebauer 2002). Moreover, its disastrous governmental experiences in Mecklenburg-Vorpommern (1998–2006) and Berlin (2001–11) weakened the local branches and tarnished the global image of the party as an alternative and consequently anti-neoliberal force.

The tide turned again with the 2003–04 wave of social mobilisation, which led to the resurgence of the PDS in the East and the rise of a new potential challenger or ally in the West, the Arbeit & soziale Gerechtigkeit – Die Wahlalternative (Electoral Alternative Labour and Social Justice, WASG). Sagely, the initially competitive relationship between the two radical left groups was rapidly steered toward an electoral alliance in Spring 2005 and a full-blown merger in June 2007 (Brie 2005; Brie et al. 2007; Ernst et al. 2012; Fülberth, 2008; Hough et al. 2007; Hübner and Strohschneider 2007; Jesse and Lang 2008; Olsen 2007; Patton 2011, 2013; Spier et al. 2007). The new party, DIE LINKE (The Left), was able to capitalise the wave of revulsion toward the SPD and embarked on a period of rapid growth (2004–09), establishing itself for the first time as a truly national political force.

The German radical left, however, largely missed the train of the post-2008 economic crisis. The momentum of 2009 was lost in internal conflicts and political paralysis, while the SPD somewhat revived its left-wing credentials and new parties (PIRATEN, AfD) claimed their share of protest vote. In the 2013 election DIE LINKE plunged back to the values of 2005.

The new German radical left

A more detailed analysis of the evolution of the systemic strength, cohesion, and political nature of the contemporary German radical left highlights its unique trajectory within the Western European party family.

Strength

The evolution of the strength of the German radical left in its various components is summarised in Table 4.1 and Figure 4.1. The almost entirety of the totals is attributable to one subject only: the PDS up to 2004, the L.PDS-WASG alliance in 2005–06, and DIE LINKE since 2007. The picture is one of a medium-small party family oscillating around 5 per cent of the total strength of German parties but following an overall trajectory of growth.

Table 4.1 Strength, German radical left

	AVERAGE 1990–2015 RESOURCES	AVERAGE 1990–2015 SYSTEMIC STRENGTH
1 ELECTORAL	votes	%
Composite (nat 60 / reg 40)		6.02
National	2,982,813	6.50
Regional	1,997,429	5.29
2 PARLIAMENTARY	seats	%
Composite (nat 60 / reg 40)		5.88
National	40.4	6.35
Regional	146.8	5.18
3 GOVERNMENTAL		%
Composite (nat 60 / reg 40)		0.68
National		0.00
Regional		1.60
4 MEMBERSHIP	members	%
	104,555	5.82
5 FINANCIAL	real 2010 euro	
Narrow measure	29,059,381	6.02
Broad measure	108,620,213	6.05
COMMUNICATION		
		medium-weak
CIVIL SOCIETY		
		medium-weak
OVERALL STRENGTH		%
Composite (average 1 to 5)		4.83

The electoral dimension was without doubt the most successful and followed a general trajectory of growth, particularly in 1994–2001 and in 2004–10. The composite indicator of electoral strength rose from 2.5 per cent in 1990 to 5.2 per cent in 2001, dipped to 4.5 per cent in 2002, soared to 7.6 per cent in 2005, continued to grow until 10.7 per cent in 2010, and then slowly declined back to 7.7 per cent in 2015. This electorate was overwhelmingly concentrated in the regions of the former GDR until 2004, geographically better distributed afterwards.

The parliamentary dimension roughly mirrored the electoral one. The radical left had a continued and generally proportional presence in the federal parliament, although the threat of exclusion was always near and almost materialised in 2002–04, when the PDS MPs were reduced to two. Its presence within regional parliaments was instead partial: permanent in the six Eastern regions, absent in three regions (Bayern, Baden-Württemberg, and Rheinland-Pfalz), and intermittent since 2005 in the remaining seven Western regions.

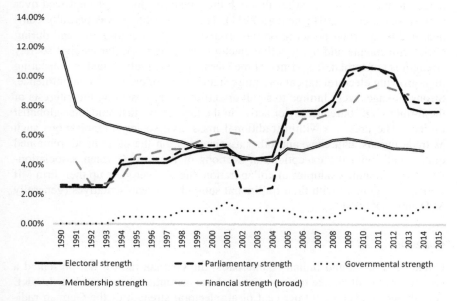

Figure 4.1 Strength evolution, German radical left

Performance in the governmental dimension was extremely weak. The composite indicator of governmental strength oscillated trendlessly from 1990 (0.0 per cent) to 2015 (1.2 per cent), with a maximum peak of 1.5 per cent in 2001. Unlike its Italian and French counterparts, the German radical left was never involved in national governmental majorities. At the regional level, governmental experiences took place but only in the East: external support in Brandenburg (1994–99), Sachsen-Anhalt (1994–2002), and Berlin (2001); direct participation in Mecklenburg-Vorpommern (1998–2006), Berlin (2002–11), and Brandenburg (2009–present); and cabinet leadership in Thüringen (2014–present).

Membership strength followed a downward course. The indicator fell from 11.7 per cent in 1990 to 4.3 per cent in 2004, recovered to 5.8 per cent in 2009, and fell again to 5.0 per cent in 2014. Initially much higher than electoral strength, it turned much lower after 2000.

Financial strength broadly followed the cue of parliamentary strength. The PDS initially inherited from the SED an enormous amount of money and assets, which were, however, immediately seized by the German state never to be returned (Behrend 2006; Bräutigam 2010). The broad measure of yearly incomes fell to a low point of 2.7 in 1992 (47.5 million real 2010 euro) but then rose, with temporary interruptions, up to a high point of 9.5 per cent in 2011 (178.9 million real 2010 euro).

Further dimensions cannot be quantified with precision, but probably were at medium-weak levels with moderately growing trends. As far as the communicative strength is concerned, the national media coverage of the radical left tended to be weak and hostile, although the situation somewhat improved over time (Hansen et al. 2010; Jandura 2011). This disadvantage was partially compensated by a strong presence on the ground in the Eastern regions and during social movements and by effective electoral campaigns. As far as civil society strength is concerned, the parties of the German radical left pained at translating their growing electoral appeal into more stable forms of organisational influence. Strong linkages were limited to small organisations representing the interests of the former GDR bureaucracy or active in the far-left, pacifist, and alter-globalist milieus. The presence within traditional mass civil society organisations such as trade unions, churches, and other associations, on the other hand, remained quite small, with the exceptions of sections of the East German associationism. Despite some examples of collaboration, these never gave up their firm – if critical – alignment with their traditional sub-cultural representatives (generally SPD and CDU/CSU).

Cohesion

Unlike its French and Italian counterparts, the German radical left presented a remarkably small degree of organisational fragmentation. The PDS/DIE LINKE contributed in average 99 per cent of all electoral strength of the German radical left, all of its parliamentary and governmental strength, and around 90 per cent of its membership and financial strength. Other radical left organisations, for instance, the communist DKP, the Maoist MLPD, and Trotskyist groups, had some weight in organisational terms, with six to ten thousand members and up to five million euro of yearly incomes, but were utterly negligible from an electoral and institutional point of view, generally refraining from electoral participation or obtaining desultory results. The big exception was the WASG in 2005–06, which might have developed into a serious competitor for the PDS but ultimately opted for an alliance and subsequent merger in 2007.

Potential moments of crisis actually abounded in the history of the PDS, but its leadership always proved flexible enough to maintain internal unity and co-opt external challenges, by means of programmatic concessions and a generous distribution of internal and public offices. In 1989–90, the SED briefly seemed to orient itself toward a self-dissolution, but the danger was ultimately averted, traditionalists and reformists were kept together under a common roof, and most of the small alternative far-left groups in the East and West were involved in the Linke Liste/PDS project and later absorbed (Bortfeldt 1992; Eckhoff 2005; Meuche-Mäker 2005: 15–16; Neugebauer and Stöss 1996: 46). In 2002–03, a split between left-wing and right-wing tendencies was narrowly avoided (Behrend 2006). In 2005–07, the alliance and merger with the WASG was successfully carried out despite strong tensions and local incidents (Heunemann 2006; Lees et al. 2010; Spier et al. 2007). In 2010–15, finally, the fiery clashes between Western radicals and Eastern pragmatists were repeatedly papered over and a precarious balance maintained.

Nature

The political nature of German radical left parties was characterised, as in the rest of Western Europe, by the transition from the legacies of the twentieth-century communist movement to the dilemmas and possibilities of the contemporary radical left landscape. The origins of the PDS as a former Soviet-bloc ruling party, however, produced marked specificities in relation to the typical patterns of the contemporary Western European radical left.

Ideologically, the German radical left was quick to ditch the legacy of the bureaucratic socialism represented by the GDR in favour of an eclectic 'radical left' programme.

Within the SED, socialism was conceived as a state-led process of accumulation and redistribution through the means of state ownership, economic planning, and party dictatorship (Dale 2004; Roesler 1991; Steiner 2010). When this model unravelled in 1989–90 under the impact of an economic, political, and geopolitical crisis, it was not clear which left-wing vision might replace it. Both the oppositional civic movements and the SED-PDS initially advanced the idea of a reformed socialist GDR (Kamenitsa 1998; Riegel 2002; Segert 2009), but its content remained vague and controversial. These debates were swept away by the unification process, which choked any hope of a reformed East German socialism and proceeded to a rapid and thorough adaptation of the country to the West German system (Abromeit 1993; Wollmann 1996).

The response of the PDS was an original theorisation of 'democratic socialism' (Klein and Brie 2007; Land 2010; Land and Possekel 1995a). This was conceived as a 'third way' between market capitalism and state socialism characterised by: (a) a wide-ranging democratisation of both state and the economy; (b) a mixed economy with a multiplicity of property forms (private, state, cooperative); (c) a developed welfare state. The vision was appealing but rather indeterminate, as the relative weight of the three theoretical poles of state intervention, market competition, and (workers' and users') self-management, as well as its difference from the models of welfarist mixed economies which predominated in Europe before the neoliberal turn, was not spelled out in detail. It could lend itself to a variety of interpretations, as the internal debates of the PDS would soon amply demonstrate (Behrend 2006; Brie 2000; Chrapa, 2000; Chrapa and Wittich 2001; Hoff 2014; Land 1995b; Prinz 2010; Sturm 2000). In practical terms, the programmatic of the PDS focused on two key areas. On the one hand, a broad anti-neoliberal catalogue of progressive measures mixing welfarist, Keynesian, and post-materialist themes. On the other hand, a particular attention to the defence of cross-class Eastern interests against the perceived economic, political, and cultural marginalisation of the area in the new German republic.

The WASG avoided any explicit commitment to a post-capitalist future, but claimed to stand for a 'new alternative social bloc of labour and knowledge' (Krämer 2004) against the intellectual hegemony of neoliberalism, and developed a coherent programme of welfarist and left-Keynesian reforms.

DIE LINKE, finally, worked out a synthesis of the main concerns of the two constituent parties, which focused on a mid-term anti-neoliberal programme (working and living conditions, the expansion of the welfare state and of state intervention, democratisation, socio-ecological restructuring, pacifism, and Eastern interests) but also retained the (vague) long-term aim of democratic socialism.

Sociologically, the German radical left has until recently diverged significantly from the Western European norm (Table 4.2).

Most contemporary radical left parties tend to have a quite heterogeneous social composition and declining links with the labour movement, but ordinary wageworkers still remain largely over-represented among their ranks and the main focus of their activity. The PDS, on the contrary, had from the start a different core constituency: the highly educated but downwardly mobile former GDR elite. The party never managed to gain a stable foothold in the Western regions, which made up at most less than 5 per cent of its members and less than 22 per cent of its voters. It also elicited a strong initial hostility from Eastern blue-collar workers, which

Table 4.2 Sociology, German radical left

	GERMAN VOTERS 1998	PDS VOTERS 1998	PDS MEMBERS 2000	GERMAN VOTERS 2009	LINKE VOTERS 2009	LINKE MEMBERS 2009
DOMICILE						
East incl. Berlin	21.7	83.0	95.2	20.0	44.4	62.1
West	78.3	17.0	4.8	80.0	55.6	37.9
GENDER						
Male	49.0	50.0	54.0	48.5	54.2	62.8
Female	51.0	50.0	45.0	51.5	45.8	37.2
AGE						
18–29	19.0	20.0	1.8	16.0	16.8	8.9
30–59	54.0	59.0	31.2	57.0	60.4	41.8
60+	27.0	21.0	67.0	27.0	22.8	49.3
CLASS						
Wageworker	50.8	61.9	29.4	50.4	58.9	36.7
Civil servant	4.1	2.6	2.5	4.4	2.6	11.5
White collar	25.3	29.4	16.1	26.6	25.7	10.8
Blue collar	16.4	17.9	4.3	16.4	22.5	6.4
Unemployed	5.0	12.0	6.5	3.0	8.0	8.0
Self-employed	6.2	5.1	1.7	7.6	5.1	5.3
Inactive	43.0	33.0	68.9	42.0	36.0	58.0
EDUCATION						
Below secondary			30.4	61.7	64.9	37.0
Secondary			4.2	20.2	19.1	17.0
Tertiary			65.4	18.1	16.0	46.0
RELIGION						
Catholic	34.5	6.6		35.1	18.7	
Protestant	40.0	15.3		37.4	30.8	
No religion	25.5	78.1		27.5	50.5	

had been among the key protagonists of the 1989–90 revolution against its predecessor, the SED. This gap was partially mended in the 1992–93 struggles against the industrial desertification of the Eastern regions, but never entirely disappeared. Altogether, PDS members remained overwhelmingly over-60 pensioners with a background as party and state cadres, with an almost equal representation of men and women, while PDS voters represented a fairly balanced cross-section of the Eastern population (except for blue-collar workers) with the addition of a small Western appendix (skewed toward wageworkers and unemployed).

The post-2005 shift significantly changed this situation, partially re-aligning the sociology of DIE LINKE with the broader radical left standards (Walter 2007). The Western regions, albeit much weaker than the Eastern ones in relative terms, in 2013 made up 38.8 per cent of party members and 50.4 per cent of its voters. The new Western members were predominantly employed wageworkers or unemployed and thus rejuvenated the overall profile of the party. Blue-collar workers became more likely to vote for DIE LINKE than the rest of the population. These developments, however, were mostly determined by the dynamism in the West; indeed, the party largely remains a *dual* entity. In the West it represents a development of the WASG: a dynamic point of attraction for broad left forces (former SPD, PDS, GRÜNE, and far-left supporters), dominated by men of the central age cohorts, with an over-representation of lower class backgrounds. In the East it remains a renamed PDS, with a declining membership dominated by gender-balanced and aging former SED members and a composite electorate mirroring the local population.

Organisationally, the German radical left was an extreme example of the crisis of twentieth-century organisational models and of the weaknesses of contemporary solutions. The key features of the SED organisation (Herbst et al. 1997) were quickly dismantled after 1989, leaving behind a largely transformed party (Gerner 1994; Neugebauer and Stöss 1996). The PDS adapted to the typical models of other German parties, with some exceptions. Its internal life was democratised and reorganised along the principles of delegate democracy (regular competitive selections of congress delegates – every two years – and electoral candidates – every election – by party members), with the addition of some elements of direct and network democracy (binding referenda, thematic groups, participation of non-members). Internal pluralism based on formal and informal tendencies was favoured over political coherence, with the aim of providing a welcoming space for the widest possible spectrum of 'broad left' traditions and sensibilities. Paramilitary and workplace cells were dissolved and replaced with territorial branches, although neighbourhood-based cells continued to exist in the East. The notion of party members as accurately screened, idealistic, obedient, and hyper-active conveyors of a central party line was completely abandoned, although most members did continue to follow in a weakened form the old patterns of activism and discipline. The party in public office, in particular the federal and regional parliamentary groups, gained ground at the expenses of the party in central office. Finally, the mode of interaction with social movements and civil society organisation moved from top-down dependence to mutual autonomy and loose punctual collaborations.

These changes transformed the PDS into a democratic and pluralist membership-based party, but failed to turn it into an attractive instrument for the self-organisation and political participation of the masses. First, the early membership collapse of 1990–93 produced a membership of aged cadres (now mostly retired) organised in close-knit cells that struggled to attract and integrate new recruits. Secondly, ordinary workers were rapidly marginalised by a highly-educated elite, withdrawing from active engagement in favour of a merely passive electoral support. Thirdly, the party was at times effective in representing social grievances in parliament, in the media, and on the streets, but lacked effective means to build solidarity and wage struggles at the level of civil society itself (either in the heavily-centralised forms typical of the twentieth-century labour movement, or in the more diffuse forms of the new social movements).

The creation of DIE LINKE did not represent an improvement in this sense. The party did manage to gain a thin coverage of the Western regions that had eluded its predecessor, experienced a temporary growth of members and of wage-workers, and strengthened its contacts with trade unions and other mass organisations. However, Western structures were much weaker and less integrative than the Eastern ones, further widening the gap between institutional activity and social participation and mobilisation.

Strategically, all three parties (PDS, WASG, and DIE LINKE) relied on the idea that a growth of the radical left, assisted by a combination of electoral, parliamentary, and extra-parliamentary pressures, would in the mid-term pull the mainstream centre-left parties to the left and create the conditions for a new progressive alliance and a 'change of direction' (*Richtungswechsel*) in governmental policies (Brie 2000, 2003, 2007; Krämer 2004). This strategy was confronted with the familiar dilemma of the contemporary European radical left. On the one hand, the strengthening of the radical left was primarily dependent on a relentless criticism of the moderate left aimed at winning over its disaffected traditional constituencies: in the German case, East German workers and unemployed (most of which were initially supportive of the CDU/CSU), the Western working class (predominantly SPD), and the educated left-libertarian strata (predominantly GRÜNE). This made friendly relationships difficult and prompted accusations of favouring the 'greater evil' of the centre-right. On the other hand, the striving toward an ideal future centre-left alliance encouraged a pragmatic attitude toward present governmental coalitions, which inevitably ended up denting the anti-neoliberal credentials of the radical left and deceiving its own supporters.

Fortunately, the German radical left parties were largely shielded from the need of making the kind of hard tactical and strategic choices that have so damaged their Italian and French counterparts. On the one hand, they were not forced to pre-electoral alliances and succeeded in maintaining an image as useful, coherent, yet non-sectarian oppositions against the Western-dominated, neoliberal, and militaristic policies embraced by the rest of the party system. Until 1997, the PDS minimised the pressures of tactical voting by stressing the importance of an East German representation in the federal parliament and by hinting that, if the situation would require it, it would not stand in the way of a minority SPD-GRÜNE government. After 1998, the PDS and DIE LINKE had a relatively easy game in pointing out the 'betrayals' of the SPD in office (with the Greens or with the CDU/CSU). On the other hand, until 2005 radical left seats were never determinant to form a centre-left governmental majority: both in 1998 and 2002 the red-green coalition won a plurality of votes but a majority of seats, thanks to the effects of the 5 per cent threshold and the additional 'overhang seats' obtained through the constituency vote.[1] After 2005, on the contrary, this situation became frequent, but DIE LINKE was helped by the staunch refusal of the SPD to even seat at the bargaining table, which allowed passing the blame for the waste of a feasible alternative majority. Thus, PDS and DIE LINKE were prevented from ever being sucked into actual experiences of governmental participation at the national level, which proved so destructive for its French (1981–84 and 1997–2002) and Italian (1997–2001 and 2006–08) counterparts, while avoiding to be labelled as sectarian spoilers.

Summary

The contemporary German radical left emerged from the unlikely reinvention in 1989–90 of a section of the Stalinist ruling party of the German Democratic Republic, the SED, as a regional democratic socialist party, the PDS. The post-unification crisis enabled it to embark on a path of vibrant growth in the Eastern regions, but its regional roots proved an obstacle for its nationwide expansion. In 2004–05, however, the huge mobilisations against the labour market reform of the Schröder government provided the adequate window of opportunity for an all-German surge of the radical left, which regrouped first into an alliance (L.PDS-WASG) and then into a unitary party (DIE LINKE) and continued to grow until 2009, deeply modifying the German political system.

The systemic strength of the radical left was altogether medium-small (4.8 per cent) but tended to follow a path of moderate growth, more than doubling between 1992 (3.0 per cent) to 2013 (6.2 per cent). Electoral, parliamentary, and financial trends were healthy, while membership figures declined and governmental strength remained extremely weak and limited to a few Eastern regions. Its organisational cohesion was almost complete, as both the PDS and DIE LINKE managed to avoid splits and find productive arrangements with potential competitors. Finally, its political nature partly followed the typical trends of the rest of the Western European party family, but with important specificities linked to its roots in the Soviet bloc.

Explaining radical left cohesion

As already remarked, one of the peculiarities of the development of the German radical left was its organisational cohesion. Instead of suffering from a destructive competition between different organisations (as in France) or from successive debilitating splits (as in Italy), the PDS managed to preserve its hegemonic status on the radical left spectrum and even to initiate significant waves of radical

94 The German radical left

left regroupment, absorbing important far-left and left social democratic currents. How was this possible?

This achievement can be explained by the interplay of six factors.

The preconditions of the processes of radical left regroupment were provided by three socio-political factors: (1) the initial crisis of the radical left in 1989–91, which reduced the salience of many of the old dividing lines, favoured processes of opening and renewal, and encouraged the pooling together of men and resources; (2) the neoliberal transformation of the SPD, which left increasing sectors of its traditional intellectual, working class, and welfarist constituencies in search of alternatives; (3) the dynamics of left-wing extra-parliamentary mobilisation that, unlike in most European countries, reached their peak in a protracted wave of protest on social issues and against a seating centre-left government (2003–05).

Strong incentives to regroupment and safeguards against splits were instead provided by three further institutional, relational, and subjective factors: (4) the attitude of the SPD, which helped to preserve the cohesion between conciliatory and intransigent tendencies by excluding the PDS from national governmental participations; (5) the electoral system, which discouraged splits and new party formations and encouraged the collaboration of radical left currents; (6) the far-sighted attitude of the PDS leadership, which consistently co-opted potential allies and defused internal tensions through programmatic compromises and generous material incentives.

The first two factors are common to all Western European countries and constitute the main drivers of the general tendency to craft, from the ruins of former communist, Eurocommunist, and far-left organisations, new 'broad left' formations with a wider appeal. The third factor played a vital role in provoking the split *to* the German radical left in 2004–05 of a small number of former social democratic cadres in the form of Oskar Lafontaine and the WASG. The German case remains to this day one of the few examples, and arguably the most successful one, of leftward splits of the European social democratic party family.[2] Radical left cohesion in Germany, however, was mainly due to the remaining three factors.

First, electoral rules, particularly the relatively high 5 per cent threshold, provided a large incentive to the regroupment of all radical left forces with the aim of obtaining parliamentary representation, visibility, and resources. Small Western radical left organisations had practically no chance to do so by going alone (they could, however, obtain state financing by winning more than 0.5 per cent), while an alliance for the PDS offered rosy prospects even to tiny groups. Conversely, for the PDS every vote counted, as it hovered close to the threshold and a success in crossing it (as in 1998 and 2005) removed the need to rely on the conquest of three 'direct seats' and brought with it symbolic and material gains (as the recognition as parliamentary Fraction instead of as mere Group). These considerations were the main drivers behind both the success of the two regroupment experiences, the Linke Liste/PDS alliance in 1990 and the L.PDS/WASG alliance in 2005, and the consensual resolution of all internal tendency wars.

Secondly, the political isolation to which the SPD subjected the PDS and DIE LINKE further helped to cement its internal cohesion. Radical tendencies had few justifications to leave, as the involvement of the parties in disastrous experiences of governmental participation was limited to a few Eastern regions and never became national or systematic. On the contrary, moderate tendencies could hardly hope to find a welcoming environment in the SPD, where anti-communist instincts ran deep.[3]

Finally, the central leadership of the PDS proved remarkably flexible and skilful, favouring internal pluralism and tolerance, seeking to compose tendency conflicts with compromise solutions acceptable to all protagonists, and proving to be prepared to offer disproportionally high rewards to prospective partners.

As long as DIE LINKE is forced to remain in the comfortable 'ghetto' of parliamentary opposition, no significant change in the level of radical left fragmentation is to be expected, regardless of the intensity of internal clashes or the magnitude of political blunders. On the other hand, a change in the attitude of the SPD and an experience of governmental participation at the national level are likely to encourage the kind of fragmentation between conciliatory and intransigent currents typical of several European countries, together with the danger of a common ruin of both contenders.

Filling the vacuum: potential and limits of radical left mobilisation

The hopes of the German radical left, as elsewhere in Europe, were pinned on the so-called 'vacuum thesis' (Brie 2000; Brie et al. 2007; Nachtwey 2009; Nachtwey and Spier 2007; Patton 2006; Stöss and Neugebauer 1998, 2002). The growing rightward shift of established catch-all parties, so went the reasoning, opened up a vacuum of political representation of working-class/welfarist interests and traditional left-wing values, which a modernised radical left should set about to fill. In Germany, this picture was enriched by the Eastern German question: on the one hand, Eastern Germans were at the forefront of the potential dissent, as they were particularly affected by neoliberal reforms and were characterised by a much more egalitarian (albeit less libertarian) political culture; on the other hand, they experienced specifically territorial problems. Thus, the radical left focused its mobilisation on three specific 'representation gaps' (*Vertretungslücken*).

The first one was the issue of cross-class East German interests. As Heidrun Abromeit (1992, 1993) convincingly showed, the mechanics of the 1990 unification led to a structural disregard for the peculiar problems and concerns of the population of those regions, which could hardly find a voice through the largely Western mainstream parties. An Eastern regional party along the lines of the Bavarian CSU might have been a logical solution, but failed to emerge in the post-unification landscape. On the contrary, representation of East German interests divided between the PDS (Neller and Thaidigsmann 2002), mainstream parties, and particularly the CDU (where Eastern politicians did ultimately rise to prominence with Angela Merkel's election as chancellor in 2005 and Joachim Gauck's election as president in 2012), and right-wing populist organisations.

96 *The German radical left*

The second one was the issue of social justice. The improvement of the working and living conditions of the working class and other subaltern strata was traditionally owned by the socialist SPD and to a lesser extent by the confessional CDU/CSU. Both parties, however, steadily turned to the right during the nineties and noughties and oversaw mass unemployment, rising social inequalities, and policies of welfare retrenchment. The PDS benefitted from these trends in the East, but failed to emerge in the West. The L.PDS/WASG alliance and DIE LINKE, on the contrary, succeeded in expanding across the whole country by mobilising on social themes.

Finally, left-libertarian issues were generally upheld by all three left-of-the-centre parties (SPD, GRÜNE, DIE LINKE) and did not offer particularly encouraging perspectives of competitive development, but the issue of pacifism could still be mobilised by the radical left against the other two parties. Both the post-1990 turn toward foreign military interventions, in particular the Kosovo (1999) and Afghanistan (2001–present) wars, and the Eastern expansion of the NATO had been spearheaded by the moderate left. Thus, pacifism became an important focus of radical left mobilisation.

In the present section I demonstrate that the vacuum theory made sense: welfarist values and interests were indeed increasingly neglected by the established parties, and radical left growth was intimately connected with its efforts on these fronts. At the same time, the radical left managed to win over only a small section of the potential welfarist constituencies disaffected by the neoliberal policies of their traditional political representatives. Why was this the case? My analysis of the electoral and organisational mobilisation of the German radical left shows that this outcome depended on a number of external and internal factors.

Contours of the vacuum

There is no doubt that the German political system, like its main European counterparts, has been evolving since the eighties in a clear rightward direction.

First, state-owned corporations – always comparatively weaker than in Italy or France – were gradually dismantled and/or aligned with shareholder models of corporate governance (Beyer and Höpner 2003; Mayer 2006; Rösler 1994). The privatisation of state-owned companies was started in the mid-eighties by the centre-right (VEBA, Volkswagen, and Lufthansa). The 1990 unification led to its sudden acceleration. In the East, the Treuhandanstalt oversaw in four years the privatisation and shutting-down of the near-totality of the local industrial sector, while follow-up institutions carried on for years with the progressive sale of Eastern real estate and agricultural land. In the West, centre-right and centre-left governments went on to partially or entirely privatise most of the remaining state-owned enterprises, including the key service providers Deutsche Post and Deutsche Telekom. Since the late noughties, only one large enterprise remains under full state ownership (Deutsche Bahn). Minority participations exist in other important companies (KfW, Deutsche Post, and Deutsche Telekom). The role of regional and local governments, however, remains strong in the banking sector, with *Landesbanken* and *Sparkassen* retaining about a third of the market share.

Secondly, public sector employment was drastically reduced. This number reached its peak in 1990, when the two German states employed more than 7 million people, but was cut to 5.4 million in 1995 and 4.6 million in 2005, stabilising afterwards.

Thirdly, welfare state reform followed a path of 'managed austerity' (Vail 2010) involving both a preservation of overall state provisions and their selective rationalisation and neoliberal recalibration. Key measures were the pension reforms of 1992, 2000, and 2006 and the labour market reforms of 2003–05 (*Agenda 2010*). It is notable that all but the first were drafted by social democratic ministers, either in centre-left or in grand coalition cabinets (Beck and Scherrer 2005; Nachtwey 2013).

Fourthly, the traditional restraint of the country in military foreign policy was reversed in the early nineties by a more assertive stance (Meiers 2010), which led to the participation to a series of minor NATO operations and to two full-fledged armed conflicts (Kosovo in 1999 and Afghanistan from 2001 onwards). Both the SPD in 1992 and the GRÜNE in 1998 abandoned their previous opposition to out-of-area military missions – in the second case, breaching one of their founding values, pacifism.

Fifthly, and most importantly, governmental parties have been less and less able to rely on the main promise of the German 'social market economy': the fact that through a regulated capitalism with a developed welfare state economic growth could be harnessed for the common good of all sectors of the population. The issue of mass unemployment, which skyrocketed for the first time with the 1982 crisis, was never tackled satisfactorily. The unemployment rate rose to 7–8 per cent of the active population in the eighties and to 9–12 per cent in the following fifteen years. After 2007 the situation significantly improved on paper, but both precarious and irregular employment and the number of people on benefits reached unheard-of levels (Eichhorst and Marx 2009). Real GDP growth continued to slow down from the very high levels of the sixties and seventies to a compound annual growth rate (CAGR) of 2.7 per cent in the business cycle 1983–93, 1.5 per cent in 1994–2003 and 0.7 per cent in 2004–09. Real wages did worse, moving from slow growth in the first two periods (CAGR 1.1 per cent and 0.7 per cent) to stagnation after 2003 (–0.2 per cent).

These trends seemed to constitute a fertile terrain for the growth of the radical left. The neoliberal shift of the established parties (Klein and Falter 2003; Nachtwey 2013; Walter 2011), however, did not necessarily create a vacuum of representation. On the one hand, the new policies and conditions might have been accepted by the affected population as hard but welcome shifts toward more competition and individual responsibility (a 'strong' neoliberal hegemony). On the other hand, they might have elicited a passive acquiescence driven by a sense of inevitability or impotence (a 'weak' neoliberal hegemony). Existing electoral and opinion poll data clearly indicate that, in fact, the disconnection between sectors of the German population and the party system did grow and was at least in part due to a growing dissatisfaction of traditional working-class and welfarist constituencies.

Support for the establishment parties (CDU/CSU, SPD, and FDP) has been constantly eroding since the early eighties, with particularly steep declines in the

98 The German radical left

periods 1983–93 and 2005–09 (Chiocchetti 2016a). Their share of the total electorate fell from 86.0 per cent in 1980 to 49.8 per cent in 2009, to the benefit of abstentions and of new parties, while their capacity to develop feelings of party identification followed the same trend, from 78.8 per cent in 1980 to 47.5 per cent in 2011 (Figure 4.2).

In addition, the weight of traditional left-wing beliefs, far from decreasing, was rather on the rise (Figure 4.3). According to the ALLBUS surveys, the difference between people identifying as left-of-the-centre and their opponents shifted from negative values in the eighties to positive afterwards (1983: –8.0 percentage points; 2006: +8.2). Germans became more and more likely to consider existing social differences as unfair rather than fair (1984: +3.2; 2008: +45.2) and socialism as 'a good idea badly implemented' rather than a bad idea (1992: –11.0; 2007: +21.9). The difference between those supporting an expansion of the welfare state and those preferring retrenchment tended to be largely positive (1990–2007 average: +13.4), with the only exception in the period 2000–04. More generally, popular criticism of social injustice, neoliberalism, and capitalism is on the rise since 1989 (*Frankfurter Allgemeine Zeitung* 2007, 2012; Glatzer 2009).

Both trends were most pronounced in the former GDR area, where particularly strong social grievances overlapped with a traditionally more egalitarian political culture. But all over Germany sizeable groups of unemployed, ordinary wage-workers, university-educated citizens, and the inactive were increasingly dissatisfied with the performance of established parties. It was up to the radical left to

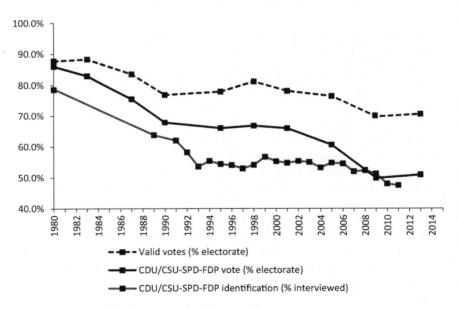

Figure 4.2 Support for German establishment parties

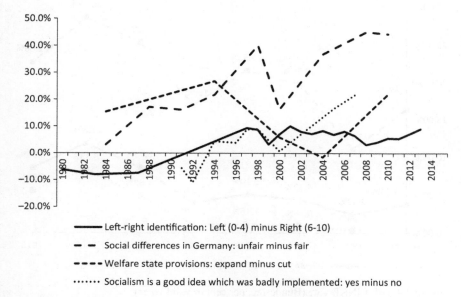

Figure 4.3 Net left-wing opinions, Germany (per cent of interviewed)

offer them a political perspective more convincing than other alternatives (critical centre-left support, political disengagement, or right-wing populism).

Electoral mobilisation

The attempts of the German radical left to fill the *electoral* dimension of the vacuum was partially successful. Despite three setbacks in late 1990, 2002, and 2013, the vote for PDS and DIE LINKE in national elections doubled from an initial level of 1,892,329 votes in early 1990 (in the GDR, corresponding to a notional all-German value of 3.8 per cent) to a final level of 3,775,699 votes (8.6 per cent) in 2013. The analysis of the geographical (Figure 4.4), social (Figure 4.5), and political (Figure 4.6) composition of this vote clearly indicates that growth was concentrated precisely among the expected groups: Eastern Germans, unemployed and blue-collar workers, and SPD voters.

The PDS suffered a precipitous electoral decline during the brief period of democratising but still-independent GDR in 1989–90. It suddenly plunged from the position of authoritarian ruler, through opinion poll values of 31 per cent in late September 1989, to 16.4 per cent of valid votes in the first free election in March 1990. It further slid to 14.6 per cent in May (local elections) and 12.7 per cent in October-December (regional elections). The party faced a marked hostility from most social categories (particularly the manual workers), which hoped for a major rise in living standards through a quick reunification with the FRG, and

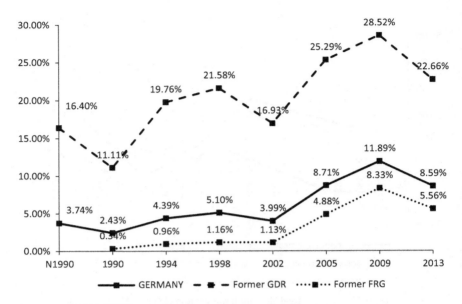

Figure 4.4 DIE LINKE vote (Bundestag, per cent of valid votes)

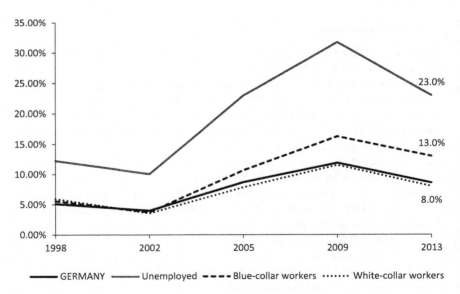

Figure 4.5 DIE LINKE vote in selected social groups (Bundestag, per cent of valid votes)

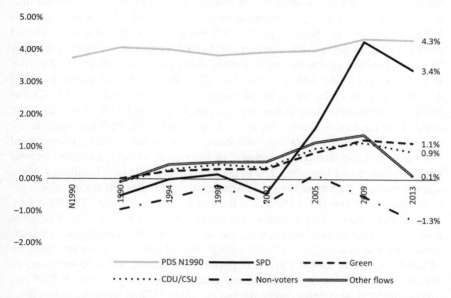

Figure 4.6 Cumulative net electoral flows of DIE LINKE (Bundestag, per cent of valid votes)

could count on the sole support of sections of the former SED members, which had benefitted from the old regime and viewed its downfall as a threat of severe downward social mobility (Goedicke 2003; Jung 1990; Solga 1995). In the first all-German federal election of December 1990, it won a national share of 2.4 per cent (11.1 per cent in the East, 0.3 in the West) and seemed doomed to a quick disappearance from the political scene, despite its success in obtaining parliamentary representation.

Starting from 1992, however, the fortunes of the party revived. It recovered its support among the former bureaucracy (now active in white-collar professions, early-retired, or unemployed), which was being significantly discriminated against in the new republic. It also managed to reach out to broader layers of the Eastern population, which felt deceived by the contrast between the early promises of a rapid socio-economic improvement and the realities of a permanently under-developed area. In particular, the involvement in the massive protest wave against Eastern deindustrialisation in 1992–93 markedly improved its image, partially mending its antagonistic relationship with the local working class. By 1998 its vote share had risen to 5.1 per cent (East 21.6, West 1.2), recovering the early losses to the SPD and scoring significant gains from CDU/CSU and new voters.

After 1998 the PDS failed to profit from the rightward shift of the seating centre-left cabinet, suffering a heavy setback in the 2002 election (4.0 per cent, East 16.9, West 1.1). In 2003 onwards, however, the tide turned again. The labour market reforms of the second Schröder cabinet provoked a crisis within the SPD, mass street protests, and the creation of the WASG. The L.PDS-WASG electoral alliance, led by Oskar Lafontaine, profited massively from this climate and soared to 8.7 per cent (East 25.4, West 4.9) in the 2005 election. This upward trend continued during the following legislature, when DIE LINKE could present itself as the only 'social' opposition against the policies of the ruling grand coalition and further rose to 11.9 per cent in the 2009 election (East 28.5, West 8.3). This period involved a qualitative shift in the nature of the German radical left. First, DIE LINKE for the first time became a truly national party, competitive both in the East and in the West of the country. Secondly, the atypical electorate of the PDS was replaced by a more typical working-class one, with strong results among both the unemployed (31.7 per cent) and blue-collar workers (16.3 per cent). Thirdly, the main electoral competitor switched from the CDU to the SPD (with a gain of 2.1 million votes!), again aligning with a more typical European pattern of intra-left competition.

In 2013, however, DIE LINKE fell back to 8.6 per cent (East 22.7, West 5.6). Internal and external factors dented the appeal of the party: the lack of tangible policy results for its two consecutive election victories; the withdrawal of Lafontaine from national politics in 2010; strong internal conflicts; a limited recovery of the SPD, due to its spell in the opposition and a mild leftward turn; and an increased competition from new protest parties. The swing voters of 2009 left toward the SPD, abstention, and AfD, but the gains of 2005 were not affected.

This electorally successfully trajectory was to a large extent the outcome of external factors over which the radical left had little influence. The growing disconnect between CDU/CSU and SPD and their traditional welfarist constituencies proceeded quite spontaneously under the impact of socio-economic trends and neoliberal policies. Mass mobilisations, particularly in 1992–93 and 2003–04, played a crucial role in turning this disaffection toward the radical left, but were predominantly initiated and led by disaffected social democrats, not by PDS members. Electoral rules endowed the PDS with a precarious but continuous representation in the federal parliament, enhancing its role as a potential left-wing alternative and pole of regroupment.[4] Finally, the SPD repeatedly squandered opportunities to check the rising competition on its left. In 1989–90, the refusal of the SDP/SPD to welcome former SED members helped to prevent a complete disarticulation of the PDS. In 2003–04, its obstinate defence of the labour market reform in the face of widespread internal and external oppositions created the conditions for the emergence of the WASG and the surge of the L.PDS/WASG alliance. In 2005, it made the huge mistake of accepting the role of junior partner in a grand coalition government with the CDU/CSU, which further dented its left-wing credential and resulted four years later in the loss of one third of its electorate and its historically lowest electoral score (23.0 per cent). More generally, an intelligent strategy of co-optation of the PDS within a broad centre-left alliance would have destabilised its electorate and split its cadres (as indeed happened in France and Italy), while the dogged refusal to even envisage a collaboration helped it to consolidate its core constituency and its anti-neoliberal appeal.

On the other hand, subjective factors did play an important subordinate role. Gregor Gysi and Lothar Bisky can deservedly claim a good share of credit for the capacity of the party to preserve its cohesion and become a pole of regroupment on the left. Where other leaders might have failed, they did almost everything right: they prevented the dissolution of the SED in 1989–90, a move which haunted the subsequent history of the PDS but gave it a solid initial base of support and a chance of parliamentary representation; they endowed it with a modern programme that combined the defence of East German interests and an all-German welfarist appeal; they relentlessly courted disaffected social democratic and green voters and social movements; and they successfully carried out the 2005–07 transition to DIE LINKE. The role of Oskar Lafontaine, in turn, was crucial for the success of the radical left in the period 2005–09. It is not coincidental that, as soon as these figures took the back seat (2002, 2013), electoral results substantially worsened.

Despite these undeniable successes, the radical left managed to tap only a small portion of the theoretical vacuum opened up by the rightward shift of the SPD and the rest of the political system. Three sets of data hint to this.

The first clue is in the relation of radical left results to a variety of indicators of left-wing opinion. In 2009 DIE LINKE obtained 5.2 million of votes, 8.3 per cent of the total electorate (including abstentions and invalid votes). These voters were fewer than people identifying as far-left or left-wing (10.6 per cent) and less than a third of people supporting an expansion of the welfare state (26.5 per cent).

The second clue is in the composition of net electoral flows of the SPD in the period 1998–2009. During that decade the SPD lost 10.2 million votes, more than half of its initial total. Only 17.6 per cent of the losses accrued to DIE LINKE; the large majority went instead to the parties of the centre-right (35.5 per cent), to abstentions (24.2 per cent), to the Greens (14.8 per cent) and to other kinds of change (7.8 per cent).

The third clue is in the sociological composition of the radical left electorate. Despite sizeable electoral gains, the core target constituency of the left (employed wageworkers) became only marginally more likely than the rest of the population to support the radical left; the success among unemployed and blue-collar workers, in particular, was not matched by results among white-collar workers (which remained slightly below-average) and civil servants (which became more and more hostile).

In other words, the potential electoral constituency of the radical left was much larger than its actual electorate, but most of it continued to prefer a vote for the moderate left (SPD and GRÜNE) or abstain.

What prevented the German radical left from exploiting more fully the disillusionment with the traditional mass parties and, in particular, from replacing the SPD as the main left-wing party?

A first problem was the nature of the PDS as the legal successor of the SED, which inevitably connected it with the discredited GDR authoritarian regime. While the party critically reassessed the Stalinist experience and sincerely converted to a liberal-democratic concept of 'democratic socialism', it nevertheless remained the main political vehicle of former bureaucrats and party members. Its opponents had, therefore, an easy task in pointing to its ambiguities, for instance, past contacts with the secret police (STASI) or neo-Stalinist internal tendencies (Jesse and Lang 2008; Knabe 2009; Lang 2003; Moreau 1998; Moreau et al. 1994; Neu 2004). This link contributed to the highly negative image of the PDS among German public opinion, particularly but not exclusively in the West.[5]

A second factor was the organisational weakness of the PDS in the West (Meuche-Mäker 2005; Neu 2000). This proved to be an insurmountable obstacle for the party, which always remained 'spiritually, politically and socially a foreign body' in the region (Brie 2000: 12). The Eastern image of the party and its lack of members and elected representatives on the ground constrained its electoral growth, which reached at its peak in 1998 just 442,136 votes (1.2 per cent), and hindered its attractiveness among disaffected SPD and Green voters. The creation of the WASG (2004) and DIE LINKE (2007) changed this situation, enabling the radical left to become a small but credible alternative across the entire national territory. Still, the roots of the new party in the West remained tenuous and determined its absence from several regional parliaments and most of the non-urban local assemblies.

The key element, however, was probably what can be defined as the *weight of tradition*. Lipset and Rokkan (1967) were the first to point out to the tendential 'freezing' of European party systems around the cleavage structure of the twenties; subsequent research on the hypothesis of a 'de-freezing' since the eighties (Drummond 2006; Mair 1993; Rose and Urwin 1970) has yielded mixed results, confirming a decline of the traditional parties but also highlighting their resilience and adaptability to new circumstances. In the German case, three countervailing factors have slowed down their electoral losses. First, voters have shown a natural wariness to give up long-lasting political allegiances forged in the formative period and consolidated by prolonged experiences of an effective (ideal and material) political representation. While the current record of established parties in securing economic growth and social welfare during the neoliberal era increasingly came under fire, their past record during the golden age continued to produce important delayed effects, particularly among the direct beneficiaries in the older age cohorts. Thus, the vote for CDU/CSU, SPD, and FDP fell between 1972 and 2009 by 27.7 percentage points among the general electorate, but only by 17.0 percentage points among over-60 voters. Secondly, the traditional (Catholic and socialist) sub-cultural networks of mass organisations and clienteles have been rapidly losing political coherence, size, and influence, but nevertheless acted as important brakes against party switching. Thirdly, by virtue of their spatial placement and resources the two main parties (CDU/CSU and SPD) were still, to a certain extent, able to polarise the competition as a choice between two alternative blocs and candidates for chancellor, thereby rallying undecided and tactical voters and penalising medium and small parties. In addition, electoral losses incurred while in government could be partially recovered through a spell in the opposition. This powerful mechanism, however, ceased to work effectively under grand coalition governments, provoking veritable electoral collapses (2009) and the proliferation of alternative options.

Organisational mobilisation

While the German radical left was partially successful in expanding in the electoral dimension of the vacuum which opened up among the deceived traditional constituencies the SPD and, in the Eastern regions of the country, of the CDU (Eastern blue-collar workers), the same cannot be said for the organisational dimension of the vacuum. The dense social linkages of the German mass parties (*Volksparteien*) have been eroding more rapidly than their own electorate; this notwithstanding, the German radical left has failed to provide a solid alternative. This section is devoted to a discussion of the two key facets of this issue, party membership and social linkages.

Like their counterparts in Western Europe, the German mass parties have suffered a strong decline in their membership levels that started in the eighties, continued in the nineties (with the brief exception of 1990, due to the massive influx of new Eastern members) and accelerated after 1999. Over the period 1990–2011, for instance, the CDU/CSU lost 34.4 per cent of its members and the SPD 48.1 per cent. Unlike the Greens, the PDS/DIE LINKE did not benefit from this situation and did much worse than its rivals, falling in absolute terms by 75.3 per cent (from 280,882 members in 1990 to 69,458 in 2011). In terms of penetration ratios (members over voters, M/V), it shifted from a membership-dense (1990: 24.9 per cent) to an intermediate (2002: 3.7 per cent) and thin (2009: 1.5 per cent) kind of party formation. Other radical left organisations, such as the orthodox DKP, followed the same trend.[6]

The cause of these problems lay in the roots of the PDS in the mass communist party *par excellence*, the SED, which in 1988 encompassed 2.3 million members, around 18.5 per cent of the GDR population. The initial choice to renew the party instead of dissolving it enabled the PDS to preserve a core of dedicated activists, but was followed only by a small fraction of the initial members (280,882 in 1990; 131,406 in 1993). Those who remained were overwhelmingly highly-educated, over-50 pensioners, and unemployed coming from the middle ranks of the former intelligentsia and bureaucracy; ordinary members deserted the party and never came back. Thus, membership decline since 1993 has been overwhelmingly dictated by natural process of aging and death of its initial core.

The winning of new members has been hindered by a series of factors. On the one hand, the general reluctance of the younger generations to join political parties, which are seen as an outmoded form of political engagement and have ceased to confer the ideational (sense of purpose and community) and material (policies and patronage) benefits of the past. On the other hand, the distinctive organisational (tightly-knit small cells), sociological (aged former bureaucrats), and geographical (overwhelmingly Eastern) set-up of the PDS, which makes it peculiarly unwelcoming for newcomers. Finally, the existence of widespread official and informal practices of discrimination, which makes radical left membership detrimental for one's life and career prospects. In the West, far-left members were thoroughly purged from civil service by the *Radikalenerlass* of 1972 (Braunthal 1990) and the political vetting of new applicants, albeit gradually loosened after

1995, remains in place in many public institutions. In the East, the 2.1 million civil servants were similarly vetted after 1990 about their role in the fallen communist regime (Crossley-Frolick 2007; Keller and Henneberger 1992; McAdams 2001). Although the number of people explicitly fired because of contacts with the STASI appears to be small – according to McAdams (2001), only 42,062 cases–, card-carrying PDS civil servants were singled out in the downsizing of the Eastern public sector, which shrunk to 1,592,546 (1991) and 861,155 (2001) employees. More generally, parts of the PDS/DIE LINKE and most smaller radical left organisations continued to be categorised as 'extremist' by the state and subjected to surveillance by the federal and regional political intelligence agencies (*Verfassungsschutz*).

Despite serious effort to turn the tide, these drawbacks proved to be insurmountable. Even at times when radical left voters and sympathisers grew rapidly, party members stagnated or continued to decline. The Western branches were more dynamic, growing to 4,708 members (2002) in the PDS, 11,250 members (2005) in the WASG and 29,551 members (2009) in DIE LINKE, but organised a paltry ratio of voters (PDS 1998: 0.68 per cent; DIE LINKE 2009: 1.00 per cent) and their growth was not strong enough to compensate for the decline of the Eastern branches. As a consequence, the total membership of DIE LINKE and of its predecessors slightly rose from 2004 (61,385) to 2009 (78,046), but the gains were completely wiped out by 2014 (60,547).

The crisis of the German mass parties was not restricted to the loss of members and entailed a deep crisis of the whole sub-cultural networks of collateral and friendly organisations (von Winter and Willems 2007). This process had three facets: (a) a *membership loss* of the sub-cultural organisations; (b) a *loosening of the ties* between organisations and members, reflected in their decreased capacity to command identification and orient behaviour; (c) a final *autonomisation* from their traditional political references, leading to a less partisan and politicised public discourse.

A good example is the trade union confederation DGB, traditionally very close to the SPD. Between 1991 and 2010 the DGB membership collapsed from 11.8 to 6.1 million members and from 35.5 per cent to 18.3 per cent of the employed workforce.[7] Despite an overwhelming majority of card-carrying SPD members among union leaders and cadres, union members have switched their political allegiance much faster than the general population, with social democratic voters falling 56 per cent in 1998 to 33.5 per cent in 2009. Finally, in 2002 the confederation discontinued the traditional practice of offering an explicit voting advice for the SPD and strongly criticised the labour market reform of 2004. The same dynamics were at play in the rest of the social democratic sub-culture, which includes an array of charities (AWO), specialised associations (VdK, SoVD, DMB, KOS), cooperatives (part of the DGRV), and other organisations and encompasses several hundred thousand cadres and several million members.

Despite its electoral surge, the German radical left was not able to expand its positions within civil society and social movement organisations and to become a serious competitor of the SPD in this domain.

The gigantic network of mass organisations controlled by the SED dissolved or merged with their Western counterparts in 1989–91, completely escaping the influence of the PDS and aligning with the new dominant parties CDU and SPD. In particular, the influence of the party among the organised labour movement was shattered (Looding and Rosenthal 2001; Wilke and Müller 1991). The only notable exception was the charity Volkssolidarität (Winkler 2010), which adopted a cross-party stance but remained politically quite close to the PDS. Although rapidly declining (853,000 members in 1991; 538,000 in 1994; 276,000 in 2009), the organisation remained a social and economic powerhouse.

In the following years, the PDS did manage to forge close links with a series of new organisations created to represent the interests of the former socialist bureaucracy (the *Ostdeutsches Kuratorium von Verbänden*, OKV), which were strategically important for their dense legal and cultural work but never gathered more than 40,000 members. Outside of this milieu, the efforts of the party tended to fall flat. Influence within traditional civil society organisations remained inexistent in the West and the federal level and very low in the East. The trade union apparatus, for instance, remained solidly controlled by the SPD, even in regions where the PDS was electorally stronger. United front movements initiated by the party also failed to take roots: the *Komitees für Gerechtigkeit*, created in 1992 to highlight the socio-economic plight of the Eastern regions, were wound up before the end of the year (Fieber and Reichmann 1995); the *Erfurter Erklärung* and the ensuing organisation *Aufstehen für eine andere Politik*, created in 1997 to spearhead centre-left unity around a common left-Keynesian programme, did not survive the 1998 election (Dahn 1997).

The founders of the WASG included a core of long-standing SPD unionists and activists, but their influence remained weak in the trade unions and other social democratic organisations and largely limited to the smallish alter-globalisation galaxy.[8] The WASG played a key role in coordinating the 2003–04 protests against the *Agenda 2010*, but these failed to coalesce into permanent social movement organisations.

DIE LINKE, finally, inherited the organisational linkages of its predecessors and experienced a moderate growth of its civil society presence. Its influence among left-leaning mass organisations, however, remained dwarfed by that of the SPD. The example of the trade union movement is again indicative. While 17.1 per cent of trade union members voted for DIE LINKE in 2009 (32.1 per cent in the East, ahead of the CDU/CSU and SPD), the 1,805 union cadres who signed the appeal '*Wir wählen links!*' consisted almost exclusively of low-ranking officials and the doors of top union organs remained closed to card-carrying LINKE supporters.[9] As far as social movement networks were concerned, the party played a central role in the 2007 G8 counter-summit at Heiligendamm and in the post-2009 anti-crisis protests (*Wir zahlen nicht für eure Krise!* in 2009–10 and *Blockupy* in 2012–13) but, again, little organisational legacy was left once the movement ebbed.

Summary

Since 1990, a growing rift has been emerging between the established catch-all parties (SPD and CDU/CSU) and large sectors of their traditional constituencies. The poor macro-economic record and the neoliberal policy orientation of the former clashed with the welfarist orientation of the latter, which personally experienced the effects of mass unemployment, wage stagnation, and welfare retrenchment or more abstractly decried the increase in insecurity and inequalities.

In electoral terms, the German radical left was to a certain extent successful, but remained well below its overall potential. Federal electoral results gradually rose from 2.4 per cent of valid votes in 1990 to 8.7 per cent in 2013, with a peak of 12.0 in 2009. In a first phase, the PDS consolidated as a strong regional party, interpreting the grievances of large sections of the East German population but failing to put down roots in the Western side of the country. In a second phase, the L.PDS/WASG alliance and DIE LINKE succeeded in becoming a medium-sized national party, soaring among the unemployed, blue-collar workers, trade unionists, and former SPD voters. This electoral growth put DIE LINKE among the most successful European radical left experiences before the post-2012 rise of SYRIZA and PODEMOS, but touched only a minority of the above-mentioned welfarist constituencies, did not fundamentally threaten the position of the SPD as the dominant left-of-the-centre and working-class force, and remained exposed to swift temporary setbacks (as in 2002 and 2013).

In organisational terms, the gains in voters and sympathisers did not translate in a parallel rise of extra-parliamentary strength. Radical left membership collapsed from 1990 to 2004 and stagnated afterwards, despite important gains in the West between 2005 and 2009. Civil society linkages experienced a moderate growth since the historical trough of 1990–91 but remained largely confined to the 'former communist' (in the East) and alter-globalist (in the West) milieus, while the bulk of mass organisations including the trade unions continued to align – albeit critically – with their traditional political representatives.

The reasons behind both successes and limits in filling the vacuum of representation of working-class and welfarist interests were partly external and partly subjective. On the one hand, the German radical left did well in softening its main handicaps (the link with the GDR dictatorship, the lack of roots in the West), exploiting major extra-parliamentary mobilisations (Eastern workers in 1992–93, unemployed and workers in 2003–04), avoiding fragmentation, and selecting popular leaders (Gregor Gysi and Oskar Lafontaine), but it failed to develop a vital mass membership and to dent the predominance of the moderate left within the organised civil society. On the other hand, favourable external conditions (general socio-economic trends and the electoral legislation) and the mistakes of the SPD helped its electoral rise, but the 'weight of tradition' (the stickiness of individual allegiances, the lingering allegiances of civil society organisations, and bipolarism) prevented it from becoming a truly competitive parliamentary and extra-parliamentary alternative.

The strategy of leftward pull

The German radical left followed, particularly since the mid-nineties, a variant of what can be defined as *strategy of (mixed) leftward pull*. In the short term, activity was primarily geared at increasing radical left strength at the electoral, parliamentary, and extra-parliamentary level. In the medium-term, this growth and the combination of a variety of pressures on the moderate left parties was supposed to affect their course and force them to undertake a turn to the left. This would create the conditions for the creation of a progressive centre-left alliance, its electoral victory, and a policy shift away from neoliberalism. In the long-term, the incremental implementation of progressive reforms through parliamentary means and extra-parliamentary mobilisations would pave the way toward a (vaguely defined) democratic socialist society.

This strategy made intuitive sense and allowed a great tactical flexibility. However, it failed to tackle satisfactorily two major problems: the decreased efficacy of grassroots struggles in the neoliberal age, and the impermeability of the moderate left to a 're-social democratisation' of its policies.

Party efforts

Several kinds of pressures can be analytically distinguished in the activity of the parties of the German radical left.

The first was the indirect pressure on the political system exerted through the electoral growth of the party and its possible influence on the 'direction of competition' (Sartori 1976). The PDS did follow an overall path of electoral growth, but its potential influence was limited by the regional nature of its support. Starting from 2005, instead, the growth of DIE LINKE constituted a direct and immediate threat to the electoral success and governmental power of the established parties, in particular the SPD.

The second element was direct influence on state policies through the building of parliamentary and governmental coalitions. The option of a tripartite centre-left alliance (SPD, GRÜNE, and DIE LINKE) was the object of much debate, but never materialised at the national level (Hirscher 2001; Hough 2010; Jesse 1997; Neu 2001; Raschke and Tils 2010; Spier 2009; Switek 2010). Until 2005 the seats of the PDS were never necessary for the formation of a centre-left parliamentary majority. Afterwards, on the contrary, the seats of DIE LINKE were vital in two out of three legislative terms (2005–09 and 2013–present). The formation of a 'red-red-green' government, however, failed on the categorical refusal of the SPD. Radical left opinions on the matter were divided, as the programmatic distance between the potential partners was huge, but the top leadership of PDS and DIE LINKE consistently signalled its openness to bargain its (probably external) support in exchange for policy concessions.[10] The SPD, however, rejected any talks and regularly preferred the role of junior partner within 'grand coalitions' with the CDU/CSU.

The third was the broader pressure exerted by public debate, alliance-building, and extra-parliamentary activities on the ideological and social balance of forces. While the radical left was isolated within the party system, it could find several allies on specific issues and social mobilisations, notably East German interests, pacifism, and the defence of the welfare state. A direct dialogue with the internal left-wing tendencies of SPD and GRÜNE was repeatedly undertaken, concretising in intellectual collaborations such as the first Crossover project (1993–99), the Erfurter Erklärung and its follow-ups (1997–2000), the second Crossover debate (2007–09), and the Institut Solidarische Moderne (2010–present). This kind of activity had, however, few direct political repercussions. Experiences of local governmental collaboration also helped to improve the acceptance of the party, but proved to be a double-edged sword. Given the balance of parliamentary strength among coalition partners and the institutional and budgetary constraints of regions and communes, this cooperation generally resulted not in the radicalisation of SPD but rather in the de-radicalisation of the PDS. In particular, the red-red coalitions in Mecklenburg-Vorpommern and in Berlin significantly damaged the credibility of the PDS as a coherent anti-neoliberal force, as they forced it to accept major welfare cuts both at the local level and in the Bundesrat (Behrend 2006: 96–118; Hildebrandt and Brie 2006). Collaboration within social movements, finally, proved to be more interesting. Although neither the PDS and the WASG nor DIE LINKE had the capabilities to initiate or sustain major grassroots struggles, they did play an important role in three of the five major cycles of contentious politics of the period (1992–93; 1997–98; 2002–05) and in a multiplicity of less prominent struggles and campaigns.

Radical left involvement in extra-parliamentary mobilisations is worth a more detailed discussion. Industrial conflict is relatively rare in Germany, due to the heavy regulation of collective bargaining and strike procedures (general strikes, for instance, are illegal) and a developed neocorporatist 'social partnership' between trade unions, employers' associations, and the state. Similarly, social movements (Roth and Rucht 2008) tend to be localised and limited to small minorities of the population. Nevertheless, five large waves of contentious politics have taken place since 1989, with major political repercussions.

The first and most important wave was the 1989–90 'peaceful revolution' in the German Democratic Republic (Dale 2006; Gehrke and Hürtgen 2001; Lohmann 1994). The mobilisation of millions of citizens in gigantic demonstrations, direct actions, and labour conflicts dealt a death blow to the ruling communist regime, forcing it first to sweeping reforms (the Modrow government from November 1989 to March 1990) and then out of office. The PDS played here an ambiguous role, being both the main target of the protesters and an actor of renewal, self-reforming and accompanying the process of democratic transition (Gysi and Falkner 1990; Segert 2008, 2009). Its efforts were, however, generally perceived as insincere and left the party enfeebled and politically isolated.

The second wave was the 1992–93 movement against the negative repercussions of the unification process (Abromeit 1992; Fieber and Reichmann 1995; Garms 1994; Gehrke 1997; Roesler 1994). More specifically, the privatisation and deindustrialisation policy of the *Treuhandanstalt* belatedly came under fire, resulting in a proliferation of local strikes, occupations, demonstrations, and hunger strikes. Some attempts to coordinate the protests were made (the *Komitees für Gerechtigkeit* and the *Ostdeutsche Initiative der Betriebs- und Personalräte*), but the movement failed to gain the support of the official trade unions and slowly died out in a swarm of localised defeats or settlements. While not very successful in industrial terms, it had, however, a significant impact on the political climate, contributing to a long-lasting shift of the East German electorate away from the CDU and toward PDS and SPD.

The third and smaller wave was the disparate anti-Kohl mobilisation of unemployed, students, leftists, and trade unionists in 1997–98 (Brandt 1998; Dahn 1997; Lahusen and Baumgarten 2006; Schulz 2008). Often explicitly conceived as a way to influence the upcoming electoral campaign, the protests were smallish and not very effective, but contributed to the victory of the red-green coalition and to the acceptance of the PDS as a peculiar but viable left-wing corrective.

The fourth wave was the generalised revival of social mobilisations of the years 2002–05. The most important movement was the one against the Agenda 2010/Hartz IV labour market reform of the Schröder government, which brought to the streets hundreds of thousands of people in a whole summer of decentralised weekly 'Monday demonstrations', several national demos, and a host of other protest actions (Burger 2008; Lahusen and Baumgarten 2006; Rink and Phillips 2007). But labour, pacifist, and alter-globalist struggles were prominent as well (Rucht and Roth 2008; Schmidt 2003; Walgrave and Rucht 2010). Despite their sometimes impressive proportions, all mobilisations ended without tangible results but had a large political resonance, providing the foundations for the rapid electoral growth of the radical left (Nachtwey and Spier 2007) and for a significant shift to the left of the public opinion.

The fifth and final wave covered on the period 2009–11 and was opened by student and anti-crisis protests (Hildebrandt and Tügel 2010; Kolisang 2013) and continued with massive environmental mobilisations (Brettschneider and Schuster 2013; Roose 2010). Unlike most of their predecessors, these were partially successful, leading, for instance, to the abolition of university tuition fees in all but one region and to a confirmation of the phasing out of nuclear energy by 2022. While DIE LINKE benefitted from the early phase of the cycle, its late phase favoured GRÜNE and SPD.

To sum up, several important broad extra-parliamentary mobilisations around 'natural' radical left issues took place in the period. These were an utter failure when measured in terms of their own goals, but helped to increase the dissatisfaction toward established parties and enhance the public profile and electoral of the radical left.

Altogether, all three forms of pressure were quite small until 2003, due to the geographical limitation of radical left activity in the little populous and poor Eastern regions, but became more sustained since 2004, when L.PDS/WASG and DIE LINKE acquired an all-German character and became a medium-sized but attractive alternative to the moderate left. To what extent were they successful?

Systemic effects

Three kinds of effects of radical left activity must be distinguished: (a) those on civil society; (b) those on official governmental policies; (c) those on the programmatic outlook of political parties, in particular the moderate left ones (SPD and GRÜNE).

With regard to the first point, the activity of the radical left had no noticeable effect. Within the workplaces, radical left activists were few, devoid of a coherent strategy of intervention, and little influential. Thus, the growth of sympathy toward the radical left among wageworkers failed to produce positive effects on the terrain of immediate class struggle: labour militancy remained very low, union density continued to fall, and working conditions (wages, contracts, unemployment, and precariousness) continued to worsen.

With regard to the second point, it is also difficult to identify clear results. Radical left mobilisation failed to prevent the implementation of the key counter-reforms of the period, such as privatisations, labour market reforms, and welfare retrenchment, and did not reverse the overall neoliberal trends. On the other hand, the pressure of the PDS and DIE LINKE might have had some indirect effects, preventing harsher cuts and pushing governmental parties to some concessions, such as the rise in the level of Eastern wages and pensions in the 1990s (which nevertheless remained clearly inferior the Western ones), the abolition of university tuition fees (2008–15), and the introduction of a federal minimum wage (2015).

With regard to the third point, finally, the growth of the radical left had some repercussions on the broader political debate, raising the profile of issues of regional and social justice, but also failed to produce a clear shift to the left of the party system. The SPD, in particular, continues to this day to cling to the policy legacy of the Schröder government and to prefer 'grand coalitions' with the CDU/CSU to 'red-red-green coalitions' with GRÜNE and DIE LINKE, although its dramatic defeat in 2009 did produce some programmatic repositioning to the left.

Altogether, the efforts of the radical left to exert a leftward pull on German politics and society were unsuccessful, and the future prospects of a wide-ranging turn from neoliberal to neo-Keynesian policies appear to be dim. There are two possible explanations for this outcome.

The first is the insufficient level of radical left pressures. At its peak in 1998, the PDS represented only about 5 per cent of the valid votes and a mere hypothetical threat to the governmental prospects of the SPD, which could reasonably hope to see it miss the electoral threshold (as it indeed happened in 2002) or to offset the losses by winning new centrist votes. After 2005, when DIE LINKE turned into a much more insidious competitor, some cracks and accommodations indeed timidly appeared in the outlook of the mainstream parties, leading for instance to the 2014 introduction of a national minimum wage. Moreover, extra-parliamentary mobilisations were all defensive and marked by a *theatrical/electoral* strategy, seeking to influence governmental policies through the exhibition of dissent and the threat of electoral losses. They rarely relied on an actual shift of the balance of forces on the ground, for instance, through industrial organisation and struggles (whose effectiveness, in turn, was dented by mass unemployment and capital mobility). The failure to obtain decisive successes, therefore, might be simply due to the insufficient systemic strength of the radical left or the wrong choice of means, and further growth might produce different incomes.

The second is a structural impermeability of European political systems to a return to classic Keynesian-welfarist policy orientations. On the one hand, until recently no moderate left party has ever reneged on its fundamentally neoliberal course, regardless of its electoral losses: good examples are the Greek PASOK, the German SPD, the Spanish PSOE, and the French PS. Some timid signs of 're-social democratisation' have appeared in 2015 with figures such as Jeremy Corbyn in the UK Labour Party or Bernie Sanders in the US Democratic Party, but their ideas remain extremely minoritarian among the leadership and cadres of their own organisations. The roots of the neoliberal orientation of the 'new' social democracy, thus, seem to run much deeper than mere electoral expediency. On the other hand, neoliberal policies are 'locked in' in a complex framework of rules, institutions, and structures (EU treaties and law, the common currency, the independence of national banks and of the European Central Bank, free trade agreements, deregulated capital markets, and global production chains) which effectively prevent national governments from pursuing independent progressive socio-economic policies. Thus, in 2015 even the Greek leftist government of SYRIZA was forced to back down and implement harsh austerity measures.

The testing of these hypotheses lies beyond the scope of the present research, but both seem to contain some elements of truth. A success of the radical left in initiating a turn away from neoliberal policies certainly requires both a revival of mass industrial militancy, and a decisive state intervention. It cannot be construed as a smooth and relatively easy outcome of predominantly electoral pressures, but requires instead a much more confrontational clash with national and international actors and structures. The German radical left, as well as the rest of the Western European party family, has so far shied away from these implications, as they would endanger its immediate electoral prospects, its efforts to build a relationship with the moderate left, and its overall acceptability among the social elites.

Summary

Despite an intensification of its pressures on the political system, the German radical left failed to make inroads toward the intermediate step of its strategy – a break of the hegemony of neoliberalism and a political change of direction toward left-Keynesian and welfarist policies. Its activity remained predominantly propagandistic and incapable of winning tangible concessions for its own core constituency. Its strategy of leftward pull failed to produce visible results, as extra-parliamentary struggles remained defensive and generally unsuccessful while electoral and institutional activities failed to provoke a change of heart of the SPD and other mainstream parties.

Concluding remarks

The post-1989 evolution of the German radical left represents a relatively successful experience within the Western European panorama. Its careful analysis, however, reveals a more nuanced picture of light and shade.

On the positive side, this political area was electorally dynamic, growing in federal elections from 2.4 per cent (1990) to 8.7 per cent (2013) of valid votes, with a peak of 12.0 per cent in 2009. It preserved its organisational cohesion and successfully aggregated around an initial core of former communist cadres successive layers of unemployed, wageworkers, disgruntled centre-left supporters, protest voters, and social movement activists. It also enriched the terms of the public debate, providing a visible political representation to themes (Eastern interests, social justice, the critique of neoliberalism and capitalism, pacifism) that had increasingly been neglected by mainstream parties.

On the negative side, however, three major problems existed. First, the electoral gains covered only a small section of its potential anti-neoliberal constituency and remained vulnerable to the dangers of de-mobilisation and tactical voting, as the deceiving results of the 2002 and 2013 general elections clearly proved. Secondly, the radical left proved unable to translate its electoral growth into tighter and more effective forms of allegiance and participation: its activists and members continued to shrink, its influence within civil society and social movement organisations remained low, and its capacity to launch or steer extra-parliamentary campaigns was limited. Thirdly, its attempts to exert a leftward pull on the political system yielded few tangible results.

Both the strength and the influence of the German radical left ultimately ran up against insurmountable ceilings caused by internal shortcomings and external constraints. The SPD is severely weakened, but DIE LINKE is still nowhere near to constituting a viable competitor. Neoliberal policies are increasingly questioned and contested among the German population, but its alternative agenda remains unconvincing and its medium-term strategy not credible. In a nutshell, DIE LINKE succeeded in becoming a relevant actor in the German party system, but failed to precipitate a reversal of neoliberal policies and trends.

Notes

1 The latter mechanism was declared inconstitutional and removed before the 2013 election.
2 Other examples are the French MDC (1993) and PG (2009) and the Greek DIKKI (1995).
3 The initial refusal of the Eastern SDP (the initial name of the social democratic party of the GDR) to accept former SED members in general and the important PDS faction of Wolfgang Berghofer in particular set the tone of the relationship. A few high-profile PDS politicians later switched to the SPD (Angela Marquardt in 2008, Sylvia-Yvonne Kaufmann in 2009), but did it individually and with meagre personal and political rewards.
4 Particularly important was the 29 September 1990 sentence of the Constitutional Court (BVerfGE 82, 322) dictating a one-off separate calculation of the 5 per cent electoral threshold in the East and in the West (including West Berlin), which enabled an initial parliamentary representation of the PDS and gave it four years to consolidate its stronghold in East Berlin (where the conquest of four 'direct seats' ensured a renewed representation in 1994).
5 In the East, negative opinions of the party rapidly fell from 61.3 per cent in 1991 to 43.6 per cent in 1994, stabilising afterwards; in the West, they never fell under 62 per

cent (2008). Similarly, positive opinions of the party reached around 40 per cent in the East (since 1994) but never exceeded 11 per cent for the PDS (2001) and 19.8 per cent for DIE LINKE (2008) in the West. The high levels of extremely negative opinions point to the fact that much of this rejection was not so much programmatic but rather of a more fundamental and emotive nature, linked to personal suffering under the GDR regime (in the East) or deeply-rooted anticommunist sentiments (in the West).
6 The large DKP membership of the eighties (42,000 in 1986, 34,000 in 1989) melted away with the fall of the Soviet bloc, leaving behind only 8,000 members in 1992. The declining trend then continued at a slower pace to this day (3,500 members in 2013).
7 As 15–20 per cent of union members are *not* employed wageworkers (e.g. unemployed, pensioners, and students), the actual share should be even lower.
8 ATTAC Deutschland, for instance, had only 14,001 members in March 2004. While refusing to formally align itself with the new party, the organisation maintained a strong informal proximity to the WASG (Nicoll 2005; Speth 2006: 96). Other alter-globalist organisations that became quite close to the WASG or the PDS (the pacifist DFG-VK, the academic BdWI, the far-left Turkish/Kurdish GDF and DIDF) had altogether less than that number of members.
9 In 2011 no card-carrying LINKE member was included in the executive of the DGB or of individual trade unions.
10 The canonic formula was that a change 'will not fail because of us' (*wird an uns nicht scheitern*), signalling a readiness to provide some initial form of external support; one of its earliest occurrences is reported in *Spiegel* (1994, March 28).

References

Abromeit, Heidrun (1993). 'Die "Vertretungslücke". Probleme in neuen deutschen Bundesstaat', *Gegenwartskunde* 42(3): 281–292.
Abromeit, Heidrun (1992). 'Zum Für und Wider einer Ost-Partei', *Gegenwartskunde* 41(4): 437–448.
Barker, Peter (ed.) (1998). *The party of democratic socialism in Germany. Modern post-Communism or nostalgic populism?* Amsterdam: Rodopi.
Beck, Stefan, and Christoph Scherrer (2005). 'Der rot-grüne Einstieg in den Abschied vom "Modell Deutschland". Ein Erklärungsversuch', *PROKLA* 35(1): 111–130.
Behrend, Manfred (2006). *Eine Geschichte der PDS. Von der zerbröckelnden Staatspartei zur Linkspartei.* Köln: Neuer ISP Verlag.
Beyer, Jürgen and Martin Höpner (2003). 'The disintegration of organised capitalism: German corporate governance in the 1990s', *West European Politics* 26(4): 179–198
Blondel, Jean (1968). 'Party systems and patterns of government in Western democracies', *Canadian Journal of Political Science* 1(2): 180–203.
Bortfeldt, Heinrich (2003). 'Die PDS am Ende?', *Deutschland Archiv* 5: 737–751.
Bortfeldt, Heinrich (1992). *Von der SED zur PDS. Wandlung zur Demokratie?* Bonn: Bouvier Verlag.
Brandt, Georg (ed.) (1998). *"Lucky Streik" – ein Kampf um Bildung: Gießener Studierende berichten.* Gießen: Focus-Verlag.
Braunthal, Gerard (1990). *Political loyalty and public service in West Germany, The 1972 decree against radicals and its consequences.* Amherst: The University of Massachusetts Press.
Bräutigam, Hansgeorg (2010). 'Die Verschleierung von SED-Vermögen', *Deutschland Archiv* 4: 628–634.

Brettschneider, Frank, and Wolfgang Schuster (eds.) (2013). *Stuttgart 21 – Ein Großprojekt zwischen Protest und Akzeptanz*. Wiesbaden: VS Verlag.
Brie, Michael (2007). 'Der Kampf um gesellschaftliche Mehrheiten', in Michael Brie, Cornelia Hildebrandt, and Meinhard Meuche-Mäker (eds.). *Die Linke. Wohin verändert sie die Republik?* Berlin: Dietz Verlag, 13–45.
Brie, Michael (ed.) (2005). *The left party in Germany: Origins, aims, expectations*. Berlin: Rosa-Luxemburg-Stiftung.
Brie, Michael (2003). Ist die PDS noch zu retten? Analyse und Perspektiven [working paper]. Berlin: Rosa-Luxemburg-Stiftung.
Brie, Michael (2000). 'Die PDS – Strategiebildung im Spannungsfeld von gesellschaftlichen Konfliktlinien und politischer Identität', in Michael Brie and Rudolf Woderich (eds.). *Die PDS im Parteiensystem*. Berlin: Dietz Verlag, 14–51.
Brie, Michael, Martin Herzig, and Thomas Koch (eds.) (1995). *Die PDS. Postkommunistische Kaderorganisation, ostdeutscher Traditionsverein oder linke Volkspartei? Empirische Befunde und kontroverse Analysen*. Köln: PapyRossa.
Brie, Michael, Cornelia Hildebrandt, and Meinhard Meuche-Mäker (eds.) (2007). *Die Linke. Wohin verändert sie die Republik?* Berlin: Dietz Verlag.
Brie, Michael, and Rudolf Woderich (eds.) (2000). *Die PDS im Parteiensystem*. Berlin: Dietz Verlag.
Burda, Michael C. (2013). 'The East German economy in the twenty-first century', in Hartmut Berghoff and Uta A. Balbier (eds.). *The East German economy, 1945–2010. Falling behind or catching up?* Cambridge: Cambridge University Press, 195–216.
Burger, Susanne (2008). *Montagsdemos – Ausdruck einer neuen Wut?* [self-published]. München: GRIN Verlag.
Bürklin, Wilhelm, and Hilke Rebenstorf (1997). *Eliten in Deutschland. Rekrutierung und Integration*. Opladen: Leske + Budrich.
BVerfGE 82, 322, 29 September 1990 [legal sentence]. Available at: www.servat.unibe.ch/dfr/bv082322.html [accessed on 01.04.2016].
Chiocchetti, Paolo (2016a). 'Measuring party strength: A new systematic framework applied to the case of German parties, 1991–2013', *German Politics* 25(1): 84–105.
Chiocchetti, Paolo (2016b). Western European radical left database. Version 2.0 (30.04.2016). Available at: www.paolochiocchetti.it/data.
Chrapa, Michael (2000). 'Interne Konfliktpotentiale und Modernisierungschancen der PDS: Situation, Anforderungen, Optionen', *UTOPIE kreativ* 113: 276–283.
Chrapa, Michael, and Dietmar Wittich (2001). Die Mitgliedschaft: der große Lümmel . . . Studie zur Mitgliederbefragung 2000 der PDS [working paper]. Berlin: Rosa-Luxemburg-Stiftung.
Crossley-Frolick, Katy (2007). 'Sifting through the past: Lustration in reunified Germany', in Vladimira Dvořáková and Anđelko Milardović (eds.). *Lustration and consolidation of democracy and the rule of law in central and eastern Europe*. Zagreb: CPI, 197–213.
Dahn, Daniela (ed.) (1997). *Eigentum verpflichtet – die Erfurter Erklärung*. Heilbronn: Distel Verlag.
Dale, Gareth (2006). *The East German revolution of 1989*. Manchester: Manchester University Press.
Dale, Gareth (2004). *Between state capitalism and globalisation. The collapse of the East German economy*. Bern: Peter Lang.
Drummond, Andrew J. (2006). 'Electoral volatility and party decline in Western democracies: 1970–1995', *Political Studies* 54(3): 628–647.
Eckhoff, Heinrich (2005). 'Was war die Linke Liste/PDS?', *Disput*, July.

Eichhorst, Werner, and Paul Marx (2009). Reforming German labor market institutions: A dual path to flexibility [working paper]. Available at: http://nbn-resolving.de/urn:nbn:de:101:1-20090403134 [accessed on 01.04.2016].
Ernst, Klaus, Thomas Händel, and Katja Zimmermann (eds.) (2012). *Was war? Was bleibt? Wege in die WASG, Wege in DIE LINKE.* Hamburg: VSA Verlag.
Fieber, Hans-Joachim, and Johannes Reichmann (1995). *'Komitees für Gerechtigkeit': Erwartungen, Meinungen, Dokumente.* Frankfurt am Main: IKO.
Förster, Peter, and Günter Roski (1990). *DDR zwischen Wende und Wahl.* Berlin: LinksDruck.
Frankfurter Allegemeine Zeitung (2012, February 22). 'Das Unbehagen am Kapitalismus' [newspaper article].
Frankfurter Allgemeine Zeitung (2007, July 18). 'Der Zauberklang des Sozialismus' [newspaper article].
Fuchs, Dieter (1999). 'The democratic culture of unified Germany', in Pippa Norris (ed.). *Critical citizens. Global support for democratic governance.* Oxford: Oxford University Press.
Fülberth, Georg (2008). *Die Linke. "Doch wenn sich die Dinge ändern".* Köln: PapyRossa Verlag.
Fülberth, Georg (1990). *KPD und DKP 1945–1990. Zwei kommunistische Parteien in der vierten Periode kapitalistischer Entwicklung.* Heilbronn: Distel Verlag.
Garms, Heinrich (1994). 'Die Ostdeutsche und Berliner Initiative der Betriebs- und Personalräte – Ein Beispiel sozialer Interessenvertretung im Transformationsprozess', *Umbruch* 8: 18–65.
Gehrke, Bernd (1997). 'Arbeitskämpfe und eigenständige Interessenvertretungen nach 1989', *Sklaven* 32–33: 4–11.
Gehrke, Bernd, and Renate Hürtgen (eds.) (2001). *Der betriebliche Aufbruch im Herbst 1989: die unbekannte Seite der DDR-Revolution.* Berlin: Bildungswerk Berlin der Heinrich Böll Stiftung.
Gerner, Manfred (1994). *Partei ohne Zukunft? Von der SED zur PDS.* München: Tilsner Verlag.
Gerth, Michael (2002). *Die PDS und die ostdeutsche Gesellschaft im Transformationsprozess: Wahlerfolge und politisch-kulturelle Kontinuitäten.* Hamburg: Verlag Dr. Kovac.
Glatzer, Wolfgang (2009). 'Gefühlte (Un)Gerechtigkeit', *Aus Politik und Zeitgeschichte*, 47.
Goedicke, Anne (2003). 'Fachexperten und Leitungskader: Karrieren von Angehörigen der oberen Dienstklasse der DDR nach der Wende', *Historical Social Research* 28(1–2): 247–269.
Gysi, Gregor, and Thomas Falkner (1990). *Sturm aufs Große Haus.* Berlin: Edition Fischerinsel.
Hansen, Mareike, Hannah Schimd, and Helmut Scherer (2010) 'Erstens: ignorieren, zweitens: diffamieren, drittens: umarmen? Eine inhaltsanalytische Untersuchung der Kommentierung der Linkspartei von 2005 bis 2009', *Publizistik* 55(4): 365–381.
Herbst, Andreas, Gerd-Rüdiger Stephan, and Jürgen Winkler (1997). *Die SED. Geschichte – Organisation – Politik. Ein Handbuch.* Berlin: Dietz Verlag.
Heunemann, Falk (2006). Die Kooperation der PDS und der WASG zur Bundestagswahl 2005 [MA thesis]. Jena: Friedrich-Schiller-Universität.
Hildebrandt, Cornelia, and Michael Brie (eds.) (2006). *Die Linke in Regierungsverantwortung. Analysen, Erfahrungen, Kontroversen.* Berlin: Rosa-Luxemburg-Stiftung.
Hildebrandt, Cornelia, and Nelli Tügel (eds.) (2010). *Der Herbst der "Wutbürger". Soziale Kämpfe in Zeiten der Krise.* Berlin: Rosa-Luxemburg-Stiftung.

Hirscher, Gerhard (2001). Jenseits der 'Neuen Mitte': die Annäherung der PDS an die SPD seit der Bundestagswahl 1998 [working paper]. München: Hanns-Seidel-Stiftung.
Hodgin, Nick, and Caroline Pearce (2011). *The GDR remembered: Representations of the East German State since 1989*. New York: Camden House.
Hoff, Benjamin-Immanuel (2014). *Die Linke. Partei neuen Typs? Milieus – Strömungen – Parteireform*. Hamburg: VSA.
Hough, Dan (2010). 'From pariah to prospective partner: The German Left Party's winding path towards government', in Jonathan Olsen, Michael Koß and Dan Hough (eds.). *Left parties in national governments*. Basingstoke: Palgrave MacMillan, 138–154.
Hough, Dan (2002). *The fall and rise of the PDS in Eastern Germany*. Birmingham: University of Birmingham Press.
Hough, Dan, Michael Koß, and Jonathan Olsen (2007). *The Left party in contemporary German politics*. Basingstoke: Palgrave Macmillan.
Hübner, Wolfgang, and Tom Strohschneider (2007). *Lafontaines Linke. Ein Rettungsboot für den Sozialismus?* Berlin: Dietz Verlag.
Jandura, Olaf (2011). 'Publizistische Chancengleichheit in der Wahlkampfberichterstattung? Eine Untersuchung zur medialen Repräsentation der im Bundestag vertretenen Parteien', *Publizistik* 56(2): 181–197.
Jesse, Eckhard (1997). 'SPD and PDS relationships', *German Politics* 6(3): 89–102.
Jesse, Eckhard, and Jürgen P. Lang (2008). *Die Linke – der smarte Extremismus einer deutschen Partei*. München: Olzog Verlag.
Jung, Matthias (1990). 'Parteiensystem und Wahlen in der DDR. Eine Analyse der Volkskammerwahl vom 18. März 1990 und der Kommunalwahlen vom 6. Mai 1990', *Aus Politik und Zeitgeschichte*, 27: 3–15.
Jünke, Christoph (2001). 'Eine kleine Geschichte der linkssozialistischen VSP von 1986 bis 2000', *Trend onlinezeitung* 4. Available at: www.trend.infopartisan.net/trd0401/t130401.html [accessed on 01.4.2016].
Kamenitsa, Lynn (1998). 'The process of political marginalisation: East German social movements after the Wall', *Comparative Politics* 30(3): 313–333.
Keller, Bernd, and Fred Henneberger (1992). 'Der öffentliche Dienst in den neuen Bundesländern: Beschäftigung, Interessenverbände und Tarifpolitik im Übergang', in Volker Eichener, Ralf Kleinfeld, Detlef Pollack, Josef Schmid, Klaus Schubert, and Helmut Voelzkow (eds.). *Organisierte Interessen in Ostdeutschland*. Marburg: Metropolis, 175–194.
Klein, Dieter, and Michael Brie (2007). Elementare Fragen neu bedenken. Kapitalismus, Sozialismus, Eigentum und Wege der Veränderung [working paper]. Berlin: Rosa-Luxemburg-Stiftung.
Klein, Markus, and Jürgen W. Falter (2003). *Der lange Weg der Grünen. Eine Partei zwischen Protest und Regierung*. München: C.H.Beck.
Knabe, Hubertus (2009). *Honeckers Erben. Die Wahrheit über DIE LINKE*. Berlin: Propyläen.
Kohl, Helmut (1990, June 10). Der entscheidende Schritt auf dem Weg in die gemeinsame Zukunft der Deutschen [speech]. Available at: www.chronik-der-mauer.de/index.php/de/Start/Detail/id/593879/page/3 [accessed on 01.04.2016].
Kolisang, Caroline (ed.) (2013). *Bundesweiter Bildungsstreik 2009. Protestbewegung – Aktionismus – Reformen der Reformen*. Wiesbaden: Springer VS.
Krämer, Ralf (2004). Für eine wahlpolitische Alternative 2006 (Version 05.02.2004). [unpublished document].
Kunze, Conrad (2008). Die postsozialistische Transformation der deutschen Elite [working paper]. Halle: Martin-Luther-Universität Halle-Wittenberg.

Lahusen, Christian, and Britta Baumgarten (2006). 'Die Fragilität kollektiven Handelns: Arbeitslosenproteste in Deutschland und Frankreich', *Zeitschrift für Soziologie* 35(2): 102–119.
Land, Rainer (2010). 'Eine demokratische DDR? Das Projekt "Moderner Sozialismus"', *Aus Politik und Zeitgeschichte*, 11: 13–19.
Land, Rainer, and Ralf Possekel (1995a). 'PDS und Moderner Sozialismus', in Michael Brie, Martin Herzig and Thomas Koch (eds.) *Die PDS. Postkommunistische Kaderorganisation, ostdeutscher Traditionsverein oder linke Volkspartei? Empirische Befunde und kontroverse Analysen.* Köln: PapyRossa, 112–130.
Land, Rainer, and Ralf Possekel (1995b). 'On the internal dynamics of the PDS: The Leninist challenge and the challenge to Leninism', *Constellations* 2(1): 51–61.
Lang, Jürgen (2003). *Ist die PDS eine demokratische Partei? Eine extremismustheoretische Untersuchung.* Baden-Baden: Nomos.
Lees, Charles, Dan Hough, and Dan Keith (2010). 'Towards an analytical framework for party mergers: Operationalising the cases of the German Left Party and the Dutch Green Left', *West European Politics* 36(6): 1299–1317.
Lipset, Seymour Martin, and Stein Rokkan (1967). 'Cleavage structures, party systems and voter alignments: An introduction', in Seymour Martin Lipset and Stein Rokkan (eds.). *Party systems and voter alignments: Cross-national perspectives.* New York: The Free Press, 1–64.
Lohmann, Suzanne (1994) 'The dynamics of informational cascades: The Monday demonstrations in Leipzig, East Germany, 1989–91', *World Politics* 41(1): 42–101.
Looding, Matthias, and Uwe Rosenthal (2001). 'Ein Jahrzehnt Gewerkschaftseinheit: ein historischer Rückblick auf Rolle und Strategien des Deutschen Gewerkschaftsbundes und zwei seiner Einzelgewerkschaften im Prozeß staatlicher und gewerkschaftlicher Vereinigung', *Beiträge zur Geschichte der Arbeiterbewegung* 43(4): 3–44.
Mair, Peter (1993). 'Myths of electoral change and the survival of traditional parties', *European Journal of Political Research*, 24(2): 121–133.
McAdams, A. James (2001). *Judging the past in Unified Germany.* Oxford: Oxford University Press.
Mayer, Florian (2006). *Vom Niedergang des unternehmerisch tätigen Staates. Privatisierungspolitik in Großbritannien, Frankreich, Italien und Deutschland.* Wiesbaden: VS Verlag.
Meiers, Franz-Joseph (2010). 'Von der Scheckbuchdiplomatie zur Verteidigung am Hindukusch. Die Rolle der Bundeswehr bei multinationalen Auslandseinsätzen, 1990–2009', *Zeitschrift für Außen- und Sicherheitspolitik* 3(2): 201–222.
Moreau, Patrick (1998). *Die PDS: Profil einer antidemokratischen Partei.* München: Hans-Seidel-Stiftung.
Moreau, Patrick, Jürgen Lang, and Viola Neu (1994). *Was will die PDS?* Berlin: Ullstein.
Meuche-Mäker, Meinhard (2005). *Die PDS im Westen 1990–2005. Schlussfolgerungen für eine neue Linke.* Berlin: Dietz Verlag.
Nachtwey, Oliver (2013). 'Market social democracy: The transformation of the SPD up to 2007', *German Politics* 22(3): 235–252.
Nachtwey, Oliver (2009). 'Die Linke and the crisis of class representation', *International Socialism Journal* 124: 24–28.
Nachtwey, Oliver, and Tim Spier (2007). 'Political opportunity structures and the success of the German Left Party in 2005', *Debatte* 15(2): 123–154.
Neller, Katja, and S. Isabell Thaidigsmann (2002). 'Das Vertretenheitsgefühl der Ostdeutschen durch die PDS: DDR-Nostalgie und andere Erklärungsfaktoren im Vergleich', *Politische Vierteljahresschrift* 43(3): 420–444.

Neu, Viola (2004). *Das Janusgesicht der PDS. Wähler und Partei zwischen Demokratie und Extremismus*. Baden-Baden: Nomos.
Neu, Viola (2001). SPD und PDS auf Bundesebene: Koalitionspartner im Wartestand? [working paper]. Sankt Augustin: Konrad-Adenauer-Stiftung.
Neu, Viola (2000). Am Ende der Hoffnung: die PDS im Westen [working paper]. Sankt Augustin: Konrad-Adenauer-Stiftung.
Neugebauer, Gero, and Richard Stöss (1996). *Die PDS. Geschichte. Organisation. Wähler. Konkurrenten*. Opladen: Leske + Budrich.
Nicoll, Norbert (2005). *Attac Deutschland. Kritik, Stand und Perspektiven*. Marburg: Tectum Verlag.
Nowak, Jörg (2015). 'Union campaigns in Germany directed against inequality: The minimum wage campaign and the Emmely campaign', *Global Labour Journal* 6(3): 366–380.
Olsen, Jonathan (2007). 'The Merger of the PDS and WASG: From Eastern German Regional Party to National Radical Left Party?', *German Politics* 16(2): 205–221.
Olsen, Jonathan (2002). 'The PDS in Western Germany: An empirical study of PDS local politicians', *German Politics* 11(1): 147–172.
Oswald, Franz (2002). *The party that came out of the cold war. The party of democratic socialism in United Germany*. Westport: Greenwood Press.
Patton, David F. (2013). 'The Left Party at six: The PDS-WASG merger in comparative perspective', *German Politics* 22(3): 219–234.
Patton, David F. (2011). *Out of the East. From PDS to Left Party in Unified Germany*. New York: State University of New York Press.
Patton, David F. (2006). 'Germany's Left Party PDS and the "Vacuum Thesis": From regional milieu party to left alternative?', *Journal of Communist Studies and Transition Politics* 22(2): 206–227.
Prinz, Sebastian (2010). *Die programmatische Entwicklung der PDS. Kontinuität und Wandel der Politik einer sozialistischen Partei*. Wiesbaden: VS Verlag.
Raschke, Joachim, and Ralf Tils (2010). 'Die Qual der Wahl: Das Debakel der SPD und strategische Optionen in der Lagerstruktur des deutschen Parteiensystems', *Forschungsjournal Neue Soziale Bewegungen*, 23(1): 11–16.
Riegel, Klaus-Georg (2002). 'Divided commitment: East German socialist intellectuals and their attitudes towards the reunification with West Germany', *Development and society* 31(1): 53–78.
Rink, Dieter, and Axel Phillips (2007). 'Mobilisierungsframes auf den Anti-Hartz-IV-Demonstrationen 2004', *Forschungsjournal Neue Soziale Bewegungen* 20(1): 52–60.
Roesler, Jörg (1994). 'Privatisation in Eastern Germany. Experience with the Treuhand', *Europe-Asia Studies* 46(3): 505–517.
Roesler, Jörg (1991). 'The rise and fall of the planned economy in the German Democratic Republic, 1945–1989', *German History* 9(1): 46–61.
Roose, Jochen (2010). 'Der endlose Streit um die Atomenergie. Konfliktsoziologische Untersuchung einer dauerhaften Auseinandersetzung', in Peter H. Feindt and Thomas Saretzki (eds.). *Umwelt- und Technikkonflikte*. Wiesbaden: VS Verlag, 79–103.
Rose, Richard, and Derek W. Urwin (1970) 'Persistence and change in Western party systems since 1945', *Political Studies*, 18(3): 287–319.
Roth Roland, and Dieter Rucht (eds.) (2008). *Die sozialen Bewegungen in Deutschland seit 1945. Ein Handbuch*. Frankfurt/Main: Campus Verlag.
Rucht, Dieter, and Roland Roth (2008) 'Globalisierungskritische Netzwerke, Kampagnen und Bewegungen', in Roland Roth and Dieter Rucht (eds.). *Die sozialen Bewegungen in Deutschland seit 1945. Ein Handbuch*. Frankfurt/Main: Campus Verlag, 493–512.

Sartori, Giovanni (1976). *Parties and party systems. A framework for analysis*. Cambridge: Cambridge University Press.
Schmidt, Rudi (2003). 'Der gescheiterte Streik in der ostdeutschen Metallindustrie', *PROKLA*, 33(3): 493–509.
Schultze, Thomas, and Almut Gross (1997). *Die Autonomen. Ursprünge, Entwicklung und Profil.* Hamburg: Konkret.
Schulz, Kristina (2008). 'Studentische Bewegungen und Protestkampagnen', in Roland Roth and Dieter Rucht (eds.). *Die sozialen Bewegungen in Deutschland seit 1945. Ein Handbuch.* Frankfurt/Main: Campus Verlag, 417–446.
Segert, Dieter (2009). 'The GDR intelligentsia and its forgotten political role during the Wende of 1989', *Debatte* 17(2): 143–157.
Segert, Dieter (2008). *Das 41. Jahr. Eine andere Geschichte der DDR.* Wien: Böhlau Verlag.
Speth, Rudolf (2006). Navigieren ohne Kompass. Strategiebildung in Parteien und NGOs [working paper]. Frankfurt: Hans-Böckler-Stiftung. Available at: www.rudolf-speth.de/images/pdf/strategiestudie.pdf [accessed on 01.04.2016].
Spiegel (der) (1994, March 28). 'Die Kader regieren mit' [newspaper article].
Spier, Tim (2009). L'impossible alliance: le SPD face à Die Linke [working paper]. Paris: Cerfa.
Spier, Tim, Felix Butzlaff, Matthias Micus, and Franz Walter (eds.) (2007). *Die Linkspartei. Zeitgemäße Idee oder Bündnis ohne Zukunft?* Wiesbaden: VS Verlag.
Solga, Heike (1995). *Auf dem Weg in eine klassenlose Gesellschaft? Klassenlagen und Mobilität zwischen Generationen in der DDR.* Berlin: Akademie Verlag.
Steffen, Michael (2002). Geschichte vom Trüffelschwein – Politik und Organisation des Kommunistischen Bundes 1971 bis 1991 [PhD thesis]. Marburg: Philipps-Universitäts Marburg.
Steiner, André (2010). *The plans that failed: An economic history of the GDR.* New York: Berghahn Books.
Stöss, Richard, and Gero Neugebauer (2002). Mit einem blauen Auge davon gekommen. Eine Analyse der Bundestagswahl 2002 [working paper]. Berlin: Otto-Stammer-Zentrum.
Stöss, Richard, and Gero Neugebauer (1998). Die SPD und die Bundestagswahl 1998. Ursachen und Risiken eines historischen Wahlsiegs unter besonderer Berücksichtigung der Verhältnisse in Ostdeutschland [working paper]. Berlin: Otto-Stammer-Zentrum.
Sturm, Eva (2000). *'Und der Zukunft zugewandt'? Eine Untersuchung zur 'Politikfähigkeit' der PDS.* Opladen: Leske + Budrich Verlag.
Switek, Niko (2010). 'Neue Regierungsbündnisse braucht das Land! Die strategische Dimension der Bildung von Koalitionen', *Zeitschrift für Politikberatung* 3: 177–196.
Thompson, Peter (2005). *The crisis of the German Left. The PDS, Stalinism and the global economy.* Oxford: Berghahn Books.
Timmer, Karsten (2000). *Vom Aufbruch zum Umbruch: die Bürgerbewegungen in der DDR 1989.* Göttingen: Vandenhoeck und Ruprecht.
Vail, Mark I. (2010). *Recasting welfare capitalism. Economic adjustment in contemporary France and Germany.* Philadelphia: Temple University Press.
von Winter, Thomas, and Ulrich Willems (eds.) (2007). *Interessenverbände in Deutschland.* Wiesbaden: VS Verlag.
Walgrave, Stefaan, and Dieter Rucht (2010). *The world says no to war. Demonstrations against the war on Iraq.* Minneapolis: University of Minnesota Press.
Walter, Franz (2011). *Die SPD. Biographie einer Partei.* 2nd ed. Hamburg: Rohwolt Taschenbuch.

Walter, Franz (2007). 'Eliten oder Unterschichten? Die Wähler der Linken', in Tim Spier, Felix Butzlaff, Matthias Micus and Franz Walter (eds.). *Die Linkspartei. Zeitgemäße Idee oder Bündnis ohne Zukunft?* Wiesbaden: VS Verlag, 325–337.

Weitz, Eric D. (1997). *Creating German communism, 1890–1990. From popular protests to socialist state*. Princeton, NJ: Princeton University Press.

Wiesenthal, Helmut (2003). 'German unification and "model Germany": An adventure in institutional conservatism', *West European Politics* 26(4): 37–58.

Wiesenthal, Helmut (1998). 'Post-unification dissatisfaction, or why are so many East Germans unhappy with the new political system', *German Politics* 7(2): 1–30.

Wilke, Manfred, and Hans-Peter Müller (1991). *Zwischen Solidarität und Eigennutz. Die Gewerkschaften des DGB im deutschen Vereinigungsprozeß*. Melle: Verlag Ernst Knoth.

Winkler, Gunnar (2010). *Zur Geschichte der Volkssolidarität 1945 bis 2010*. Berlin: Volkssolidarität Bundesverband e.V.

Wollmann, Hellmut (1996). 'Institutionenbildung in Ostdeutschland: Neubau, Umbau und "schöpferische Zerstörung"', in Max Kaase, Andreas Eisen, Oscar W. Gabriel, Oskar Niedermayer and Hellmut Wollmann (eds.). *Politisches System*. Opladen: Leske + Budrich, 47–105.

5 The Italian radical left
The story of a failure

The contemporary Italian radical left inherited only a fraction of the pre-1989 strength of the Italian Communist Party, but its subsequent development made it a far from marginal force within Italian and European politics. On the one hand, its electoral strength fluctuated around mid-range levels, but was big enough to make it a vital element for the formation of centre-left majorities and entrusted it with a disproportionate amount of governmental strength at both regional and national levels. On the other hand, its major party, the Party of Communist Refoundation, played an important role in the transnational coordination of the contemporary radical left, both within the Party of the European Left (2004–present) and within the alter-globalist movement (1999–2004).[1] Despite its promising beginnings, however, the Italian radical left failed to consolidate its positions and progressively fell prey to fragmentation, strategic helplessness, and political marginality.

The discussion is structured as follows. First, I briefly introduce the historical context in which the parties 'new' Italian radical left emerged and had to operate. Secondly, I track more in detail the evolution of their systemic strength, cohesion, and political nature. Thirdly, I explain the remarkably high levels of radical left fragmentation with the specificities of the Italian bipolarism. Fourthly, I analyse the validity of the 'vacuum thesis' with reference to the Italian case. I show that radical left growth unquestionably relied on the neoliberal turn of established parties and the resulting vacuum of political representation of working-class and welfarist interests. However, structural factors heavily constrained this expansion and ultimately reversed it. Fifthly, I assess the strategies of the main radical left organisations, showing each of them failed to noticeably influence either the social balance of force, state policies, and the dynamics of political competition. Finally, I summarise and discuss the main findings.

The analysis is based on a large amount of primary evidence. Due to space constraints, references in the text are generally limited to the secondary literature. Primary data, together with sources, notes, and elaborations, are accessible through the Western European Radical Left Database (Chiocchetti 2016).

The national context

The Italian context since 1989 was characterised by wide-ranging economic and political shifts, to which the Italian radical left struggled to respond adequately.

The four main developments concerned the weakening of Italian capitalism, the neoliberalisation of public policy, the transformation of the political system, and the progressive shift of the Italian Communist Party from Eurocommunism to an American-style left-of-the-centre party. While each of these four trends represented a dramatic setback for traditional left-wing interests and values, the reconstituted radical left that emerged from the ruins of the pre-1989 communist and far-left traditions could reasonably expect to benefit from them. These hopes were not entirely unfounded, but proved to be overly optimistic. A vacuum of political representation of working-class and welfarist interests indeed materialised, but the Italian radical left failed to durably exploit it.

The starting point in the late eighties was a radical left that remained very strong but was afflicted by a deep identity crisis. Unlike all other communist parties in Western Europe, the Partito Comunista Italiano (Italian Communist Party, PCI) withstood the decade with relative grace. Despite a strong decline since its historical peak in 1976, by 1987 the party could still boast more than 10 million votes (26.6 per cent), 1.5 million members, a strong network of subcultural organisations (such as the trade union CGIL, the cooperative federation Legacoop, and the recreational federation ARCI), and an important presence in regional and local governments (in the 'red regions' of Central Italy and in some other big cities). Its crisis was less a material one than one of identity (Agosti 2000; Lazar 1992; Magri 2013; Morando 2010; Vittoria 2006). In 1989–91, the party leadership seized the opportunity of the fall of the Eastern bloc, renamed itself Partito Democratico della Sinistra (Democratic Party of the Left, PDS), and abandoned communism and the radical left for a broadly social-democratic orientation. This bold move was a unique example within the Western European radical left, as the historical weakness and ultimate collapse of Italian reformist socialism offered an opportunity that was barred elsewhere (comparable cases can be found among Eastern European former ruling parties). The Italian far left galaxy, in turn, lost the mass dimension and influence it had enjoyed in the seventies (Balestrini and Moroni 1997; Bianchi and Caminiti 2007, 2008; Gambetta 2010), but remained one of the strongest in Europe (Billi 1996; Moroni et al. 1996; Pucciarelli 2011). Democrazia Proletaria (Proletarian Democracy, DP) had in 1987 641,901 voters (1.7 per cent), 9,153 members, and an independent parliamentary representation, while a subculture of workerist, autonomist, and Marxist groups remained active in squats, universities, and workplaces. The ideological crisis was, however, visible in these quarters as well, with extra-parliamentary groups drifting toward lifestyle politics and half of DP splitting in 1989–90 toward the Greens.

Against this background, a variety of sensibilities in the left wing of and to the left of the old PCI converged in 1991 in the Partito della Rifondazione Comunista (Party of the Communist Refoundation, PRC) (Bertolino 2004, 2008; Cannavò 2009; Dalmasso 2002; De Nardis 2009; Dormagen 1996; Favilli 2011; Valentini 2000). The neo-communist party immediately rose to the status of significant political player, winning 2,201,482 votes (5.6 per cent) and 117,551 members in 1992. It was, however, soon faced with a dilemma that would determine its entire subsequent evolution: should it join the emerging centre-left pole of the bipolar competition, or should it try to build an anti-neoliberal third pole? The PRC was unable to find a satisfactory solution. It constantly oscillated between the two options, losing credibility and votes during its experiences of governmental participation (1996–98; 2006–08), suffering debilitating splits when it opted for an intransigent course, and collapsing in 2007–10, with only a rump organisation surviving afterwards.

The organisations that emerged from these travails sought to solve the contradictions of the PRC, but failed as well. Right-wing splits remained small, hovering at best around 2–3 per cent of valid votes, and were in time either absorbed by the moderate left or forced back into a more confrontational stance. The Movimento dei Comunisti Unitary (Movement of Unitary Communists, MCU), established in 1995, soon merged into the DS. The Partito dei Comunisti Italiani (Party of the Italian Communists, PdCI), established in 1998 (Bordandini and Di Virgilio 2007; Cossu 2004), also collapsed and split in 2008–09, shifting to a more confrontational course and rebranding in 2014 as Partito Comunista d'Italia (Communist Party of Italy, PCd'I). Sinistra Ecologia Libertà (Left Ecology Freedom, SEL), established in 2009 from the convergence of a variety of splinter organisations (Bordandini 2013; Damiani 2013), gradually emerged as the main radical left player and in 2013 regained parliamentary representation through an alliance with the PD. Ironically, however, it soon found itself back to square one, as the very idea of a centre-left alliance was buried by its partner and the party was forced into an increasingly vocal opposition to seating 'grand coalition' governments. Left-wing splits, in turn, were frequent, but never really took off, due to the relatively high number of signatures required to run for election and the periodic return of their larger competitors to a more confrontational stance.[2] Far-left organisations not connected with the PRC, finally, were also small and exclusively extra-parliamentary.[3]

A simplified diagram of these evolutions is depicted in Figure 5.1. Altogether, the trajectory of the Italian radical left began with an initial phase of growth around the PRC (1992–96), proceeded with a long period of ample oscillations of the couple PRC and PdCI (1997–2007), and ended with a final phase of unprecedented weakness and fragmentation (2008–present).

The new Italian radical left

A more detailed analysis of the evolution of the systemic strength, cohesion, and nature of the contemporary Italian radical left underscores both its similarities and peculiarities compared to the rest of the Western European party family.

Strength

The evolution of the systemic strength of the Italian radical left in the period 1992–95 is summarised in Table 5.1 and Figure 5.2. Like its German counterpart, this can be shown to occupy a medium-small space of about 5 per cent. Its trajectory was broadly parabolic, moving from an initial period of growth after 1992, through oscillations at relatively high levels after 1997, to a final period of crisis since 2008.

126 *The Italian radical left*

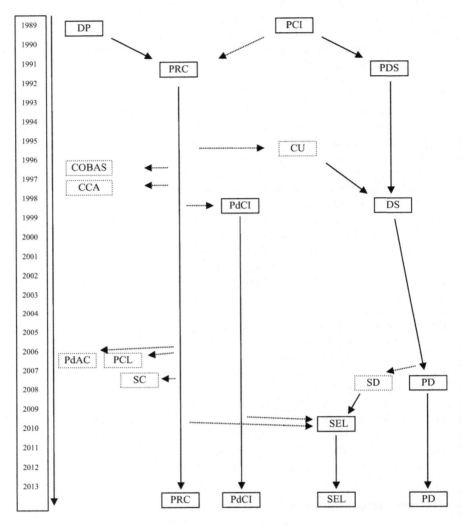

Figure 5.1 Family tree of the Italian post-communist left

Electoral strength averaged 6.4 per cent over the period 1992–2015. It initially fell from 26.9 per cent in 1990 (PCI and DP) to 1.5 per cent in 1991 (DP). It then steadily grew to 8.4 per cent in 1996, as the PRC gradually stood for election at all levels and increased its vote shares. It then fell to 6.7 per cent in 2001, but recovered to 7.9 per cent in 2006. Finally, after 2008 it dipped catastrophically. While formal levels remained between 4.8 and 5.6 per cent, the strength of groups issued from the PRC can be estimated below 4 per cent, with the rest covered by previously extraneous forces that joined at one time or the other the radical left in various electoral coalitions (Verdi, IdV, and DS/PD splinter groups).

Table 5.1 Strength, Italian radical left

	AVERAGE 1992–2015 RESOURCES	AVERAGE 1992–2015 SYSTEMIC STRENGTH
1 ELECTORAL	votes	%
Composite (nat 70 / reg 30)		6.36
National – Camera	2,421,636	6.45
Regional	1,836,566	6.14
2 PARLIAMENTARY	seats	%
Composite (nat 70 / reg 30)		4.32
National – Camera	27.7	4.40
National – Senato	10.3	3.28
Regional	57.4	5.44
3 GOVERNMENTAL		%
Composite (nat 70 / reg 30)		3.90
National – Camera		3.40
National – Senato		2.77
Regional		5.80
4 MEMBERSHIP	members	%
	111,857	6.41
FINANCIAL		medium-weak
COMMUNICATION		medium-weak
CIVIL SOCIETY		medium-weak
OVERALL STRENGTH		%
Composite (average 1 to 4)		5.25

Parliamentary strength was substantially lower, averaging 4.3 per cent. It fell from 28.7 per cent in 1990 to 2.2 per cent in 1991, grew to 5.8 per cent in 1995, declined to a low point of 3.5 per cent in 2002, rose to an extraordinary 11.7 per cent in 2007, dipped again to 1.2 per cent in 2012, and recovered to 3.7 per cent in 2015. Three factors account for these discrepancies. First, the electoral legislation strongly penalised smaller and non-aligned forces, but these effects could be mitigated and reversed with a strategy of centre-left alliances. Secondly, the increased fragmentation of the radical left led to many instances of reduced or absent representation, most spectacularly in the 2008 general election. Thirdly, the low faithfulness of Italian elected representatives led to continuous flows of defections to and from the radical left, particularly in 1991 (from PCI to PRC) and 2007 (from DS to the SD splinter group).

Governmental strength was the most dynamic of all dimensions. Its average level was low (3.9 per cent), but its peaks were notable. In the context of a tight bipolar competition, the contribution of the radical left was often indispensable

128 *The Italian radical left*

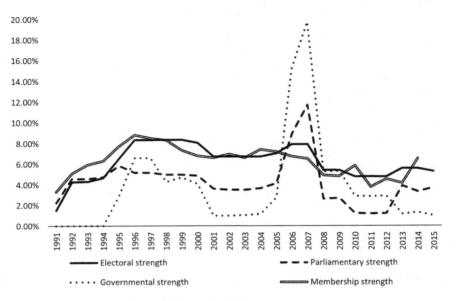

Figure 5.2 Strength evolution, Italian radical left

to ensure the formation of centre-left governmental majorities. Although many leftists were opposed to a centre-left alliance, which they deemed to inevitably be subservient to neoliberal ideology and centrist parties, this did not prevent a growing governmental involvement. Composite governmental strength went up from 0.0 per cent in 1994 to 6.6 per cent in 1996, fell back to 1.0 per cent in 2001, rose to 19.7 per cent in 2007, collapsed to 2.9 per cent in 2010, and slowly declined to 1.0 per cent in 2015. At the national level, radical left organisations supported six cabinets: Dini in 1995–96 (MCU); Prodi I in 1996–98 (PRC); D'Alema I, D'Alema II and Amato II in 1998–2001 (PdCI); Prodi II in 2006–08 (PRC, PdCI, and SD). National governmental weight thus peaked at 8.2 per cent in 1996 and at 23.2 per cent in 2007. Moreover, the boundaries between opposition and external support were often blurry: both the PRC toward Dini and far-left dissidents toward Prodi II behaved as opposition parties, but usually sought to ensure the cabinet's survival in confidence votes through a variety of parliamentary tactics. At the regional level, the radical left directly participated in countless cabinets after 1995. The peak was reached in 2009, with a regional governmental strength of 17.7 per cent, a coverage of over two-thirds of the Italian population, and the presidency of the Puglia region (with Nichi Vendola, PRC then SEL).

Membership strength broadly followed electoral results, averaging 6.4 per cent of the total party membership. In relative terms, it rose from 3.3 per cent in 1991 to 8.8 per cent in 1996, oscillated around 7 per cent until 2006, fell to 4.1 per cent in 2013, and rose again to 6.5 per cent in 2014. This was due not so much to specific efforts, but rather to the wild evolution of the membership of other parties, which more than halved in 1990–95, boomed in 2006–11, and halved again afterwards. In absolute terms, radical left membership remained fairly stable around 120,000 members from 1991 to 2007 and then slowly declined, reaching a trough of 63,992 members in 2014.

Further dimensions cannot be quantified with precision. Financial data are available but incomplete, covering only a small portion of total party incomes. It can be assumed that radical left financial strength generally moved at a level between its electoral and parliamentary strength, the two major sources of funds. In absolute terms, it rose until 2007 and collapsed afterwards, constraining in a major way party activities.[4] Communication strength was also probably similar to parliamentary strength. Party-owned communication channels were weak, but exposure in the mass media was relatively good, although uneven (stronger for parties within centre-left alliances, weaker for independent forces) and often with a negative bias. Finally, civil society strength was paradoxically one of the weakest points of radical left parties. Despite the central role of the PRC in the alter-globalist and pacifist mobilisations of the 1999–2004 period, the direct influence of card-carrying radical left members within civil society and social movement organisations was negligible. Generally speaking, the leadership and cadres of traditional mass organisations remained solidly aligned with their usual (post-communist and Christian democratic) political referents. A subordinate role was played by 'critical currents' that were programmatically quite close to the radical left, but generally opted for a continued political allegiance to the PDS/DS/PD.

In conclusion, the trajectory of radical left societal weight can be usefully divided in three distinct sequences.

A first ascending period (1991–97) covered the emergence of the PRC under the 'First Republic' and its consolidation under the 'Second Republic'. The party cultivated an image of externality and antagonism toward the rest of the political system while duly participating to left-wing (1994) and centre-left (1996) alliances geared at defeating the right. The victory of the latter and the creation of the first organic centre-left cabinet of the Second Republic (Prodi I, 1996–2001), which the PRC supported externally, rapidly highlighted the ambiguity of the party's positioning and increased the centrifugal pressures on it, leading to the crisis of 1998 and the opening of a new phase.

The second period (1998–2007) was characterised by a significant organisational fragmentation, pro-cyclical oscillations at high levels, and a growing integration within the centre-left. The radical left space was now occupied by two main organisations (PRC and PdCI), which lost weight while in office and recovered it while in opposition to right-wing governments. The PdCI was from the start a loyal partner of the centre-left. The PRC, despite the apparent intransigent turn of 1998–2003, did not resist the political and material incentives provided by centre-left alliances and was also increasingly involved in regional and national governmental participations.

The third period (2008–present), finally, was characterised by an overall lack of influence and existential uncertainty. The electoral defeats of 2008–10 led to a permanent loss of resources and coherence, which were never truly recovered.

Cohesion

As already remarked, the Italian radical left followed a path of increasing organisational fragmentation. A visual representation of this evolution (national level only) is provided in Figure 5.3.

From 1991 to 1997, one neo-communist organisation (the PRC) completely dominated, despite a number of small and short-lived splits to the right (MCU) and to the left (COBAS and CCA). The years from 1998 to 2006 saw a sustained competition between two neo-communist parties, the more modern and radical PRC and the more traditionalist and conciliatory PdCI. A third phase (2007–13) was characterised by a simultaneous splintering of existing parties and frantic but ultimately unsuccessful attempts toward unity. In 2006–07, a number of small left-wing currents left the parties in protest against the experience of governmental participation (PCL, PdAC, SC, and PBC). At the same time, the traditional radical left (PRC and PdCI), the ecologists, and Sinistra Democratica (Democratic Left, SD) – an important split of the DS – converged in the electoral cartel La Sinistra – l'Arcobaleno (The Left – The Rainbow, SA). In 2008–09, the SA cartel collapsed, with half of its participants giving birth to a new unified party (SEL) and the other half regaining their organisational autonomy (the 'rump' PRC, PdCI, and Verdi).

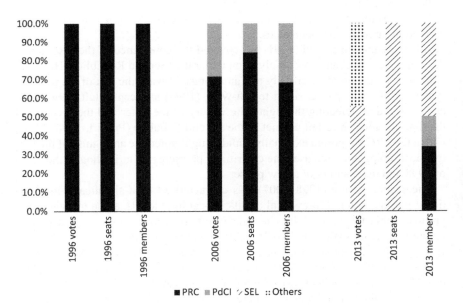

Figure 5.3 Fragmentation (national level), Italian radical left

While SEL managed to acquire a certain stability and coherence, the other groups further declined and lost themselves in a whirlwind of short-lived electoral alliances: the Federazione della Sinistra (Federation of the Left, FdS) between PRC and PdCI in 2008–12; and Rivoluzione Civile (Civic Revolution, RC) between the two latter parties, Verdi, and various fragments issued from the left-liberal IdV in 2013. Since 2014, finally, efforts toward a reunification of the whole radical left picked up speed, but have not resulted in clear progress yet. The moderate turn of Renzi's PD pushed the traditional radical left closer and led to the creation of new splinter groups, such as Fassina's Futuro a Sinistra (Future to the Left, FaS) and Civati's Possibile (Possible). However, political divergences and organisational jealousies have so far prevented a stable convergence. On the one hand, the electoral coalition L'Altra Europa con Tsipras (The Other Europe with Tsipras, AET) succeeded in presenting a united front at the European and several regional elections, but was marred by conflicts between SEL and the other partners and never evolved toward a unitary subject. On the other hand, the recent project of an enlarged SEL, with the provisional name of Sinistra Italiana (Italian Left, SI) has been met with scepticism by many of the existing organisations.

This fragmentation was not necessarily damaging from the point of view of electoral results, but severely limited the institutional and extra-parliamentary influence of the radical left.

Nature

The nature of the Italian radical left followed the normal Western European patterns of anti-neoliberal renewal, with two specificities: a strong, although poorly defined, communist identity; and a high level of internal conflict between intransigent and conciliatory wings which was heightened by the specificities of Italian bipolarism.

Ideologically, the Italian radical left continuously oscillated between the legacy of twentieth-century communism and the pursuit of a more modern radical left worldview.

In terms of identity, traditionalism and innovation coexisted in an uneasy mixture. On the one hand, an intense emotional reaction to the shelving of the communist identity by the leadership of the old PCI in 1989–91 had been at the heart of the establishment of the PRC (Dormagen 1996, 1998) and conditioned its whole subsequent development, provoking strong resistances to attempts to contaminate it with other traditions (such as non-violence in the early noughties) or dilute it into broader organisational vehicles (such as SA and SEL in the late noughties). On the other hand, what communism actually meant was not at all clear. The early PRC welcomed a broad range of Ingraians, Togliattians, Marxist-Leninists, Trotskyists, left-socialists, post-operaists, and left-libertarians, whose positions on the matter differed widely. Moreover, radical left activists agreed that communism was in need of a 'refoundation', but this task was rarely taken seriously. In the end, parties concentrated on short-term tactical and policy issues and ideological elaboration remained superficial, with some groups reviving pretty traditional forms of Togliattism (PdCI) or Trotskyism (PCL), others simply juxtaposing heterogeneous references (PRC), and some ultimately abandoning any anti-capitalist perspective (SEL). Finally, the communist label and symbols represented an obstacle for projects of broader radical left regroupment, but retained a strong emotional value for a core constituency: their progressive abandonment since 2008 favoured unity, but certainly contributed to the electoral losses of the period.

In terms of long-term goals, anti-capitalism was initially retained as the fundamental aim of the parties, but played little role in their internal and public life and was partly abandoned in recent years. Until the late noughties, all parties maintained a clear formal reference to the overcoming of capitalism and to the attainment of a future socialist or communist society in their statutes and programmatic documents: for the PRC, 'the transformation of capitalist society in order to achieve the liberation of women and men through the establishment of a communist society'; for the PdCI, the 'fight for socialism and communism'; for the PCL, the 'achievement of communism as a superior form of civilisation'.[5] As in most of the contemporary radical left thinking, however, the exact contours of the anti-capitalist project and its links with day-to-day political activity remained unclear. Since 2008, this perspective was increasingly superseded by a more straightforward anti-neoliberal one. SEL, in particular, merely advocated a generic 'alternative to modern capitalism' in the form of a '"social" market economy', while many of the new allies attracted by the radical left completely bypassed the question of socialism.

In terms of medium-term goals, the Italian radical left pursued an eclectic yet coherent assemblage of Keynesian, welfarist, workerist, and left-libertarian themes that pointed to a break with neoliberalism and turn toward progressive policies. In this field, what distinguished individual parties was not so much real programmatic disagreements but rather their acknowledgement of external constraints: thus, the acceptance of centre-left alliances and the EU framework progressively forced them to moderate and fudge their demands, turning from a full-blown 'New Deal' package in the early nineties to vague redistributive proposals in the mid-noughties.

Sociologically, the Italian radical left retained a focus on a broad welfarist coalition of active wageworkers and other welfarist allies (Table 5.2). The relative backwardness of Italian society was reflected in several elements of the structure of the electorate, such as the high number of female homemakers, pensioners, self-employed, and unemployed, the low educational levels, and the high levels of religiosity. Consequently, wageworkers made up barely half of the radical left voters and members, and employed 'core' wageworkers (excluding the middle management and the unemployed) less than 40 per cent. While blue-collar workers remained strongly over-represented, the centre of gravity further shifted over time from the lower working-class strata to other social groups: the inactive; relatively well-off groups such as teachers, civil servants, and professionals; the highly-educated but economically weak youth precariat; and critical intellectuals and professionals. The geography of the radical left vote inherited from the PCI strong results in the 'red area' of Central Italy and weak results in the 'white area' of Northeast Italy, but the share of the Centre-South grew constantly. Another

Table 5.2 Sociology, Italian radical left

	ITALIAN ELECT. 1996	RL VOTERS 1996	RL MEMBERS 1999	ITALIAN ELECT. 2006	RL VOTERS 2006	RL MEMBERS 2006
AREA						
North-West	26.0	26.8	19.9	26.2	26.5	18.4
North-East	11.5	7.8	6.5	11.6	8.1	6.4
Red area	17.3	23.1	27.8	17.4	22.0	27.2
Centre-South	45.2	42.3	45.5	44.8	43.4	47.8
GENDER						
Male	50.2	54.9	73.5	48.9	56.4	69.2
Female	49.8	45.1	26.5	51.1	43.6	30.8
AGE						
<25	13.4	20.6	10.2	11.9	15.8	12.0
25–64	74.4	74.3	70.7	68.7	71.3	70.9
>64	12.2	5.1	19.0	19.4	12.9	17.2
CLASS						
Wageworker	41.9	50.9	50.0	42.6	51.0	46.1
White-collar	19.5	21.2	17.8	21.4	22.0	22.4
Blue-collar	14.1	22.3	22.5	12.5	19.0	16.1
Unemployed	8.3	7.4	9.7	8.7	10.0	7.6
Employer and self-employed	12.5	6.9	8.2	12.8	9.0	10.4
Inactive	45.6	42.3	41.8	44.6	40.0	43.6
Pensioner	20.4	12.0	29.9	24.0	21.0	25.2
Student	9.2	16.0	9.3	6.2	9.0	14.2
Other	16.1	14.3	2.6	14.4	10.0	4.2
EDUCATION						
Below secondary	70.0	68.0	66.6	54.3	47.6	49.5
Secondary	23.2	25.1	31.2	35.8	40.6	37.8
Tertiary	7.8	6.9	7.2	9.9	11.9	12.8
RELIGION						
Practicing Catholic	57.1	30.8		50.0	33.3	
Non-practicing Catholic	34.3	41.4		42.6	53.9	
Other religion	0.9	2.4		3.0	4.9	
No religion	7.7	25.4		4.4	7.8	

peculiarity was the strong results among students and the youth, which seemed to bode well for the long-term development of the Italian radical left but did not prevent the post-2008 collapse among senior citizens and the working-age population.

Organisationally, the Italian radical left emerged in 1991 virtually from scratch. It therefore completely bypassed the typical features and tendencies of twentieth-century communist mass parties and broadly followed a 'modern cadre party' model (Bertolino 2004; Bordandini 2013; Bordandini and Di Virgilio 2007; Calossi 2007; PRC 2007; Transform! Italia 2004). More specifically: a predominantly territorial structure instead of a mixed structure based on territorial branches and workplace cells; a vibrant tendency-based internal democracy instead of democratic centralism (with the exception of the PdCI); a stratarchical autonomy of territorial (local federations) and functional (the party in public office) structures instead of the concentration of power in the hands of the central office; a personalised style of leadership around charismatic figures such as Fausto Bertinotti (PRC) and Nichi Vendola (SEL) instead of a collegial/bureaucratic style (Calise 2010; Damiani 2011; Gerbaudo 2011; Newell 2010); a strong dependence from the state (party financing) and external actors (the mass media, professional consultants); and weak organisational linkages through collateral or sympathising mass organisations.

This had both positive and negative long-term consequences. On the positive side, the Italian radical left remained organisationally flexible and attractive, as attested by the ability of each party to win an adequate initial membership (PRC in 1991, PdCI in 1999, and SEL in 2009), continuously refill its ranks with new and young members, and escape the general tendency of European parties to age and shrink. On the negative side, party membership was comparatively low, the radical left was initially dwarfed by the PDS, with clear consequences in terms of electoral results and civil society links, and its weak cohesion encouraged splits of minority tendencies and the autonomisation and defection of its elected representatives.

Relatively viable until 2007, the parties were hit hard by the post-2008 crisis and survived as mere shadows of their former selves. This led to experiments pushing the boundaries of the party-form, such as 'personal' primary election committees in SEL (Damiani 2011; Romano 2009), a clear separation of roles between the extra-parliamentary party and broader electoral coalitions in the PRC, and forms of assembly and internet democracy. None of them, however, could solve the problems of the radical left, which essentially derived from its political orientation and identity rather than from its modes of organisation.

Strategically, the chickens came home to roost. All parties shared a similar analysis of the conjuncture, characterised by an unfavourable balance of forces between classes, the predominance of neoliberal policies, and a rapid rightward drift and bipolarisation of the Italian political system. They decried the course of the PDS/DS/PD, and saw in it an opportunity to reclaim for themselves the traditional redistributive and welfarist themes once expounded by the PCI. Finally, they generally believed that an appropriate mix of electoral, parliamentary, and extra-parliamentary pressures could stop and reverse these trends, leading in the medium term to a successful turn toward anti-neoliberal policies. However, the identification of the correct strategy and tactics to reach this goal remained controversial.

Most of the radical left, while strongly critical of the orientation of the moderate left, nevertheless believed that a *strategy of leftward pull* could in time lead to its 're-social democratisation'. Only minority groups such as the PCL insisted to see it as an inevitable adversary, advocating the construction of an autonomous anti-capitalist pole and refusing any collaboration.

More importantly, however, opinions differed on the attitude toward electoral and parliamentary tactics. Left-wing currents advocated a *semi-intransigent stance* toward the moderate left, refusing direct governmental participation and envisaging at best limited electoral agreements and weak forms of parliamentary support. Right-wing currents advocated instead a *conciliatory stance*, believing that the building of centre-left alliances was required to defeat the right and might offer important room for manoeuvre. The central majority of cadres, members, and voters aimlessly oscillated between these two poles.

All options, however, proved unstable and ineffective. The (actual and potential) radical left constituency was traversed by contradictory tendencies, with a strong disgust toward the politics of moderate left coexisting with a deep-seated fear toward the right-wing coalition led by Silvio Berlusconi. Thus, radical left supporters warmed up to centre-left alliances during periods of seating right-wing governments, but regularly ended up bitterly disappointed by the record of resulting centre-left governments. In addition, the choice for a conciliatory or an intransigent stance inevitably led to splits by dissenting tendencies. The PRC sought to respond to this situation with a middle course of 'radicalism and unity', but degenerated into a progressive loss of strength and political coherence. Intransigent splits (COBAS and CCA in 1996–97; PdAC, PCL, and SC in 2006–08) initially seemed to have some room for manoeuvre, but were regularly wrong-footed by the prompt return of the PRC in the opposition. The position of conciliatory splits (MCU in 1995; PdCI in 1998; SEL in 2009), on the other hand, was unsustainable in the long term: these organisations were gradually weakened by their association with the centre-left, and ultimately had to choose between being absorbed or revert to a more militant stance.

Summary

The contemporary Italian radical left emerged in 1991 from the convergence within the PRC of diverse currents opposed to the mutation of the Italian Communist Party. The rapid rightward drift of the political system sustained its growth until 1997, but the majoritarian shift of the electoral legislation and the consolidation of a pattern of bipolar competition progressively constrained its options. The PRC sought to navigate a narrow course between the need for a clear anti-neoliberal orientation and strong pressures toward centre-left alliances, but progressively fragmented into a number of competing organisations. Altogether, the radical left remained relatively strong between 1995 and 2007, but collapsed to a state of semi-marginality after 2008.

Overall systemic strength averaged 5.25 per cent, close to the median level of the Western European radical left. One remarkable aspect lay in its membership, which was quite dynamic and broadly followed its electoral vicissitudes. Another lay in its governmental strength, with relatively high levels of involvement at the regional level and a surprisingly high overall peak in 2007 (19.7 per cent).

Cohesion was quite low and followed a declining path. The initial dominance of the PRC was challenged after 1998 by the presence of a smaller competitor (PdCI) and ended after 2008 in a confused whirlwind of challenges and regroupment projects, with SEL gradually emerging as the largest group.

The political nature of the Italian radical left, finally, broadly conformed to the general reinvention of the Western European party family as an anti-neoliberal force, but struggled more than other countries with typical dilemmas on identity and strategy.

Explaining radical left fragmentation

Like its Western European counterparts, the Italian radical left was characterised by two intrinsic political tensions. The first and major one concerned the question of the relationship with the moderate left. The programmatic gulf was huge and never ceased to grow, as the two families advocated diametrically opposite solutions to the problems of the country, be it on macro-economic and fiscal policy, economic dirigisme, welfare reform, redistribution, institutional issues, and foreign policy. Therefore, attempts to govern together (1995–96, 1996–98, 1998–2001, and 2006–08) were brief, conflictual, and almost farcical, with the moderate left efficiently pursuing the bulk of its programme while the radical left screamed on the sidelines, trying to mitigate the scope and pace of neoliberal reforms or spin them in a more favourable light. At the same time, a number of reasons encouraged the pursuit of some form of understanding: *lesser evilism*, the fear of a right-wing coalition that was exaggeratedly presented as a mortal danger for the working class and for democracy; *damage reduction*, the effort to exert a constraining influence on centre-left policies; and *long-term strategic calculations*, in which an alliance was seen as an important stepping stone toward a gradual change of heart and 're-social democratisation' of the moderate left.

The second and minor one concerned the choice between ideological and organisational self-sufficiency and radical left regroupment. On the one hand, the communist identity of the PRC was to a certain extent an obstacle in winning over potential allies, but the adoption of a generic 'left' identity (as most organisations did after 2008) clashed with the founding myth of the party, questioning its initial battle against the name change of the Italian Communist Party. On the other hand, the dialogue between rival radical left organisations and tendencies was made difficult by the past history of clashes and by existing political differences and organisational jealousies.

What made these dilemmas intractable was the tremendous pressure exerted by the political system.

First, the majoritarian electoral laws in place from 1993 to 2014 strongly encouraged the establishment of a bipolar competition between two broad and heterogeneous centre-left and centre-right alliances (Fusaro 2009).[6] Parties opting for a non-aligned course had to face medium-sized electoral thresholds, brutal losses in terms of seats, and justified accusations of playing a spoiler role against their less distant competitors. In turn, even tiny organisations could gain representation by joining one of the larger coalitions, either as hosts in the electoral lists of their allies or through lower electoral thresholds (after 2005). Not surprisingly, the number and weight of non-aligned forces in the far left, far right, and centre of the political spectrum steadily declined from 1992 to 2006, before picking up steam again after 2008 thanks to the delegitimation of traditional parties and coalitions due to the economic crisis, legal scandals, infightings, and 'grand coalition' governments.

Secondly, the weakness of the moderate left made the contribution of the radical left vital both for electoral victory and for the parliamentary survival of a centre-left government. As a result, the Italian radical left could not afford itself the luxury of mobilising on its own themes while postponing its parliamentary choices to future circumstances and negotiations. If it wanted to prevent a right-wing victory, it had to join pre-electoral centre-left alliances with a common programme and partly common lists, and offer an unambiguous parliamentary support to the resulting government, at least in confidence votes. A refusal of doing this, in turn, automatically meant electoral defeats and cabinet crises.

Thirdly, the centre-left consciously exploited this situation to divide and weaken the radical left. On the one hand, it continuously encouraged conciliatory splits from the PRC with the promise of substantial parliamentary and governmental offices (MCU in 1995, PdCI in 1998, SEL in 2009, and other splinter groups in 2008 and 2014). On the other hand, it intermittently tried to solve the problem of unreliable radical left allies at its roots. In 2001 and 2008, when its electoral defeat was all but certain, it refused any alliance with the radical left and sought to downsize it with appeals to tactical voting; the second attempt was successful, determining a temporary loss of parliamentary representation (2008–13). In 1999 and 2000, it supported referendums on the abolition of the proportional part of the electoral law (25 per cent of seats), which narrowly failed due to low participation. In a later phase, finally, it pushed for a shift from a bipolar to a two-party political competition, through the unification of most centre-left forces in the Democratic Party (Bordandini et al. 2008), a failed electoral referendum in 2009, and a new electoral law in 2015, which automatically attributes 54 per cent of the seats to the most voted list (in the first round if it reaches at least 40 per cent of the votes, in the second round otherwise).

The inevitable consequence of these preconditions was a growing fragmentation and organisational instability of the radical left. On the one hand, the PRC progressively splintered in a number of competing organisations, which in turn later suffered further divisions. In all cases, the main dividing line was the question of the attitude toward the centre-left alliance, with cultural differences and organisational jealousies further complicating the picture.

On the other hand, the numerous attempts to carry out processes of radical left regroupment between 1998 and 2013 failed for the same reasons.[7] Although radical left organisations (PRC, PdCI, SEL, and other minor groups), left-wing factions of the PDS/DS/PD, the Verdi, and sections of the left-wing organised civil society all shared broadly similar anti-neoliberal values and programmes, their unity was impossible as long as some remained within the framework of a centre-left coalition and others outside of it. From 1998 to 2003, the hostility between the PRC and the centre-left prevented any progress on this front. From 2004 to 2007, when the PRC joined the centre-left alliance and later the Prodi II government, regroupment *within the centre-left* became for the first time feasible. Nevertheless, a successful merger was delayed by lingering strategic differences (with the PRC strongly conflicted about its recent turn, and far left splinter groups squarely opposing it), organisational jealousies (with the leading role of the PRC challenged by other partners), and identity issues (with strong resistances to the disappearance of communist and ecologist markers under a generic 'left' label). A hurried forced unity was finally reached in 2008 with the creation of the Rainbow Left electoral cartel, as the radical left organisations were wrong-footed by the call of early elections and the option of Veltroni's PD for a narrow coalition excluding them. This settlement, however, fell apart soon afterwards, leading to the re-emergence in 2009–13 of a competition between a post-ideological and conciliatory pole represented by SEL (which succeeded in mending the rift with the PD) and a variety of other organisations, which oscillated between intransigent stances and the pursuit of looser forms of understanding with the PD, often coalescing into shifting improvised coalitions at election times. After 2014, finally, the way to a regroupment *outside of the centre-left* was paved by the soon-to-be-approved reform of the electoral law, which ultimately abolished pre-electoral coalitions, made radical left parliamentary support redundant, and encouraged a pooling of resources of all groups refusing to be absorbed by Renzi's PD. However, unity was again delayed by some uncertainty about the rules of the game,[8] competition among existing organisations (particularly around the leading role of SEL), and further political and identity differences. The situation is due to remain fluid until the next general election, planned for 2018 but with some probability of an early date.

Filling the vacuum: potential and limits of the radical left mobilisation

The political and economic trends since 1989 sketched a worrying picture for the Italian radical left but simultaneously offered important chances of revival and growth.

The growing economic problems of the country, which hit heavily the medium-low salaried strata and the younger sections of the active population, shook the popular confidence in the ability of Italian capitalism to ensure an adequate growth and a wide distribution of material welfare. The policy responses of the state, marked by a mix of austerity and neoliberal reforms, aggravated the situation. Finally, the rapid rightward shift of the political system created a vacuum of political representation of working-class and welfarist interests.

A more detailed analysis shows that, despite some promising experiences, the electoral and organisational mobilisation of the Italian radical left failed to convince its potential constituencies, which fragmented between an unenthusiastic support for centre-left parties, political disengagement, and more recently a fascination for Grillo's Movimento 5 Stelle (5 Stars Movement, M5S).

Contours of the vacuum

Since the early nineties Italy suffered a progressive deterioration of its industrial structure, international competitiveness, productivity, and macro-economic performance (Amyot 2003, 2014; Bagnai 2016; Barca 1997; De Cecco 2007; Gallino 2006; Mucchetti 2003; Praussello 2015; Rangone and Solari 2012). Real GDP growth rates went from vibrant until 1989 to paltry afterwards, turning negative after 2007. The large industry gradually lost out to international competitors, while the more dynamic small industry was decimated by the Great Recession. Trade competitiveness ceased to be bolstered by currency devaluations, while internal demand was compressed by restrictive fiscal policies. Public debt, whose monetisation was now prevented by the autonomy of the Italian (1981) and European (1999) central banks and whose weight was magnified by slow economic growth, rose to the unheard-of levels of 121.2 per cent of GDP in 1994 and 132.4 per cent of GDP in 2015. Job creation was poor, with official unemployment rates usually above 9 per cent and most of the new jobs offered in low-skilled and precarious positions. Real wages stagnated, with an annual growth of just 0.2 per cent between 1993 and 2009. Altogether, the Italian share of the world GDP fell from 4.54 per cent in 1987 to 2.77 per cent in 2014.

This decline was accompanied, and in part caused, by a progressive shift of Italian economic policy from a dirigiste developmentalist to a neoliberal orientation, which began hesitantly in the eighties but became dominant only after the fiscal and currency crisis of 1992. As in the rest of Western Europe, neoliberalisation did not entail an overall reduction of the economic centrality of the state, but rather a change in the means and goals of its intervention.[9] The strong state-owned sector was dismantled through privatisations and liberalisations (Barucci and Pierobon 2007; Mediobanca 2000; Valle 2002). Public employment fell from 3.8 million in 1992 (17.8 per cent of total employment) to 3.2 in 2011 (14.1 per cent). Welfare reforms sought to curb the growth and ultimately reduce the cost of social expenditures (Ascoli and Pavolini 2015; Ferrera and Jessoula 2007). The main area of retrenchment was that of pensions, where retirement age was increased, the indexation of existing pensions weakened, and replacement rates for future pensioners slashed. Labour market reforms deregulated hiring and firing procedures and created a large pool of precarious wageworkers with low salaries and few rights (Accornero 2006; Gallino 2007). Wage restraint was institutionalised with the abolition of wage-price indexation in 1992–93 and a targeting of pay rises on planned inflation. Periodic devaluations were barred by the adoption of fixed exchange rates and the ultimately the euro (1999), which led to a strong loss of price competitiveness in relation to the country's European trading partners. EU constraints to deficit financing led to a highly restrictive fiscal policy, which compressed domestic demand and investment.

Unlike other Western European countries, this policy shift was not carried out by existing political forces, but entailed instead a veritable revolution in the political system. Between 1989 and 1996 the actors, ideologies, rules, and patterns of competition of the so-called 'First Republic' were swept away and replaced by a 'Second Republic' that remained in a state of continuous and unstable transition (Bartolini and D'Alimonte 1995; Calise 2006; Ceccanti 2016; Ginsborg 2001; Grilli di Cortona 2007; Gundle and Parker 1996; Newell and Bull 2005; Revelli 1996; Waters 1994). Traditional mass parties collapsed and were superseded by fickle organisations with vague ideologies, shallow social roots, and leader-centred organisations. The national electoral system was modified three times (1993, 2005, and 2015), from an initial non-selective proportional representation to various majoritarian arrangements. And the pattern of blocked competition dominated by the Christian Democracy and its centrist allies gave way to a prevailing pattern of bipolar alternation between centre-left and right-wing coalitions, with frequent interludes of technocratic 'grand coalition' cabinets.

Abstractly, these developments seemed to create a huge potential vacuum of representation of working-class and welfarist interest, which the radical left could set about to exploit.

First, former communist voters (at least a quarter of the total voters) could be reasonably expected to be alienated by the progressive rightward shift of the PDS/DS/PD (Bellucci et al. 2000; Bordandini et al. 2008; Bordignon 2014; Ignazi 1992; Liguori 2009) and attracted to the radical left, which proudly identified with the radical and classist streaks of the legacy of the old Italian Communist Party. Starting from 1989, the majority of the PCI sought to overcome its permanent exclusion from governmental power through a radical ideological renewal, a change of the rules of the game, and a bold strategy of alliances. In the early nineties, it abandoned communism, renamed itself Partito Democratico della Sinistra (Democratic Party of the Left, PDS), joined the social democratic mainstream, spearheaded the majoritarian reform of the electoral law, and forged a short-lived left-wing alliance (i Progressisti, the Progressives). In the mid-nineties, it cut a deal with large sections of the old establishment, contributed to the creation of a centre-left alliance with Christian democratic and liberal currents (l'Ulivo, the Olive Tree), became the main supporter of the pro-EU neoliberal shift of the country, and changed its name again to Democratici di Sinistra (Democrats of the Left, DS). In the late noughties, finally, it merged with its allies first in a loose federation (also called l'Ulivo) and then in the US-style Partito Democratico (Democratic Party, PD), and unsuccessfully attempted to force a shift from a bipolar to a two-party kind of political competition. In psychological terms, the break with communism was hard to accept for many traditional voters, and was made more painful by the deletion of the last reference to the communist roots in the DS party symbol (1998), the subordination to and merger with the Christian democratic rivals (1996–2007), and the final loss of control of post-communists on the PD (2013).[10] In political terms, the renewal of the party progressively broke with many key traditional left-wing values, such as workerism, welfarism, pacifism, and proportional representation. In terms of alliances, in its pursuit of power the party was prepared to go very far, allying not only with the old centrist establishment (informally in 1992–93, formally since 1996), but also with centrist sections of the new right-wing coalition (1995, 1998, 2013), the Northern League (briefly in 1995), and Berlusconi himself (1995, 2011–13).

Secondly, low growth and neoliberal reforms hit hard large sections of the Italian population, particularly the younger generations, the unemployed and underemployed, the South, private-sector wageworkers, and public-sector wageworkers. The collapse of traditional centrist parties in 1992–94 freed them from traditional political allegiances, and the performance of successive centre-left, right-wing, and 'grand coalition' governments only fuelled their potential dissatisfaction.

Thirdly, additional issues offered interesting perspectives: pacifism, where the 1990 turn of all parties toward foreign military interventions (Ignazi et al. 2012) clashed with constitutional constraints and widespread popular opposition, and alter-globalism, which acquired a sizeable support between 1999 and 2005.

In practice, it can be shown that the Italian population was indeed increasingly dissatisfied with mainstream political parties and continued to expound broadly progressive socio-economic positions.

Electoral support for mainstream parties collapsed twice, in 1994 and 2013 (Figure 5.4). The old centrist establishment (*pentapartito*) fell from 48.5 per cent of the electorate in 1987 to 15.8 per cent in 1994, when voters resoundingly rewarded the new right-wing alliance between the populist Forza Italia (Forward Italy, FI), the post-fascist Alleanza Nazionale (National Alliance, AN), and the right-regionalist Lega Nord (Northern League, LN) (Bartolini and D'Alimonte 1995). In the following two decades, Italian politics was dominated by an unstable bipolar alternation of a centre-left and a right-wing coalition: the boundaries of each of them continuously shifted, most governments crumbled before the end of their term (1995, 1998, 2008, 2011), and each coalition was voted out at the next general election (Bellucci and Segatti 2010). The concept of a mainstream is elusive in these decades, as the level of social acceptability of many parties remained low: most components of the right-wing coalition were treated as dangerous outsiders by large parts of the domestic and international elites, and the communist roots of the PDS/DS/PD were abhorred in conservative circles. Nevertheless, centre-left, centrist, and right-wing parties (excluding the radical left,

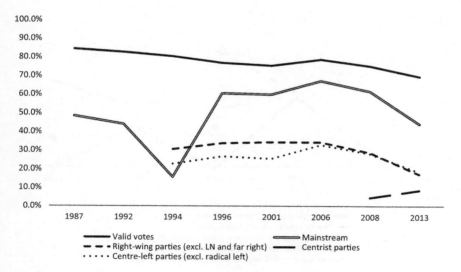

Figure 5.4 Support for Italian establishment parties (per cent of the electorate)

the LN, and minor far-right forces) remained stable for two decades around 60–70 per cent of the electorate. In 2014 the sum of all these forces, which had governed together since 2011 in the Monti cabinet, suddenly fell to just 44.1 per cent of the electorate, as voters flocked to the new anti-system movement M5S and abstention (Bordignon and Ceccarini 2013; De Sio et al. 2013; ITANES 2013).

Although the electoral shift in 1994 seemed to reward right-wing forces, whose programmes included strong anti-state, anti-welfare, and anti-union themes, popular opinions on socio-economic themes actually remained well anchored in the old welfarist consensus (Figure 5.5). Despite the contrary positions of much of the political elite, media, academia, and business community, the data of the ITANES surveys shows that Italians continued to support more state intervention in the economy (net value of +28.0 per cent in 2008), a public healthcare system (+51.0 per cent in 2006), more regulation of the labour market (+9.2 per cent in 2008), and the status quo on welfare retrenchment (+2.6 per cent in 2001 on the trade-off more welfare versus less taxes). Self-identification on the left-right scale was also often tilted toward the left. Pacifist opposition to military missions abroad was overwhelming.

Finally, the Italian civil society was prepared to act on these opinions and engaged in important waves of left-leaning mass mobilisation against government policies (Albertazzi et al. 2009; Alteri and Raffini 2014; Della Porta et al. 2003, 2006; Ghezzi and Guiducci 2007; Roccato and Fedi 2007). Like elsewhere in Western Europe, these tended to flare up mainly when right-wing governments were in office. The first Berlusconi cabinet (1994–95) was welcomed by

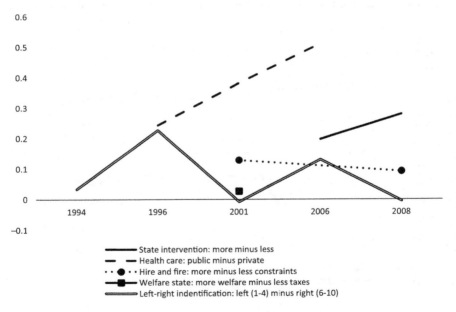

Figure 5.5 Net left-wing opinions, Italy (per cent of interviewed)

anti-fascist demonstrations and a large general strike against its pension reform, which led to the defection of the Northern League and its fall soon thereafter. The second Berlusconi government (2001–06) was confronted with a generalised flourishing of social movements against labour market reform, welfare cuts, the Iraq war, capitalist globalisation, and education reforms. Opposition to the third Berlusconi government (2008–11) was more limited, but nevertheless included important student, trade union, and anti-corruption mobilisations. Centrist (Amato and Ciampi in 1992–94), centre-left (Prodi, D'Alema, and Amato in 1996–01, Prodi in 2006–08, Renzi since 2014), and 'grand coalition' (Dini in 1995, Monti and Letta in 2011–13) cabinets, on the contrary, engendered widespread dissatisfaction but comparatively little protest, as the support of much the traditional left-wing subculture (parties, trade unions, associations, and movements) effectively contained open dissent and resistance. Ironically, it was precisely this kind of governments that went further in the implementation of austerity and neoliberal reforms, while the open neoliberal rhetoric of the right remained largely on paper.

The favourable conditions to benefit from the disaffection of former communist and other welfarist voters toward mainstream parties were there. The results of the radical left mobilisations, however, turned out to be limited and uncertain until 2007, and negative after 2008.

Electoral mobilisation

The *electoral* mobilisation of the Italian radical left was initially successful, but hit a ceiling in 1996 and faltered after 2008.

Results in national elections (first chamber, proportional part) are reported in Figure 5.6. These grew from 2,201,428 votes in 1992 (5.6 per cent) to 3,213,748 in 1996 (8.6 per cent), then oscillated for a decade on slightly lower levels, and collapsed to 1,657,629 votes in 2008 (4.4 per cent), with a small final recovery in 2013 (1,990,212 votes, 5.6 per cent). Vote shares in 2008 and 2013 are inflated by the contribution to the SA, SEL, and RC lists of currents previously extraneous to the radical left (SD and Verdi in both elections; IDV in 2013; and other minor groups).

The analysis of the class dimension (Figure 5.7) and origin (Figure 5.8) of the radical left vote confirms that, in its best moments, this party family succeeded in making some inroads among the disaffected welfarist and ex-communist constituencies. On the one hand, the social groups most penalised by the post-1992 neoliberal trends generally displayed a stronger propensity to vote for the radical left than the general population. In 1996, results were excellent among blue-collar workers (11.6 per cent), white-collar workers (10.9 per cent), and students (13.6 per cent). In 2006, support remained strong among blue-collar workers (10.8 per cent) and students (11.0 per cent), dropped among white-collar workers (7.7 per cent), but rose among the unemployed and precarious workers (9.6 per cent). The 2008 collapse, however, frustrated two decades of efforts among all social categories. On the other hand, the radical left indeed made big gains among former PCI and current PDS/DS/PD voters. Data on electoral flows are not very reliable, due

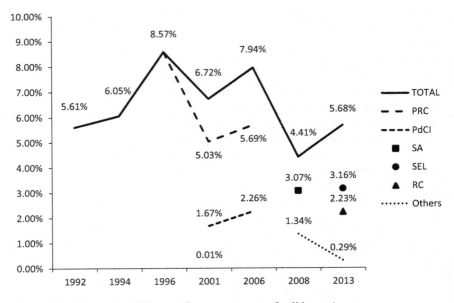

Figure 5.6 Italian radical left vote (Camera, per cent of valid votes)

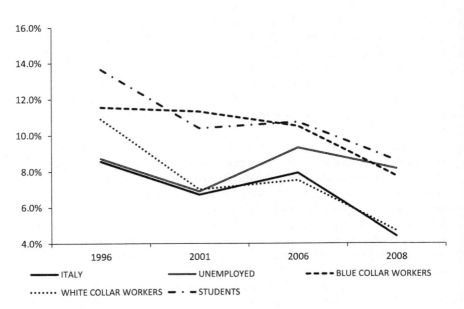

Figure 5.7 Italian radical left vote in selected social groups (Camera, per cent of valid votes)

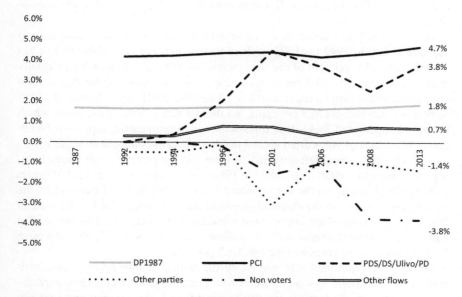

Figure 5.8 Cumulative net electoral flows of the Italian radical left (Camera, per cent of valid votes)

to small samples, incomplete options, and large discrepancies between reported and real results. My estimate of cumulative net flows based on the ITANES surveys would suggest a gain of 1.6 million votes from the PCI in 1992 (4.2 per cent of valid votes). Further hefty gains were made from the PDS/DS between 1994 and 2001 (1.7 million votes, 4.5 per cent), but partially melted away in 2008. Small gains were also generally made with generational replacement. However, these progresses were dampened after 1996 by a negative balance toward other parties (in 2013 0.5 million votes, −1.4 per cent) and huge losses toward abstention (in 2013 1.3 million votes, −3.8 per cent).

As a general rule, radical left parties slowly grew while in opposition to rightwing or grand coalition governments (1992–96; 2001–06; 2008–13) and collapsed while involved in supporting centre-left governments (1996–98; 1998–01; 2006–08). They also clearly benefitted from left-leaning mass social movements (1995; 2001–04). The problem was that the very dynamics that fuelled their growth also pushed them toward an alliance with the moderate left to defeat the right-wing, thereby engendering most of their subsequent problems. The hopes built up in the former periods were thus periodically shattered in the latter, pushing large sections of their constituency toward abstention and leading to an increasingly negative long-term balance.

Even at its peaks in 1995–96 and 2005–06, the Italian radical left managed to fill just a small portion of the potential vacuum left by the neoliberal turn of mainstream political parties. A few data from the ITANES surveys of the persuasively make the point.

First, relatively few disaffected ex-communist voters shifted their allegiance to the radical left. In 1992 the PRC retained a mere 16.0 per cent of the PCI voters of 1987 (and 15.6 per cent of the DP voters). By 2001 the situation was virtually unchanged, with only 15.7 per cent of people having supported the PCI at least once in the past opting for the radical left.[11] The 1992–2001 net gains from the PDS were more substantial (26.3 per cent), but did not really damage the latter, which broadly compensated these departures with new more centrist supporters. After 2001, this source of votes dried up and net flows became stagnant or negative.

Secondly, the radical left attracted an even smaller portion of all voters holding left-wing and welfarist opinions. In 1996, for instance, 36.4 per cent of voters self-identified clearly on the left (position 1–3 over 10) and 12.1 per cent on the far left (position 1), but the electoral results of the PRC stopped at 8.6 per cent. In 2001, 55.5 per cent of the interviewed favoured a more regulated labour market and 51.3 per cent an expansion of the welfare state; still, the PRC gathered a mere 5.0 per cent of valid votes and the PdCI 1.7 per cent.

Thirdly, the prominent role played by the radical left in several mass anti-neoliberal mobilisations was rewarded with electoral gains well below expectations. In 1995–96, the battle of the PRC against the pension reforms and austerity policies of the Berlusconi and Dini governments was followed by an increase of 2.5 percentage points. In 1998–99, the intervention of the PRC in the movement against the war in Kosovo did not prevent a severe defeat in the contemporary European Parliament elections. The most deceiving period was, however, that between 2001 and 2006, when alter-globalist, pacifist, and labour movements in which PRC and PdCI played a key role reached an unprecedented level of visibility and support. In 2003, for instance, about 28 per cent of the electorate supported an unsuccessful referendum extending the protection of workers against unlawful dismissal, and about 20 per cent actively participated to anti-war protests. Still, the radical left vote in 2006 stopped at 8.0 per cent of valid votes, with an increase of only 1.3 percentage points.

In a nutshell, although many post-communist and welfarist voters disagreed with the policy course of their old and new political representatives, few of them were actually prepared to switch allegiance to the parties of the radical left.

The explanation of this behaviour is not entirely clear.

A first possible factor was the ability of mainstream parties to deflect criticism by affirming the inevitability or understating the pain implied by their policies. On the one hand, as elsewhere in Europe, reforms were often framed as perhaps unpleasant but unescapable necessities imposed by external constraints: the threat of the international financial markets; the unsustainable level of public debt; the global industrial competition; and the rules of the European Union. On the other hand, most of their advocates emphatically denied the intention to dismantle the post-war European model of welfarist mixed economy, arguing that sacrifices were aimed at specific regulatory excesses and corporative privileges[12], were altogether modest, were temporary, or would be compensated in the medium-term by a revival of economic growth. In addition, most neoliberal policies, such as the abolition of wage-price indexation (1984–93), the liberalisation of hiring procedures (1987–96), the flexibilisation of labour contracts (since 1997), and the increase of retirement age and reduction of pension replacement rates (since 1995), were purposely implemented in a very gradual manner, starting with interventions of small entity affecting a limited number of persons and progressively deepening and widening their effects. An abstract support for traditional expansionary and dirigiste policies, thus, could well coexist with an acceptance of limited and temporary steps in the opposite direction, particularly if left-wing and confessional parties guaranteed that they were adopted in good faith. In fact, evidence points out that the centre-left succeeded in convincing substantial parts of its electorate both of the sound nature of its neoliberal reform, and of its continued left-wing credentials.

A second possible factor was the capacity of mainstream parties to preserve the allegiance of their welfarist constituency *despite* their policy orientation. On the one hand, traditional ideological rivalries and subcultural allegiances in part survived the collapse of the party system in 1992–94. Thus, loyalty to 'the party' (PDS/DS/PD), confessional attachment, anti-communism, and the advice of trusted civil society organisations constrained a shift toward the radical left. On the other hand, the new ideology of 'anti-Berlusconism' helped to rally disaffected left-leaning voters around the centre-left alliance and technocratic governments resulting from internal crises of the right-wing bloc (Dini in 1995–96, Monti in 2011–13). Finally, the very dynamic of bipolar alternation squeezed non-aligned forces, encouraged a tactical voting for the 'lesser evil', and channelled dissatisfaction away from party switch and toward coalition switch and abstention.

Finally, a major problem was the association of the radical left with the centre-left alliance, which tarnished its anti-neoliberal credibility and limited its appeal among swing voters. A more independent stance would have eliminated some of the reasons behind the defeats of 2001 and 2008, and would have put the radical left in a better position to exploit the political turmoil of 1992–1995 and 2008–2015, when establishment parties were rocked by the effects of economic crises, austerity policies, and corruption scandals. Yet, it is not sure that this course was actually viable. In the long-term, the Italian radical left might have shared the fate of SYRIZA or PODEMOS, emerging from the Great Recession as an anti-establishment third pole in place of the Five Stars Movement. From 1994 to 2008, however, the already mentioned constraints of the new bipolar competition made an autonomous stance almost impracticable, as it would have implied an automatic victory of the right-wing coalition, a serious electoral squeeze due to tactical voting, more conciliatory splits, and the possible loss of parliamentary representation. Most radical left leaders indeed believed that this path was too risky, and therefore opted for conciliatory (PdCI, SEL) or dynamic (PRC) alliance strategies.

Organisational mobilisation

The *organisational* mobilisation of the Italian radical left was even less successful than its electoral one. In the original split of 1991, the overwhelming majority of communist members and ancillary organisations sided with the PDS, leaving the

148 The Italian radical left

PRC bereft of followers and linkages. Subsequent efforts led to some gains in the early nineties and mid-noughties, but came nowhere near to challenging the continued predominance of its moderate competitors and were widely reversed after 2007. While sizeable strata of left-wing party and social activists held a certain sympathy for their positions, existing radical left parties never found the way to forge a solid common framework for electoral and extra-parliamentary activities.

Results in terms of membership development were mixed (Figure 5.9).

As already remarked, radical left membership rose modestly from 117,551 in 1992 to 130,509 in 1997, oscillated until 2006 (136,323), and collapsed afterwards (63,992 in 2014). On the positive side, it escaped for about 15 years the general tendency of European parties to shrink and age. On the negative side, it completely failed to challenge the organisational supremacy of its moderate left competitors. First, these levels never exceeded a tiny 9 per cent of the 1989 membership of PCI and DP, which predominantly stuck with the PDS or retreated from active partisan engagement. Secondly, they reached at their peak in 2006 only 18.9 per cent of the total membership of 'left' parties (including the radical left, the greens, and the PCI/PDS/DS/PD). The latter party lost about 62 per cent of its members between 1989 and 2006 (from 1,421,230 to 543,907), recovered after the PD merger (831,042 in 2009), and lost again about 56 per cent until 2015 (366,641). However, after the initial wave in 1991 few of these disaffected members and activists switched to the radical left. From 1992 to 2006 a number of important post-communist figures (Fausto Bertinotti, Pietro Ingrao, Aldo Tortorella, Pietro Folena) did defect from the PDS/DS, but either refrained from engaging in existing radical left parties or proved to be generals without troops.

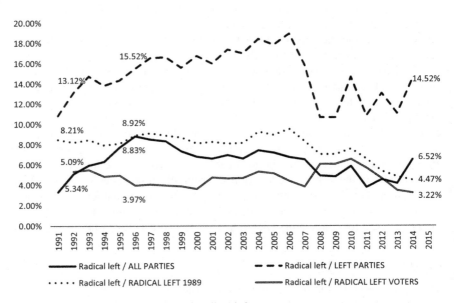

Figure 5.9 Membership ratios, Italian radical left

After 2007, on the other hand, several organised tendencies (SD, Socialismo 2000, FaS, Possibile) switched from the PD to the radical left, but only a fraction of their former supporters followed them in their new home.

Results in terms of social linkages were fairly negative. Within the trade union movement, the influence of the radical left started from weak positions and stagnated over time. Radical trade unions (Choi and Mattoni 2010; Manicastri 2014) often cooperated with official radical left parties in extra-parliamentary mobilisations and referendums, but encompassed at best 0.3 million workers and generally refrained from party and electoral politics.[13] The former communist union CGIL (Ghezzi and Guiducci 2007), which counted 5.8 million members in 2011, half of which were active workers, staunchly supported the PCI majority in its long march from communism to neoliberalism. At the peak of its influence in 1996, the PRC 'controlled' only 13.7 per cent of CGIL members (PDS: 44.9 per cent), 2.9 per cent of officials, 3.7 per cent of managing committee members, and no secretariat member (PDS: 77.8 per cent). The broader 'CGIL left' (Andruccioli 2008; Cremaschi 2000; Lacoppola 2010), which included other groups close to DS factions or unaffiliated, was more substantial but never went above 18 per cent of congress votes and secretariat members (2002).[14] An important area of progress was the metalworkers' union, whose leadership shifted in 1997 on 'critical' positions and partially aligned with the radical left after 2007 (PRC, then SEL); other categories, however, did not budge. To sum up, the radical left was relatively weak, fragmented in a myriad of rivalling organisations and tendencies, and rarely in the condition of challenging the moderate course of the main union leaderships. The CGIL, in particular, was very active in mobilisations against right-wing governments, but played a key role in assisting centre-left and centrist governments in the smooth implementation of social dialogue (*concertazione*), wage restraint, fiscal austerity, and neoliberal reforms (Baccaro 2002; Leonardi 2013). A unique window of opportunity for the radical left was represented by the years 1992–95, when the acquiescence of the trade unions to the abrupt neoliberal turn in the Italian political economy was met with widespread grassroots dissent and resistance. Once this battle was lost, the social relation of forces and stringent legislative constraints drastically reduced the space for and success chances of subsequent labour struggles, leading to two decades of gradual retreat of workers' militancy, rights, and conditions.

Within other civil society organisations, the situation was similar. The post-autonomist subculture of social centres (*centri sociali*) and cultural initiatives remained vital but altogether marginal (Mudu 2004, 2012). The traditional communist subculture, as well as parts of the Catholic one, remained overwhelmingly loyal to the parties of the centre-left (PDS/DS, DL, and PD), although important organisations (such as FIOM, ARCI, Rete Lilliput) became increasingly open to collaborations with the radical left on specific issues or in loose movement networks.

The only area where the radical left was visibly successful was in the fluid context of social movement events. Between 1999 and 2004, in particular, the PRC was prominent in the alter-globalist and pacifist movements, won the sympathy of a majority of their active participants, and acquired a key role in their organising structures (Della Porta et al. 2003, 2006). In a survey conducted during the Genova counter-summit in 2001, for instance, 63.5 per cent of the respondents declared their proximity with the PRC and only 10.2 per cent opted for the DS. In turn, the party member Vittorio Agnoletto was selected as the spokesperson of the Genova Social Forum (2001) and the Italian Social Forum (2001–04), two broad consensus-based coordination bodies. This, however, soon proved to be an optical illusion, as the retreat of the movements left small behind several sympathising personalities, but no veritable affiliated mass organisation, with the partial and belated exception of the metalworkers' union FIOM.

Summary

As elsewhere in the industrialised world, Italy has experienced since 1989 the emergence of a growing rift between neoliberal elites and the interests of large sections of its population. The attempts of the radical left to fill the resulting vacuum of representation of working-class and welfarist themes were theoretically facilitated by a number of specific national features: the existence until 1991 of a communist party with 1.4 million members and 8–10 million votes; the collapse of existing political parties in 1992–94 and 2011–15 in the midst of economic crises and corruption scandals; two large anti-neoliberal extra-parliamentary movements in the early nineties and early noughties; and the increasingly dismal macro-economic performance of the country.

Despite these advantages, the PRC and its successor organisations failed to profit from the travails of establishment parties. From an electoral point of view, the radical left initially won over a small fraction of the former communist electorate, modestly grew until 1996, stagnated until 2007, and declined afterwards. From an organisational point of view, it failed to provide an effective alternative to the crisis of Fordist organisational models and remained dwarfed by its moderate left competitors, with a medium-weak membership strength and very weak social linkages.

The reasons behind this failure had mainly to do with the dynamics of the new post-1994 political system. On the one hand, this stabilised for almost two decades a bipolar competition between broad centre-left and right-wing coalitions, pressuring minor forces to join or face a serious threat of demise. On the other hand, the same mechanisms progressively destroyed the anti-neoliberal and anti-establishment credibility of the radical left, associating it with the implementation of neoliberal policies at both national and regional levels, and progressively fragmented it into a variety of small and ineffective rival organisations.

The strategy of leftward pull

Despite its deceiving results in winning over disaffected former communist and welfarist voters, the size and strategic importance of the Italian radical left in the post-1994 bipolar competition placed it in a unique position to try to influence state policies and the course of its moderate partners.

As already remarked, the bulk of the Italian parties (PRC, PdCI, and SEL) followed a *strategy of leftward pull*, attempting to use their electoral, parliamentary, and extra-parliamentary strength to pull the PDS/DS/PD to the left and toward traditional welfarist values and policies. Each party, however, adopted a distinctive vision of the kinds of pressures and devices most likely to lead to the wished-for aim. Under the leadership of Fausto Bertinotti, the PRC followed a dynamic course which foresaw hard bargaining tactics, sharp tactical turns, moments of alliance followed by moments of contraposition, and a strong reliance on extra-parliamentary mobilisations (Cannavò 2009). It was also fairly optimistic on its capacity, with the help of DS internal tendencies, the trade unions, and social movements, to influence the course of the centre-left alliance and bring about a 'new reform course' or the first elements of a medium-term anti-neoliberal 'alternative of society'. Its right-wing splits followed a more conciliatory course, seeing themselves as constitutive parts of the centre-left alliance. The PdCI was more traditional and pessimistic, considering the centre-left as a 'trench' against the greater evil of the right-wing and pursuing the best possible compromises in a generally unfavourable situation. SEL, on the other hand, gambled for a long phase on a *leveraged buyout* of the centre-left through the mechanism of open coalition primaries. Only the small far-left splinter groups followed an intransigent course of opposition to the centre-left, which, however, did not completely rule out weak forms of collaboration, such as partial stand-down agreements or benign parliamentary abstentions on confidence votes.

None of these strategies proved successful.

Party efforts

The parties of the Italian radical left deployed a variety of means and activities to pursue their goals.

A first group of pressures related to party building. At a general level, the mere growth of their electoral and social support was supposed to pull the direction of competition to the left. More specifically, electoral losses for the centre-left parties were supposed to encourage a change of heart of their cadres and leaders away from their neoliberal orientation. Thus, the parties of the radical left targeted the working-class and welfarist constituencies bearing the brunt of low growth and neoliberal reforms with policies of public investment, fiscal stimulus, wealth redistribution, welfare expansion, and re-regulation; they specifically courted the voters of the PDS/DS/PD; and they sought to engineer splits of its left-wing internal tendencies. These efforts were initially somewhat successful, but foundered afterwards.

In its initial phase of development, the electoral strength of the PRC rose to 5.6 per cent (1992) and 8.6 per cent (1996) in national elections, to 7.7 per cent in regional elections (1995), and 6.1 per cent (1994) in European elections. There is also some evidence that its hard bargaining tactics toward the Prodi I government in 1996–97, where the party won a formal commitment to the introduction of the 35-hour working week (then reneged) and some funds for public employment programmes, pushed the voting intentions for the PRC up in the opinion polls. This experience, however, ended in a debacle, forcing the party to support harsh budgets and reforms and leading to the early exit from the majority and to the split of the PdCI. The whole radical left, despite the influx of new groups, never recovered the electoral levels of 1996, and the second governmental experience in 2006–08 produced a further fall below the levels of 1992.

In addition, the electoral losses of the PDS/DS/PD to the left were more than compensated by gains from the centre or through the mechanism of tactical voting. The PDS initially fell from 26.6 per cent in 1987 (PCI) to 16.1 per cent in 1992, but then recovered to 21.1 per cent in 1996. The new decline to 16.6 per cent in 2001 did not benefit the radical left, which also lost heavily. The subsequent federation and merger with its centrist allies, far from producing a haemorrhage of votes, led to modest losses in 2006 (30.4 per cent) or growth (33.1 per cent in 2008): in the latter case, mostly thanks to former leftist scared by the possible return of Berlusconi. The post-2011 policies of the PD disoriented parts of its traditional electorate (25.5 per cent in 2013), but were followed by extraordinary gains among centrist and centre-right voters (40.8 per cent in the 2014 European election).

Finally, the attempts to win over organised centre-left groups were either unsuccessful or fruitless. The courting of the Ingraian minority of the PDS in 1992–96 did not produce any notable split, as did the courting of the *correntone* of the DS in 2001–06. An important group, Democratic Left (SD), did ultimately refuse to join the PD in 2007, joining the SA electoral cartel and then SEL, but carried with it only a fraction of its theoretical strength (15.1 per cent of congress votes) and did not prevent an overall collapse of radical left votes. The same was true for the convergence of external allies (most of the former Verdi, in some occasions IdV and PSI, and other 'civic' groups) in the 'radical left' lists since 2008. The weight of the most recent PD splinter groups (FaS and Possibile) cannot yet be established with certainly, but it is unlikely to be large.

A second group of pressures related to political alliances. Given the structural weakness of its moderate partners, the radical left constantly enjoyed the role of kingmaker, as its support was essential both for an electoral victory of the centre-left coalition and for the survival of a centre-left government. Instead of opting for a course of fundamental opposition, it generally sought to make use of this position to affect the orientation of both the alliance and of state policies.

The PRC tried to influence the PDS/DS/PD with a combination of friendly negotiations, threats of a break, and incentives for a rapprochement. At the national level, full agreements were reached for the participation to the 1994 electoral alliance and to the Prodi II government (2006–08). A partial agreement was reached for the external support of the Prodi I government, which, however, fell apart after two years of strained relations (1996–98). Most of the time, the party ran for elections outside of the centre-left alliance (1992, 2001, 2008, 2013) and opposed left-leaning governments (Ciampi in 1993–94; Dini 1995–96; D'Alema and Amato in 1998–01), while at the same time showing its readiness to accept less moderate policies and offering technical electoral arrangements to defeat the right-wing. At the regional and local levels, the party initially adopted a policy of case-by-case alliances, moved to generalised electoral and governmental alliances in 2000, and swung back to a predominantly solitary course after 2014.

The PdCI opted instead for a complete and loyal support to the centre-left, hoping to obtain acceptable compromises through the control of portfolios and joint efforts with other left-wing elements of the coalition, such as the DS minority factions, the Greens, and the IdV. This stance was rewarded with a disproportional amount of offices but, given the tiny electoral weight of the party, was not likely to produce major policy effects.

SEL followed the conciliatory example of the PdCI, but also tried to subvert the centre-left from the inside through the mechanism of open coalition primaries (Damiani 2011; Sandri and Seddone 2015; Seddone and Valbruzzi 2012). These had already been successfully exploited by Nichi Vendola in 2005 to win the nomination as president of the Puglia region. Subsequent attempts, such as the 2005 national run of Fausto Bertinotti, had been much less impressive, and the small size of the party did not bode well for the success of its strategy. In 2010–11, however, the weakness of the PD did in fact allow a second victory of Vendola in Puglia and surprise victories by personalities close to SEL in the cities of Milano, Genova, and Cagliari. The national run of Vendola in 2012 started with good voting intentions, but ultimately stopped at only 15.6 of primary voters. Thereafter, SEL became a mere uninfluential appendage of the centre-left and never again managed to threaten its moderate leaderships.

A third group of pressures related to the use of referendums, which circumvented issues of tactical voting and party loyalty and enabled voters to freely express their opinions and dissatisfaction. The referendum campaigns of 1995 on workplace democracy (proposed by PRC and radical unions) and 2011 on economic, environmental, and legal themes (proposed by a broad alter-globalist network) gained the support of most political forces and won the vote. More significantly, the 2003 referendum campaign on the extension of protections against unfair dismissals – proposed by the PRC and opposed by most parties – created a rift within the DS (the party majority opposed it, the minority and the CGIL trade union supported it) and, while losing the vote, gathered a respectable 10.5 million of yes votes. Most core issues of the radical left, however, could not be subject to a referendum due to constitutional constraints, which forbid popular votes on budgetary issues and international treaties.

A final group of pressures relied on the ability extra-parliamentary mobilisations to win concrete concessions from civil society actors (for instance, entrepreneurs) or from the public authorities.

As far as workplaces were concerned, the radical left completely failed to build large militant structures, struggles, and successes. As already remarked, both the radical trade unions and the CGIL left wing remained weak and the moderate main trade union confederations (CGIL, CISL, and UIL) maintained a solid control of workers' representation and collective bargaining. Labour conflicts continued their long-term precipitous fall, with the number of working hours lost through strikes falling from 129.2 million in the seventies to 45.2 million in the eighties,

10.8 million in the nineties, and 5.4 million in the noughties. Collective agreements and actual working conditions worsened substantially and uninterruptedly.

Non-workplace movements were more vital. The radical left was, for instance, prominent in the support of autonomous social centres, movements of squatters and migrants, new forms of ethical consumption, and environmental mobilisations (Della Porta and Piazza 2008). These activities, however, were generally limited to small groups and had little impact on the overall course of national politics.

Mass social movements directed at directly impacting on governmental policies were instead frequent and important, but often tended to complicate rather than facilitate the problems of the radical left. Large social movements repeatedly flared up during the tenure of right-wing governments. Some were successful (against the 1994 pension reform), some partially (against the 2003 labour market reform), other unsuccessful (alter-globalists, pacifists, students, anti-Berlusconists), but all crucially contributed to cabinet crises and/or subsequent heavy electoral defeats of the right-wing. One of their indirect consequences, however, was to revive the image of moderate left parties without really changing their orientation, thus backing the radical left into unsustainable alliances. Protests against centre-left and grand coalition governments were generally small, given the lack of support of trade unions and other civil society organisations. Thus, they always failed to influence state policies, but embarrassed those radical left parties that were actually part of those governments: emblematic were the clashes with antimilitarist (1999, 2007–08) and No-TAV (2007) activists.

Systemic effects

None of the above-mentioned efforts led to visible positive results.

Far from responding to the pressures of the radical left, the PDS/DS/PD continued to evolve along a steady rightward trajectory. Attempts to split it won over some generals but no foot soldiers. The centre-left alliance also drifted to the right, progressively englobing new centrist and centre-right elements and, after 2008, squeezing out its old left-wing ones. Grand coalition cabinets supported by the moderate left (1992–94, 1995–96, and 2011–14), but also centre-left cabinets proper, were disastrous from an anti-neoliberal standpoint, dismantling piece by piece most elements of the legislative legacy of the Fordist period and showing no noticeable radical left policy influence. Neither conciliatory nor intransigent tactics worked. Political discourse did briefly shift to the left in the high tide of extra-parliamentary mobilisations or referendum campaigns, but immediately swung back after their ebbing. Social movements themselves had a large impact on public opinion and electoral trends, but did not fundamentally impact on centre-left orientations. Crucially, the CGIL trade union maintained an industrially and politically moderate course at times of centre-left or centrist governments, with the only partial exception of the metalworkers' union FIOM and some stirrings since 2014. As a matter of fact, it was the radical left that was gradually pulled to the right and undermined by its partners.

As in the German case, this strategic failure depended both on an insufficient level of pressures and on the structural impermeability of the political system and of the centre-left to a Keynesian-welfarist revival.

On the first account, the Italian radical left never went beyond a medium-small 8.6 per cent of valid votes, its crucial position of kingmaker was undermined by the readiness of many of its elected representatives to defect in case of a break, and its extra-parliamentary forces were too weak to affect mass organisations, social movements, and governmental policies.

On the second account, a change of direction in socio-economic policy was made arduous by a number of structural and ideological factors. First, the centrist governments of the eighties and the centre-left governments of the nineties anchored their neoliberal reforms in a complex legal and institutional framework: in particular, the independence of the Bank of Italy, the liberalisation of banking controls and capital movement restrictions, the EU legislation on competition and state aid, EU and WTO trade regulations, the euro convergence criteria, and the final relinquishment of sovereign monetary with the adoption of the euro. Secondly, a government determined to renegotiate these internal and international commitments would still have to face the constraints of an unfavourable international regime (globalisation and financialisation) and the lack of technical tools and expertise (due to the privatisation of state-owned enterprises and the withering of the old dirigiste bureaucracy). Finally, these moves profoundly shaped the very identity of the centre-left, which included key neoliberal technocrats as leaders (Amato, Ciampi, Andreatta, Prodi, Padoa-Schioppa) or more autonomous fellow travellers (Dini, Monti) and came to equate its mission with a market-friendly, pro-EU modernisation of the country.

Summary

The varied and often creative attempts of the Italian radical left to exert a leftward pull on the moderate left and the rest of the political system were completely unsuccessful. On the contrary, it was the centre-left that increasingly neutralised the radical left, splitting it into rival tendencies, involving it in unpopular governmental coalitions, and ultimately marginalising it after 2013.

Concluding remarks

The analysis offered in this chapter shows that the trajectory of the Italian radical left since 1989 was indeed a spectacular failure. The legacy of the strongest communist party in Western Europe was overwhelmingly retained by PDS/DS/PD and did not facilitate its subsequent growth. Its systemic strength always remained medium-small, following a growth path until 1996, oscillating for two decades around average Western European levels, and collapsing after 2007. Its organisational cohesion degenerated in a chaotic competition of splinter groups, dubious allies, and failed regroupment attempts. Its political and strategical coherence was shattered by the centripetal pressures of the new bipolar competition, which first ensnared it piece by piece in the cold embrace of the centre-left alliance and then relegated it to the fringes of national political life. Its attempts to fill the growing vacuum of representation of working-class and welfarist interests and to exert a leftward pull on the political system were both unsuccessful. These disaffected constituencies remained sceptical, preferring a critical support for the centre-left, the vote for a variety of right-wing or left-wing populist parties (Northern League, Forward Italy, IdV, M5S), or abstention. The moderate left, in turn, stuck to a steady rightward course that made it the leading actor of the neoliberal transformation of the country.

The reasons for this failure were essentially structural, although subjective choices and the skilful countermeasures of centre-left parties played a subordinate role. The Italian bipolarism did not give the radical left the breathing space needed to consolidate and grow, undermining its cohesion and credibility, squeezing its support, and making it bear the brunt of the tensions produced by unpopular centre-left governments. The growing involvement in the centre-left pole was a tragic mistake, but the path of political independence was fraught with material and political dangers that radical left leaders generally preferred to avoid. Finally, the repeated attempts of the centre-left to marginalise the radical left through changes to the electoral law or the mechanism of tactical voting narrowly failed until 2008, determined its temporary loss of parliamentary representation in 2008–12 and, if the proposed constitutional reform will be approved in the coming referendum, will probably confine it to the role of an irrelevant political force after 2017.

Notes

1 The PRC was the only political party in the world to be allowed to sign the final declaration of the first World Social Forum in 2001 and was instrumental in organising its largest European mobilisations (the Genoa counter-summit in 2001 and the Florence European Social Forum in 2002).
2 The dissidences of the 1996–1998 period (COBAS and CCA) were insignificant and short-lived. The dissidences of the 2006–2009 period, on the contrary (PdAC, PCL, SC, PBC, and PC), rose to 1.3 per cent of the valid votes in the 2008 general election, but gradually faded afterwards.
3 Noteworthy are the quasi-bordigist Lotta Comunista (Communist Struggle), active since 1965, the orthodox Rete dei Comunisti (Communist Network, RdC), created in 1998, and the Federazione Anarchica Italiana (Italian Anarchist Federation, FAI), established in 1945. Shifting networks within the *centri sociali* galaxy were important within social movements but never took the form of party organisations, sometimes supporting the PRC or SEL.
4 Nominal annual incomes of the central parties (excluding local structures, all parliamentary groups, and other incomes), for instance, fell from 27.4 million euro in 2007 to 3.8 million euro in 2011, then stabilising around that level.
5 The quotations are taken from recent party programmes.
6 At the national level, the proportional electoral law of 1946 (D.P.R. 361/1957) was changed first in 1993 (legge Mattarella, L. 276/1993 and L. 277/1993, so-called *Mattarellum*) and again in 2005 (legge Calderoli, L. 270/2005, so-called *Porcellum*). The latter was declared partially inconstitutional in 2014, marking a provisional return to proportional representation (C.cost. 1/2014, so-called *Consultellum*). A new two-round majoritarian law was approved in 2015 for the lower chamber (L. 52/2015, so-called

Italicum), while the higher chamber will continue to be regulated by the Consultellum until the end of its direct election, foreseen in a constitutional reform that will be the object of a referendum in October 2016. The electoral law for ordinary regions was changed in 1995 (legge Tatarella, L. 43/1995, so-called *Tatarellum*) and liberalised in 2001, with several of them later adopting minor or major variants. The electoral law for local administrations also experienced a majoritarian turn in 1993 (L. 81/1993).

7 The most notable of them were the *Italian Social Forum* coordination (2001–03); the *Lavoro e Libertà* (2003) and *Sezione italiana della Sinistra Europea* (2004–07) associations; the *Forum Programmatico per una Alternativa di Governo* (2003–04), *Camera di Consultazione della Sinistra* (2004–05), and *Costituente della Sinistra* (2007–08) discussion bodies; and the *La Sinistra – L'Arcobaleno* (2008), *Federazione della Sinistra* (2009–12), and *Rivoluzione Civile* (2013) electoral cartels.

8 Initial versions of the *Italicum* maintained the possibility of pre-electoral coalitions. The final version, approved in May 2015, has into force only in July 2016 and remains incomplete until the implementation of the Senate reform, approved in April 2016 and suspended until the October 2016 referendum.

9 In the period 1993–2009 state revenues (45.2 per cent of GDP), expenditures (49.1 per cent of GDP), and gross debt (110.8 per cent of GDP) remained at historical peak levels.

10 Non post-communist interim party secretaries briefly held office in 2009 (the Christian democrat Dario Franceschini) and 2013 (the socialist Guglielmo Epifani); in 2013, the Christian democrat and post-ideological Matteo Renzi conquered the party and confined much of the traditional DS leadership to the role of uninfluential internal minority.

11 Former PCI voters amounted to 38.0 per cent of the sample: 37.8 per cent opted for the Left Democrats, 11.4 per cent for the centre-left Daisy, 18.3 for Forward Italy, 10.5 per cent for other parties, and 6.3 per cent abstained.

12 The Northern League adopted a variant of this frame, pitting hard-working Northerners against undeserving Southerners and migrants.

13 The main organisations were the CUB (industry), RdB (public sector), Conf. Cobas (teachers), SLAI Cobas and subsequent splits (autoworkers), SULT (transport workers), and USB (a 2010 merger of some of the above).

14 The main groups were Fausto Bertinotti's *Essere Sindacato* (1991–96), Gianpaolo Patta's *Alternativa Sindacale* (1996–2000) and *Lavoro Società* (2000–07), Ferruccio Danini's *Area dei Comunisti* (1996–2000), Giorgio Cremaschi's *Rete28Aprile* (2005–present), and the new leadership of the metalworkers' union FIOM (1997–present).

References

Accornero, Aris (2006). *San Precario lavora per noi*. Milano: Rizzoli.

Agosti, Aldo (2000). *Storia del Partito Comunista Italiano, 1921–1991*. Bari: Laterza.

Albertazzi, Daniele, Clodagh Brook, Charlotte Ross, and Nina Rothenberg (eds.) (2009). *Resisting the tide. Cultures of opposition under Berlusconi (2001–2006)*. New York: Continuum Books.

Alteri, Luca, and Luca Raffini (2014). *La nuova politica. Mobilitazioni, movimenti e conflitti in Italia*. Napoli: Edises.

Amyot, Grant (2014). 'The transformation of Italian capitalism in the global financial crisis', in Richard Westra, Dennis Badeen, and Robert Albritton (eds.). *The future of capitalism after the financial crisis. The varieties of capitalism debate in the age of austerity*. Abingdon: Routledge, 96–113.

Amyot, Grant (2003). *Business, the state and economic policy: The case of Italy*. London: Routledge.

158 *The Italian radical left*

Andruccioli, Paolo (2008). *Spine rosse. Breve storia della minoranza congressuale della CGIL (1978–2006)*. Roma: Ediesse.
Ascoli, Ugo, and Emmanuele Pavolini (2015). *The Italian welfare state in a European perspective. A comparative analysis*. London: Policy Press.
Baccaro, Lucio (2002). 'The construction of "democratic" corporatism in Italy', *Politics & Society* 30(2): 327–357.
Bagnai, Alberto (2016). 'Italy's decline and the balance-of-payments constraint: A multi-country analysis', *International Review of Applied Economics* 30(1): 1–26.
Balestrini, Nanni, and Primo Moroni (1997). *L'orda d'oro 1968–1977. La grande ondata rivoluzionaria e creativa, politica ed esistenziale*. Milano: Giangiacomo Feltrinelli Editore.
Barca, Fabrizio (ed.) (1997). *Storia del capitalismo italiano*. Roma: Donzelli Editore.
Bartolini, Stefano, and Roberto D'Alimonte (eds.) (1995). *Maggioritario ma non troppo. Le elezioni politiche del 1994*. Bologna: Il Mulino.
Barucci, Emilio, and Federico Pierobon (2007). 'Privatizations in Italy: Planning or improvisation? Efficiency gains or rents?', *Review of Economic Conditions in Italy* 61(3): 341–369.
Bellucci, Paolo, Marco Maraffi, and Paolo Segatti (2000). *PCI, PDS, DS. La trasformazione dell'identità politica della sinistra di governo*. Roma: Donzelli.
Bellucci, Paolo, and Paolo Segatti (2010). *Votare in Italia: 1968–2008. Dall'appartenenza alla scelta*. Bologna: Il Mulino.
Bertolino, Simone (2008). 'The PRC: Emergence and crisis of the antagonistic left', in Uwe Backes and Patrick Moreau (eds.). *Communist and post-communist parties in Europe*. Göttingen: Vandenhoeck & Ruprecht, 215–244.
Bertolino, Simone (2004). *Rifondazione Comunista. Storia e organizzazione*. Bologna: Il Mulino.
Bianchi, Sergio, and Lanfranco Caminiti (eds.) (2007, 2008). *Gli autonomi: le storie, le lotte, le teorie* (3 volumes). Roma: DeriveApprodi.
Billi, Fabrizio (1996). *Camminare eretti: democrazia proletaria e comunismo, da DP a Rifondazione Comunista*. Milano: Punto Rosso.
Bordandini, Paola (2013). *La spada di Vendola. Una risorsa o un problema per il centrosinistra?* Roma: Donzelli.
Bordandini, Paola, and Aldo Di Virgilio (2007). 'Comunisti italiani: ritratto di un partito di nicchia', *Rivista Italiana di Scienza Politica* 37(2): 262–296.
Bordandini, Paola, Aldo Di Virgilio, and Francesco Raniolo (2008). 'The birth of a party: The case of the Italian Partito Democratico', *South European Society and Politics* 13(3): 303–324.
Bordignon, Fabio (2014). 'Matteo Renzi: A "leftist Berlusconi" for the Italian Democratic Party?', *South European Society and Politics* 19(1): 1–23.
Bordignon, Fabio, and Luigi Ceccarini (2013). 'Five stars and a cricket. Beppe Grillo shakes Italian politics', *South European Society and Politics* 18(3): 427–449.
Calise, Mauro (2010). *Il partito personale. I due corpi del leader*. Bari: Laterza.
Calise, Mauro (2006). *La terza repubblica. Partiti contro presidenti*. Bari: Laterza.
Calossi, Enrico (2007). 'Rifondazione Comunista e Comunisti Italiani', in Luciano Bardi, Piero Ignazi, and Oreste Massari (eds.). *I partiti italiani. Iscritti, dirigenti, eletti*. Milano: Università Bocconi, 218–247.
Cannavò, Salvatore (2009). *La Rifondazione mancata. 1991–2008, una storia del PRC*. Roma: Edizioni Alegre.
Ceccanti, Stefano (2016). *La transizione è (quasi) finita*. Torino: Giappichelli.

Chiocchetti, Paolo (2016). Western European radical left database. Version 2.0 (30.04.2016). Available at: www.paolochiocchetti.it/data.
Choi, Hae-Lin, and Alice Mattoni (2010). 'The contentious field of precarious work in Italy: Political actors, strategies and coalitions', *WorkingUSA* 13: 213–243.
Cossu, Andrea (2004). ' "Tenetela cara questa bandiera!". Simbolismo politico e ricorso al rituale nella scissione del Partito dei Comunisti Italiani', *Polis* 18(2): 207–236.
Cremaschi, Giorgio (2000). 'Riflusso e possibile ripresa', *la rivista del Manifesto* 3.
Dalmasso, Sergio (2002). *Rifondare è difficile. Dallo scioglimento del PCI al 'movimento dei movimenti'*. Boves (CN): CIPEC.
Damiani, Marco (2013). 'Vendola, la forma partito e il modello di leadership. Una sinistra "in movimento" tra partecipazione e personalizzazione politica', *SocietàMutamentoPolitica* 4(7): 307–329.
Damiani, Marco (2011). 'Nichi Vendola: For the new "laboratory" of the Italian Left', *Bulletin of Italian Politics* 3(2): 371–390.
De Cecco, Marcello (2007). 'Italy's dysfunctional political economy', *West European Politics* 30(4): 763–783.
Della Porta, Donatella, Massimo Andretta, and Lorenzo Mosca (2003). 'Movimenti sociali e sfide globali: Politica, antipolitica e nuova politica dopo l'11 settembre', *Rassegna italiana di sociologia*, 44(1): 43–75.
Della Porta, Donatella, Massimiliano Andretta, Lorenzo Mosca, and Herbert Reiter (2006). *Globalization from below. Transnational activism and protest networks*. Minneapolis: University of Minnesota Press.
Della Porta, Donatella, and Gianni Piazza (2008). *Le ragioni del no. Le campagne contro la Tav in Val di Susa e il Ponte sullo Stretto*. Milano: Feltrinelli.
de Nardis, Fabio (2009). *La Rifondazione Comunista. Asimmetrie di potere e strategie politiche di un partito in movimento*. Milano: FrancoAngeli.
De Sio, Lorenzo, Matteo Cataldi, and Federico De Lucia (eds.) (2013). *Le elezioni politiche del 2013*. Roma: CISE.
Dormagen, Jean-Yves (1998). 'Parcours, culture et opinions des cadres du Parti de la refondation communiste', *Communisme* 51/52: 151–168.
Dormagen, Jean-Yves (1996). *I comunisti. Dal PCI alla nascita di Rifondazione comunista*. Roma: Koinè.
Favilli, Paolo (2011). *In direzione ostinata e contraria. Per una storia di Rifondazione Comunista*. Roma: DeriveApprodi.
Ferrera, Maurizio, and Matteo Jessoula (2007) 'Italy: A narrow gate for path-shift', in Ellen M. Immergut, Karen M. Anderson, and Isabelle Schulze (eds.). *Handbook of West European pension politics*. Oxford: Oxford University Press, 396–453.
Fusaro, Carlo (2009). 'Party system developments and electoral legislation in Italy (1948–2009)', *Bulletin of Italian Politics* 1(1): 49–68.
Gallino, Luciano (2007). *Il lavoro non è una merce. Contro la flessibilità*. Bari: Laterza.
Gallino, Luciano (2006). *L'Italia in frantumi*. Bari: Laterza.
Gambetta, William (2010). *Democrazia Proletaria. La nuova sinistra tra piazze e palazzi*. Milano: Punto Rosso.
Gerbaudo, Paolo (2011). 'Berlusconi of the left? Nichi Vendola and the "narration" of the new Italian Left', *Soundings* 48(11): 87–96.
Ghezzi, Carlo, and Marica Guiducci (2007). *La strada del lavoro. Fatti e persone nella CGIL da piazza Fontana all'articolo 18*. Milano: Baldini Castoldi Dalai.
Ginsborg, Paul (2001). *Italy and its discontents, 1980–2001*. London: Penguin Books.

Grilli di Cortona, Pietro (2007). *Il cambiamento politico in Italia. Dalla Prima alla Seconda Repubblica.* Roma: Carocci.
Gundle, Stephen, and Simon Parker (eds.) (1996). *The new Italian republic.* London: Routledge.
Ignazi, Piero (1992). *Dal PCI al PDS.* Bologna: Il Mulino.
Ignazi, Piero, Giampiero Giacomello, and Fabrizio Coticchia (2012). *Italian military operations abroad. Just don't call it war.* Basingstoke: Palgrave MacMillan.
ITANES (2013). *Voto amaro: disincanto e crisi economica nelle elezioni del 2013.* Bologna: il Mulino.
Lacoppola, Gianluca (2010). The evolution of the CGIL left. Available at: www.s-gs.de/wordpress/wp-content/uploads/2010/04/Lacoppola-Evolution-of-the-CGIL-Left.doc [accessed on 01.04.2016].
Lazar, Marc (1992). *Maisons rouges. Les Partis communistes français et italien de la Libération à nos jours.* Paris: Aubier.
Leonardi, Salvo (2013). 'Gli anni della concertazione: un excursus storico-politico', *Alternative per il Socialismo* 25.
Liguori, Guido (2009). *La morte del PCI.* Roma: Manifestolibri.
Magri, Lucio (2013). *The tailor of Ulm. Communism in the twentieth century.* London: Verso.
Manicastri, Steven (2014). '*Operaismo* revisited: Italy's state-capitalist assault on workers and the rise of COBAS', in Immanuel Ness (ed.). *New forms of worker organization: The syndicalist and autonomist restoration of class-struggle unionism.* Oakland: PM Press, 20–38.
Mediobanca (2000). *Le privatizzazioni in Italia dal 1992.* Milano: Ricerche e Studi S.p.A.
Morando, Enrico (2010). *Riformisti e comunisti? Dal Pci al Pd. I 'miglioristi' nella politica italiana.* Roma: Donzelli.
Moroni, Primo, Consorzio AAster, Centro Sociale Cox18, and Centro sociale Leoncavallo (1996). *Centri sociali: geografie del desiderio.* Milano: Shake.
Mucchetti, Massimo (2003). *Licenziare i padroni?* Milano: Feltrinelli.
Mudu, Pierpaolo (2012). 'I centri sociali italiani: Verso tre decadi di occupazioni e di spazi autogestiti', *Partecipazione e Conflitto* 5(1): 69–92.
Mudu, Pierpaolo (2004). 'Resisting and challenging neoliberalism: The development of Italian social centers', *Antipode* 36(5): 917–941.
Newell, James L. (2010). Getting personal? The case of Rifondazione Comunista. Paper presented at the 60th annual conference of the UK Political Studies Association (PSA), Edinburgh, 29 March–1 April.
Newell, James, and Martin Bull (2005). *Italian politics: Adjustment under duress.* London: Polity.
Praussello, Franco (2015). 'The impact of the Eurozone crisis on a periphery country: The case of Italy', in Savvas Katsikides and Pavlos I. Koktsidis (eds.). *Societies in transition.* Cham: Springer, 57–86.
PRC (2007). *L'inchiesta sul partito.* Roma: O.GRA.RO.
Pucciarelli, Matteo (2011). *Gli ultimi Mohicani. Una storia di Democrazia Proletaria.* Roma: Edizioni Alegre.
Rangone, Marco, and Stefano Solari (2012). 'From the Southern-European model to nowhere: The evolution of Italian capitalism, 1976–2001', *Journal of European Public Policy* 19(8): 1188–1206.
Revelli, Marco (1996). *Le due destre.* Torino: Bollati Boringhieri.

Roccato, Michele, and Angela Fedi (2007). ' "Not in my name?" The Italians and the war in Iraq', *Journal of Community & Applied Social Psychology* 17(3): 229–236.
Romano, Onofrio (2009). 'Le fabbriche di Nichi. Fenomenologia di una comunità politica postdemocratica', *Democrazia e Diritto* 3–4: 151–175.
Sandri, Giulia, and Antonella Seddone (eds.) (2015). *The primary game. The case of the Italian democratic party.* Novi Ligure: Epoké.
Seddone, Antonella, and Marco Valbruzzi (ed.) (2012). *Primarie per il sindaco. Partiti, candidate, elettori.* Milano: Egea.
Transform! Italia (2004). Ricerca sull'innovazione nel PRC [working paper]. Amsterdam: Transnational Institute.
Valentini, Alessandro (2000). *La vecchia talpa e l'araba fenice.* Napoli: La città del sole.
Valle, Leonardo (2002). 'Club privé. A cosa sono servite le privatizzazioni delle banche italiane', *Proteo* 1.
Vittoria, Albertina (2006). *Storia del PCI. 1921–1991.* Roma: Carocci Editore.
Waters, Sarah (1994). 'Tangentopoli and the emergence of a new political order in Italy', *West European Politics* 17(1): 169–182.

6 The French radical left
Success or failure?

The contemporary French radical left presents a strange paradox. On the one hand, its extra-parliamentary influence was beyond compare in the Western European landscape. First, radical left activists maintained a strong presence on the ground and were prominent in civil society and social movement organisations, from the traditional communist subculture to the movementist and alter-globalist galaxy. Secondly, the latter groups contributed to an unparalleled level of resistance to neoliberalism, with periodic mass anti-government mobilisations (1986–88, 1993–95, 2002–03, 2005–06, 2009–10, 2015) and a myriad of other contentious events by public sector workers, private sector workers, students, ethnic minority youth, migrants, the unemployed, peasants, environmentalists, and single-issue campaigners. Thirdly, radical left personalities and themes were quite influential in academia and in the public discourse. Fourthly, radical left campaigns had the capacity of gaining a majority support, as attested, for instance, by the victory in the 2005 European Constitution referendum. On the other hand, the electoral strength of the radical left always remained medium-small, oscillating between 7 and 14 per cent of valid votes, and its success in bringing about positive social change (as opposed to hindering negative developments) was scarce. In this chapter I analyse the reasons behind this disconnect and answer the question of whether this trajectory must be qualified as a success or as a failure.

The discussion is structured as follows. First, I briefly introduce the historical context in which the parties of the 'new' French radical left emerged and had to operate. Secondly, I track in more detail the evolution of their systemic strength, cohesion, and political nature. Thirdly, I provide an explanation of the growing fragmentation of this party family and of the failure of various regroupment projects. Fourthly, I analyse the validity of the 'vacuum thesis' with reference to the French case. Fifthly, I assess the success of the efforts of each of the radical left organisations to influence the social balance of forces, the dynamics of political competition, and state policies. Finally, I summarise and discuss the main findings.

The analysis is based on a large amount of primary evidence. Due to space constraints, references in the text are generally limited to the secondary literature. Primary data, together with sources, notes, and elaborations, are accessible through the Western European Radical Left Database (Chiocchetti 2016).

The national context

France is a country with strong left-wing and radical left traditions, which made a deep mark on its intellectual, political, and social history (Becker and Candar 2005). Plebeian and working-class radicalism played an important role in the revolutions of the eighteenth and nineteenth century (1789–96, 1830–32, 1848–49, and 1871). In the period of the Second International, the class left remained relatively weak, due to the competition of left-wing republicans and strong internal divisions between rival parties and tendencies. This delay was caught up in the post-World War I decades, and from 1936 to 1981 the French left became remarkably strong, with a large communist party, vital far-left and left-socialist currents, and three huge semi-revolutionary movements (the Popular Front strikes of 1936, the armed anti-fascist resistance in 1940–44, and May 1968).

During the eighties, however, the strength and influence of the radical left collapsed. In 1983, the Socialist Party (PS) abruptly shifted from outspokenly anticapitalist to broadly centrist position. The Communist Party (PCF) and the far left, in turn, entered into a profound crisis and their electoral strength fell from 23.9 per cent in 1978 to 11.3 per cent in 1986. The end of the Eastern bloc in 1989–91 did not produce the kind of organisational and electoral upheavals that befell most other Western European counterparts, but further compounded the disarray in their ranks.

Starting from 1993–95, the wheel turned and the political life of the country came to be dominated by a continuous and generally inconclusive clash between elite attempts to introduce neoliberal reforms and sustained popular resistances. The revival of labour militancy, social movements, and critical thought created a favourable environment for the radical left, whose strength and influence suddenly recovered. As in Italy, however, the dynamics of the bipolar political competition constrained its momentum and progressively undermined its political coherence and organisational cohesion.

The 'new' French radical left was essentially composed by old organisations, which retained their traditional names and most of their political culture but tried to adapt their image, discourse, and organisational practices to the requirements of the changed historical period.[1]

The main player was the Parti communiste français (French Communist Party, PCF) (Andolfatto 2005; Bell 1998, 2004; Courtois and Lazar 2000; Delwit 2014; Lavabre and Platone 2003; Lazar 1992; Martelli 2009, 2010; Pudal 2009). Born in 1920, in the seventies it was still one of the strongest communist parties of Western Europe, sitting halfway between pro-Soviet orthodoxy and Eurocommunism. The crisis of the eighties destroyed this position, but the decline slowed down in 1986 and stopped in 1995. The party seized the opportunity provided by the revival of left-wing social movement to try a belated reconversion into a modern anti-neoliberal party. However, the disastrous governmental participation in the Jospin government (1997–2002) and many local administrations, and its lacklustre leadership and profile, exposed it to a strong competition by alternative radical left organisations and determined a further progressive decline.

On the far left, three Trotskyist organisations always maintained a small core of supporters and boomed between 1995 and 2010 (*Cahiers Leon Trotsky* 79/2002; *Dissidences* 6/2009; Lanuque 2002; Nick 2002; Pina 2005, 2011; Raynaud 2006; Reynié 2007; Salles 2012; Sperber 2010; Tiberj 2004; Turpin 1997; Ubbiali 2008). The strongest was Lutte Ouvrière (Workers' Struggle, LO) (Barcia 2003; Choffat 1991, 2012; Ubbiali 2002). Established in 1956, it expounded a distinctive brand of Trotskyism derived from the legacy of the tiny Barta group (1939–52). During the seventies and eighties, it managed to develop into a small national organisation with a decent electoral support and a popular figurehead, Arlette Laguiller. Its electoral results sharply rose in 1995, but faded again after 2002 due to the squeeze of tactical voting for the PS and an increased radical left competition. The second strongest was the Ligue communiste révolutionnaire (Revolutionary Communist League, LCR), re-established in 2009 as Nouveau parti anticapitaliste (New Anticapitalist Party, NPA) (Bonnemaison 2012; Filoche 2007; Johsua 2004, 2015; Krivine 2006; Salles 2005). Created in 1969 through the merger of an older organisation (1944) and a recent group of students (1966), it was the French section of the official Fourth International. The group had its first place in the sun in the post-1968 decade, rapidly declined from the late seventies to the mid-nineties, and boomed again after 2002. The 2008–09 refoundation initially had promising results, but the party narrowly failed to come up ahead of the Front de Gauche (FdG) in the 2009 European election, and progressively lost to it most of its voters and members. The smallest organisation was the Parti des travailleurs (Workers' Party, PT), rebranded in 2008 as Parti ouvrier indépendant (Independent Labour Party, POI) (Campinchi 2000; Landais 2013). Born in a 1965 split of the Fourth International, it followed a minority interpretation of Trotkyism known as 'Lambertism', from the name of its historical leader Pierre Boussel a.k.a. Lambert. Despite its sometimes substantial influence in terms of membership and organisational linkages, particularly in the student union UNEF and the trade union FO, it never went beyond 0.5 per cent of votes in national elections.

Left-socialist and other non-communist forces also played a non-negligible role in the French radical left. The Parti socialiste unifié (Unified Socialist Party, PSU) was an important left-socialist organisation from 1960 to 1981, but dramatically declined in the eighties and dissolved in 1990 (Kernalegenn et al. 2010). Some of its activists, however, joined forces with communist and far-left dissidents and created an 'eco-socialist' milieu that survived in various forms until the present day, often with national elected representatives.[2] The Parti de gauche (Left Party, PG) was created in 2008–09 by a split from the PS of another left-wing leader, Jean-Luc Mélenchon (Alemagna and Alliès 2012; Escalona and Vieira 2014). While much weaker than either the PCF or the NPA, the organisation managed to exploit its strategic position and the charismatic figure of its leader to become an important actor of the contemporary radical left. In 2012, in particular, Mélenchon was selected as the presidential candidate of the FdG, obtaining an excellent 11.1 per cent of valid votes. In 2015, the similar left-socialist group Nouvelle

Gauche Socialiste (New Socialist Left, NGS) split from the PS; its importance and future prospects are, however, not clear.

Several other groups are excluded by this analysis, due to their uncertain political positioning. The Mouvement des citoyens (Citizens' Movement, MDC) was created in 1993 by the split from the PS of its historical left-wing leader Jean-Pierre Chevènement (Verrier 2003). It embodied a 'left-republican' ideology oscillating between the radical left, the PS, and a 'neither left nor right' sovereignism; some splinter groups did later join the PG. Autonomous communist, ex-communist, and left-independentist parties of the overseas territories were negligible at the national level, but often sizeable in their specific field of activity.[3] Solid allies of the radical left up to the early eighties, they subsequently oscillated between PCF, PS, and other forces in response to local concerns. Nouvelle Donné (New Deal, ND) was created in 2013 by disaffected socialist members; despite a clear Keynesian and welfarist programme, the party avoids any anti-capitalist reference and has not developed a tight relationship with the rest of the radical left.

Finally, while a number of attempts of regroupment failed during the nineties and the noughties, after 2008 the vast majority of the radical left gradually came together in a loose radical left coalition, the Front de Gauche (Left Front, FdG) (Marlière 2012; Martelli 2012). Despite its growing success in 2009–12, this alliance remained traversed by serious tensions between orientations (the relationship with PS and Verts) and organisations, and by 2016 was moribund, with Mélenchon announcing an 'insurgent' presidential candidacy and the PCF wavering uncertainly between him, a broader left-wing coalition, and the Socialist Party.

The new French radical left

A more detailed analysis of the evolution of the strength, cohesion, and nature of the contemporary French radical left shows a fluid situation, marked by both continuities and discontinuities with the pre-1989 past.

Strength

The evolution of the systemic strength of the French radical left in the period 1993–2015 are summarised in Table 6.1 and Figure 6.1 below. The overall indicator defines a medium-sized political area with an average strength of 10.7 per cent – about twice the size of its German and Italian counterparts – following a broadly declining trajectory.

Electoral strength was in average 9.9 per cent, with a sharp turning point in 2002. Four periods can be distinguished. In an initial phase (1986–94), marked by a deep crisis of international communism and of the French left, results in all kinds of elections slowly declined, but less than in most other European countries. Legislative vote shares fell from 11.7 per cent in 1988 to 11.0 per cent in 1993. In a second phase (1995–2002), marked by the boom of anti-neoliberal movements, results improved and stabilised at higher levels. Presidential vote shares rose from 11.2 per cent in 1988 to 13.9 per cent in 1995 and 13.9 per cent in 2002.

Table 6.1 Strength, French radical left

	AVERAGE 1993–2015 RESOURCES	AVERAGE 1993–2015 SYSTEMIC STRENGTH
1 ELECTORAL	votes	%
Composite (pres. 20 / nat. 60 / reg. 20)		9.85
Presidential	3,962,495	12.40
Legislative	2,410,740	9.39
Regional	1,946,152	8.79
2 PARLIAMENTARY	seats	%
Composite (nat. 75 / reg. 25)		5.12
National	23	3.90
Regional	155	8.79
3 GOVERNMENTAL		%
Composite (pres. 20 / nat. 60 / reg. 20)		3.31
President		0.00
National		1.96
Regional		10.66
4 MEMBERSHIP	members	%
	150,059	24.36
FINANCIAL		strong
COMMUNICATION		medium
CIVIL SOCIETY		medium
OVERALL STRENGTH		%
Composite (average 1 to 4)		10.66

The trauma of 21 April 2002 (Perrineau and Ysmal 2003) opened a third period of weakness (2002–08), as radical left voters rallied to the socialist candidates to prevent a repeat of the centre-right vs. far right second round of the 2002 presidential election. Legislative vote shares fell to 7.6 per cent in 2002 and 8.0 per cent in 2007; presidential vote shares followed at 9.0 per cent in 2007. The last period (2009–15), finally, was characterised by contradictory developments, with swift recoveries in European (12.6 per cent in 2009) and presidential (12.8 per cent in 2012) elections coexisting with a stagnation of legislative results (7.9 per cent in 2012) and heavy losses in subsequent European and local elections. Interestingly, the radical left usually performed well in presidential and European elections, where a variety of competing organisations ran appealing candidates and effective campaigns focused on mobilising their core constituency and winning the anti-establishment vote. Legislative results were much lower, due to a lower turnout of radical left voters, the poor results of non-communist organisations (who lacked

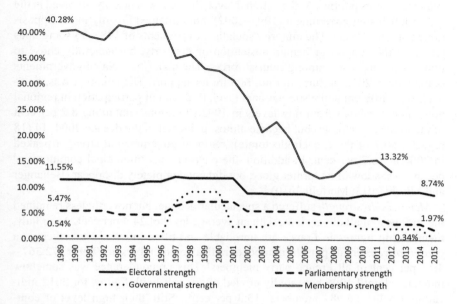

Figure 6.1 Strength evolution, French radical left

the resources to field candidates and campaign in all constituencies), and the pressure toward tactical voting. In regional and local elections, finally, the PCF often opted for unitary centre-left lists from the first round, thus driving down official radical left results.

Parliamentary strength was much lower: in average 5.1 per cent, with a strong declining tendency since 2002. At the national level, results stagnated from 4.3 per cent in 1988 to 4.0 per cent in 1993, increased to 6.3 per cent in 1997, and then collapsed to 3.8 per cent (2002), 3.1 per cent (2007), and 1.7 per cent (2012). This decline almost cost the PCF its parliamentary group, which was saved after 2007 by a reduction of the minimum number of members and by 'technical' agreements with other smaller organisations. At the regional level, results were propped up by the strategy of centre-left alliances adopted by the PCF and other smaller groups between 1992 and 2010.[4] Thanks to frequent common lists at the first round or mergers (*fusions*) in the second, the radical left retained a regional parliamentary strength of 7.2 per cent in 1992, 10.7 per cent in 1998, 10.6 in 2004, and 7.2 per cent in 2010; in 2015, when it ran everywhere separate from the PS, the level collapsed at 2.7 per cent. The effects of the majoritarian electoral legislation were in both cases decisive, virtually denying representation to non-aligned forces and making the more conciliatory organisations heavily dependent from the outcome of pre-electoral negotiations on joint lists and mutual stand-down agreements.

Governmental strength was also low: in average 3.3 per cent, with a 9.3 peak in 1998. No French president has ever hailed from the radical left or shown any sympathy for its politics. At the national level, the PCF was heavily involved in the centre-left Jospin government (1997–2002), but remained broadly in the opposition in all other years. The minority socialist governments of 1988–93 sometimes relied on the support or benign abstention of the party, but generally chose to find the missing votes among centrist forces. The majority socialist governments seating since 2012, in turn, did not require its support. The situation was, however, very different at the sub-national level. Radical left participation in regional governments started from tiny levels in 1992 (2 regions containing 8.2 per cent of the French electorate) but became almost universal in the decade 2004–14 (18 regions, 86.7 of the French electorate); regional governmental strength peaked in 2004 at 16.7 per cent. In addition, the once-famous 'municipal communism' became a shadow of its former glory, but did not completely disappear (Bellanger and Mischi 2013; Martelli 2010).[5]

Membership strength suffered a spectacular decline, but nevertheless remained the strongest of all dimensions, with an average level of 24.4 per cent. As in Italy, membership figures in France are unreliable and often inflated. Nevertheless, a *conservative* estimate puts the number of radical left members in 1989 at 372,367 – 40.3 per cent of all French party members! This preponderance was somehow maintained until 1996 but rapidly eroded afterwards, with figures for 2012 indicating a paltry 86,984 members (13.3 per cent). Still, their high level of commitment and the existence of large groups of close sympathisers and activist of minor groups endowed radical left parties with crucial advantages in the political competition, which became very visible at times of electoral campaigns and extra-parliamentary mobilisations.

Further dimensions cannot be ascertained with precision. Financial data for the period 2003–10 suggest a very strong position, with average real yearly incomes 41.8 million euro (19.6 per cent of all party incomes). This was the result of the enormous accumulated resources of the PCF, a strong self-financing capacity (contributions of elected representatives, commercial activities, membership fees, and donations), and a fairly liberal party financing law. Media outreach declined strongly, but radical left parties still controlled important communication tools: the quite intensive official electoral propaganda (video and radio ads, home-delivered leaflets, placards), reimbursed by the state and providing a basic level playing field between all candidates; PCF's daily newspaper l'Humanité, with a distribution of about 50,000 copies; its annual festival Fête de l'Humanité, with half a million declared visitors, and LO's network of biweekly workplace leaflets (*bulletins d'entreprise*), with an estimated outreach of several hundred thousand readers. The mainstream press and television was skewed toward the two major governmental parties, but did cover the radical left and offered it from time to time a large audience, particularly before presidential elections. Finally, the strength of social linkages collapsed since the mid-eighties, but the legacy of a shared political culture facilitated informal dialogue and collaborations. On the one hand, the vast network of communist unions and mass organisations weakened and clearly distanced itself from the PCF during the nineties but, unlike its homologues in Italy and Eastern Germany, did not dissolve or unambiguously switch allegiance to other political forces. On the other hand, the smaller but substantial social movement and alter-globalist milieu was also jealous of its autonomy, but broadly identified with the radical left and was not alien to double memberships and direct electoral interventions.

To sum up, the brutal electoral, institutional, and membership decline of the period 1981–86 slowed down afterwards and was briefly reversed after 1995. In the early and mid-nineties, the French radical left was much weakened compared to the seventies, but remained one of the strongest in Western Europe and quite influential in terms of organisational strength, social linkages, and local strongholds. The post-1995 recovery, however, was wasted by the devastating double impact of governmental participation and pro-socialist tactical voting. All indicators of systemic strength quickly moved to catch up with the new situation, leaving it in tatters after 2002. This notwithstanding, its constituent organisations still play a prominent role in extra-parliamentary political life and mobilisations, and their former members and supporters are not permanently lost to the cause, as demonstrated by the short-lived surge of 2008–12.

Cohesion

One of the main problems of the French radical left was its growing fragmentation into rival organisations, traditions, and strategic orientations. A visual representation of this evolution (national level only) is provided in Figure 6.2.

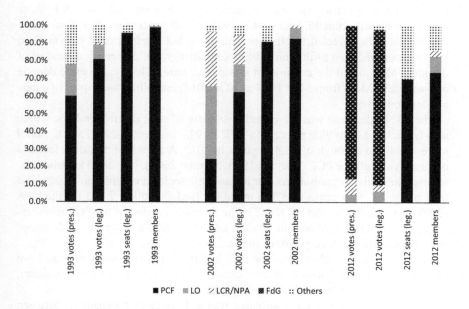

Figure 6.2 Fragmentation (national level), French radical left

The PCF had always held an absolutely hegemonic position within this area, although alternative organisations such as the PSU or the Trotskyist far left had managed to build up some following during the seventies. Starting from the late-eighties, however, this predominance was gradually eroded by a variety of challengers.

The first to go was its lead in presidential elections. The share of its candidates dropped from 81.8 per cent in 1981 (Georges Marchais) to 60.2 per cent in 1988 (André Lajoinie), 62.0 per cent in 1995 (Robert Hue), 24.4 per cent in 2002 (Robert Hue), and 21.4 per cent in 2007 (Marie-George Buffet). Alternative candidates such as Pierre Juquin (PCF dissident), Arlette Laguiller (LO), Olivier Besancenot (LCR/NPA), and José Bové (alter-globalist), despite hailing from tiny organisations, performed well, often beating them into second or third place. Shaken by these disasters, the party ended up rallying to the 2012 candidature of the left-socialist Mélenchon (PG), who finally succeeded in reunifying the radical left vote (86.7 per cent).

The decline of the PCF was less pronounced in legislative elections, where it could better exploit the advantages of a solid national organisation and of local incumbents; still, the weight of communist candidates dropped from 92.2 per cent in 1981 to 80.8 per cent in 1993, 62.7 per cent in 2002, and 53.4 in 2007. In 2012, the party rallied to the FdG coalition, but results were mixed. While its share of the radical left vote indeed recovered at 87.6 per cent, vote shares remained well below those of Mélenchon and barely improved for recognisable communist candidates.

None of the above made any difference in terms of MPs, as the chance of ordinary challengers to win seats remained non-existent. Still, the PCF share decreased as well, from 95.7 per cent in 1993 to 70.0 per cent in 2012. First, some communist MPs defected to other organisations but retained their personalised local support and their affiliation to the communist group.[6] Secondly, a handful of dissident MPs joined the communist group over time.[7] Thirdly, the mere decline of communist MPs (from 34 in 1997 to 10 in 2012) magnified the impact of external developments.

The last to decrease was the communist share of radical left members, which slowly declined from 98.9 per cent in 1993 to 94.3 per cent in 2001, and then fell more rapidly to a trough of 73.8 per cent in 2012. A stream of dissident factions progressively left the PCF (Dreyfus 1990; Mermat 2005), but failed to build substantial alternative organisations. Far left and left-socialist organisations grew, but only modestly, with peaks of 8,700 members for LO (2006), 9,123 for the NPA (2009), and 12,000 for the PG (2012). The dramatic erosion of the PCF membership (from 298,991 members in 1993 to 64,184 in 2012), however, made out of any minor challenge a very serious threat.

The progressive weakening of the PCF highlighted the necessity of a decisive reorganisation or regroupment of the radical left. A partial solution to the problem, however, came very late and remained fragile.

From 1995 to 2009, what dominated was a destructive competition between rival radical left organisations (Geay and Willemez 2008; Kouvelakis 2007, 2012;

Mathieu 2015; Wolfreys 2003, 2008). First LO (1995–2002) and then the LCR/NPA (2002–10) sought to challenge the role of the PCF as the main radical left force but, despite some successes, failed to win over enough members and voters or to force it to a subordinate alliance. At the same time, various attempts at radical left regroupment failed on substantial political issues and organisational jealousies. The 1995 social movement pushed toward a convergence of the radical left, but divisions were soon exacerbated by the experience of the Jospin government. An alternative 'pole of revolutionaries' between LO and LCR never went beyond an intermittent electoral alliance. The 2005 referendum campaign again pushed toward a convergence, but intense negotiations left behind LO and the PS-left and ultimately broke down, leading to three rival presidential candidates. The disastrous results of the 2007 elections finally led to more flexibility, but the result was not one but two competing projects, the NPA and the FdG.

From 2010 to 2015, on the contrary, the FdG coalition gradually outcompeted LO and NPA, attracting most radical left organisations and activists and occupying the overwhelming majority of the radical left space (Marliére 2012; Martelli 2012; Mathieu 2015). However, the opportunity to develop into a unitary party or a more structured alliance was wasted and its unity was progressively undermined by a number of imbalances: between a clear autonomous profile and the need to save its parliamentary representation through alliances with the Socialist Party or minor centre-left forces (in legislative and sub-national elections); between the overwhelming institutional and organisational strength of the PCF and its weak electoral appeal; and between its main party (PCF) and its most popular spokesperson (Mélenchon). At every election since 2012, competing lists resurfaced, and the coalition all but broke down in 2016.

Nature

As in the rest of Western Europe, the contemporary French radical left is characterised by a significant break with the typical features of the twentieth-century communist movement and a – still unachieved – effort of renewal and reconfiguration.

Ideologically, the French radical left progressively shifted toward a modern 'broad left' anti-neoliberal programme, but several differences remained on its precise content and implications.

The PCF radically renewed its ideological outlook between 1994 and 2002 under the leadership of Robert Hue (Andolfatto 2005; Mermat 2005; Mischi 2003). The repudiation of the Soviet model and the opening to radical-democratic and left-libertarian themes, however, did not coalesce into a clear alternative idea of society. On the one hand, the long-term goal of a 'communism which will free mankind' continued to be formally affirmed in its statutes and internal documents, but its contours were not further elaborated and references to Marxism, working-class agency, anti-capitalism, and communism were progressively de-emphasised in its public discourse, to be replaced by vague statements of humanistic and progressive values. On the other hand, the anti-neoliberal character of its medium-term programme was clear, with a typical catalogue of demands centred on state intervention, job creation, social protection, and redistribution, but the credibility of its implementation was dented by the readiness of the PCF to compromise with the PS (as shown in its governmental experience of 1997–02) and its reluctance to provide precise answers on how to overcome EU constraints. Finally, the links between one stage and the other were left indefinite.

The renewal of the LCR was more superficial (Bonnemaison 2012; Johsua 2015; Ubbiali 2008). The organisation somewhat downplayed its references to revolutionary communism, Trotskyism, and the Fourth International and refocused on anti-neoliberal themes but, behind various stylistic innovations, its traditional goals and strategy remained clearly recognisable. On the one hand, LCR and NPA continued to identify with an anti-capitalist perspective rooted in socialisation, planning, and socialist democracy. On the other hand, they insisted on structuring their medium-term programme not around relatively feasible anti-neoliberal reforms, but rather around radical transitional demands that could rapidly lead to a break with capitalism.

LO, on the contrary, changed little of its political culture and ideology (Choffat 2012; Ubbiali 2008). While its public profile was characterised by a radical workerist and populist discourse, the organisation never really saw itself as anti-neoliberal, openly sticking to its distinctive conception of Trotskyism and following the traditional blueprint of a Leninist party, workplace intervention, transitional demands, a proletarian revolution, a council-based socialist democracy, and the gradual withering away of class boundaries and the state.

The case of the PG was quite interesting (Escalona and Vieira 2014). This organisation rapidly evolved from a mild anti-neoliberalism toward a radical eco-socialist programme combining a green dirigiste welfarism ('ecological planning'), radical-democratic goals ('civic revolution' and 'sixth republic'), a break with EU institutions, and anti-capitalist insights. While its sources of inspiration were eclectic and the contours of its vision vague, the party actually went further than the PCF in its advocacy both of medium-term reforms and of a long-term democratic road to socialism.

Sociologically, some tension developed between electoral constituency, party organisation, and political discourse (Table 6.2).

Altogether, the radical left electorate remained solidly 'proletarian', with the share of employed and unemployed wageworkers oscillating between 55 and 65 per cent of the total. The decline of blue-collar workers was compensated by the rise of white-collar workers and intermediate professions. The dramatic shift of the PCF from a party of the working class to a party of pensioners and other inactive persons, in turn, was compensated by the large gains of other far-left and left-socialist organisations among all categories of wageworkers. The weight of wageworkers and of the youth increased in elections dominated by the latter (e.g. 2002 and 2007 presidential elections) and decreased in those dominated by the former (e.g. legislative and sub-national elections).

Radical left organisations, on the contrary, saw a collapse of the traditional predominance of blue-collar workers and a surge of pensioners and educated elites

Table 6.2 Sociology, French radical left

	FRENCH ELECT. 1978	RL VOTERS 1978	PCF MEMBERS 1979	FRENCH ELECT. 2002	RL VOTERS 2002	PCF MEMBERS 1997
GENDER						
Male	48.1	52.8	65.0	45.9	42.9	60.0
Female	51.9	47.2	35.0	54.1	57.1	40.0
AGE						
<30	24.8	35.8	24.5	19.6	22.3	10.5
30–59	52.0	50.3	59.9	54.1	65.0	65.1
>59	23.2	13.9	15.6	26.3	12.7	24.4
CLASS						
Wageworker	40.5	57.3	59.9	46.9	63.4	43.7
Intermediate	10.0	11.7	10.2	14.7	17.2	10.3
White-collar	12.3	13.4	17.6	15.5	20.9	17.1
Blue-collar	13.5	24.9	32.1	11.4	18.8	16.3
Unemployed	4.7	7.3		5.3	6.5	
Employer and self-employed	11.2	3.7	5.9	2.7	0.8	2.5
Professional	4.8	3.8	3.4	7.9	6.5	5.9
Inactive	43.4	35.2	30.8	42.5	29.3	47.9
Pensioner	18.7	12.6	15.5	27.9	14.1	24.5
Student	2.4	3.3		6.4	7.4	
Other	22.3	19.3	15.3	8.2	7.8	23.4
EDUCATION						
Below secondary	74.7	77.5		53.7	57.3	
Secondary	14.1	12.3		16.4	17.4	
Tertiary	11.2	10.2		29.9	25.2	
RELIGION						
Practicing Catholic	17.0	3.0		10.6	5.1	
Non-practicing Catholic	65.5	62.7		57.2	47.5	
Other religion	3.7	2.0		5.8	4.3	
No religion	13.8	32.3		26.4	43.0	

(intellectuals and professionals). Among PCF members, blue-collar workers declined from 32.1 per cent in 1979 to 16.3 in 1997, while the inactive rose from 30.8 per cent to 47.9 per cent (Platone and Ranger 2000). Among communist MPs, former blue-collar workers vanished (32.6 per cent in 1979, 14.7 per cent in 1997, 0.0 per cent in 2012) to the benefit of intermediate and upper professions (36.1 per cent in 1979, 71.8 per cent in 1997, 71.4 per cent in 2010), and the average age markedly increased (51.4 years old in 1979, 55.4 in 1997 and 61.7 in 2012). The professional background of PCF secretaries shifted from metalworker (before 1994) to nurse, civil servant, and journalist (after 1994). During the eighties and the nineties, the party lost contact with the life-worlds of ordinary workers and, crucially, progressively shelved its voluntarist policies aimed at their schooling and promotion to positions of responsibility (Ethuin 2003; Mischi 2010; Pudal 2002).

LO also experienced some growth of teachers and pensioners, but its membership seems to have remained overwhelmingly composed by blue-collar and white-collar workers (Choffat 2012). Within the LCR/NPA, the weight and visibility of ordinary wageworkers gradually increased since 2002, but upper-intermediate professions and students remained absolutely predominant (Johsua 2015).

The discourse of the parties, finally, ranged from an absolute focus on the working-class for LO, to a mixture of workerist and movementist themes for the LCR/NPA, to broader reference to 'the people' or 'the citizens' for PCF, PG, and the FdG coalition.

Organisationally, the transition from mass to modern cadre parties was more gradual than in Germany and Italy but reached similar results. The PCF lost both negative and positive aspects of its tradition between 1994 and 2002 (Andolfatto 2005; Pudal 2009). On the one hand, it shelved its Stalinist monolithism and embraced internal democracy and pluralism; on the other hand, its identity and cohesion, militant resources, electoral support, and social linkages all evaporated at the same speed, leaving behind an empty shell of disoriented cadres. LO clung to the tradition of the Leninist 'cadre party' (Ubbiali 2002). Despite a strong growth of sympathisers and members without voting rights, it failed to substantially expand and renew its activist core. The LCR/NPA strongly relaxed its Leninist norms between 1998 and 2009, seeking to become the core of a reconfiguration of the French radical left (Johsua 2015; Rizet 2007). The marked progresses in terms of members and connections were erased by the subsequent crisis, when its membership fell back to the 2003 levels and many of its historic cadres left to join the FdG. The PG broadly continued the organisational practices of its socialist predecessor. Its initial surge was also short-lived, fading after 2012.

Overall, each organisation failed to provide a solution to the key issues created in the radical left by the decline of the communist mass party model: the disconnect between electoral support and partisan engagement; the shrinking of parties to the milieu of professional politicians or semi-professional activists, to the exclusion of ordinary citizens; the autonomisation of central leaders and elected representatives from grassroots members; and the growing gap between parties and civil society organisations. The periodic surges of interest for and participation in radical left politics were not consolidated in stable partisan or associational structures, as local committees and national networks regularly fell apart and left behind few organisational benefits. The promising unitary framework established by the FdG in the 2012 presidential campaign, finally, was equally incapable to create stable attachments and effective mobilisation tools, remaining a mere unstable alliance of small and shrinking organisations.

Strategically, the various organisations were sharply divided on their plans to bring about an anti-neoliberal or anti-capitalist turn.

On the one hand, LO advocated a strategy of *anti-capitalist alternative* and the consolidation of a 'workers' camp' against both poles of the bourgeois alternation. On the other hand, the leadership of the PCF decisively turned in the mid-nineties toward a strategy of *conciliatory leftward pull*, generalising centre-left electoral alliances, becoming a junior partner of the socialists in the Jospin cabinet

(1997–2002) and in most regional and local administrations (1998–2014), and trying to influence them through dialogue, friendly pressures, and agreements with other smaller left-wing forces (Becker 2005; Boy et al. 2003). Most radical left members and voters remained in the middle of the road, despising the 'social liberalism' of the PS but nevertheless being ready to help its victory against the right.

These contradictory strategies were one of the main reasons behind both the increasing fragmentation of the French radical left, and the failure or fragility of the various attempts of radical left regroupment.

Summary

The making of the contemporary French radical left, unlike most European cases, was not marked by a sharp break with the past under the impulse of the fall of the Eastern bloc in 1989–91. The main organisations of the previous period survived intact and provided the framework for the subsequent recovery, although their political nature gradually adapted to the new conditions and their absolute and relative strength radically shifted.

Their systemic strength was relatively high, but fragile and strongly unbalanced. Electoral results oscillated between 7 and 13 per cent, charting an uncertain path between a large popular sympathy for their programmes, the constraints of the majoritarian bipolar political competition, and brutal disillusionments (2002). The legacy of the PCF inexorably eroded, but left behind several pockets of strength: large financial resources, local strongholds, an initially huge membership, and vast but loosened social linkages. Other parties (LO, LCR/NPA, and PG) rose swiftly, but failed to translate their electoral growth into solid organisational and institutional positions. The radical left as a whole could from time to time seduce the left-wing opinion during extra-parliamentary mobilisations and referendums, but did not come close to denting the socialist supremacy in elections and representative institutions.

In terms of political nature, this political area oscillated between anti-capitalism and anti-neoliberalism, workerism and populism, intransigence and centre-left integration, never finding that elusive balance that could have satisfied all sections of its potential constituency.

In terms of cohesion, the rapid electoral and membership decline of the PCF paved the way for a variety of challengers, which, however, all failed to establish their predominance. The result was a pulverisation of the partisan radical left in rival groups, cultures, and strategic visions, which subsequent regroupment attempts could only superficially paper over.

Explaining radical left fragmentation

The progressive fragmentation of the French radical left and of its electorate can be traced back to the interplay of three main factors.

The first one was the dilemma of the attitude to be adopted toward the Socialist party, which led to a differentiation between intransigent and conciliatory strategies and unsuccessful attempts to conciliate both. On the one hand, the conciliatory turn of the PCF during the nineties, with its convinced participation to the *gauche plurielle* and its prominent involvement as junior governmental partner at the national and sub-national level, destroyed its credibility and opened its flank to more intransigent organisations: first LO (1995–2002), then LCR/NPA (2002–10), and finally the PG (2011–present). On the other hand, the regroupment of the whole radical left in a united *anti-neoliberal pole* was undermined by the same tensions. Regroupment within the centre-left, as variously attempted during the nineties, was not acceptable for the far left. Regroupment outside of the centre-left, in turn, was highly problematic. The PCF agreed to it in principle after 2002, but never ceased to participate to centre-left governmental alliances at the local level and unsuccessfully pursue a revival of the plural left at the national one. LO usually refused any electoral contamination with the socialist party, which other minor groups, the PG, and parts of the LCR/NPA were instead prepared to accept to a certain extent.[8] The choice of autonomy, finally, was often an obstacle to the dialogue with external forces, such as the left wing of the PS or some of its smaller allies (MDC, Verts).

The second one was the contradictory impact of institutional rules and regulations. The fairly permissive legislation on party and campaign financing (Lehingue 2008; Phélippeau and François 2010) encouraged the proliferation of radical left candidates and offered to medium-small organisations the access to a reasonable amount of resources.[9] The effects of electoral legislation (Brechon 2009), in turn, varied widely according to the specific rules of each kind of election and the chances of each organisation to gain representation and other material benefits. Presidential elections favoured competing candidatures and the dispersion of votes in the first round. The single-member two-round system used in legislative and cantonal elections had normally the same effects outside of the constituencies of seating radical left MPs, but higher hurdles and lower rewards limited the number of non-communist candidates and their total vote shares. European elections and regional elections until 1998, with their PR system with medium-level electoral thresholds, promoted the pooling of the resources to gain representation: for instance, LO-LCR alliances, PCF 'open lists', or FdG lists. The effects of the majority bonus system in place for big cities and regional elections since 2004, finally, depended on the local balance of forces, encouraging sometimes alliances, other times a proliferation of candidates, and still other times joint radical left lists with the defection of the PCF or PCF dissidents to the main centre-left list.

The third one was the lack of will or incapacity of the existing radical left organisations to find reasonable compromises to their political and material conflicts. The partial convergence of most of the French radical left around a common 'broad left' identity and anti-neoliberal programme was clear since the mid-nineties, when the PCF gave up its hostility to the far left, different political cultures (communism, left-socialism, Trotskyism, welfarism, ecologism, left-libertarianism) started to mingle, and unity of action was reached in mass mobilisations. While disagreements on long-term goals and medium-term strategies were important, in the short-term a minimum level of unity was certainly feasible, as proved by contemporary European developments and the later experience of the FdG. In particular, the PCF could have limited its involvement in centre-left alliances at the national and regional level to an external support without governmental participation, and the far left could have downplayed the divide between anti-neoliberalism and anti-capitalism. However, each major organisation (PCF, LO, LCR/NPA, and PG) hoped to be able to outmanoeuvre the others and become the core of a future regroupment, and therefore tended to emphasise the dividing points between them. The PCF, in view of its important history and clear institutional-organisational supremacy, was reluctant to rally behind a non-communist presidential candidate (which it did only in 2012) and to dissolve itself in a broader organisation (which it refused to do). In addition, the potential benefits of an alliance were unclear: a stronger image, certainly, but slightly less resources (campaign financing, TV spaces) and considerably fewer elected representatives (due to an absence of alliances with the PS).

The consequence of these pressures was a growing fragmentation of the French radical left. In the nineties, the supremacy of the PCF vanished and was replaced by a violent competition between groups allied with the ruling Socialist Party and groups opposed to it. After the 2002 defeat, more credible attempts at an anti-neoliberal regroupment repeatedly collapsed due to persisting strategic differences and organisational rivalries. From 2009 to 2014, a formal convergence was finally reached through the FdG, which narrowly defeated the rival NPA project and absorbed most radical left organisations and voters. However, it failed to solve underlying divergences and to institutionalise common participatory and decisional structures. After 2015, finally, the tension between the PCF and Mélenchon exploded, leading to a virtual end of the alliance.

Filling the vacuum: potential and limits of the radical left mobilisation

Like most advanced economies, France has experienced since the eighties a worsening of its macro-economic performance, mass unemployment, deindustrialisation, wage restraint, and some neoliberalisation of its political economy. Three specificities, however, stand out. First, negative trends affecting wageworkers and the welfare state were much less pronounced than in most other Western European countries, and real living standards, career perspectives, and the level of social protection continued to moderately grow. Secondly, neoliberal reforms were predominantly introduced by right-wing governments, while socialist governments generally pursued centrist policies, favouring financial and trade deregulation and Europeanisation but trying to compensate their effects with active budgetary, industrial, and social policies. Thirdly, the level of popular resistance to neoliberalism was unparalleled, with periodic social movements of a huge size and often successful character.

The challenge for the French radical left was thus different than in Germany or Italy, as support for progressive policies remained widespread, but the rift between these welfarist constituencies and the political elite interested more the centre-right than the centre-left. The dull profile of the Socialist Party kept its first-round results low, but the overwhelming majority of left-of-centre voters remained ready to support it in the second round.

A more detailed analysis of this problem shows that the radical left completely failed to expand its support among working-class and welfarist constituencies, with relatively well-off groups sticking to traditional parties, and the core working class increasingly abstaining or opting for the far-right FN.

Contours of the vacuum

At the level of political economy, the neoliberal transition affected France in a much less pronounced way than most of its Western counterparts.

The shift away from the traditional *dirigiste* state was gradual and incomplete (Berne and Pogorel 2005; Clift 2012; MacLean 1997; Schmidt 1996; Smith 1990). When the neoliberal counter-revolution of Thatcher and Reagan was in full swing, the French socialist government actually embarked on a programme of large-scale nationalisations (1981–82) which consolidated the French state-owned sector as one of the largest in Europe. With the socialist electoral defeat of 1986, the tide changed and in the following decades a widespread process of total and partial privatisations reversed the situation. The bulk of it was conducted by centre-right cabinets; centre-left ones initially positioned themselves on a defence of the status quo (1988–93) but later enthusiastically adapted to the trend (1997–2002). This notwithstanding, the French state-owned sector remained proportionally quite large and bigger than in most other advanced industrial countries.

Welfare state restructuring was milder than in Italy or Germany and often counterbalanced by an actual expansion of welfare provisions (Cole 1999; Vail 2010). Total governmental expenditures between 1994 and 2009 hovered around a very high 53.4 per cent of GDP, broadly following the economic cycle. Public employment remained one of the highest in Europe, continuously expanding from 4,257,700 in 1990 (18.3 per cent of total employment) to 5,640,700 in 2014 (21.2 per cent). Aggressive labour market and pension reforms were often attempted by right-wing cabinets, but only partially implemented. Socialist governments until 2012, in turn, tended to avoid direct clashes with their traditional constituencies, maintaining existing programmes and protections and often expanding them, as in the 1988 introduction of a guaranteed minimum income and the 1998 introduction of the 35-hour working week.

Macro-economic developments were also not unambiguously negative, until the great recession. The international weight of the country declined, but its economy remained competitive and its large corporations successful. Between 1993 and 2009, GDP growth was slower than in the post-war golden age or in the seventies but remained at acceptable levels (1993–2009: 1.8 per cent). Wage growth was slower but positive (0.6 per cent) and referred to a reduced number of working hours. The wage share and income inequality remained broadly stable, while poverty was kept at bay by the growth of the legal minimum wage and the existence of a strong safety net. The main problem was unemployment, which remained high throughout the period (1994–2014 average: 8.9 per cent). Precarious work contracts also increased, reaching in 2011 about 12 per cent of the workforce.

At the level of political behaviour, the disconnect between political elites and welfarist constituencies was similarly ambiguous.

Traditional centre-right parties – the Gaullist Rassemblement pour la République (Rally for the Republic, RPR), the centrist Union pour la démocratie française (Union for French Democracy, UDF), and their 2002 successor Union pour un mouvement populaire (Union for a Popular Movement, UMP), renamed in 2015 Les Républicains (the Republicans, LR) – strongly alienated their supporters in the working class and the youth with aggressive labour market, pension, and education reforms, which sparked huge mobilisations in the streets, workplaces, and educational establishments (1986, 1994–95, 2003, 2006, 2009–10) and usually led to heavy defeats in the subsequent election (1988, 1993, 2012, but not in 2007).

Public perception of moderate left parties (PS, Verts, and left-radicals) was different. Disappointment for the 'austerity turn' of the Mitterrand presidency in 1983 and its failure to tackle mass unemployment was mitigated by a strong appreciation for its social reforms of 1981–82 (Ross et al. 1987). Mixed feelings characterised all subsequent socialist governments (1988–93, 1997–02, 2012–present), which slowly drifted to the right on socio-economic themes but mobilised a rhetoric of social justice and partially followed through with pieces of legislation and spending decisions. Generally speaking, the PS supported pro-business, pro-finance, and pro-EU economic policies, but sought to compensate their adverse social effects with a moderate expansion of state expenditures, employment programmes, low- and middle-class incomes, and welfare provisions (Abdelal 2007; Bergounioux and Grunberg 2007; Vail 2010). In addition, the return to the opposition periodically boosted its image and support. Only the recent Hollande governments, which were forced to open austerity policies and neoliberal reforms under the pressure of slow growth and EU constraints, seem to be in the process of breaking with their traditional welfarist constituencies.

At the extra-parliamentary level, resistance against neoliberal trends was strong and periodically turned into mass movements of a magnitude unmatched in any other European country outside of Greece.

The first and main actor were wageworkers in the public sector, transport sector, and (to a less extent) private sector (Andolfatto and Labbé 2011a; Béroud 2008; Béroud et al. 2008; Kouvelakis 2007; Mouriaux 2008). Overall strike activity remained vibrant, with major peaks in 1989, 1995, 2003, and 2010 (Figure 7.3).[10] In localised industrial conflicts, strikes were sometimes accompanied by hunger strikes, occupations, and kidnappings; national conflicts, in turn, combined general or public sector strikes and protracted cycles of anti-government demonstrations (Filleule and Tartakowsky 2008). Between 1986 and 1989, a series of generally successful sectorial movements were launched by transport and industrial workers, nurses, teachers, and employees of the Ministry of Finances, with a prominent role played by grassroots networks (Denis 1996). In 1995, an enormous

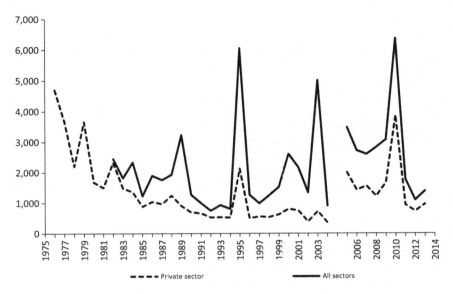

Figure 6.3 Industrial conflicts in France (thousand days lost to strikes)

mobilisation of public sector workers led to the withdrawal of the pension reform of the Juppé government (Béroud and Mouriaux 1998). Other massive but unsuccessful mobilisations of the public sector against further pension reforms were launched in 2003 (Gordon and Mathers 2004) and 2010 (Ancelovici 2011; Andolfatto and Labbé 2011b). In 2009, anti-crisis movements developed in the French Antilles (Monza 2009) and on mainland France (Béroud and Yon 2012). In early 2016, finally, a sizeable movement against the labour market reform of the socialist government started to develop.

The second important actor was the youth. University and high-school students were behind important movements in 1986 (Devaquet university reform), 1994 (CIP job contract), 1998 (Allègre education reform), 2002 (anti-FN demonstrations), 2005 (Fillon education reform), 2006 (CPE job contract), 2007 (Pécresse university reform), and 2016 (El Khomri labour market reform) (Gemie 2003; Legois et al. 2007; Obono 2008). Minority youth, in turn, were behind Marches for Equality in 1983–84 and major urban riots in 1981 and 2005 (Béaud and Masclet 2006; Hargreaves 1991; Le Goaziou and Mucchielli 2006).

Other notable movements included the diffuse mobilisations of the *"sans"* in the period 1991–98 – undocumented migrants, homeless people, and the unemployed (Garcia 2013; Mathieu 2012; Mouchard 2009; Waters 2006); the alterglobalist movement in the period 1999–2004 (Agrikoliansky 2007; Agrikoliansky et al. 2005); and the 2004–05 grassroots campaign for a 'left no' to the EU constitution referendum (Crespy 2008; Dufour 2010).

Did this situation create a favourable environment for the growth of the radical left?

According to the CDSP surveys, approval for welfarist and dirigiste opinions ran high among the French electorate, moving from 40 to 70 per cent according to the specific issue and framing: large minorities disapproved profits (48.7 per cent in 1995; 48.1 per cent in 2007) and approved nationalisations (46.6 per cent in 1995), more state intervention on firms (44.4 per cent in 2002), and a ban on layoffs (44.8 per cent); majorities disapproved privatisations (from 44.2 per cent in 1995 to 66.1 per cent in 2007), approved more taxes for the rich (57.4 per cent in 2007) and a reduction of wealth inequalities (65.1 per cent), and valued wage rises more than competitiveness (68.2 per cent); support for more general values such as equality or solidarity was overwhelming. However, voters did not necessarily see these values as threatened by the traditional parties of the left (PS) and of the right (RPR/UMP/LR, UDF). The former was generally considered in tune with social justice issues, despite its privatisation policies of the nineties. The latter were more criticised, but their rhetoric and record on wages, welfare expenditures, and solidarity was not entirely implausible. In 1995, for instance, a majority of the French with a negative opinion of profits found that Jospin and Chirac had the best solutions for social protection (61.9 per cent), salaries (58.1 per cent), and unemployment (57.9 per cent). In 2007, only a minority of the French favouring salaries over competitiveness thought that Royal and Sarkozy had the best overall solutions for the country (37.9 per cent), but 51.5 nevertheless found Sarkozy's socio-economic programme convincing.

In terms of actual voting behaviour, the electoral support in the first round for the three main establishment parties RPR/UMP/LR, UDF, and PS, which have long dominated French political institutions at all levels, strongly declined after 1978 (Figure 6.4). In presidential elections, their share on total registered voters fell from 56.3 per cent in 1988 to 33.2 per cent in 2002, recovered to 47.1 per cent in 2007, and fell again afterwards (43.5 per cent in 2012). Their share in legislative elections also declined, although with a different timing: down from 46.6 per cent in 1988 to 33.5 per cent in 1997, up to 39.1 per cent in 2002, and down again to 31.8 per cent in 2012. The main beneficiaries were abstention, the far-right FN, and a variety of smaller parties and candidates. The shock of the 2002 presidential election provoked a medium-term countervailing movement (2002–07), with a rise of political participation and a backlash against minor parties, but did not change the long-term trend. Each party tended to lose heavily when in government and recover less when in opposition, with the decade 1997–2007 being a partial exception. However, the same parties still managed to preserve an overwhelming level of support in the second round, when most voters of other parties could happily or reluctantly bring themselves to converge on their candidates. In presidential elections, for instance, the share of PS and RPR/UMP candidates on total registered voters in the second round declined from 81.1 per cent in 1988 to 74.9 per cent in 1995, dropped to 62.0 per cent in 2002 (when, for the first time, one of the candidate was the outsider Jean-Marie Le Pen), but recovered to the previous range afterwards (80.4 per cent in 2007, 75.7 per cent in 2012).

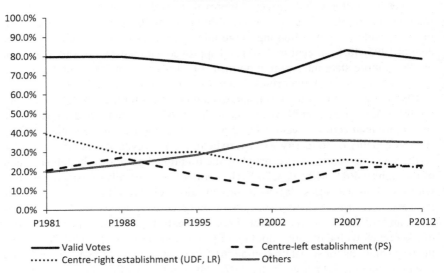

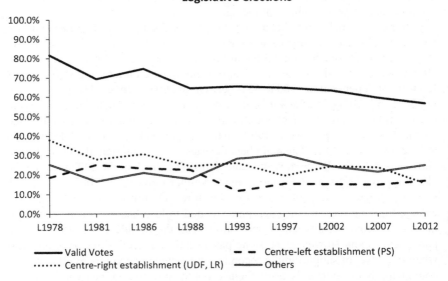

Figure 6.4 Support for French establishment parties (per cent of registered voters)

To sum up, until the great recession the French population displayed a high level of sympathy for the anti-neoliberal issues put forward by the radical left and a high readiness to engage in anti-neoliberal movements, but generally continued to see established parties and candidates as adequate representatives of those very same issues. The left-wing electorate, in turn, was quite happy to nudge the PS to the left by voting for radical left (1995–2002, 2009–12) or other left-wing candidates (such as ecologists or left-republicans), but did not widely share their harsh criticism of the PS as a bourgeois or 'social liberal' force and continued to perceive it as an acceptable welfarist option. Two exceptions existed to this overall absence of a clear vacuum of representation of welfarist issues. The first was the issue of EU integration, where the pro-European course of the establishment parties was contested by many political actors (the radical left, left sovereigntists such as Chevènement, left-wing currents of the PS, several Gaullist figures, and the FN) and rejected by about half of the voters (49.2 per cent voted against the ratification of the Maastricht Treaty in 1992; 54.7 did the same against the proposed European Constitution in 2005). This hostility was overwhelmingly motivated by the perceived threat of EU integration to the French social and economic model, although nationalist motives played a secondary role (Crespy 2008). The second was the developments since 2008. As elsewhere in Europe, establishment parties proved incapable to kick-start a durable recovery, saw the margins for autonomous national policies squeezed by old and new European constraints (euro, Fiscal Compact), scrambled to implement unpopular policies (2010 pension reform, 2011 budget cuts, 2016 labour market reforms), and progressively lost the confidence of their supporters.

Electoral mobilisation

The *electoral* mobilisation of the French radical left was altogether deceiving.

Results in legislative and presidential elections are shown in Figure 6.5.The radical left vote was stable from 1986 to 1993 (11.0 per cent), grew a little in the 1995 presidential election (13.9 per cent), was again stable until the 2002 presidential elections, and crashed around 8.0 per cent afterwards, with the exception of the 2012 presidential election (12.8 per cent). In other words, it failed both to reconquer the radical electorate of the seventies (1978: 23.9 per cent) and to profit from the electoral weakening of established parties.

Dissatisfaction and extra-parliamentary mobilisations against centre-right governments generally increased its vote share, but much less than that of moderate left parties. Legislative gains were 0.4 percentage points (against 4.0) in 1986–88, 1.5 points (against 10.3) in 1993–97, 0.4 points (against −1.3) in 2002–07, and -0.1 points (against 8.9) in 2007–12. In other kinds of elections results were often better, but never exceeded the barrier of 13.9 per cent (1995).

Periods of socialist governments, in turn, ranged from mildly (1988–93: −0.7 points) to highly (1997–2002: -4.9 points) negative. Direct governmental participation was an unmitigated disaster. The legislative vote share of the PCF had already collapsed between 1981 (16.1 per cent) and 1986 (9.5 per cent); it halved again

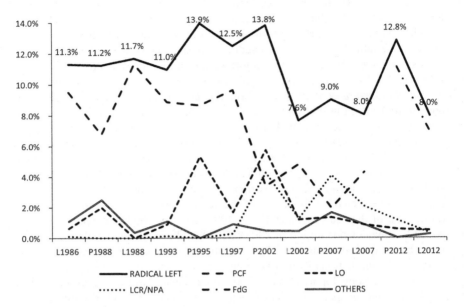

Figure 6.5 French radical left vote (per cent of valid votes)

between 1997 (9.6 per cent) and 2002 (4.8 per cent). Oppositional forces, however, rarely drew major benefits from their stance. The Trotskyist far left stagnated in 1981–86; the radical left in its entirety did the same in 1988–93; only the 1997–2002 period saw a boom of far-left candidates. The current period (2012–present) has so far conformed to these trends, with stagnant or declining values of the FdG and other organisations in European and sub-national elections and in voting intentions.

At the level of individual parties, the situation was extremely fluid. The PCF was predominant until 1997, although it struggled in presidential elections. In 1997–2002 it collapsed, paving the way to dangerous but smallish far-left challengers (LO until 2002, the LCR/NPA until 2009). Since 2010, finally, the space was reunified by the FdG alliance.

This failure of the radical left to expand its electoral support is easily explained.

Firstly, the Socialist Party was able to remain the main beneficiary of popular dissatisfaction and mobilisation against the policies of right-wing governments. Politically, the party generally defended a programme of modest Keynesian and welfarist expansion that was broadly in tune with the interests of employed and unemployed wageworkers, despite its refusal to tackle the structural determinants of their problems (EU constraints, trade and financial liberalisation, the retreat of the state-owned sector). In its electoral campaigns, it promised wage and pension rises, employment programmes, and an increase of public investments and welfare provisions. Its governmental record was mixed, but not devoid of progressive measures (such as the 35-hour working week) and, since 1993, infrequent (1997–2002, 2012–present). Systemically, the party was weak by European social democratic standards, but benefitted from its position of main left-wing force in the bipolar left-right competition. Unattached voters seeking a governmental change naturally turned to the PS for an alternative, as its candidates were usually the best placed to win presidential elections, legislative seats, and a national parliamentary majority. Supporters of radical left or of other left-wing parties (Verts, left-radicals, MDC, and so on), in turn, were often led to vote for it by the specificities of the French electoral system. In itself, the two-round majoritarian system allowed a relatively free expression of voters' preferences in the first round, intervening only in the second round to force a convergence around either of the two or three remaining options; its main goal was not to shape first preferences, but to drastically limit parliamentary representation to least disliked 'centrist' candidates. However, the PS benefitted from a number of mechanisms. Left-wing competition was low in many legislative constituencies, where minor organisations did not have boots on the ground and failed to field competing candidates. Formal centre-left alliances were sometimes reached, with joint candidates or mutual stand-down agreements in some or all of legislative constituencies: junior partners could hope to gain representation in a few places, but had to boost the socialist vote everywhere else.[11] The very decline of the socialist vote, finally, contained a self-correcting tendency. Centre-left voters were not averse to switching to minor parties; for most of them, however, splitting the left-wing vote made sense only as far as the presence of the socialist candidate in the second round was not in doubt. In the 2002 presidential election this did not happen: Lionel Jospin was narrowly eliminated, and the run-off took place between Jacques Chirac (UMP) and Jean-Marie Le Pen (FN). The shock provoked by these events led to a much more tactical voting behaviour of the French electorate in two-round competitions, boosting socialist candidates to the detriment of the radical left.

Secondly, the same mechanisms made it difficult for the radical left to profit from the tenure of socialist governments. Direct involvement, as in the case of the PCF in 1981–84, 1997–2002, and many regional and local administrations, combined the worst of the two worlds, with satisfied voters switching to the socialists and disaffected ones to abstention or the far left. The benefits of non-involvement, in turn, were limited and short-lived, as the failures of the PS reflected badly on the left as a whole (including parties that were not in government or parliament, but had helped to get it into power in the second round) and hostility toward it gradually waned after a spell in the opposition.

Thirdly, the very format of legislative elections drove down the support for the radical left. On the one hand, only the PCF had the capacity of fielding candidates and campaigning throughout the country. Other organisations generally competed only in a selected number of constituencies, and not all their supporters were ready to transfer their vote to other radical left candidates, preferring instead to abstain or to vote socialist. On the other hand, the dim chance of winning any parliamentary seat outside of a few communist strongholds discouraged the turnout of radical left voters. Finally, the holding of a legislative elections right after two rounds of the presidential ones (which happened occasionally before 2002, normally afterwards) further depressed the turnout of the electorate as a whole, of the defeated pole, and of minor parties.

Fourthly, the high level of fragmentation of the radical left was not negative in the short-term, but prevented the long-term accumulation of forces that could have made its candidates competitive for the second round and threatened the entrenched primacy of the Socialist Party.

For all these reasons, the French radical left failed to establish a stable 'fourth pole' of the political competition (Grunberg and Schweisguth 2003), oscillating between dependence from the socialist party and futile protest and strongly weakening in the negative post-2002 conjuncture. Promising results in presidential elections (Laguiller in 1995 and 2002; Besancenot in 2002 and 2007; Mélenchon in 2012) could not change these structural constraints and were therefore relatively short-lived. The hopes of the period 2005–06, with the victory in the EU referendum and in the labour market reform mobilisation, failed to produce any gain in 2007. The collapse of the popularity of the Hollande government after 2013, finally, has so far been wasted by internal divisions – although the emerging movement of 2016 may still bear some fruit. Establishment parties were weakened but remained firmly in control, and the only party that fully profited from their slow decline was the far-right FN (Fysh and Wolfreys 2003; Shields 2007).

Organisational mobilisation

The *organisational* mobilisation of the French radical left was similarly unsuccessful. The strong membership and social linkages of the PCF continued to erode, while the gains of other organisations remained tiny. The vitality of left-wing protests and social movements did not affect this conclusion, as no party managed to translate the sympathy it often elicited among participants and activists into new forms of stable attachment or collaboration.

Membership decline was relentless (Figure 6.6).

The PCF had already strongly weakened in the eighties, falling from its all-time high of 566,492 members in 1978 to 368,609 in 1986, and briefly stabilising until 1989 (369,167). Decline resumed with force in 1990, reducing the number of dues-paying membership to 92,772 in 2003 and 64,184 in 2012. The crisis of communist identity, an unfavourable demographic composition, the electoral and institutional decline of the party, and dissatisfaction with its politics led to the departure of about 82 per cent of the original 1989 members. Crucially, in 2002 the PCF was overcome by the PS for the first time since the thirties and never recovered its past dominance. Although no precise data on the subsequent trajectory of former communist members are available, it seems that the vast majority simply retreated from active partisan or political engagement, with only a tiny fraction switching to other radical left or left-wing organisations.

The rest of the radical left failed to profit from the membership crisis of the Communist Party. LO strengthened its network of activists (from 650 to 2,000)

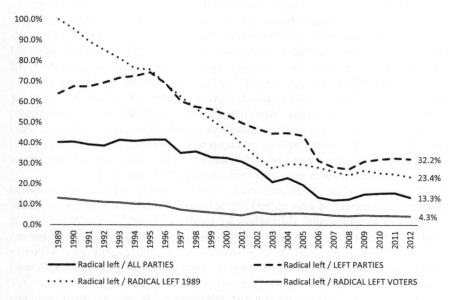

Figure 6.6 Membership ratios, French radical left

and formal members (from 1,000 to 7,000) between 1980 and 2002. The LCR rose from 1,041 members in 1997 to 2,640 in 2007, and again to 9,123 in 2009 (after its rebranding as NPA), before plunging back to about 3,000 in 2012. The PG peaked at 12,000 declared members in 2012. In all three cases, membership gains were insignificant compared to electoral ones, and these alternative organisations remained dwarfed by the communist one.

Organisational linkages of radical left parties also suffered a very profound decline.

Just like the Italian PCI, from 1945 to the early eighties the French PCF could boast a massive network of collateral or friendly mass organisations embracing several million communist and non-communist members and covering all major social categories and issues: wageworkers (CGT), teachers (FSU), pensioners (UNRPA), women (UFF), the youth (MJCF), veterans (ARAC, FNACA), tenants (CNL), sportspeople (FSGT), volunteers (SPF), and so on. The electoral and membership decline of the party was accompanied by a crisis of these linkages (Andolfatto 2008; Borrel 1999; Brodiez 2006; Mischi 2010). The process went through two phases. Until the early nineties, these organisations remained under the tight control of the PCF, but suffered a decline of communist sympathies in their ranks and heavy membership losses. From the mid-nineties onwards, in turn, they stabilised their condition, but only to the price of a progressive autonomisation from the party and depoliticisation of their activities. The best example of this process is provided by the CGT, the largest French trade union confederation. Between 1978 and 1995 the union suffered a veritable haemorrhage, plunging from 1.3 million to a mere 480 thousand members. Simultaneously, the vote of union members for communist presidential candidates collapsed from very high levels (57 per cent in 1981, 49 per cent in 1988) to medium-low ones (35 per cent in 1995, 18 per cent in 2002, and 7 per cent in 2007). As a reaction, starting in 1993 its leaders Louis Viannet and Bernard Thibault undertook a slow but decisive process of autonomisation from their former political patron (Andolfatto 1997, 2008). Today, the union remains an important reference point for anti-neoliberal mobilisations, but has given up any privileged link with the radical left and has ceased to act as a relay for radical left identification (although many of its leaders and cadres remained card-carrying PCF members).

The decline of the traditional communist subculture was not compensated by the development of new radical left networks. Post-1968 'new social movements' did institutionalise themselves in a variety of single-issue organisations and converged over time around loose anti-neoliberal and alter-globalist networks (Agrikoliansky et al. 2005; Crettiez and Sommier 2006; Geay and Willemez 2008; Mouchard 2009).[12] Despite many personal and ideological links with radical left organisations, however, these groups were as jealous of their autonomy and pluralism as the former communist organisations. In addition, their influence generally remained limited to a small stratum of highly educated and politicised citizens, so that even the choice of an open political engagement to the side of the radical left would have made little difference in electoral and organisational terms.[13]

Both processes were caused by two main factors. On the one hand, general national and international trends affecting all traditional forms of engagement and organisation hit the communist subculture, which embodied old conceptions in an almost idealtypical manner, with particular harshness: the declining attractiveness of traditional social and political mediations (parties, unions, churches, and so on); a growing rift between groups with high and low cultural and social capital on the value of traditional sociabilities, professionalisation, and representativeness; the move from totalising worldviews to fragmented causes; and the shift from traditional to 'distanced' activism (Ion 1997).

On the other hand, party members and collateral organisations simply caught up with and adapted to – with a delay – the continuous decline of the electoral appeal and general attractiveness of the radical left,

Summary

The French radical left failed to durably profit from the rightward shift of established political parties and the high level of popular resistance against neoliberal reforms. In electoral terms, its scores were generally higher than the Western European average, but successes (1993–2002; 2009–12) were limited, while the 2002 defeat led to long-term downsizing. In organisational terms, the communist subculture progressively disintegrated while the connection with new forms of social and political engagement remained tenuous.

The roots of this failure are multiple.

First, the French Socialist Party progressively shifted to the right since 1983, but did not entirely abandon a perspective of Keynesian and welfarist compensations of the adverse social consequences of neoliberalised capitalism. As a consequence, the party was heavily contested for its moderation when in government, but quickly recovered its positions when in opposition. Voters advocating a more radical course often switched to minor far-left or left-wing competitors when the stakes were low, but overwhelmingly returned to the fold when the real left-right competition took place. This progressive image shattered after 2013, when the deteriorating macro-economic situation led the Hollande government to aggressively pursue fiscal discipline and labour market reforms; the long-term implications of this turn are, however, not yet clear.

Secondly, the French electoral system was problematic, making the conquest of parliamentary representation heavily dependent on an agreement with the PS (outside of a few remaining communist strongholds) and encouraging the direct or indirect involvement of the radical left in the success of centre-left coalitions. As a consequence, the radical left could not credibly present itself as a 'fourth pole' of the political competition, forfeiting potential voters to the far right, abstention, and the periodic left-right alternation.

Thirdly, the PCF paid a heavy price for its excessive proximity to the socialist party, with two experiences of national governmental participation and countless ones at the regional and local level. Its incapacity to define a clear boundary with the moderate left, and the apparent incoherence of its 'zigzags' between conciliatory and intransigent strategies, progressively disoriented its electorate and provoked a double exodus: to the left, toward shifting radical challengers (LO, LCR/NPA, PG), and to the right, toward the socialist party itself. The resulting fragmentation and imbalances of the radical left further limited its influence and attractiveness. There is no doubt that the PCF made major mistakes; it should have minimised its direct governmental involvement and worked much earlier toward a relatively intransigent 'broad left' regroupment along the lines of the FdG. This might have led to long-term gains, as the case of the FN clearly suggests, but was difficult to sustain in the short-term, as it clashed with the widespread anti-right sentiments of its electorate and would have meant to forfeit much of its existing institutional positions.

Fourthly, the radical left failed to devise viable new political visions, modes of extra-parliamentary intervention, and forms of social and political engagement. As a consequence, its role in local and national mobilisations often led to short-term gains in terms of sympathy and electoral support, but did not produce permanent electoral and institutional advances.

The strategy of leftward pull

The French radical left did not have a shared and coherent strategy to achieve its political goals. Different assessment existed on the relative importance of electoral-parliamentary activities and extra-parliamentary mobilisations, the adoption of conciliatory or intransigent attitudes toward the socialist party, the likelihood of its future radicalisation, and the precise link between anti-neoliberal and anti-capitalist goals. Moreover, party programmes remained vague on key issues of implementation. At a more general level, however, all organisations believed that a combination of extra-parliamentary, electoral, and institutional pressures could affect the social and political balance of forces and pave the way for a turn toward progressive or revolutionary measures.

In fact, none of the means and strategies deployed proved to be entirely successful, contributing to block or slow down the implementation of unpopular reforms but failing to initiate major policy reversals.

Party efforts

A first group of pressures aimed at indirectly influencing the direction of competition through the mere growth of radical left systemic strength. These, however, never came close to represent a serious threat for establishment parties. As I have shown in the previous section, the electoral strength of the French radical left increased very little in the nineties, and strongly declined after 2002. Moreover, the two-round electoral system made any force below 15–20 per cent of valid votes largely irrelevant in both presidential and legislative elections, provided that its voters were prepared to converge on the least-distant competitor in the second round. Mainstream parties could maintain a virtual monopoly on parliamentary seats and executive offices even with very low levels of support, and were little impressed with the performance of a medium-sized but fragmented radical left.

A second group of pressures aimed at directly influencing other parties and governmental policies through electoral and parliamentary tactics. These could assume the form of organic centre-left alliances or attempts to wrestle policy concessions from the Socialist Party lending or withdrawing weaker forms of support. The PCF wanted to create the conditions for a progressive alliance and tried out a variety of different tactics: from direct governmental participation (1981–94 and 1997–02) and external support (1984–86), through case-by-case parliamentary support (1989–93), to a benign opposition (2012–present), and from joint first-round lists to a sustained competition in both rounds. The far left strongly opposed governmental involvement and was more sceptical on the role of the PS: it generally tried to pressure it by threatening to spoil its electoral victory, but was not entirely hostile to limited electoral arrangements. The PG adopted a more intransigent variation of the communist line, seeking to favour a medium-term reconfiguration of the centre-left on the ruins of existing orientations and leaderships.

A third group of pressures concerned the intervention in extra-parliamentary mobilisations. In the nineties, the PCF still had the capacity to unleash the CGT trade union against unwanted governmental policies. Progressively, however, social movements came to be led by broad coalitions of trade unions, other civil society organisations, or unattached personalities. All radical left organisations heavily intervened with their members at both the top and the grassroots levels, but could not shape much the course of national events, retaining a leading role only in specific local mobilisations.

Systemic effects

These activities brought little tangible results.
The policy course of the Socialist Party does not seem to have been significantly affected by radical left pressures. As already remarked, the PS followed until recently a centrist socio-economic programme combining both neoliberal and welfarist elements. Over time, however, the former took more and more precedence over the latter, with a progressive shift toward fiscal and monetary discipline, free movement of goods and capitals, privatisations, and labour market flexibility. The presence of the PCF in government did not prevent major negative policy shifts, such as the 'austerity turn' of the Mauroy cabinet in 1983 or the European negotiations and privatisations of the Jospin cabinet in 1997–2002. Progressive measures, in turn, were autonomously conceived by the PS with little input from its junior partners.

The mass extra-parliamentary mobilisations that periodically rocked the country since 1986 were sometimes successful in forcing right-wing governments to retreat unpopular reforms (for instance, the 1995 pension reform and the 2006 labour market reform) or in wresting limited concessions. The contribution of the radical left was minoritarian but important. However, the movements remained exclusively defensive, failures became more and more frequent (for instance, the 2003 and 2010 protests against pension reforms), and most electoral benefits accrued to the Socialist Party.

The radical left also played an important role in the large no vote of the 1992 and 2005 referendums on EU treaties, but these manifestations of dissent did not affect the further course of French integration in the constraining legal and institutional framework of the Union.

This failure to exert a visible leftward pull on French politics and society was common to all radical left parties and strategies. Two main elements explain this outcome.

On the one hand, it may simply derive from an insufficient level of pressures. The electoral strength of the radical left followed a long-term downward trend, settling in 2015 around medium-small levels to be divided among a number of competing organisations. The electoral system bolstered the dominant position of the Socialist Party within a loose centre-left pole, squeezed radical left representation, and made it largely irrelevant for final outcomes. Its votes in the second round could be largely taken for granted: only LO consistently refused to support the socialist candidates, and most radical left voters did so anyway. Its few MPs, in turn, were sometimes relevant for the formation of governmental majorities (1988–93, 1997–2002), but the threat of a no-confidence vote was employed only twice (1990 and 1992) and with little success. More aggressive tactics would have been dangerous in the short-term, determining a loss of both votes and elected representatives. Finally, its organisational decline deprived it of the capacity to force concessions out of governments or employers through targeted extra-parliamentary mobilisations.

On the other hand, the option for a more decisive Keynesian and welfarist stimulus would have meant an inevitable clash with a whole framework of international commitments and institutions: the European Monetary System (EMS) and Economic and Monetary Union (EMU); trade and capital liberalisation; and large parts of the European treaties and secondary legislation. This was unthinkable for mainstream parties, as it would have run against the interests of the highly internationalised French large corporations, threatened the Franco-German axis, and undermined the result of decades of French diplomatic efforts. Thus, French governments often sought to compensate the internal losers of Europeanisation and globalisation, but could not tackle the underlying structural causes of their problems.

Summary

The various means and strategies deployed by the radical left failed to pull French politics and society to the left. The cross-party strength of anti-neoliberal opinions and mobilisations among the French population certainly helped to slow down the pace of reforms and ensure the survival of many key elements of the post-war socio-economic model, but the contribution of the radical left to this outcome was altogether minoritarian and could not reverse the progressive right-ward shift of the Socialist Party. This depended partly on an insufficient level of pressures, and partly on the structural constrains narrowing the margins for expansive policies, particularly in times of crisis.

Concluding remarks

The French national context since 1989 exhibited several typical features of contemporary Western European developments: moves toward a neoliberal restructuring of state and society; a rightward shift of the political system, including social democratic parties; and an electoral weakening of mainstream political traditions. Some key differences were, however, evident. Firstly, opposition and resistance to neoliberalism has remained very strong, with a constant background of localised movements by wageworkers, the youth, and other social subjects and cyclical waves of mass extra-parliamentary mobilisation (1994–95, 2003, 2005–06, 2009–10, 2016). Secondly, the pace of the process of neoliberalisation has been slow and its extent incomplete, leaving behind several key elements of the previous developmental model. Thus, the French economy powerfully shifted in the direction of the private sector, deregulation, and internationalisation, but the state continued to intervene massively to sustain domestic demand and investment, create employment, and guarantee a growth of living standards and extensive welfare provisions.

In this context, the French radical left sought to recover from the crisis of the eighties and early nineties, winning over the disaffected welfarist constituencies of establishment parties and charting a path toward an anti-neoliberal or anti-capitalist policy turn. Its initial trajectory was promising, but ended in a complete failure.

The persistence of the communist subculture endowed the PCF with an extraordinarily favourable starting position in terms of membership, financial resources, social linkages, and localised institutional strongholds; the hiatus of the mid-nineties, however, was short-lived, and all indicators of societal strength soon resumed their decline. The recurrent electoral surges of alternative far-left or left-socialist parties (LO, LCR/NPA, and PG) remained unstable and did not translate in a parallel organisational consolidation. The level of fragmentation into competing organisations rose steadily, reducing the potential influence and perspectives of this political area; a belated regroupment under the banners of the FdG (2009–15) briefly papered over the key underlying problems but was progressively undermined by political divergences, organisational rivalries, and the lack of a veritable institutionalisation. Overall electoral strength first stabilised around 11 per cent (1988–94), then modestly rose to almost 14 per cent (1995–2002), collapsed at around 8 per cent in 2002, and oscillated between the last two values afterwards.

The attempt to become a credible alternative to the mainstream failed for a number of reasons: the nature of the PS; the mechanisms of the French electoral system and political competition; strategic mistakes; and a failure to devise appealing new forms of social and political engagement.

Its efforts to pull the political system and society to the left, finally, failed as well, due to an insufficient level of pressures and structural constraints.

In conclusion, the French radical left failed to morph into a solid 'fourth pole' capable of realistically challenging both right-wing and left-wing candidates. It periodically oscillated between promising and poor electoral result, excitement and gloom, fragmentation and regroupment, dependency from the PS and sterile isolation, faithfully measuring shifts in the public mood but remaining altogether of little relevance for the fate of its country.

Notes

1 The literature produced by and on radical left organisations since 1917 is immense. Good bibliographies are Souillard and Carreau (2011) on the PCF and Lanuque et al. (2011) on the Trotskyist far left.
2 Its main embodiments were Juquin's *Nouvelle gauche* (NG) in 1988–89; the *Alternative rouge et verte* (AREV) in 1989–98; *Les alternatifs* (1998–present); the *Convention pour une alternative progressiste* (CAP) in 1994–2012; the presidential campaign of Bové in 2007; the *Fédération pour une alternative sociale et écologique* (FASE) in 2008–13; and *Ensemble!* since 2013.
3 The most relevant organisations are the *Parti communiste réunionnais* (PCR), *Parti communiste guadeloupéen* (PCG), *Parti progressiste démocratique guadeloupéen* (PPDG), *Parti communiste martiniquais* (PCM), *Mouvement indépendantiste martiniquais* (MIM), and *Mouvement de décolonisation et émancipation sociale* (MDES). They are very little studied, a praiseworthy exception being Gauvin (2000).

4 The frequency of joint centre-left list peaked in 1998 (all 22 metropolitan regions) and then slowly declined.
5 Communist-led city councils administered 9.5 per cent of the French population in 1989 and 5.2 per cent in 2008, and the coverage of communist-led departments went from 4.9 per cent in 1998 to 2.1 in 2015, with the lone stronghold of Val-de-Marne resisting the socialist and conservative competition.
6 Examples are Ernest Moutoussamy (PPDG, 1991–2002), Jean-Pierre Brard (CAP, 1996–present), Maxime Gremetz (PCF dissident, 2007–11), and three FASE MPs in 2010, two of which were re-elected in 2012.
7 Examples are Jacques Desallangre (ex-MDC, then independent and PG, 2002–12), Marc Dolez (ex-PS, then PG and independent, 2008–present), and Martine Billard (ex-Verts, then PG, 2009–12).
8 The LCR/NPA and the PG broadly refused governmental alliances with the PS, for different reasons, but generally supported 'technical' joint lists or constituency-sharing agreements (particularly in legislative constituencies with a danger of a far-right victory), 'technical' list mergers in the second round of regional and municipal elections, and the principles of 'republican discipline' (a vote for the best placed left-leaning candidate in the second round). LO opposed all of the above, although it sometimes made exceptions (in 1981 and again in 2007–08).
9 Between 1993 and 2008 four groups have managed to regularly gain access to state financing: LO, LCR/NPA, PT, and SEGA (a technical regroupment of the eco-socialist milieu).
10 The series combines sectoral data from several official sources. In the private sector, administrative data had a growing tendency to underestimate strike levels, which was corrected in 2005 with a shift to survey data. In the public sector, administrative data are fairly complete and homogeneous. Data for specific sectors are not available (agriculture, local government, companies below 10 employees) or only intermittently (hospitals until 1990 and since 2009, private sector participation to general strikes in 1996–2004, nationalised companies until 2006).
11 The votes won by these candidates were generally attributed to the party they individually belonged to.
12 Notable organisations emerged among activists focusing on anti-racism (GISTI, MRAP, RESF, RLF), unemployment (APEIS, MNCP, AC!), housing rights and exclusion (DAL, DD!!), HIV (ACT UP), global finance (ATTAC), wageworkers (Solidaires), and peasants (CP).
13 At its peak in 2008, the alternative union Solidaires had about 80,000 members; still a dwarf compared to the formerly communist union CGT in the same year (620,000). Figures for other organisations were much lower: ATTAC had at most 30,000 members (2003); the CP around 10,000; AC!, RLF, and DD!! were informal networks of local collectives without a clearly defined membership. At another level, the poor performance of Bové in the 2007 presidential elections (483,008 votes, 1.32 per cent) was an eloquent reflection of the shallow roots of the alter-globalist movement.

References

Abdelal, Rawi (2007). *Capital rules: The construction of global finance.* Cambridge: Cambridge University Press.
Agrikoliansky, Eric (2007). 'L'altermondialisme en temps de crise', *Mouvements* 50(2): 33–41.
Agrikoliansky, Eric, Olivier Filleule, and Nonna Mayer (eds.) (2005). *L'altermondialisme en France. La longue histoire d'une nouvelle cause.* Paris: Flammarion.
Alemagna, Lilian, and Stéphane Alliès (2012). *Mélenchon le plébéien.* Paris: Robert Laffont.

Ancelovici, Marcos (2011). 'In search of lost radicalism. The hot autumn of 2010 and the transformation of labor contention in France', *French Politics, Culture & Society* 29(3): 121–140.
Andolfatto, Dominique (2008). 'Trade unions and communism in Spain, France and Italy', in Uwe Backes and Patrick Moreau (eds.). *Communist and post-communist parties in Europe*. Göttingen: Vandenhoeck and Ruprecht, 483–500.
Andolfatto, Dominique (2005). *PCF: de la mutation à la liquidation*. Paris: Editions du Rocher.
Andolfatto, Dominique (1997). 'Les doubles dirigeants de la CGT et du Parti communiste', *Communisme* 51/52: 125–156.
Andolfatto, Dominique, and Dominique Labbé (2011a). *Histoire des syndicats (1906–2010)*. Paris: Éditions du Seuil.
Andolfatto, Dominique, and Dominique Labbé (2011b). 'Retraites: les faux-semblants d'un mouvement social', *Le Débat* 163(1): 72–80.
Barcia, Robert (Hardy) (2003). *La véritable histoire de Lutte Ouvrière*. Paris: Denoel.
Béaud, Stéphane, and Olivier Masclet (2006). 'Des "marcheurs" de 1983 aux "émeutieurs" de 2005. Deux générations sociales d'enfants d'immigrés', *Annales* 61(4): 809–843.
Becker, Jean-Jacques (2005). 'La gauche plurielle (1995–2002)', in Jean-Jacques Becker and Gilles Candar (eds.). *Histoire des gauches en France*. Paris: La Decouverte, 295–310.
Becker, Jean-Jacques, and Gilles Candar (eds.) (2005). *Histoire des gauches en France*. Paris: La Découverte.
Bell, David Scott (2004). 'The French Communist Party within the left and alternative movements', *Modern & Contemporary France* 12(1): 23–34.
Bell, David Scott (1998). 'The French Communist Party in the 1990s', *Journal of Communist Studies and Transition Politics* 14(3): 126–133.
Bellanger, Emmanuel, and Julian Mischi (eds.) (2013). *Les territoires du communisme. Élus locaux, politiques publiques et sociabilités militantes*. Paris: Armand Colin.
Bergounioux, Alain, and Gérard Grunberg (2007). *L'ambition et le remords: les socialistes français et le pouvoir (1905–2005)*. Paris: Hachette Littératures.
Berne, Michel, and Gérard Pogorel (2005). Privatization experiences in France. CESifo Working Paper 1195. Available at: http://ssrn.com/abstract=553962 [accessed on 01.04.2016].
Béroud, Sophie (2008). 'La décennie des 'victoires défaites' (1995–2007) ou les effets du découplage entre mobilisations sociales et dynamiques syndicales', in Bertrand Geay and Laurent Willemez (eds.). *Pour une gauche de gauche*. Bellecombe-en-Bauges: Éditions du Croquant, 19–34.
Béroud, Sophie, Jean-Michel Denis, Guillaume Desage, Baptiste Giraud, and Jérôme Pélisse (2008). *La lutte continue? Les conflits du travail dans la France contemporaine*. Bellecombe-en-Bauges: Éditions du Croquant.
Béroud, Sophie, and René Mouriaux (eds.) (1998). *Le souffle de décembre*. Paris: Syllepse.
Béroud, Sophie, and Karel Yon (2012). 'Face à la crise, la mobilisation sociale et ses limites. Une analyse des contradictions syndicales', *Modern & Contemporary France*, 20(2): 169–183.
Bonnemaison, Didier (2012). 'De la Ligue Communiste Révolutionnaire au Nouveau Parti Anticapitaliste', in Jean-Michel De Waele and Daniel-Louis Seiler (eds.). *Les partis de la gauche anticapitaliste en Europe*. Paris: Economica, 305–322.
Borrel, Marianne (1999). Sociologie d'une métamorphose: la Fédération Sportive et Gymnique du travail entre société communiste et mouvement sportif (1964–1992) [PhD thesis]. Paris: IEP.

Boy, Daniel, Henri Rey, François Platone, Françoise Subileau, and Colette Ysmal (2003). *C'était la gauche plurielle*. Paris: Presses de Sciences Po.
Brechon, Pierre (2009). *La France aux urnes*. Paris: la Documentation française.
Brodiez, Axelle (2006). *Le Secours populaire français, 1945–2000. Du communisme à l'humanitaire*. Paris: Presses de Sciences Po.
Cahiers Leon Trotsky, 79/2002. Special issue: 'L'histoire de l'extrême gauche française: le cas du "trotskysme". Une histoire impossible?'.
Campinchi, Philippe (2000). *Les lambertiste: un courant trotskiste français*. Paris: Balland.
Chiocchetti, Paolo (2016). Western European radical left database. Version 2.0 (30.04.2016). Available at: www.paolochiocchetti.it/data.
Choffat, Thierry (2012). 'Lutte Ouvrière, entre continuité et renouvellement', in Jean-Michel De Waele and Daniel-Louis Seiler (eds.). *Les partis de la gauche anticapitaliste en Europe*. Paris: Economica, 292–304.
Choffat, Thierry (1991). Lutte Ouvrière [DEA thesis]. Nancy: Université de Nancy II.
Clift, Ben (2012). 'Comparative capitalisms, ideational political economy and the French post-*dirigiste* responses to the financial crisis', *New Political Economy* 17(5): 565–590.
Cole, Alistair (1999). 'French socialists in office: Lessons from Mitterrand and Jospin', *Modern & Contemporary France* 7(1): 81–87.
Courtois, Stéphane, and Marc Lazar (2000). *Histoire du Parti communiste français*. 2nd ed. Paris: PUF.
Crespy, Amandine (2008). 'La cristallisation des résistances de gauche à l'intégration européenne: les logiques de mobilisation dans la campagne référendaire française de 2005', *Revue internationale de politique comparée* 15(4): 589–603.
Crettiez, Xavier, and Isabelle Sommier (2006). *La France rebelle. Tous les mouvements et acteurs de la contestation*. Paris: Michalon.
Delwit, Pascal (2014). 'Le parti communiste français et le Front de gauche', in Pascal Delwit (ed.). *Les partis politiques en France*. Bruxelles: éditions de l'Université de Bruxelles, 59–85.
Denis, Jean-Michel (1996). *Les coordinations. Recherche désespérée d'une citoyenneté*. Paris: Syllepse.
Dissidences 6/2009. Special issue: 'Trotskysmes en France'.
Dreyfus, Michel (1990). *PCF: Crises et dissidences: de 1920 à nos jours*. Paris: Éditions Complexe.
Dufour, Pascale (2010). 'The mobilisation against the 2005 treaty establishing a Constitution for Europe: A French mobilization for another Europe', *Social Movement Studies* 9(4): 425–441.
Escalona, Fabien, and Mathieu Vieira (2014). 'Le sens et le rôle de la résistance a l'UE pour le Parti de Gauche', *Politique européenne* 43(1): 68–92.
Ethuin, Nathalie (2003). À l'école du parti. L'éducation et la formation des militants et des cadres du PCF (1970–2003) [PhD thesis]. Lille: Université de Lille II.
Filleule, Olivier, and Danielle Tartakowsky (2008). *La manifestation*. Paris: Presses de Sciences Po.
Filoche, Gérard (2007). *Mai 68, histoire sans fin (Tome 1)*. Dijon: Gawsevitch.
Fysh, Peter and Jim Wolfreys (2003). *The politics of racism in France*. 2nd ed. Basingstoke: Palgrave Macmillan.
Garcia, Guillaume (2013). *La cause des 'sans'. Sans-papiers, sans-logis, sans-emploi à l'épreuve de médias*. Rennes: Presses Universitaires de Rennes.
Gauvin, Gilles (2000). 'Le parti communiste de la Réunion (1946–2000)', *Vingtième Siècle* 68(1): 74–94.

Geay, Bertrand, and Laurent Willemez (eds.) (2008). *Pour une gauche de gauche*. Bellecombe-en-Bauges: Éditions du Croquant.
Gemie, Sharif (2003). 'Anti-Le Pen protests: France, April-May 2002', *Journal of Contemporary European Studies* 11(2): 231–251.
Gordon, Alex, and Andy Mathers (2004). 'State restructuring and trade union realignment. The pension struggle in France', *Capital & Class* 83: 9–18.
Grunberg, Gérard, and Étienne Schweisguth (2003). 'La tripartition de l'espace politique', in Pascal Perrineau and Colette Ysmal (eds.). *Le vote de tous le refus. Les élections présidentielle et législatives de 2002*. Paris: Presses de Sciences Po, 339–362.
Hargreaves, Alec G. (1991). 'The political mobilization of the North African immigrant community in France', *Ethnic and Racial Studies* 14(3): 350–367.
Ion, Jacques (1997). *La fin des militants?* Paris: L'Atelier.
Johsua, Florence (2015). *Anticapitalistes. Une sociologie historique de l'engagement*. Paris: La Découverte.
Johsua, Florence (2004). La dynamique militante à l'extrême gauche: le cas de la Ligue Communiste Révolutionnaire [working paper]. Paris: Cahiers du CEVIPOF.
Kernalegenn, Tudi, François Prigent, Gilles Richard, and Jacqueline Sainclivier (eds.) (2010). *Le PSU vu d'en bas. Réseaux sociaux, mouvement politique, laboratoire d'idées (années 1950 – années 1980)*. Rennes: Presses Universitaires de Rennes.
Kouvelakis, Stathis (2012). 'Échecs et recomposition de la gauche radicale', *Mouvements* 69(1): 19–25.
Kouvelakis, Stathis (2007). *La France en révolte. Luttes sociales et cycles politiques*. Paris: Textuel.
Krivine, Alain (2006). *Ça te passera avec l'âge*. Mayenne: Flammarion.
Landais, Karim (2013). *De l'OCI au Parti des Travailleurs*. Paris: Ni Patrie Ni Frontières.
Lanuque, Jean-Guillaume (2002). 'Marges et replis dans le mouvement ouvrier français: le cas de l'extrême gauche', in Claude Pennetier (ed.). *Marges et replis, frontières, cas limites, dans la gauche française: l'apport des itinéraires militants*. Paris: Centre d'histoire sociale du XXe siècle, 51–57 .
Lanuque, Jean-Guillaume, Christian Beuvain, Jean Hentzgen, Stéphane Moulain, Jean-Paul Salles, Georges Ubbiali, and Jean Vigreux (2011). 'Bibliographie: les trotskysmes en France', *Dissidences* 2. Available at: http://revuesshs.u-bourgogne.fr/dissidences/document.php?id=587 [accessed on 1.04.2016].
Lavabre, Marie-Claire, and François Platone (2003). *Que reste-t-il du PCF?* Paris: Autrement.
Lazar, Marc (1992). *Maisons rouges. Les Partis communistes français et italien de la Libération à nos jours*. Paris: Aubier.
Le Goaziou, Véronique, and Laurent Mucchielli (eds.) (2006). *Quand les banlieues brûlent... Retour sur les émeutes de novembre 2005*. Paris: La Découverte.
Legois, Jean-Philippe, Robi Morder, and Alain Monchablon (eds.) (2007). *Cent ans de mouvements étudiants*. Paris: Syllepse.
Lehingue, Patrick (2008). 'Les déterminants matériels de l'activité politique. Ce que nous disent les comptes publics des partis', in Bertrand Geay and Laurent Willemez (eds.). *Pour une gauche de gauche*. Bellecombe-en-Bauges: Éditions du Croquant, 113–146.
MacLean, Mairi (1997). 'Privatisation, *dirigisme* and the global economy: An end to French exceptionalism?', *Modern & Contemporary France* 5(2): 215–227.
Marlière, Philippe (2012). 'Le Front de gauche au miroir de Syriza', *Transform!* 10: 219–225.

Martelli, Roger (2012). 'Front de gauche, aube ou crépuscule?', *Mouvements* 69(1): 101–108.
Martelli, Roger (2010). *L'empreinte communiste. PCF et société française (1920–2010)*. Paris: Les Éditions sociales.
Martelli, Roger (2009). *L'archipel communiste. Une histoire électorale du PCF*. Paris: La Dispute.
Mathieu, Lilian (2012). *L'espace des mouvements sociaux*. Bellecombe-en-Bauges: Éditions du Croquant.
Mathieu, Romain (2015). 'Tous ensemble!'? Les dynamiques de transformation de la gauche radicale française [PhD thesis]. Nancy: Université de Lorraine.
Mermat, Djamel (2005). Les imaginaires du changement dans les discours communistes. Le cas du PCF: 1976–2004 [PhD thesis]. Lille: Université de Lille.
Mischi, Julian (2010). *Servir la classe ouvrière. Sociabilités militantes au PCF*. Rennes: Presses Universitaires de Rennes.
Mischi, Julian (2003). 'La recomposition identitaire du P.C.F.', *Communisme* 72/73: 71–99.
Monza, Rosan (2009). 'Géopolitique de la crise guadeloupéenne: Crise sociale et/ou postcoloniale?', *Herodote* 135(4): 170–194.
Mouriaux, René (2008). *Le syndicalisme en France depuis 1945*. Paris: La Découverte.
Nick, Christophe (2002). *Les trotskistes*. Paris: Fayard.
Obono, Danièle (2008). 'Une nouvelle génération politique: les étudiants et le mouvement anti-CPE en France', *JHEA/RESA* 6(273): 157–181.
Perrineau, Pascal, and Colette Ysmal (eds.) (2003). *Le vote de tous le refus. Les élections présidentielle et législatives de 2002*. Paris: Presses de Sciences Po.
Phélippeau, Eric, and Abel François (eds.) (2010). *Le financement de la vie politique française. Des régles aux pratiques (1988–2009)*. Saint-Denis: WEKA.
Pina, Chistine (2011). 'L'extrême gauche, la vraie gauche?', in Pierre Bréchon (ed.). *Les partis politiques français*. Paris: La Documentation française, 181–203.
Pina, Christine (2005). 'L'extrême gauche en France: entre permanence et évolutions', in Pierre Bréchon (ed.) *Les partis politiques français*. Paris: La Documentation française, 179–200.
Platone, François, and Jean Ranger (2000). Les adhérents du Parti communiste français en 1997: enquête [working paper]. Paris: CEVIPOF.
Pudal, Bernard (2009). *Un monde défait. Les communistes français de 1956 à nos jours*. Bellecombe-en-Bauges: Éditions du Croquant.
Pudal, Bernard (2002). 'La beauté de la mort communiste', *Revue française de science politique* 52(5): 545–559.
Raynaud, Philippe (2006). *L'extrême gauche plurielle. Entre démocratie radicale et révolution*. Paris: CEVIPOF.
Reynié, Dominique (2007). *L'extrême gauche, moribonde ou renaissante?* Paris: PUF.
Rizet, Stéphanie (2007). 'Qu'est-ce qui fait courir les militants de la Ligue communiste révolutionnaire?', *Sociologies pratiques* 15(2): 69–81.
Ross, George, Stanley Hoffmann, and Sylvia Malzacher (eds.) (1987). *The Mitterrand experiment*. New York: Oxford University Press.
Salles, Jean-Paul (2012). 'Actualités: les élections 2012: Une extrême gauche réduite à l'état gazeux?', *Revue électronique dissidences* 4. Available at: http://revuesshs.u-bourgogne.fr/dissidences/document.php?id=2457 [accessed on 1.04.2016].
Salles, Jean-Paul (2005). *La Ligue communiste révolutionnaire (1968–1981). Instrument du Grand Soir ou lieu d'apprentissage?* Rennes: Presses Universitaires de Rennes.

Schmidt, Vivien A. (1996). *From state to market? The transformation of French business and government.* Cambridge: CUP.
Shields, James (2007). *The extreme right in France: From Pétain to Le Pen.* Abingdon: Routledge.
Smith, W. Rand (1990). 'Nationalizations for what? Capitalist power and public enterprise in Mitterrand's France', *Politics & Society* 18(1): 75–89.
Souillard, Sabine, and Pascal Carreau (2011). *État bibliographique sur le communisme français.* Seine-Saint-Denis: Archives départementales de la Seine-Saint-Denis.
Sperber, Nathan (2010). 'Three million Trotskyists? Explaining extreme left voting in France in the 2002 presidential election', *European Journal of Political Research* 49(3): 359–392.
Tiberj, Vincent (2004). L'extrême gauche et la recomposition de la gauche traditionnelle à la veille des élections régionales. [working paper]. Paris: CEVIPOF.
Turpin, Pierre (1997). *Les révolutionnaires dans la France social-démocrate, 1981–1995.* Paris: L'Harmattan.
Ubbiali, Georges (2008). 'Les usages du trotskisme dans l'extrême gauche française', in Bertrand Geay and Laurent Willemez (eds.). *Pour une gauche de gauche.* Bellecombe-en-Bauges: Éditions du Croquant, 261–275.
Ubbiali, Georges (2002). 'Militer à GC-UC-VO-LO, ou les trois états de la matière', *Cahiers Leon Trotsky* 79: 55–70.
Vail, Mark I. (2010). *Recasting welfare capitalism. Economic adjustment in contemporary France and Germany.* Philadelphia: Temple University Press.
Verrier, Benôit (2003). Loyauté militante et fragmentation des partis. Du CERES au MDC [PhD thesis]. Strasbourg: Université de Strasbourg III.
Waters, Sarah (2006). *Social movements in France: Towards a new citizenship.* Basingstoke: Palgrave Macmillan.
Wolfreys, Jim (2008). 'Regroupment and retrenchment on the radical left in France', *Journal of Contemporary European Studies* 16(1): 69–82.
Wolfreys, Jim (2003). 'Beyond the mainstream: *la gauche de la gauche*', in Jocelyn Evans (ed.). *The French party system.* Manchester: Manchester University Press, 91–104.

7 Filling the vacuum?
The trajectory of the contemporary radical left in Western Europe

The key findings of the empirical analysis of the contemporary radical left carried out at an aggregate level (Western Europe, chapter three) and at a country level (the three case studies of Germany, Italy, and France, chapters four to six) are brought together in this chapter. The four trajectories are compared, making explicit the implicit comparative focus of the rest of the book. Robust conclusions on the nature, success, and limitations of this party family are reached, and their implications are discussed.

First, I summarise how this work contributes to illuminate some questions on the meaning of the Western European radical left that emerge from the existing scholarly literature. Secondly, I examine the main trends of its political nature, highlighting both the potential and the limits of its new anti-neoliberal orientation. Thirdly, I track the evolution of radical left strength, confirming the presence of a real, yet uneven recovery since 1994. Fourthly, I identify the main determinants of cohesion and fragmentation. Fifthly, I illustrate the main determinants of electoral success. Sixthly, I assess the failure of the radical left to exert a significant influence on Western European politics and society. The primary data with sources, notes, and elaborations are available in the Western European Radical Left Database (Chiocchetti 2016).

The radical left party family and its meaning

The analysis of the trajectory of Western European radical left parties since 1989 confirms the emergence of a renewed party family from ruins of twentieth-century communism. This conclusion was initially rejected by the literature (Bull 1994), then discussed (Botella and Ramiro 2003; Hudson 2000), and finally accepted (De Waele and Seiler 2012; Hudson 2012; March 2012; March and Mudde 2005). This book makes a three-fold contribution to this debate.

Firstly, it identifies the forces that make the Western European radical left not a mere collection of disparate organisations and tendencies, but a composite yet relatively coherent party family. To a certain extent, the radical left indeed appears as a residual category, grouping together a motley crew of parties with different historical origins and current ideological orientations, united only by their spatial position on the left of mainstream social democracy and by their common opposition to the economic, social, and political trends labelled as neoliberalism.

It is not accidental that, unlike its predecessors, it often defines its project not with positive qualifiers (communism, socialism) but with negations (alternative, anti-neoliberalism, anti-capitalism). My analysis, however, has shown that an underlying field of forces shapes with its contradictory tendencies the nature and behaviour of all the components of the radical left. The result is a number of fundamental commonalities: the effort to represent the working-class and welfarist constituencies neglected by the rightward shift of mainstream political parties; the development of an anti-neoliberal programme from a matrix of different traditions (communist, far-left, social democratic, and left-libertarian) and social groups (the Fordist working class, public sector employees, the unemployed, the new precariat, intellectual strata, and the inactive population); attempts to reconcile anti-neoliberalism and anti-capitalism, traditional legacies and new realities; strong pressures toward an organisational regroupment in 'broad left' parties or coalitions; and an unresolved relationship with the moderate left, with continuous oscillations between conciliatory and intransigent attitudes.

A corollary of this analysis is that differences between parties are real and important, but their classification into stable ideological sub-groupings (Gomez et al. 2016; March 2012) is not tenable, for three reasons. First, virtually all large parties (an exception might be the Greek KKE after 1991) continuously experiment with different combinations of common elements, mixing old and new left, communist and social democratic, rationalist and populist, Marxist and ecologist themes. Secondly, different ideological tendencies can consolidate into different organisations or coexist within the same party or coalition, depending on the external circumstances and the flexibility of the common working framework. Thirdly, even parties with very different political orientations are usually faced with the same dilemmas: in particular, that between anti-neoliberal coherence and left unity.

Secondly, this plural and fluid landscape highlights the importance of an aggregate approach focusing on the interaction between all kinds of radical left organisations and factions, not discriminating against smaller or extra-parliamentary forces. Such an approach can contribute to a better understanding of questions of strength, fragmentation, strategy, and behaviour.

Thirdly, opinions still differ on an assessment of the deeper meaning of the post-1989 mutation of the Western European radical left.

Early observers interpreted it as an incoherent and centripetal adaptation to the collapse of the Soviet bloc, stressing the multiplicity of paths and outcomes (Bull 1995; Botella and Ramiro 2003; Marantzidis 2004). Others described it as a 'social democratisation' based on a discontinuity with their past (Arter 2002; Fülberth 2008), or as a revival of 'left reformism' that carried on earlier practices (Callinicos 2012). A final group points instead to a continuation under a new guise of traditional anti-capitalist ideals: a case of a wolf in sheep's clothing (Backes and Moreau 2008) or of the reinvention of a 'socialism for the twenty-first century' (Hudson 2012). Most authors stress the compresence of all three elements (March and Mudde 2005).

The German, Italian, and French experiences seem to suggest that the answer is none of the above. The early divergences in ideology and identity unevenly but progressively turned into a convergence around a similar anti-neoliberal programme and a generic 'left' identity (DIE LINKE, FdG, SEL, FdS). Differences persisted, but could usually be managed within the common working framework of a unitary party or a looser alliance. When this did not happen, it was due more to strategic differences and organisational jealousies than to ideological issues. Anti-capitalism, in turn, was retained by virtually all parties as a marker of difference and as a vague long-term aspiration, but very little work went into elaborating the blueprint of a concrete alternative model to capitalism and Soviet socialism. Finally, the programme of the radical left was undoubtedly characterised by a focus on anti-neoliberal reforms, but these remained largely on paper: whenever in government, radical parties were forced to go along with the neoliberal policies proposed by their larger allies (the Italian PRC in 1996–01) or imposed by the international context (the Greek SYRIZA since 2015). In my opinion, the Western European radical left is better characterised as an *electoral thermometer* of popular dissatisfaction toward neoliberalism, which registers changes in the public mood but has not (yet?) found a convincing solution to the riddles of anti-neoliberal politics.

A mixed anti-neoliberal reconversion

The analysis of the three case studies confirms both the tentative convergence of the Western European radical left toward a common anti-neoliberal perspective, and the obstacles to the development of a credible political alternative.

Political project: an incomplete anti-neoliberalism

In terms of political project, most parties moved toward the advocacy of a medium-term anti-neoliberal programme that could appeal to the discontents of the neoliberal transition and of the rightward shift of mainstream parties.

This encompassed three main groups of issues. The first was a set of Keynesian and welfarist demands related to employment, wages, job security, working and living conditions, welfare provisions, public services, and social and regional inequality. The second was a set of left-libertarian values related to peace, global justice, civil and democratic rights, minority rights, environmental protection, and secularism. The third one was related to the discussion of an alternative developmental model (financialisation, globalisation, social and environmental sustainability, quality and direction of economic growth, and democratic ownership and control of the means of production). The reference to a long-term anti-capitalist perspective, variously defined as 'communism', 'democratic socialism', 'eco-socialism', or in vaguer terms, remained in the statutes and official programmes of virtually all parties, with the partial exception of SEL in Italy. However, its contours remained vague and its practical importance – outside the relatively small Trotskyist and far left circles – was progressively downplayed. At a time when models of 'really-existing socialism' had collapsed and struggles entirely focused on the defence of existing levels of social protection against the onslaught of neoliberal reforms, the issue appeared largely academic. Generally speaking, most radical leftists believed that such debates could be postponed to a future stage, after the successful implementation of a minimum neoliberal programme and a recovery of organised popular participation and militancy; others believed that a coherent anti-neoliberal programme would in and of itself put to the centre stage the question of a rupture with capitalism; a final group was probably content with a set of partial reforms.

This perspective had three weak points. First, such a broad programme naturally aspired to represent the interests of the vast majority of the population, as neoliberalism was understood to work for the benefit of a small minority of domestic and international capitalists. However, in practice it was generally difficult to simultaneously represent each heterogeneous component: employed wageworkers, the unemployed, and the inactive; public and private sector workers; relatively protected Fordist workers and the new precariat; young and old; men and women; workerists and post-materialists; anti-capitalists and reformists; regional interests; and so on. Secondly, a fundamental dilemma related to the readiness to seek compromises with other parties in view of obtaining short-term policy gains. Conciliatory currents actively sought to participate in centre-left alliances but, given the existing balance of forces, ended up supporting policies diametrically opposed to their stated aims. Intransigent currents, on the other hand, were often perceived as advocates of a sterile opposition lacking any concrete strategic perspective. Thirdly, programmes were mostly thought as mobilising tools and were rarely clear on key issues of implementation. The issue of budgetary and other structural constraints became increasingly relevant. These were duly criticised, but no clear strategy to circumvent them was outlined. Thus, every time they acceded to governmental offices radical left parties found themselves in a predicament: fiscal austerity automatically ruled out most their policies, but its overcoming required an overhaul of deep-seated economic structures and of a whole gamut of national, EU, and international rules (balanced budgets, trade and capital deregulation, fixed exchange rates, central bank autonomy, competition law) that they were not ready to challenge. As a consequence, they tended to give in on structural issues (such as budget cuts and privatisations), while seeking to mitigate their social effects or win modest redistributive compensations.

Constituency: a composite welfarist coalition

The difficulty in conciliating the different sections of the anti-neoliberal constituency appears clearly from an analysis of the social composition of the German, French, and Italian radical lefts.

The weight of the theoretical 'core socio-economic constituency' and its main components (blue-collar worker, white-collar workers, and the unemployed) on radical left voters and members is summarised in Table 7.1. The table also reports in brackets the degree of over- or under-representation of each category compared to the total valid votes.

In average, the electorate of the radical left retained a strong working-class bias: wageworkers were over-represented, with an index of 133 in France, 126 in Italy and 113 in Germany; employers and self-employed strongly under-represented; the most over-represented categories were the unemployed and blue-collar workers. The total share of this core constituency (62.4 in Germany, 58.3 in France, 48.8 in Italy) was virtually unchanged compared to the pre-1989 figures. This marked class

Table 7.1 Core constituencies, Germany, France, and Italy

	GERMANY		FRANCE		ITALY	
VOTERS	RL 1998–2009	RL 1978	RL 1995–2007	RL 1987	RL 1996–2008	
	4 elections		3 elections		4 elections	
CORE CONSTITUENCY	62.4 (113)	57.3 (140)	58.3 (133)	48.4 (122)	48.8 (126)	
EMPLOYED	50.4 (101)	49.9 (138)	50.7 (132)	44.7 (122)	39.7 (126)	
White-collar	29.6 (93)	25.1 (112)	32.8 (121)	10.7 (71)	20.1 (108)	
Blue-collar	20.8 (116)	24.9 (180)	17.9 (158)	34.0 (158)	19.6 (153)	
UNEMPLOYED	11.9 (256)	7.3 (159)	7.6 (144)	3.7 (126)	9.1 (127)	
MEMBERS	SED 1988	RL 1998–2009	PCF 1979	PCF 1997	PCI 1987	PRC 1999–2006
		2 surveys		1 survey		3 surveys
CORE CONSTITUENCY	75.8	31.6	59.9	43.7	52.4	48.2
EMPLOYED	78.5	25.1	59.9	43.7	52.4	40.3
White-collar		19.9	27.8	27.4	11.1	20.0
Blue-collar		5.2	32.1	16.3	41.3	20.3
UNEMPLOYED		6.5				7.8

character, however, was exposed to some tensions. First, 40–50 per cent of the radical left electorate was constituted by 'secondary' constituencies: inactive persons (pensioners, students, homemakers), self-employed, and professionals. Secondly, the internal composition of the core constituency was increasingly segmented, with a strong decline of blue-collar workers and a rise of white-collar workers and the unemployed. Thirdly, the average figures hide important shifts over time: blue-collar workers, for instance, were a relatively weak constituency for the German PDS until 2005; the unemployed, in turn, abandoned the Italian radical left in 1996 and 2001. Fourthly, the different components of this constellation were unequally divided among various radical left competitors: in France, for instance, the salaried strata tended toward the far left, while the PCF was dominated by pensioners and the inactive.

The composition of the radical left membership, instead, attests to a clear loosening of the traditional links with the working class. The German SED, the French PCF, and the Italian PCI, despite profound differences, had unquestionable working-class roots: wageworkers made up a majority of their membership, with a prominent role of blue-collar workers; part of their organisation was structured along the workplace principle (workplace cells); and cadres with a working-class background were schooled and promoted to significant leadership positions. Within their contemporary heirs, instead, employed workers have become a minority while the weight of the inactive and professionals has soared.

If we broaden the scope of the analysis of the radical left electorate to other socio-demographic characteristics, the class appeal appears to be coexisting with

Table 7.2 Significant determinants of the radical left vote, Germany, France, and Italy

	GERMANY 1998, 2002, 2005, 2009 (legislative)	ITALY 1996, 2001, 2006 (legislative)	FRANCE 1995, 2002, 2007 (presidential)
GEOGRAPHY			
Positive	Eastern regions RL 65.6% – index 314	Red area RL 22.7% – index 123	-
Negative	Western regions RL 34.4% – index 43	North-East RL 8.3% – index 69	-
GENDER			
Positive	-	-	-
Negative	-	-	-
AGE			
Positive	-	<25 years old RL 16.9% – index 138	-
Negative	-	>64 years old RL 10.2% – index 63	>59 years old RL 15.6% – index 57
RELIGIOUS PRACTICE			
Positive	Non-religious RL 61.2% – index 228	Non-believers RL 16.3% – index 295 Non-practicing Catholics RL 18.1% – index 152	Non-believers RL 42.4% – index 170
Negative	Catholics RL 13.0% – index 37 Protestants RL 25.8% – index 68	Practicing Catholics RL 31.4% – index 60	Practicing Catholics RL 4.2% – index 38 Other religion RL 4.2% – index 78 Non-practicing Catholics RL 49.2% – index 83
EDUCATION			
Positive	-	University degree RL 9.8% – index 128	-
Negative	-	-	University degree RL 20.0% – index 82
PROFESSION			
Positive	Unemployed RL 11.9% – index 258	Students RL 12.0% – index 151 Blue-collar workers RL 19.8% – index 146	Blue-collar workers RL 18.1% – index 158 Unemployed RL 8.2% – index 140 White-collar workers RL 19.2% – index 129

(*Continued*)

Table 7.2 (Continued)

	GERMANY 1998, 2002, 2005, 2009 (legislative)	ITALY 1996, 2001, 2006 (legislative)	FRANCE 1995, 2002, 2007 (presidential)
Negative	Civil servant RL 2.8% – index 61 Self-employed RL 4.8% – index 68	Self-employed RL 8.0% – index 59	Self-employed RL 1.6% – index 35 Retired RL 17.3% – index 64
SELF-POSITIONING			
Positive	n.a.	Left (1+2) RL 73.7% – index 364	Far-left RL 18.5% – index 426 Left RL 52.4% – index 155
Negative	n.a.	Centre (5+6) RL 4.6% – index 26 Centre-right (7+8) RL 1.6% – index 7 Right (9+10) RL 0.6% – index 5	Centre RL 13.8% – index 63 Right RL 4.9% – index 16 Far-right RL 0.2% – index 7

a strong influence of other variables. Table 7.2 reports the variables that unambiguously influenced the likelihood of a vote for the radical left (±9 per cent on index in all elections).

The strongest and most constant influence was exerted by two ideological variables: ideology and religious affiliation/practice. Not surprisingly, parties drew the overwhelming majority of their support among voters on the 'far-left' or 'left' end of the political spectrum and rapidly lost support among those on the centre, right and far-right. Non-believers were very likely to vote for the radical left, practicing Catholics avoided it, while the effects of other confessions and degrees of religious practice varied.

Geographical sub-cultures were very relevant, but their persistence suffered a partial erosion. The support for the PDS was largely concentrated in the small territory of the former German Democratic Republic (more than 75 per cent of its votes), but this share dropped to around 50 per cent with the alliance and merger with the WASG; over-representation of Eastern voters steadily declined from 406.5 per cent (1990) to 235.1 per cent (2013). The support for the Italian radical left was better distributed geographically. The PRC and its various splinter groups generally enjoyed strong results in the 'red' central regions (former PCI strongholds) and weak ones in the 'white' North-East (former DC and current right-wing strongholds), but the over-representation of the red area almost completely disappeared (from 149.8 per cent in 1992 to 106.2 per cent in 2013). In France, traditional communist strongholds were spatially very fragmented: roughly speaking, one area in the North, one in the Centre and one on the Mediterranean coast. Here as well, the differences seem to have gradually decreased over time (Brechon 2009; Martelli 2009).

The radical left electorate was on average slightly masculine, but counter-examples abounded: good gender balance was achieved in Italy in 1996 and in Eastern Germany throughout the period, and a female majority was reached in the French 2002 presidential election.[1]

As far as age is concerned, over-60 tended to be strongly reluctant toward the radical left in Italy, France, and Western Germany, but not in Eastern Germany. Supportive groups also varied from country to country and from election to election. The youth (under-24) was consistently favourable in Italy, generally favourable in France (except in 1995) but generally hostile in Germany. The working-age population (25–59) gave inconclusive results, with the weight of older age brackets slightly on the rise.

As far as educational levels were concerned, holders of a university degree were more likely than the average voter to support the radical left in Italy and less likely in France; in Germany, the strongly favourable attitude of graduates toward the PDS was reversed with DIE LINKE.

Finally, the influence of class on the radical left vote was moderately strong and usually consistent, but not completely uniform. Employers and self-employed were overwhelmingly repelled by the radical left. The success among the different sectors of employed wageworkers, instead, varied: largely limited to blue-collar workers in Italy; broader (blue-collar and white-collar) in France; evolving in Germany, where the hostility of blue-collar workers toward the PDS turned to a strong attraction toward DIE LINKE. The unemployed were strongly favourable in Germany and France but not in Italy. Students were very supportive in Italy but inconsistent in the other two countries. Finally, the remaining sections of the economically inactive population tended to be quite hostile in France and Italy but not necessarily so in Germany.

Altogether, the radical left electorate was fairly composite, reflecting a mixture of class (blue-collar workers and the unemployed) and ideological (left-wingers and secularists) appeals. This coalition was consistent with the anti-neoliberal discourse of the parties, but success among the different social categories was not uniform, and the preferences of the two groups sometimes diverged. The French radical left presented the most marked class profile. The Italian radical left was more split between manual workers on the one hand, and a precarious educated youth on the other. The German radical left started out as the mouthpiece of a very peculiar social stratum, the downwardly-mobile former bureaucracy of the GDR, and progressively expanded its support among the unemployed and blue-collar workers (particularly after 2005).

The radical left membership, on the other hand, did not reflect well the working-class focus of radical left parties and was increasingly dominated by pensioners and intellectual workers.

Strategy: the key dilemma

In terms of strategical mediations, the three case studies confirm that most radical left parties broadly agreed on a strategy of leftward pull aimed at gradually influencing the course of the moderate left through a combination of parliamentary and extra-parliamentary, friendly and hostile pressures. Only a minority of far-left groups expounded instead a strategy of anti-capitalist alternative, bypassing the moderate left with a course of rigorous political independence and transitional watchwords preparing a pre-revolutionary situation.

This agreement, however, broke down on the veritable bone of contention of the contemporary radical left: the degree of intransigence required to precipitate a 're-social democratisation' of the moderate left. Conciliatory voices declared the unavoidability of strategies of organic centre-left alliances, hoping to prevent a greater evil (a right-wing government) and to influence policies from the inside. Intransigent voices, on the contrary, tended to reject electoral and above all governmental coalitions on grounds of anti-neoliberal coherence. Most of the parties constantly oscillated between the two poles.

No satisfactory solution was found to this problem. The conciliatory path profoundly damaged the internal cohesion and external image of the radical left, proving unsustainable in the long-term. Those who chose it either ended up merging into larger moderate left parties (MCU in 1995–98, various dissident groups) or had to revert to a more independent stance to avoid disaster (PdCI in 2008, PCF in 2010, and SEL in 2014). A hard-line anti-capitalist path had little chances of reaching out beyond the few converts, as proved by the marginalisation of LO after 2002, the Italian far left after 2008, and the NPA in 2009–12. Some pieces of evidence point to the potential of a populist strategy combining an intransigent attitude toward the moderate left coupled with a relatively moderate programme: often adopted by radical right parties, it recently contributed to the extraordinary successes of SYRIZA in Greece, PODEMOS in Spain, and (outside of the radical left) the M5S in Italy. Promising in the long-term, this strategy was however risky in the short-term, as large sections of the anti-neoliberal electorate remained attached to some form of united front against the right and many electoral systems (France, Italy) threatened a bloodbath of elected representatives and resources for non-aligned forces.

Summary

In the nineties, the Western European radical left sought to recover its lost strength by formulating a modern anti-neoliberal programme and by appealing to the neglected working-class and welfarist constituencies of mainstream parties. As I will show in the next sections, the efforts were initially successful, as they allowed the various parties to benefit from the rise of dissatisfaction and resistance against neoliberal reforms and to initiate processes of regroupment. However, some key strategic and programmatic flaws contributed to an interruption of these trends in the noughties, and a subsequent stagnation and fragmentation of the radical left in several countries.

The uneven development of radical left strength

This section explicitly compares the trajectories of radical left strength in Western Europe, Germany, Italy, and France. These were characterised by both similarities

Filling the vacuum? 209

and differences, highlighting the combined role of cross-national trends and national specificities in shaping radical left development.

Electoral strength: a real but uncertain recovery

Scholarly assessments on the electoral success of the contemporary Western European radical left have varied over time. Initial observers stressed its swift decline (Bull 1995). Subsequent analyses detected contradictory tendencies, remaining cautious on the overall direction of change (March and Mudde 2005). Recent contributions emphasise instead modest or strong recovery trends (De Waele and Seiler 2012; March and Keith 2016). The new methodology adopted in this book, with the use of Western European aggregate weighted figures and the simultaneous analysis of national variations and cross-national trends, clarifies the issue and enables a fine-grained appreciation of the radical left trajectory.

This can be periodised in four main stages (Figure 7.1). In the first period (1989–93), the radical left – despite a small initial 'Gorbachev bump' – suffered a swift, heavy, and almost universal decline. The aggregate value fell from 9.4 per cent in 1988 to 5.1 in 1993; the average value from 7.9 to 5.4 per cent; and 14 out of 17 countries experienced losses.[2] Most of the aggregate decline was due to defections from the party family, particularly that of the majority faction of the Italian PCI, but the overwhelming majority of parties lost moderately or heavily. In the second period (1994–99), the radical left embarked instead on a strong recovery path. The aggregate value rose to 7.2 per cent; the average value to 7.0 per cent; and 14 out of 17 countries experienced gains.[3] Aggregate results remained lower than in

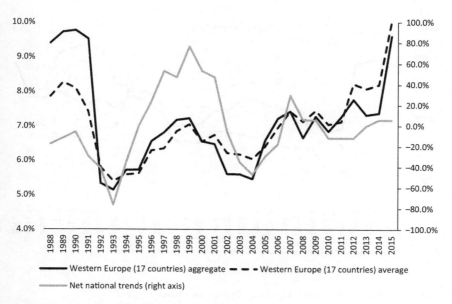

Figure 7.1 Electoral strength, Western Europe

210 *Filling the vacuum?*

1988, but represented a 40 per cent increase on 1993, and eight countries outperformed their 1988 results. In the third period (2000–07), little progress was made. The aggregate value plunged back to 5.5 in 2004 and entirely recovered to 7.4 in 2007; cross-national trends were visible but weaker; and national trajectories more asynchronous and volatile. In the fourth period (2008–15), finally, cross-national trends broke down and a trendless volatility imposed itself. Countries and individual parties experienced unprecedented short-term gains and losses. The effects of the Great Recession led to extraordinary gains in some Mediterranean countries (Greece, Spain, and Portugal) and a re-emergence as relevant party family in two other countries (Belgium and Ireland), but left it stagnant or declining in the rest of the continent (in particular, in the populous Germany, France, Italy, and the UK). The aggregate value was stuck until 2014; it shot up in 2015 (9.6 per cent), but largely because of the results of a single Spanish party (PODEMOS and its connected alliances).

To sum up, the recovery of the radical left since its low point in 1993 emerges clearly from the empirical evidence, but remains to the present day uneven and unstable. The first aggregate momentum was cross-national but broke down in 1999. The second aggregate momentum started around 2012, but national results remained highly volatile and showed increasing signs of divergence between peripheral and core countries.

The trajectories of the three case studies confirm this general assessment (Figure 7.2). Across the period 1994–2015, average electoral results – including both sub-national and presidential elections – were medium-small: 9.8 per cent in

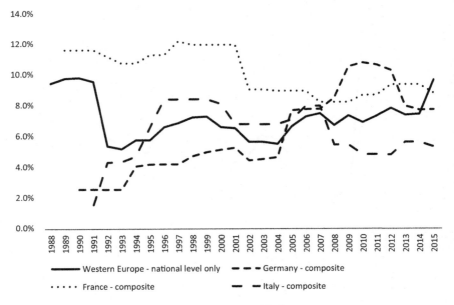

Figure 7.2 Electoral strength, Germany, France, and Italy

Filling the vacuum? 211

France; 6.7 per cent in Germany; 6.5 per cent in Italy. The radical left massively improved on its pre-1989 results in Germany, thanks to the consolidation of a territorial appeal in the new Eastern regions and a post-2005 surge in the Western regions, but never recovered the strength of its communist predecessors in Italy and France. All three countries grew in the nineties and fell in the early noughties. Thereafter, national paths diverged: Germany grew substantially until 2012 but fell below 8 per cent afterwards; Italy grew less until 2006, collapsed in 2008, and remained around 5 per cent ever since; France never recovered from the shock of 2002, stagnating around 8–9 per cent.

Institutional strength: a double-edged sword

This book provides the first quantification of the aggregate parliamentary and governmental strength of the radical left. The issue of parliamentary representation has been touched only marginally and with reference to individual national cases; governmental participation has been researched extensively and comparatively (Bale and Dunphy 2011; Olsen et al. 2010), but without clear quantitative indicators of national and aggregate strength.

Parliamentary strength broadly followed electoral movements, but at a substantially lower level (Figure 7.3). Average 1994–2015 values were 4.7 per cent for Western Europe (national level only), 6.5 per cent for Germany, 5.1 per cent for France, and 4.3 per cent for Italy. These disproportionalities were essentially due to the working of electoral legislations (majoritarian system, small constituency

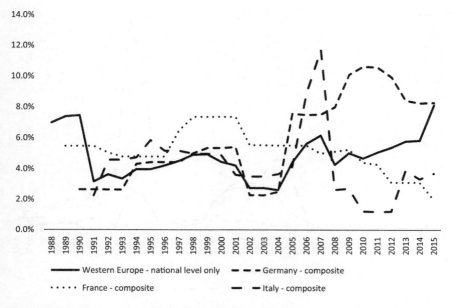

Figure 7.3 Parliamentary strength, Germany, France, and Italy

size, electoral thresholds) and to a growing fragmentation of the radical left in competing electoral lists. In the three case studies, the risk of a loss of national parliamentary status was always present: it materialised once in Italy (2008–12), was constant in Germany until 2005, and became progressively closer in France (only 10 MPs in 2012). Switches of allegiance were rare in Germany and France, but frequent in Italy. Presence in regional parliaments was weaker in Germany (due to problems in the Western regions) but stronger in France and Italy (due to widespread strategies of centre-left alliances).

Hurdles to parliamentary representation had an important effect on the development of the radical left, weakening its financial and communication resources, depressing the electoral results of smaller parties and whole countries (Austria, Belgium, France, Ireland, Switzerland, and the UK), and often encouraging regroupment processes.

Governmental strength was limited, due to the parliamentary weakness of the radical left and the preference of many social democratic parties for pure centre-left or grand coalition alliances (Figure 7.4). The average 1994–2015 value for Western Europe (national level only) was 1.8 per cent, much higher than in the eighties but nevertheless quite marginal. In seven years, however, peaks above 3 per cent were reached, and the sheer number of experiences of direct governmental participation and external support increased mightily, encompassing nine of the total seventeen countries.

The analysis of the three case studies is particularly instructive. On the one hand, national governmental experiences were absent (Germany) or rare (Italy

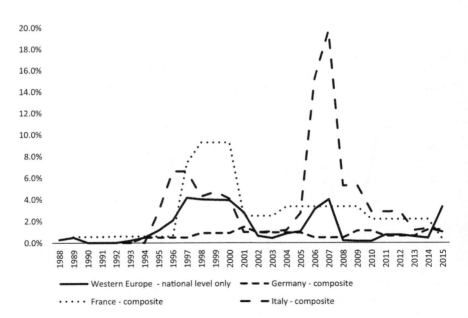

Figure 7.4 Governmental strength, Germany, France, and Italy

and France), and radical left parties always remained small junior partners in the resulting governmental majorities. On the other hand, national data systematically understate the level of radical left involvement, which can be shown to be substantially higher in regional governments. Including the regional level, the average 1994–2015 values rise to 0.8 per cent in Germany, 3.4 per cent in France, and 4.3 per cent in Italy, with peaks of 9.3 per cent (1999–2000) in the second and of 19.7 per cent (2007) in the third country. Alliances at the regional level were less controversial for both radical left and social democratic parties: the lure of victory and resources often trumped programmatic differences, which in any case predominantly related to national and international issues.

Governmental participation had major effects on the development of the radical left. Despite their rare frequency, national experiences caused heavy electoral losses in the short term and often involved the occurrence of party splits and the rise of more intransigent challengers. The consequences of regional experiences were similar but more attenuated. Nevertheless, in cases when this involvement extended to most of the national territory (France in 2004–14, Italy in 2005–10), it certainly weakened the public perception of the radical left as an 'anti-system' force and exposed it to an enhanced competition from other protest movements (FN in France, M5S in Italy).

Organisational strength: no solution to the crisis of the communist mass party model

Organisational dimensions of radical left strength are extensively researched at the level of individual parties but rarely in comparative and aggregate terms. My analysis has made a first step in this direction, but more research on these issues is needed, as primary data are often non-comprehensive, inhomogeneous, and unreliable. Nevertheless, the evidence points to the fact that attempts to respond to the irreversible crisis of the communist mass party model have failed, resulting partly in a continued decline of organisational strength, and partly in an uneasy adaptation to the patterns of 'normal' modern cadre parties.

With regard to membership strength, results were an unmitigated disaster (Figure 7.5). Data for nine countries (Austria, France, Germany, Italy, the Netherlands, Portugal, Spain, Sweden, and the UK) show a continuous decline from 2.1 million members in 1988 (17.1 per cent of all party members) to about 830,000 in 1993 (9.1 per cent), 530,000 in 2003 (6.8 per cent), and 430,000 in 2013 (6.0 per cent). National numbers fell by 95 per cent for Italy (1988–2013), 75 per cent for France (1988–2013), and by 77 per cent for Germany (1990–2013). Patterns were different but outcomes were broadly similar. Three facts are remarkable. First, aggregate membership strength was much stronger than electoral strength before 1989, but became slightly weaker in the noughties. Secondly, parties with deep communist roots invariably declined and aged, proving incapable to renew their organisational legacy. Thirdly, new parties and parties with different roots often grew. Their membership gains, however, were proportionally lower than their electoral ones and rarely compensated the decline of their communist

214   *Filling the vacuum?*

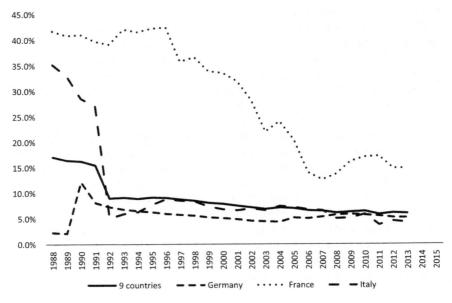

Figure 7.5 Membership strength, Germany, France, and Italy

cousins. Fourthly, the encapsulation ratios of radical left parties (M/V) generally declined from the high levels typical of twentieth-century mass parties (6–15 per cent) to those of modern cadre parties (3–5 per cent) or vanguard parties (below 2 per cent). No organisational innovation managed to reverse the long-term decline of party activism, which affected all party families (Ion 1997; Van Biezen et al. 2012) but radical left parties to a special degree. Alternative forms of left-wing political engagement (NGOs, local groups, loose social movements, and individual efforts) remained relatively vital, but could not be transformed into stable partisan links.[4]

From many points of view, this was a minor problem: members are increasingly marginal for the financing and running of Western political parties, and a small membership makes electoral results more volatile but does not affect the chances of electoral success. For the radical left, however, it constituted a major ideological and strategic hurdle, as its political perspective heavily relied on grassroots participation and extra-parliamentary mobilisations. A possible solution is the one recently offered by PODEMOS in Spain (and the M5S in Italy): the abolition of any distinction between members and sympathisers, with the hope recreating under different forms the kind of passive but stable attachment that characterised much of the membership of traditional mass parties. Other counter-examples are provided by the revival of party membership in semi-revolutionary situations (as in the Venezuelan PSUV, the Nepali UCPN-M, or the Bolivian MAS): these cases, however, are so far limited to developing countries. For the foreseeable future, the Western European radical left will tend to be dominated by increasingly small political organisations, often capable of significant electoral exploits but unable to translate this superficial sympathy into more solid and stable relations of allegiance and activism.

With regard to sub-cultural linkages, the tight links of communist parties with friendly civil society organisations collapsed during the nineties and new relations remained quantitatively and qualitatively limited. An adequate measurement of this variable is at present impossible, as it would require both a comprehensive census of the membership figures of each organisation (partial data are available through administrative and survey sources) and an operationalisation of the intensity of each link between party and organisation (very difficult in a period when most of the latter have switched from formal affiliation to autonomy). Nevertheless, it is absolutely evident that not much remains today of the strong and tightly-knit sub-cultural networks that dominated Western European politics from the late nineteenth century to the nineteen-seventies (Hellemans 1990). As I have shown in previous chapters, this process was characterised by three overlapping trends: (a) a quantitative decline of the membership of friendly mass organisations; (b) the autonomisation of these organisations from their traditional partisan referents; (c) the de-ideologisation of civil society organisations themselves, which replaced strong worldviews with a more prosaic role of providers of individual and collective services. The outcome was a new model of looser, more punctual, and constantly renegotiated relations between increasingly autonomous organisations and social spheres, couched in terms of a celebration of the nonpartisan and apolitical character of civil society activity and in the rhetoric of the autonomy of social movements.

Radical left parties have been considerably weakened by this shift. In Italy, the PRC was deprived from the start of any influence within the imposing network of collateral organisations of the Italian PCI, which was entirely inherited by the rival post-communist party (PDS). Over the subsequent decades, radical left parties made a constant effort to rebuild solid relations with old and new civil society organisations, but progress was limited. Relations of affinity and collaboration were indeed established with a variety of societal milieus (for instance, the alter-globalist galaxy), but the groups were smallish and the linkages weak. The trade union movement, in particular, overwhelmingly continued to support the PDS/DS/PD, albeit with frequent critical remarks. In Germany, the totalising control of the SED on the Eastern civil society was shattered by revolution and re-unification. The PDS retained tight links with a small network of organisations representing the former bureaucracy and with the largest Eastern charity, but lost all influence in the organised labour movement and in other societal milieus. Over the following decades, radical left parties established good working relations with large sections of the German civil society, particularly in the East, but these continued to concentrate their support on their traditional representatives (SPD, CDU/CSU, and GRÜNE), albeit in a more critical and de-emphasised way. In France, finally, the old network of collateral organisations of the PCF was not immediately destroyed by the implosion of the Soviet bloc, but progressively lost weight and coherence. The outcome was often paradoxical, as these organisations effectively ceased to act as relays of communist influence and moved toward more moderate orientations, but leaders and cadres retained a vague communist culture and often a formal party membership. Thus, linkages remained stronger than in the other two countries, but their practical impact limited.

With regard to financial and other organisational resources data are sketchy and inhomogeneous. Generally speaking, the financial strength of radical left parties seems to have hovered somewhere between their parliamentary and electoral strength, the two main sources of incomes. Parties became overwhelmingly dependent from direct and indirect sources of state funding, with a marginal contribution of membership dues and donations. This fact enhanced the importance of winning parliamentary representation, producing differentiated consequences according to the specific context. In some cases, it encouraged processes of regroupment (Germany). In other cases, it strengthened the split of the radical left between predominantly parliamentary and predominantly extra-parliamentary currents (France). In most cases, it enhanced the appeal of centre-left alliances, which could ensure survival and resources even in the presence of weak and declining electoral results. Human resources probably declined compared to the eighties and broadly followed the evolution of financial resources since the noughties. Communication strength, in turn, suffered from the decline of membership strength and of party-owned media, many of which have closed or are in crisis, but may have been compensated by a stronger mass media exposure.

Summary

The Western European radical left slowly recovered from the long decline of the eighties and early nineties, but patterns varied in time, space, and dimension. At the electoral level, a strong and universal recovery in the nineties left space to more differentiated national trajectories afterwards. Aggregate strength oscillated between 5 and 7 per cent, with a sudden spike to 9.6 per cent in 2015. National results became increasingly volatile and divergent. Importantly, the radical lefts of the three case studies are caught up since 2012 in stagnating or declining trends and do not seem to be benefitting from the surge of their Mediterranean counterparts (Greece, Spain, and Portugal). At the institutional level, the radical left remained a weak-to-marginal actor, with a parliamentary strength substantially lower than its electoral one and a governmental strength on the rise but small. At the organisational level, the crisis of the communist mass party model still exerts its effects three decades after the fall of the Soviet bloc. Parties have been unable to turn their enhanced image and electoral support into stable forms of individual (membership) and collective (sub-cultural linkages) attachment, and predominantly remain electoral organisations with little organised following.

The three case studies followed in many respects the broader Western European trends, but were characterised by important national specificities. First, the organisational legacy of the communist predecessors had an important impact both on the starting point and on the subsequent development of the radical left in each country and in all dimensions. Secondly, mass extra-parliamentary mobilisations and governmental participations strongly influenced the timing of electoral success and failure. Thirdly, electoral systems and the strategy of alliances of the moderate left affected the translation of votes into parliamentary and governmental strength. The most successful case was the most unlikely, that of the German radical left. Despite its roots in a Stalinist regime, the PDS skilfully managed to exploit mass protests to develop first a regional (1992–93) and then an all-German (2004) appeal, expanding its electoral support among dissatisfied voters in relative isolation from the rest of the party system. The French and Italian radical lefts, on the other hand, suffered under the constraints of majoritarian electoral systems and bipolar competition patterns, losing their momentum in the governmental experiences of the late nineties (at the national level) and noughties (at the regional level) and arriving to 2015 in a state of unprecedented weakness. None of the parties was entirely successful in offering a credible challenge to the moderate left which, despite its many predicaments, remained hegemonic on the left-wing spectrum.

Determinants of radical left cohesion and fragmentation

The degree of fragmentation of the Western European radical left is underestimated by existing scholarship, which systematically excludes from the analysis minor and extra-parliamentary parties (De Waele and Seiler 2012; March 2012). My analysis shows that this level has constantly increased since 1993, producing an often destructive competition between existing parties, splinter groups, far-left challengers, and new organisations. The contentious points have been broadly similar in all countries, but their outcomes have produced strikingly different national trajectories.

The three case studies are good cases in point. In France, the competition between the communist PCF and other radical left actors (LO, LCR/NPA, PT, PG, and PCF dissidents) became entrenched during the eighties and grew larger in the following decades. Regroupment efforts failed in 1995–97 and 2005–07. They finally succeeded in 2009–12, leading to the convergence of most organisations and voters under the banners of the FdG. The alliance, however, never evolved toward a permanent coalition (like the Spanish IU) or a merger (like the German DIE LINKE), was plagued by internal conflicts, and is currently moribund. In Italy, the whole radical left spectrum initially converged in the neo-communist PRC, but this progressively fragmented in a variety of competing parties, micro-parties, and temporary electoral cartels. A first unification attempt took place and failed in 2008 (the SA alliance); a second attempt is currently underway (SI), but its chances do not look too bright. In Germany, on the contrary, the democratic socialist PDS avoided major splits, and twice absorbed its potential competitors in its ranks (1990 and 2007). Violent internal conflicts repeatedly erupted, but were always defused or papered over.

The case for a regroupment of forces of different origin and sensibility in a common 'broad left' party or coalition is simple: the end of the Soviet Union downplayed one of the historically most contentious issues between communists, Trotskyists, Maoists, and left-socialists; all groups now identified with a medium-term anti-neoliberal programme, in more radical or moderate variants; all of them tried to reclaim the representation of working-class and welfarist strata from neoliberalised mainstream parties; and the relative weakness of each of them favoured the pooling of forces. While a number of political and material questions produced tensions and fostered vocal debates, temporary compromise solutions were often within reach.

The establishment and preservation of radical left unity overwhelmingly depended on three factors: (a) the ability of the main radical left party to ensure a reasonable distribution of political and material resources among existing tendencies and potential partners; (b) the incentives provided by the political system, particularly those concerning the access to state financing and parliamentary representation; (c) the saliency of the question of centre-left alliances and governmental participation.

The behaviour of the biggest radical left party in each country (PDS, PRC, and PCF) was of crucial importance. A modernised ideology, a pluralist internal organisation, and the willingness to reward potential partners with adequate resources and visibility were crucial to the success of regroupment processes. In Italy, the open and flexible attitude of the PRC helped to keep together a variety of communist and far left currents in the early nineties, before fragmenting under the pressure of bipolarism. In France, the PCF regularly wasted many opportunities through its insistence on leading the process and the few incentives it could offer to potential allies; a belated regroupment occurred only in 2012, when it agreed to rally behind the left-socialist Mélenchon as its presidential candidate. In Germany, the leadership of the PDS was willing to grant important programmatic, symbolic, and material concessions to its allies, which greatly facilitated the success of its successive mergers.

The presence of institutional incentives was also very important in ensuring the cohesion (or lack thereof) of radical left forces. In Germany, the 5 per cent electoral threshold discouraged potential competitors to the PDS and favoured radical left regroupment. In Italy, the electoral system deterred competitors to the left of the PRC (the 4 per cent thresholds), but lured moderated factions and individuals toward conciliatory splits (lower barriers to representation for members of the centre-left coalitions). After 2007, this encouraged both the creation of heterogeneous electoral coalitions geared at gaining parliamentary representation, and the break-up of said coalitions through offers by the PD of a place at the table. In France, the extremely high barriers to representation discouraged competing candidatures in legislative elections but encouraged them in presidential ones, as a common candidate would have reduced the media exposure and financial prospects of each individual organisation.

Finally, the saliency of the central political fault line of the radical left, the question of a conciliatory or intransigent attitude toward the moderate left, varied sharply according to the context. Whenever the electoral and parliamentary contribution of the radical left became determinant for the formation or survival of a centre-left government, powerful centrifugal pressures were set in motion; in other cases, a formal unity could be more easily preserved. In Germany, the PDS had the luck of being considered as *nicht koalitionsfähig* (not a viable coalition partner) by the SPD, which agreed to alliances only in a few Eastern regions. This greatly alleviated the pressures on the cohesion of the party, where factions continuously clashed on the issue but could not openly break on the basis of a merely theoretical possibility. In Italy, the radical left was always determinant for the success of centre-left coalitions, leading to frequent governmental participations and splits. In France, finally, the two-round electoral system of presidential and legislative elections generally enabled the PS to govern alone or with minor allies, without the direct support of the radical left. When this did not happen (1997–02), the result was a major split between PCF and its far-left competitors. At the regional level, in turn, the situation was similar to that in Italy.

On the basis of the aforementioned considerations, the trajectories of the three countries become easy to understand. The unity of the Italian radical left was progressively destroyed by the salience of the issue of governmental participation and by the selective incentives offered by the electoral system to right-wing splits. The unity of the German radical left was preserved by the absence of the first pressure, by the positive effects of the electoral system, and by the willingness of the PDS to reward potential allies with material resources and a political role well above their effective contribution. In the case of France, finally, the many chances of regroupment of the radical left between 1993 and 2007 were scuppered partly by the issue of governmental participation and partly by the incapacity of the various potential partners to reach a balanced compromise; the latter element, in turn, largely derived from disproportions in their respective societal strength.[5] It was only when the bad memories of the Jospin period waned and when a weakened PCF was ready to agree to important material concessions that the partial regroupment of the FdG could take place (2009–12).

The welfarist vacuum and its limitations

The initial hypothesis of this book was that the rightward shift of mainstream party families during the eighties and nineties opened up a potential vacuum of political representation of working-class and welfarist constituencies, which the radical left sought to fill with its anti-neoliberal mobilisation (chapter one).

The analysis of the cases of Germany, France, and Italy supports the empirical existence of such a vacuum, showing that from 1994 to 2015 more than half of the electorate continued to exhibit traditional welfarist opinions, was increasingly dissatisfied with mainstream parties, and repeatedly engaged in mass mobilisations against specific neoliberal reforms. It also confirms that, under certain conditions, the radical left was able to exploit the popular rejection of neoliberalism to make inroads among disaffected voters of social democratic and other mainstream parties. The case of the German radical left is exemplary: in 2002–09 DIE LINKE made a net gain of 3.2 million votes, 64.3 per cent of which were former SPD supporters. The gains of the PRC were smaller, but had a similar composition: 0.9 million votes in 1994–96, 69.4 per cent of which former PDS supporters. French data on electoral flows are less precise, but also indicate a predominant interchange with the PS. Such successes, however, were always of a limited magnitude and short-lived. A long-term upward movement is visible only in Germany (with two interruptions); in Italy and France, the long-term trend was rather flat or declining. In other words, the vacuum proved to be much more difficult to fill than expected. Why was it so?

The study of the preconditions of radical left electoral success points to three major possible avenues of growth.

The first avenue was represented by an overall shift of the political mood to the left, with both moderate and radical left parties benefitting from the swing. These conjunctures generally resulted from major reform proposals by seating right-wing governments, which elicited large movements of resistance: examples are the years 1995–97 and 2009–12 in France, the years 1993–98 in Germany, and the years 1994–96 and 2002–05 in Italy.

The second avenue was represented by a shift of moderate left voters toward the radical left, motivated by the desire of punishing the mainstream parties for their governmental policies or of nudging them to move to the left. The most favourable environment was provided by grand coalition governments, when both the stabilising effects of the left-right competition and the pressure toward left unity faltered, fuelling the rise of anti-establishment parties of all hues. Examples are Germany (2005–09), to a less extent Italy (1994–96) and, outside the three countries, Greece (2009–12). The Italian radical left wasted an extraordinary opportunity to exploit a similar situation which occurred after 2011. Its opposition to the Monti and Letta cabinets was not very credible, in view of its past and present links with the centre-left coalition and its unprecedented organisational and parliamentary weakness; the chance was instead seized by Grillo's M5S. A path of head-on confrontation with a seating centre-left government could also bear fruit (Germany 2002–05; the French far left in 1997–02); in absence of a minimum level of confidence, however, it could lead instead to demobilisation or adaptation to a 'lesser evil' perspective (Italy in 1999–2001 and 2008; Germany in 2002).

The third avenue was represented by a growth of the radical left beyond the confines of the secular and progressive left-wing voters. The strategies employed and the success met varied for each party. The French far-left candidates (Laguiller, Besancenot) were the most successful in appealing to class and attracting a core constituency of economically active wageworkers.[6] The German PDS, on the other hand, saw the predominance of a regional (East German interests) over a class appeal, with strong but socially undifferentiated results among the Eastern voters and a nation-wide over-representation only among the unemployed. The Italian radical left, finally, showed a decreasing capability to attract specific social constituencies (except for the youth) and remained predominately characterised by its left-wing ideological positioning.

The problem with most of these strategies was that they were self-moderating: they could give good results in the short-term, but inevitably led to equal or stronger losses in the medium-term.

The very electoral success of the radical left parties tended to make them determinant, in the ballot box and in parliament, for the formation of a centre-left governing coalition – the more so, the more successful they were at contending the typical electorate of mainstream left parties. The choice to exploit this situation as a powerful lever to influence the policies of a victorious centre-left coalition invariably turned out to be a poisoned chalice. Both external support (Italy in 1996–98) and direct governmental participation (France in 1997–2002, Italy in 1998–2001 and 2006–08) yielded few visible material results, destroyed the credibility of the parties in the eyes of their electorate, and led them to electoral disasters at the subsequent election. The opposite choice of intransigence, on the other hand, risked to expose the parties to accusations of playing into the hands of the enemy and to a subsequent squeeze due to anti-right tactical voting. The French radical left experienced this brutal pressure after the 2002 presidential election: the shock of the elimination of Lionel Jospin from the second round led to an immediate loss of almost half of its electorate, mainly in the direction of the Socialist Party, and its effects appear to be long-lasting.[7] The Italian radical left also suffered heavily from this mechanism in 2008, when it lost at least 0.7 million votes to the Democratic Party;[8] more frequently, the choice of intransigence meant painful splits (the MCU in 1995; the PdCI in 1998; SEL in 2008–09) of the tendencies which were determined to maintain a close alliance with the centre-left. The threat was somewhat minimised only in the German case, as it was the SPD that consistently refused a governmental alliance with the radical left.[9] Crucially, the oppositional stance which might work well at times of centre-left governments became less practical and rewarding at times of strong rejection and mobilisation against right-wing ones; conversely, the unitary posture which yielded fruits against the right became catastrophic as soon as it morphed into governmental participation.

An additional problem was provided by the fact that the sudden surges of enthusiasm obtained through a convincing electoral or extra-parliamentary campaign, a popular leader, or a new partisan project were difficult to sustain for a longer period. As neither conciliatory nor intransigent organisations managed to win immediate, concrete, and visible policy concessions for their constituency, the hopes raised by an initial bout of electoral growth tended to wear off quickly, while the newly-won supporters went back to abstention or more mainstream political options.

A further obstacle was the response of mainstream centre-left forces to the competition on their left. Veritable shifts to the left were minimal, even at a rhetorical level. However, the mere return to opposition after an electoral defeat generally enabled them to win back a section of their former disaffected supporters (Italy in 2001–06; France in 1993–97 and 2002–12; Germany in 2009–13), although it was rarely sufficient to entirely recover the past losses. Moreover, the fact that the parties retained declining but strong linkages with the workers' movement (trade unions, cooperatives, associations) and other civil society and social movement organisations enabled them to preserve the loyalty of critical strata which might have otherwise gone over to their more radical competitors.

Finally, the rightward shift of mainstream political parties was to some extent accompanied by a parallel rightward shift of their constituencies. The proactive role of moderate left leaders in driving the neoliberal adaptation of their parties (e.g. the role of Achille Occhetto and Walter Veltroni in Italy and Gerhard Schröder in Germany) tended to run against an often intense initial resistance by their activists, members, and voters. Over time, however, part of the critics came around to the new course or put up with the changes. In other words, neoliberal reforms created short-term windows of opportunity for the radical left, but that opening tended to significantly narrow in the medium-term.

The failure of the strategy of leftward pull

The radical left was not very effective in pushing forward its political programme and shaping Western European politics and society.

At the level of extra-parliamentary mobilisation, the radical left parties were very active in their support and participation to a broad range of struggles and social movements. This involvement was generally regarded as constructive by the participants, won them new allies, and often significantly increased their electoral audience. The link between electoral gains and left-leaning social mobilisations emerges very clearly in all three countries. In France, the two electoral peaks of the radical left (1995–2002 and 2009–12) are tightly correlated to massive anti-right mobilisations led by the labour movement (1995 and 2009–10). In Italy, the two peaks (1995–96 and 2004–06) neatly followed large anti-Berlusconi mobilisations by trade unions (1994 and 2002) and pacifist networks (2002–04). In Germany, finally, the two largest increases of the vote for the PDS/DIE LINKE (1994 and 2005) were direct consequences of the 1992–93 anti-Treuhand, of the 2003 pacifist, and of the 2003–04 anti-Hartz mobilisations.[10]

The organisational and strategic benefits of such an involvement, however, remained limited. First of all, the parties largely failed to translate the gains of sympathy into more stable linkages, such as new members and activists, the establishment of new collateral and friendly organisations, or the conquest of leadership positions within the existing social movement organisations. The trade union movement, in particular, remained closely aligned with the moderate left, and the influence of radical left activists stagnated (Germany, France) or even declined (Italy). Secondly, all but one major mobilisation was directed against seating right-wing governments; as a consequence, they primarily benefitted the main opposition party (SPD, PS, PD) and increased the pressures on the radical left to join centre-left electoral and governmental alliances. Thirdly, despite their mass character, many of the union-based movements were ultimately either unsuccessful (France in 2003 and 2009–10, Germany in 1993 and 2004) or circumvented by subsequent trade union negotiations (Italy in 1995). In short, the radical left was altogether unable to make use of extra-parliamentary mobilisations to improve its long-term ability to achieve its aims; the benefits, therefore, remained generally limited to short-term electoral gains, which disappeared as the general mood turned from optimism to pessimism and resignation.

At the level of electoral and parliamentary mobilisation, the radical left parties were similarly unable to alter the 'direction of competition' (Sartori 1976) and to put a halt to the main trends of the neoliberal era. In all three countries, the ruling elite was broadly successful in pushing forward a major reconfiguration of class power, reversing the post-war balance between public and private sector, making labour cheaper, more flexible, and less influential and shifting the burden of taxation away from capital and managerial incomes. Some legacies of the Fordist social model live on, but the overall direction of change remains highly unfavourable to the radical left project.

This insufficient record is explained by two factors.

On the one hand, the failures of the radical left have depended, of course, on the altogether limited levels of its societal weight. As a medium-small political family representing between 4 and 13 per cent of the electorate, often fragmented in competing organisations, and lacking the capacity to independently initiate social mobilisations, the pressures it could exert on the social and political system were naturally modest. Its leftward pull on the moderate left was hampered by additional factors: the lack of vitality of social democratic internal left-wing tendencies; the hostility of the leadership of key civil society organisations, in particular of the trade union movement; the general weakness (with the exception of France) and ineffectiveness of labour conflicts; the capacity of the moderate left to retain its traditionalist supporters through lesser-evilism (the German SPD in 2002; the French PS after 2002; Veltroni's PD in 2008) or to compensate their departure with gains at the centre (Mitterrand, Schröder, Prodi); finally, the continuous strategic oscillations of radical left parties between conciliatory and intransigent strategies.

On the other hand, the recent experience of SYRIZA in Greece conclusively proves that the impermeability of the European political systems to popular pressures toward redistribution and social protection have deeper roots. Slow growth, capital mobility, fixed exchange rates, open economies, trade deficits, central bank independence, weak state-owned sectors: these typical features of the neoliberal model naturally curtail the space for redistributive and interventionist policies. In addition, however, these features tend to be entrenched in complex institutional frameworks that are virtually impossible to change and costly to abandon: notably the Eurozone, the European Union, and the WTO. Initially very Eurosceptic, most radical left parties converted in the eighties and nineties to a critical Europeanist strategy based on a long-term process of change of the neoliberal orientation of the EU (Dunphy 2005).[11] This option was relatively innocuous in periods of sustained growth, when the parties could avoid structural issues and concentrate on redistributive ones, but had devastating consequences after the start of the Great Recession, when a relaunch of growth and employment required fiscal, currency, and industrial policies that were explicitly barred by EU law and institutions.

Thus, in absence of a major organisational, theoretical, and strategical rethinking, the radical left seems condemned to a growing helplessness and marginality.

Notes

1 Sperber (2010) has emphasised the strong showing of the far left among the female electorate in this election, due to its success among the highly feminised 'service proletariat'. This outcome, however, was partially counter-balanced by the (masculine) communist electorate and was not replicated in 2007 and 2012.
2 Germany grew, but only thanks to the entry of the Eastern PDS; Luxembourg held its first election after the fall of the Eastern bloc only in 1994 (where it lost heavily); the UK was already so low that the trend made no difference (0.1 per cent in 1987).
3 Norway declined; Denmark and Switzerland remained stable.
4 In all probability, these forms of political engagement did not compensate the decline of traditional organisations (parties, unions, churches, and associations). Given their predominantly informal and punctual nature, however, their extent is difficult to quantify.
5 The PCF, a giant from the point of view of membership, resources, and institutional presence, could not envisage an equal partnership with groups which could score well electorally (in presidential and European elections) but were dwarves in all other respects. The far left, on the other hand, hoped to use the lever of its electoral popularity to split the communist constituency and pave the way for a deeper reconfiguration.
6 It was this appeal which enabled LO and LCR to obtain much better results than the PCF among non-left voters (identifying as 'neither left nor right', 'centrist', and even 'right-wing') and 'semi-practicing Catholics'.
7 From 2002 to 2008 its scores in all kinds of elections oscillated between 7.6 per cent and 9.2 per cent of valid votes (against an excellent 13.8 per cent of the 2002 presidential first round), and legislative results in 2012 remained stuck at 7.9 per cent (despite a strong upswing in 2009–12).
8 The figure refers to the net losses of PRC and PdCI only; voters of the other partners of the SA cartel largely shifted to the PD.
9 Pro-SPD swings were modest (0.3 million votes in 2002, 0.4 million in 2013) and roughly equivalent to those toward abstention.
10 A significant exception to this trend is provided by the important French mobilisations of the period 2003–06 (2003 labour and 2006 anti-CPE mobilisations), which failed to produce a positive impact on the radical left vote. The reason for this was probably the 2002 presidential election, which led to a mid-term shift of many former radical left voters toward the Socialist Party.
11 Exceptions can be found in the Nordic countries and in most orthodox and far-left parties.

References

Arter, David (2002). 'Communists we are no longer, social democrats we can never be: The evolution of the leftist parties in Finland and Sweden', *Journal of Communist Studies and Transition Politics* 18(3): 1–28.
Backes, Uwe, and Patrick Moreau (eds.) (2008). *Communist and post-communist parties in Europe*. Göttingen: Vandenhoeck and Ruprecht.
Bale, Tim, and Richard Dunphy (2011). 'In from the cold? Left parties and government involvement since 1989', *Comparative European Politics* 9(3): 269–291.
Botella, Juan, and Luis Ramiro (eds.) (2003). *The crisis of communism and party change: The evolution of Western European communist and post-communist parties*. Barcelona: ICPS.
Brechon, Pierre (2009). *La France aux urnes*. Paris: la Documentation française.
Bull Martin J. (1995). 'The West European Communist movement in the late twentieth century', *West European Politics* 18(1): 78–97.

Bull, Martin J. (1994). 'The West European communist movement: Past, present, future', in Martin J. Bull and Paul Heywood (eds.). *West European communist parties after the revolutions of 1989*. London: Macmillan, 203–222.

Callinicos, Alex (2012). 'The second coming of the radical left', *International Socialism Journal* 135: 10–22.

Chiocchetti, Paolo (2016). Western European radical left database. Version 2.0 (30.04.2016). Available at: www.paolochiocchetti.it/data.

De Waele, Jean-Michel, and Daniel-Louis Seiler (eds.) (2012). *Le partis de la gauche anticapitaliste en Europe*. Paris: Economica.

Dunphy, Richard (2005). *Contesting capitalism: Left parties and European integration*. Manchester: Manchester University Press.

Fülberth, Georg (2008). *Die Linke. "Doch wenn sich die Dinge ändern"*. Köln: PapyRossa Verlag.

Gomez, Raul, Laura Morales, and Luis Ramiro (2016). 'Varieties of radicalism: Examining the diversity of radical left parties and voters in Western Europe', *Western European Politics* 39(2): 351–379.

Hellemans, Staf (1990). *Strijd om de moderniteit. Sociale bewegingen en verzuiling in Europa sinds 1800*. Leuven: Leuven University Press.

Hudson, Kate (2012). *The new European left. A socialism for the Twenty-First century?* Basingstoke: Palgrave Macmillan.

Hudson, Kate (2000). *European communism since 1989: Towards a new European left?* Basingstoke: Palgrave MacMillan.

Ion, Jacques (1997). *La fin des militants?* Paris: L'Atelier.

Marantzidis, Nikos (2004). 'Exit, voice or loyalty? Les stratégies des partis communistes d'Europe de l'Ouest après 1989', *Communisme* 76/77: 169–184.

March, Luke, and Daniel Keith (eds.) (2016). *Europe's radical left. From marginality to the mainstream?* London: Rowman and Littlefield.

March, Luke (2012). *Radical left parties in contemporary Europe*. Abingdon: Routledge.

March, Luke, and Cas Mudde (2005). 'What's left of the radical left? The European radical left after 1989: Decline *and* mutation', *Comparative European Politics* 3: 23–49.

Martelli, Roger (2009). *L'archipel communiste. Une histoire électorale du PCF*. Paris: La Dispute.

Olsen, Jonathan, Michael Koß, and Dan Hough (2010). *Left parties in national governments*. Basingstoke: Palgrave Macmillan.

Sartori, Giovanni (1976). *Parties and party systems. A framework for analysis*. Cambridge: Cambridge University Press.

Sperber, Nathan (2010). 'Three million Trotskyists? Explaining extreme left voting in France in the 2002 presidential election', *European Journal of Political Research* 49(3): 359–392.

van Biezen, Ingrid, Peter Mair, and Thomas Poguntke (2012). 'Going, going . . . gone? The decline of party membership in contemporary Europe', *European Journal of Political Research* 51(1): 24–56.

Conclusion

This concluding chapter summarises the main findings of the analysis and discusses their implications.

The year 2015: a turning point

The year 2015 represents a major turning point in the history of the contemporary Western European radical left. In three Mediterranean countries, this party family experienced an extraordinary success. National electoral results surged to 45.0 per cent in Greece, 25.8 per cent in Spain, and 21.5 per cent in Portugal. As a consequence, continental electoral strength rose to 9.6 – for the first time, above the levels of 1988. The Greek SYRIZA formed a coalition government headed by its leader Alexis Tsipras; the Portuguese BE and PCP offered an external support to a minority socialist government; and the Spanish PODEMOS came close to beating the socialists into second place, gearing up for an early election in June 2016. Meanwhile, their counterparts in the three main countries of the Eurozone – Germany, France, and Italy – stagnated and struggled in face of rising competitors: the right-wing populism of the FN, LN, and AfD; the generic populism of the M5S; and the centrist populism of the Italian Prime Minister Matteo Renzi. After years of trendless and relatively small oscillations, the Great Recession finally caught up with the Western European radical left, opening up unprecedented opportunities but laying bare its flaws and limits.

These events confirmed the validity of a number of points made in the previous chapters. First, the radical left entered in 2007 in a phase of trendless fluctuations and increased volatility. The Great Recession deepened the legitimacy crisis of neoliberal policies and mainstream parties, but the course taken by the resulting dissatisfaction was not preordained. Like in the thirties and in the seventies, swift rises and falls became easier, but relied more and more on the capacity of parties to provide convincing solutions to the question of a return to growth. The radical left was indeed an electoral thermometer of the popular dissatisfaction toward neoliberalism – but not the only one.

Secondly, the presence of left-leaning mass mobilisations was an essential precondition for strong radical left growth. The successes of SYRIZA and PODEMOS were directly linked to the anti-austerity movements of 2010–12; the link for the Portuguese BE was less clear but might also be construed as a delayed result of the 2011 protests.

Thirdly, the political colour of the seating government was also important. All three countries presented favourable short-term combinations: a grand coalition government in Greece and centre-right governments in Spain and Portugal. The latter, however, are problematic in the medium-term, as they enhance the pressure toward centre-left alliances (chapter seven). This is exactly what happened in both countries. In Portugal, the radical left was forced into an external governmental participation, which does not bode well for its future development. In Spain, a complex political arithmetic and a failure of negotiations led to early elections, postponing PODEMOS's predicament.

Fourthly, the combination of a clear anti-establishment profile and a relatively moderate programme helps explain the success of PODEMOS over IU (which was somewhat tarnished by experiences of national and regional governmental participation) and of SYRIZA over its more radical competitors.

Fifthly, a large residual cannot be explained with external conditions and is likely to derive from the concrete agency of each specific party. For instance, SYRIZA fully profited from the grand coalition governments of 2011–15, but the German and Italian radical lefts did not.

Sixthly, the tragic failure of the SYRIZA government, which within six months had to renege all its commitments and rally to harsh austerity policies, highlighted a crucial weakness in the programme and strategy of the radical left. The question of the tight constraints imposed by the EU and Eurozone framework to the implementation of any anti-neoliberal programme was put in the limelight, and the flaws of the critical Europeanist perspective of most radical left parties revealed. The turn to sovereigntist solutions is still limited to minority currents, but the issue is likely to dominate future discussions and become a major fault line of this party family.

Findings

This book has endeavoured to provide a convincing interpretation of the overall trajectory of the Western European radical left party family from 1989 to 2015. The approach triangulates between case (Germany, Italy, and France), aggregate (17 Western European countries), and comparative analysis, combining the advantages of rich contexts, comparison, and appropriate benchmarks.

In chapter one, I present an innovative theoretical framework for the conceptualisation and analysis of the radical left party family. I propose a slightly amended definition of the radical left as a party family situating itself in the tradition of the 'class left' and organising as a separate tendency to the left of mainstream social democracy. I thereby acknowledge its constitutive pluralism and historicity. I stress the need of a multi-level, aggregate analysis focusing on the interaction between individual parties, party families, and underlying fields of forces structuring their boundaries and internal vectors. I suggest an approach for the analysis of party nature based on four dimensions: social constituency, political project, organisational mediations, and strategic mediations. I identify an anti-neoliberal field of forces originated by the triple crisis of international communism, the Fordist social model, and neoliberalism. This field marks the difference between old and new radical left, creating a potential vacuum of political representation of working-class and welfarist constituencies but at the same time preventing a neat separation between radical and moderate left. It also overdetermines the behaviour of radical left parties by imposing the coexistence of partially contradictory elements: anti-neoliberal coherence and centre-left unity; anti-neoliberalism and anti-capitalism; old traditions and new realities. Finally, I introduce a new methodology for the measurement of the strength of political parties and party families.

In chapter two, I briefly review the roots of the contemporary radical left in the historical evolution of the Western European landscape (17 countries) over the period 1914–1988. I discuss the transformation of contexts, main actors, and radical left nature, providing the first measurement of the long-term evolution of four components (electoral, parliamentary, governmental, and membership) of radical left aggregate strength.

In chapter three, I survey the evolution of the said Western European landscape (17 countries) over the period 1989–2015, identifying the key features of the historical context, radical left strength, nature, and cohesion. I highlight the interaction of party agency and competition, national factors, and cross-national trends in shaping its development. I detect a succession of distinct medium-term phases of electoral development: an initial collapse in 1989–93, a substantial recovery in 1994–99, a period of increasing volatility in 2000–07, and a disappearance of all cross-national trends during the Great Recession. I also stress the growing fragmentation of this party family between 1995 and 2004, only superficially contained afterwards.

In chapter four, I analyse the trajectory of the German radical left since 1989. This can be defined as a success story, as the PDS progressively managed to expand its electoral support from a relatively small stratum of former party cadres to large sections of the Eastern population and, since the creation of DIE LINKE in 2005–07, to medium-small segments of the Western society. Although DIE LINKE failed to move closer to its anti-neoliberal aspirations, it consolidated as an important political player and shattered the bipolar dynamics of the German party system.

In chapter five, I examine the trajectory of the Italian radical left since 1989. Once considered among the most vital and interesting in Europe, this gradually fragmented into a number of rival parties and grouplets and resoundingly crashed in the 2008 election. The roots of this failure are identified in the pervasive effects of Italian bipolarism, which constantly undermined the cohesion and coherence of the PRC. Thus, the radical left arrived at the appointment with the Great Recession weak, splintered, and discredited; a pending constitutional reform, if approved, will permanently condemn it to a state of political irrelevance.

In chapter six, I investigate the trajectory of the French radical left since 1989. This is the most difficult case to assess, as success and failure varied widely according to the moment and dimension selected. Altogether, the radical left had a promising beginning in the nineties, was shattered by the combined effects of PCF's governmental participation (1997–02) and the 2002 presidential election, and never fully recovered its former strength. However, its broader intellectual, political, and extra-parliamentary appeal remains much larger than its actual strength, ensuring it an important place in the political life of the country.

In chapter seven, I explicitly compare the four trajectories in Western Europe, Germany, Italy, and France, drawing robust conclusions on the nature, success, and limitations of the radical left party family. This can be characterised as an electoral thermometer of popular dissatisfaction toward neoliberalism, sensible to changes in the public mood but not yet able to provide a convincing solution to the concerns of its potential constituency. Despite a partial electoral recovery and the recent breakthroughs in Southern Europe, the Western European radical left taken as a whole has mostly failed to develop coherent anti-neoliberal projects, effective strategies, and solid organisational mediations, remaining a medium-sized but relatively uninfluential political actor.

Contributions

The contribution of this analysis to the existing scholarship is twofold.

On the one hand, I add to the growing literature on the Western European radical left (Backes and Moreau 2008; De Waele and Seiler 2012; Escalona et al. 2017; Hudson 2012; March 2012; Mannewitz 2012; March and Keith 2016) by offering a number of new resources, tools, analyses, and findings.

First, I supply the first comprehensive collection of primary data on radical left strength and sociology in contemporary Germany, Italy, and France (1989–2015). Less detailed data on electoral, parliamentary, and governmental strength are available for seventeen Western European countries and a longer period (1919–2015). These resources can be accessed through the Western European Radical Left Database (Chiocchetti 2016).

Secondly, I offer the first accurate measurement of aggregate (weighted) radical left strength and other indicators of strength, geographical distribution, fragmentation, and trends, including minor parties and the regional level.

Thirdly, I provide detailed and nuanced political science analyses of the long-term trajectory of the radical left in Western Europe (chapter two and three), Germany (chapter four), Italy (chapter five), and France (chapter six).

Fourthly, I contribute to the ongoing discussion on the origin and nature of the contemporary radical left party family.

Fifthly, I advance the study of some little-researched aspects of the radical left: parliamentary and governmental under-representation, the regional level, small parties, fragmentation, strategy, and extra-parliamentary activities.

Finally, I provide new findings and working hypotheses on the determinants of radical left success, behaviour, and fragmentation, which may be tested and integrated into existing predictive statistical models (March and Rommerskirchen 2015; Ramiro 2016). In particular, the evidence provided on the important role played by cross-national trends, neoliberal policies, welfarist opinions, left-wing mass mobilisations, and governmental participation should lead to further research and attempts at their operationalisation into quantitative variables.

On the other hand, I contribute to the broader literatures on party politics and Western European politics in four respects.

First, I apply the systematic framework for the measurement of party strength presented in Chiocchetti (2016b) to a larger sample, demonstrating its flexibility and analytic power. This enables an accurate and coherent comparison of party strength across dimensions (electoral, parliamentary, governmental, and membership), levels (national and regional), institutions, and countries. Moreover, it enables the aggregation of individual series into composite (weighted) series. The toolbox of indicators can be usefully applied or adapted to the analysis of a large number of political problems, improving the quality of results.

Secondly, I propose a simplified model for the study of the 'nature' of political parties, understood as complex tools enabling collective action and mediating between civil society and authoritative decision-making. Reorganising a number of established lines of inquiry on party politics, I develop the concept of party nature as the interaction of four components: social constituency, political project, organisational mediations, and strategic mediations. Whether this is a useful narrative and analytical model, I leave to the judgement of the reader.

Thirdly, I hypothesise that the behaviour of the members of the radical left party family is affected by an underlying 'field of forces' determined by the spatial positioning of national parties and voters on the political spectrum, ideological beliefs, voters' strategic behaviour, and macro-historical processes. The three case studies of Germany, France, and Italy offer some support to this hypothesis, but more research is required to confirm the reality of these forces and to flesh out their nature and mechanics. If the claim were corroborated, it would open up the question of the existence of similar fields for other party families or socio-ideological spaces.

Finally, I add to the understanding of contemporary Western European, German, Italian, and French politics by exploring the debates, strength, and impact of an important but relatively little studied component of those party systems.

Concluding remarks

The Western European radical left has emerged from the analysis as a medium-sized party family playing a role, not decisive but significant, in all sectors of political and social life: elections, parliaments, governmental formation, extra-parliamentary mobilisation, and public debate. Moreover, its strength has considerably recovered since 1993, although in an uneven and discontinuous manner.

At the same time, none of the parties in Germany, France, and Italy has so far succeeded in making decisive progresses toward their proclaimed goals: to fill the vacuum of representation left by the neoliberal transformation of mainstream political parties; to challenge the dominance of social democratic parties on the left side of the political spectrum; to stimulate a renewal of working-class and radical democratic politics; to precipitate an anti-neoliberal turn in public policy; and to devise a credible vision of a post-capitalist transition.

The next couple of years might well prove to be decisive. The steep decline of mainstream parties opens up new possibilities for the radical left, but this party family still lacks concrete answers to the questions of relaunching growth, ending the Eurozone crisis, and moving toward a new developmental model.

In any case, its experience – with its successes and shortcomings – represents an important piece of contemporary political history and shines a revealing light on the challenges and possibilities of Europe's present – and Europe's future.

References

Backes, Uwe, and Patrick Moreau (eds.) (2008). *Communist and post-communist parties in Europe*. Göttingen: Vandenhoeck and Ruprecht.

Chiocchetti, Paolo (2016). Western European radical left database. Version 2.0 (30.04.2016). Available at: www.paolochiocchetti.it/data.

Chiocchetti, Paolo (2016b). 'Measuring party strength: A new systematic framework applied to the case of German parties, 1991–2013', *German Politics* 25(1): 84–105.

De Waele, Jean-Michel, and Daniel-Louis Seiler (eds.) (2012). *Le partis de la gauche anticapitaliste en Europe*. Paris: Economica.

Escalona, Fabien, Luke March, and Mathieu Vieira (2017). *The Palgrave Handbook of radical left parties in Europe*. London: Palgrave.

Hudson, Kate (2012). *The new European left. A socialism for the Twenty-First century?* Basingstoke: Palgrave Macmillan.

Mannewitz, Tom (2012). *Linksextremistische Parteien in Europa nach 1990. Ursachen für Wahlerfolge und -misserfolge*. Baden-Baden: Nomos.

March, Luke (2012). *Radical left parties in contemporary Europe*. Abingdon: Routledge.

March, Luke, and Daniel Keith (eds.) (2016). *Europe's radical left. From marginality to the mainstream?* London: Rowman and Littlefield.

March, Luke, and Charlotte Rommerskirchen (2015). 'Out of left field? Explaining the variable electoral success of European radical left parties', *Party Politics* 21(1): 40–53.

Ramiro, Luis (2016). 'Support for radical left parties in Western Europe: Social background, ideology and political orientations', *European Political Science Review* 8(1): 1–23.

Index

anarchism *see* far left
anti-capitalism *see* political project; vacuum of representation
anti-neoliberal field of forces 14–19, 201, 227–8
anti-neoliberalism *see* political project; vacuum of representation

Bertinotti, Fausto 134, 148, 151, 153
Besancenot, Olivier 170, 186, 220
Bové, José 170

civil society organisations *see* extra-parliamentary mobilisations; social linkages
cohesion: concept 19; France 169–70, 175–7; Germany 88, 94–5; Italy 130–1, 136–8; Western Europe 54, 75–7, 200–2, 217–19
collateral organisations *see* extra-parliamentary mobilisations; social linkages
communication resources: concept 21; France 168; Germany 86–8; Italy 129; Western Europe 216
communism: cohesion 54, 75–7; crisis 1, 14–15, 35–6, 60–2; electoral strength 37–41, 64–9; governmental strength 41–3, 70–1; history 29, 30–6; membership strength 43–4, 71; organisational mediations 50–1, 73–4; parliamentary strength 41–2, 69–70; party family 9–10; political project 48–50, 72–3; renewal 9–10, 60–2, 72–5, 200–8; social constituency 46–8, 73; strategic mediations 51–3, 74; *see also* PCF; PdCI; PDS; PRC; Western European radical left
communist dissidences *see* far left

democratic socialism (Germany) 89
DIE LINKE (Die Linke): cohesion 88, 93–5; electoral strength 86, 99–104; governmental strength 86–7; history 84–5; influence 111–13; membership strength 86–7, 105–6; organisational mediations 91–2; parliamentary strength 86–7; political project 89–90; social constituency 90–1; social linkages 87, 106–7; strategic mediations 92–3, 108–11
DKP (Deutsche Kommunistische Partei) 88, 105

electoral strength: concept 20–1; France 165–7, 183–6; Germany 86–7, 99–104; Italy 126–8, 143–7; Western Europe 37–41, 64–9, 209–11
Eurocommunism *see* communism
extra-parliamentary mobilisations: France 163, 179–80, 183, 188, 190–2; Germany 82–5, 107–8, 110–11; Italy 142–3, 145–6, 149–50, 153–4; Western Europe 1–2, 23, 30–6, 52–3, 63–4, 68–9, 220–3, 226–7

far left: France 163–4, 170–2, 176–7, 184, 190, 193–4; Germany 84, 88, 94, 105–6; history 31–2, 34–6, 61, 217–20; Italy 124–5, 128, 131–2, 151, 156n3; nature 49–54, 72–5, 201–2, 208; party family 9–11, 16–17; *see also* LO; NPA; PG; WASG; Western European radical left
FdG (Front de gauche): development 164–5, 169–71, 174, 177, 189, 193; electoral strength 184

Index 233

financial resources: concept 21; France 168; Germany 86–8; Italy 129; Western Europe 216
fragmentation *see* cohesion
France: neoliberal shift 163, 177–80; social movements 179–80; vacuum of representation 180–9
French radical left: cohesion 169–71, 175–7; electoral strength 165–6, 183–6; governmental strength 166–8; history 163; influence 191–2; membership strength 166–8, 186–7; organisational mediations 174; parliamentary strength 166–7; political project 171–2; social constituency 172–4; social linkages 168–9, 187–8; strategic mediations 174–5, 190–1

German radical left: cohesion 88, 93–5; electoral strength 86, 99–104; governmental strength 86–7; history 84–5; influence 111–13; membership strength 86–7, 105–6; organisational mediations 91–2; parliamentary strength 86–7; political project 89–90; social constituency 90–1; social linkages 87, 106–7; strategic mediations 92–3, 108–11
Germany: neoliberal shift 82–4, 95–7; social movements 82–5, 107–8, 110–11; vacuum of representation 97–9, 100–4, 105–8
governmental participation *see* governmental strength; strategic mediations
governmental strength: concept 20–1; France 165–8; Germany 86–7; Italy 127–8; Western Europe 41–4, 70–1, 211–13
Gysi, Gregor 85, 102–3, 108

Hue, Robert 170–1

ideology *see* political project
influence: concept 22; France 190–2; Germany 109–13; Italy 151–5; Western Europe 222–4
Italian radical left: cohesion 130–1, 136–8; electoral strength 126–7, 143–7; governmental strength 127–8; history 114–16; influence 154–5; membership strength 127–9, 148; organisational mediations 133–4;

parliamentary strength 127–8; political project 131–2; social constituency 132–3, 204; social linkages 129, 149–50; strategic mediations 134–5, 150–4
Italy: neoliberal shift 123–4, 138–40; social movements 142–3, 145–6, 149–50, 153–4; vacuum of representation 140–3, 143–7, 147–50, 150–1

Jospin government 163, 174–5, 179, 181, 185

KPD (Kommunistische Partei Deutschlands) 31, 32, 44–5, 47–8

Lafontaine, Oskar 81, 83, 94, 102–3, 198
Laguiller, Arlette 164, 170, 186, 200
LCR (Ligue communiste révolutionnaire) *see* NPA
left-nationalism *see* far left
left-socialism *see* far left
leftward pull *see* strategic mediations
LO (Lutte Ouvrière): cohesion 169–71, 175–7; electoral strength 165–6, 183–6; governmental strength 166–8; history 163; influence 191–2; membership strength 166–8, 186–7; organisational mediations 174; parliamentary strength 166–7; political project 171–2; social constituency 172–4; social linkages 168–9, 187–8; strategic mediations 174–5, 190–1

Maoism *see* far left
MCU (Movimento dei Comunisti Unitari) 125, 128, 130, 135, 137
Mélenchon, Jean-Luc 164–5, 170, 177, 218
membership strength: concept 20–1; France 165–8, 186–7; Germany 86–7, 105–6; Italy 127–9, 147–9; Western Europe 43–4, 71, 213–15
methodology: cohesion 19–20; explanatory variables 23; field of forces 14–17; influence 22; levels of analysis 17–18; party family 9–11; party nature 11–14; research object 6–8; strength 20–2, 37, 43; summary 227–9

234 Index

nature: concept 11–14; France 171–5; Germany 89–93; Italy 131–6; Western Europe 53–4, 72–5
neoliberalism *see* vacuum of representation
new left *see* far left
NPA (Nouveau parti anticapitaliste): cohesion 169–71, 175–7; electoral strength 165–6, 183–6; governmental strength 166–8; history 163; influence 191–2; membership strength 166–8, 186–7; organisational mediations 174; parliamentary strength 166–7; political project 171–2; social constituency 172–4; social linkages 168–9, 187–8; strategic mediations 174–5, 190–1

organisation *see* organisational mediations
organisational mediations: concept 13–14; France 174; Germany 91–2; Italy 133–4; Western Europe 50–1, 73–4
overall strength: concept 20–1; France 165–9; Germany 85–8; Italy 125–30

parliamentary strength: concept 20–1; France 165–7; Germany 86–7; Italy 127–8; Western Europe 41–2, 69–70, 211–13
party family: concept 6–11; France 163–5; Germany 84–5; Italy 124–5; Western Europe 29–36, 60–4, 200–2, 226–9
party models *see* organisational mediations
party nature *see* nature
party strength *see* strength
PCF (Parti communiste français): cohesion 169–71, 175–7; electoral strength 39–40, 43, 165–6, 183–6; governmental strength 42–3, 166–8; history 31–3, 35, 163; influence 191–2; membership strength 44, 166–8, 186–7; organisational mediations 174; parliamentary strength 166–7; political project 61, 171–2; social constituency 47, 172–4, 204; social linkages 168–9, 187–8; strategic mediations 174–5, 190–1
PCI (Partito Comunista Italiano): governmental participation 42–3; history 31–6, 61, 124, 140; social constituency 27, 204; strength 39–40, 44–5, 62, 124, 126, 152
PCL (Partito Comunista dei Lavoratori) 130, 132, 134–5, 165n2

PdCI (Partito dei Comunisti Italiani): cohesion 130–1, 136–8; electoral strength 126–7, 143–7; governmental strength 127–8; history 114–16; influence 154–5; membership strength 127–9, 148; organisational mediations 133–4; parliamentary strength 127–8; political project 131–2; social constituency 132–3; social linkages 129, 149–50; strategic mediations 134–5, 150–4
PDS (Partei des Demokratischen Sozialismus): cohesion 88, 93–5; electoral strength 86, 99–104; governmental strength 86–7; history 84–5; influence 111–13; membership strength 86–7, 105–6; organisational mediations 91–2; parliamentary strength 86–7; political project 89–90; social constituency 90–1, 204; social linkages 87, 106–7; strategic mediations 92–3, 108–11
PG (Parti de Gauche): cohesion 169–71, 175–7; electoral strength 165–6, 183–6; governmental strength 166–8; history 163; influence 191–2; membership strength 166–8, 186–7; organisational mediations 174; parliamentary strength 166–7; political project 171–2; social constituency 172–4; social linkages 168–9, 187–8; strategic mediations 174–5, 190–1
POI (Parti ouvrier indépendant) 165
political project: concept 12–13; France 171–2; Germany 89; Italy 131–2; Western Europe 48–50, 72–3, 200–3
PRC (Partito della Rifondazione Comunista): cohesion 130–1, 136–8; electoral strength 126–7, 143–7; governmental strength 127–8; history 114–16; influence 154–5; membership strength 127–9, 148; organisational mediations 133–4; parliamentary strength 127–8; political project 131–2; social constituency 132–3, 204; social linkages 129, 149–50; strategic mediations 134–5, 150–4
Prodi I government 128, 129, 151, 152
Prodi II government 128, 137, 152
programme *see* political project

radical left *see* French radical left; German radical left; Italian radical left; party family; Western European radical left
regroupment *see* cohesion

SA (Sinistra Arcobaleno) 130, 138
Schröder government 81, 83–4, 85
SED (Sozialistische Einheitspartei Deutschlands) 61, 81–4, 87–9, 91, 102–5, 110
SEL (Sinistra Ecologia Libertà): cohesion 130–1, 136–8; electoral strength 126–7, 143–7; governmental strength 127–8; history 114–16; influence 154–5; membership strength 127–9, 148; organisational mediations 133–4; parliamentary strength 127–8; political project 131–2; social constituency 132–3; social linkages 129, 149–50; strategic mediations 134–5, 150–4
social constituency: concept 11–12; France 172–4; Germany 90–1; Italy 132–3; Western Europe 46–8, 73, 203–7
social linkages: concept 13–14, 21; France 168–9, 187–8; Germany 86–9, 106–7; Italy 129, 149–50; Western Europe 68, 73, 215–16
social movements *see* extra-parliamentary mobilisations; social linkages
sociology *see* social constituency
splits *see* cohesion
Stalinism *see* communism
strategic mediations: concept 14; France 174–5, 190–2; Germany 91–3, 108–11; Italy 134–5, 150–5; Western Europe 51–3, 74, 208–9, 222–3
strategy *see* strategic mediations
strength: concept 20–2; France 165–9; Germany 85–8; Italy 125–30; Western Europe 45, 71–2, 216–17

trade unions *see* extra-parliamentary mobilisations; social linkages
Trotskyism *see* far left

vacuum of representation: concept 14–17, 23; France 177–83, 183–6, 186–8, 188–9; Germany 95–9, 100–4, 105–7, 107–8; Italy 138–43, 143–7, 147–50, 150–1; Western Europe 219–22, 230–1
Vendola, Nichi 128, 134, 153

WASG (Arbeit & soziale Gerechtigkeit – Die Wahlalternative): cohesion 88, 93–5; electoral strength 86, 99–104; governmental strength 86–7; history 84–5; influence 111–13; membership strength 86–7, 105–6; organisational mediations 91–2; parliamentary strength 86–7; political project 89–90; social constituency 90–1; social linkages 87, 106–7; strategic mediations 92–3, 108–11
welfare state *see* vacuum of representation
Western European radical left: cohesion 54, 75–7, 200–2, 217–19; eighteenth century 29–30; eighties 35–6; electoral strength 37–41, 64–9, 209–11, 219–22; fifties 33–4; findings 227–9; forties 32–4; governmental strength 41–3, 70–1, 211–13; influence 222–3; membership strength 43–4, 71, 213–15; nineties 60–3; noughties 62–3; organisational mediations 50–1, 73–4, 213–16; parliamentary strength 41–2, 69–70, 211–13; party family 6–11, 29–36, 60–4, 200–2, 226–9; political project 48–50, 72–3, 200–2, 202–3; seventies 34–5; sixties 34–5; social constituency 46–8, 73, 203–7; social linkages 215–16; strategic mediations 51–3, 74, 207–8; thirties 31–2; twenties 31–2; twenty-tens 63, 226–7; world war one 30–1; *see also* French radical left; German radical left; Italian radical left
working class: France 172–4, 177–80, 187–8, 192; Germany 90–2, 95–7, 99–103, 106, 114; Italy 132–3, 139–41, 143–6, 149, 150, 153–4; Western Europe 45–8, 52–3, 73, 77, 201, 203–7, 220–1, 230–1